POSITIVELY PAGE

THE DIAMOND DALLAS PAGE JOURNEY

POSITIVELY PAGE
A Positive Publications Book

Positively Page by Diamond Dallas Page with Larry Smokey Genta.
Copyright © 2000 by Positive Publications.

ISBN: 1-880325-28-4

Library of Congress Catalog Number: 99-098059

Front cover designed by Diane Baklor.
Back cover concept by Robin Genta.
Dust jacket layout by Tom Monteleone.
Cover photograph by Ernest Washington.
Typesetting, layout, interior design
   by Tom and Elizabeth Monteleone of Borderlands Press.

Printed in the United States of America
First Edition, January, 2000

Positive Publications, 9505 Reisterstown Rd, Owings Mills MD 21117
877-337-2264

POSITIVELY PAGE

THE DIAMOND DALLAS PAGE JOURNEY

DIAMOND DALLAS PAGE
with Larry "Smokey" Genta

Positive Publications
Baltimore, Maryland

January, 2000

Life has taken me almost to the penthouse and back to the sh**house so many times, my life feels like a yo-yo. Since my earliest recollections, it's been up and down, and then up again. Lately though, the string has been getting shorter and shorter.

— "Diamond Dallas" Page Falkinburg

December 1998

Acknowledgments

I want to thank the team who was responsible for *Positively Page*, mainly my circle of friends who contributed in so many ways to the writing and photos that make this book so special. I especially want to thank Chip and Renee Silverman, as well as Carol Tracey, for their long hours and input with the editing, proofing, and layout. Thanks also to Elizabeth and Tom Monteleone for dealing with a bunch of wide-eyed rookies who wanted to publish their own book. I am fortunate to have the support and help of people like Carole and Chris Imperiale, Myers and Todd Armstrong, and their families. Thanks to Brad Small, Gunnar Erickson, and his staff for providing guidance and friendship.

The families of my bro's, Smokey and Kent, made tremendous sacrifices. Tons of hugs and kisses go to Robin, JJ, and Lauren Genta, and Diane, Kali, and Kendall Baklor. You can have your husbands and daddies back now . . .

—*Page*

I could not have completed this effort without the blessing and support of my dad, who remains the coolest cat I know. I will always be indebted to the guy I call "The Boss," Frank Ormstead and his girl, Dee. They continue to make me realize "it's no sin to be glad you're alive." Thanks also to Kent Baklor and Family, Brad Small, Bob Ochsendorf Promotions, Rob LaRe, and brother, Jeff LaRe, Carole and Christopher Imperiale, Bigg, Stallion, Little T-Rick, all the people who took the time to be interviewed, and those who contributed photos and time to make this effort a reality. More thanks to Maryann O'Brien, Courtney Jones, Marty Adams, Jeremy Ramsey, Johnny "Delta" Moreno, Darcy, Linda, and Zane at Awesome Productions, Rich Schmick, Brian Bentley, and Craig Grialou.

I can't forget Chachi's care packages, Tim Cammel and the boys at Mandalay Bay, Adam Hirschfelder, Lee Marshall, Muff Pallagrosi, Terry McGovern, all my old pals at National Distributing and The Coffaro Beer Company, and Gary Juster, J.J. Dillion, and the entire staff at WCW.

It was Renee Silverman and her husband, Chip, who made a long story a better one, and Carol Tracey who banged the keyboard late into many nights to get us to print.

I am so thankful that I had the support and understanding of the love of my life, my wife Ro, and our two "squirrels," JJ and "The Loop." It's the kids who remind me of how important it is to be a man, and it's my wife who makes me glad that I am one.

I dedicate this to my masterpiece, Lauren Renee Genta.

—*Smokey*

Dedication

To my grandmother, Doris "Gram" Seigel,
the lady who was always there when I needed her.
Thank you. I love you, and it will always show in my words and actions.

CONTENTS

FOREWORD

This guy is nuts.

He is possessed.

Diamond Dallas Page has more energy pumping through his veins than anyone I know, and I "get off" just watching him. Just talking to him is a shot of adrenaline for me, sometimes, and his intensity almost reaches the point of "wacko."

In over 20 years in professional wrestling, I have never seen anyone like Diamond Dallas Page. He is a guy who really had nothing going for him in the beginning. He was misunderstood, called a "quack," and for a long time, wasn't taken seriously.

Looking back now, Page was a quack in the same way that Einstein was. He knew what he was doing all along, learning and preparing for the day that he could take all of the negatives surrounding him and turn them into positives.

His love for every facet of the business is unmatched, and his hunger to learn and absorb put him in a position where his hard work has paid off. He did it with guts, determination, and a willingness to work toward perfection. Page has learned from every one of his mistakes, and will make it a point to *triple* correct every one of them. He is a relentless individual who turned everyone around him into believers.

Once you get to know Page, you realize that *if* he ever lacked anything that it takes to be a superstar . . . he has it all now. The most important thing that Page learned is that this is a give-and-take business. But unlike so many of the people in our business, he is smart enough and secure enough to constantly give back to the future of professional wrestling.

If there was one guy who I could clone, or if there was someway that his love and passion for the essence of our business could be injected into every wrestler, the future of wrestling would look a whole lot brighter.

As I see it, Page is responsible for everything he has achieved, and it continues to be rejuvenating to all of us to watch what he has accomplished.

As life in and out of the ring continued to deal him so many negatives, he has always remained . . . "Positively Page."

Hogan

—Terry "Hulk Hogan" Bollea

PREFACE

THE FRONT PAGE OF THE JOURNEY

The most important words that I have ever spoken were not in any wrestling ring or arena.

Positively Page is the story of my personal quest from the seaside Jersey Shore town of Pt. Pleasant, where I grew up, through my life in the nightclub business, to the creation of the professional wrestler, Diamond Dallas Page.

My life has been a yo-yo, with so many ups and downs that to be writing this intro is, by far, one of the proudest moments of my life.

Positively Page was co-authored by one of my closest friends, Larry "Smokey" Genta. He has not only done an unbelievable job of putting my story together, but he conducted countless hours of research and taped interviews of the many people who have become so much a part of my life. Our friendship goes back to the nightclub days when we shared the philosophy that "the team that has the most fun . . . wins." Smokey's been my bro since we first met 15 years ago.

Of all my accomplishments in life, from the successes in the nightclub business to all the championship belts, awards, and accolades, this book is my second proudest moment. My proudest moment, however, and of all the decisions that I have made in my yo-yo life, was my decision to say the words "I do" to Kimberly Lynn Bacon.

She is my lover, my partner, and most of all, my best friend. Kimberly has been with me for almost every pop and drop of the yo-yo, and she has weathered the storms better than I. She has been inspirational and continues to encourage my passion in everything I do.

I had trouble reading as a kid, and, for that reason, I've elected to focus my attention on literacy in America; helping teach kids the enjoyment and benefits of reading. With the assistance of a few friends, I was able to establish a grass-roots charity foundation in 1998. *Bang It Out For Books* was formed to help provide books and other educational materials to children, their families, and schools in need. By purchasing this book, you will contribute to those efforts.

I encourage you to contact the foundation to find out how you can help in our efforts to spread the word to kids that "Reading is knowledge, and knowledge is the power to create your own destiny."

I want to take this opportunity to thank everyone who has joined me on my journey. Thanks also to all those friends and fans who I have met along the road while living my "American Dream."

And, finally, I want to thank all the skeptics who said I would never . . . or could never . . . .

Because nothing or nobody . . . could have motivated me more!

Bro's in the bar business in 1985 . . .
co-authors in 1999. Larry "Smokey"
Genta and I have always clicked—
like "words and music."

CHAPTER ONE

MY LIFE WITH GRAM AND OTHER REALITIES

My early life may have been an indication of what was ahead . . . it was the beginning of "the yo-yo." During my childhood, I bounced from house to house and family to family.

I don't remember a great deal about being a little kid, but one thing that stands out is that I loved to lay in front of the TV watching wrestling. I watched my heroes on TV. I wanted to be like them. I wanted to be a wrestler.

When I was eight years old, my father dropped me off at my grandmother's house. I'm sure he dropped me off on other occasions, but I just don't remember them.

Page Joseph Falkinburg — nine months. An early start to Sturgis?

Larry "Smokey" Genta*
Biographer:

The Diamond Dallas Page story began before that day when Page Joseph Falkinburg went to live with his grandmother and the brother and sister he never knew.

"Little Page" was a child born to two children. His father, known as "Page One," and mother, Sylvia, were high school sweethearts, discovering fast cars, backseat love, and parenthood before they found out about adulthood. The times were different then. Young couples struggled without relying on marriage counselors or government agencies. Licensed day care wasn't available. Birth control was more of a mathematical equation than a part of our culture. Divorce was taboo, especially in the blue-collar beach resorts of the shores of New Jersey. Often, young couples would reconcile their differences and attempt to solidify their union by adding responsibility. And having more children.

Eighteen months after Page was born, a second son, Rory, arrived, and a little more than one year later came a baby girl, Sally. Those times were rocky, with fights, breakups, and many nights waiting for Daddy to come home. When he wasn't working hard, Page One was playing hard. Life for the young father of three centered around excessive hours of work and the games he was playing. If it was summertime, he preferred to play those games away from home.

Page One and Sylvia were parents three times before she reached twenty-one. They separated and divorced during Sylvia's final pregnancy. There had been plenty of fresh starts for the young family, and a couple of changes in scenery. As the children came and the responsibility mounted, the pressures magnified. Kids were shuffled back and forth between grandparents and family friends during the good times as well as the bad. But throughout the union of Sylvia Seigel and Page Falkinburg, their three kids never lacked attention, love, or money.

The Falkinburg family was well-known in the beach towns of Asbury Park, Belmar, and Pt. Pleasant, New Jersey. Page One

---

*Throughout this book, the text is marked in three typestyles: normal for DDP's story in his own words, san serif for my narrative, and italics for everyone else's quotes.

was the younger of two sons born to Sally Wilson and Bill Falkinburg, a hardworking Dutch immigrant. Not only were they well-known, they were well-off—not as a result of Sally's blue-blooded background, but because of Bill Falkinburg's work ethic.

Falkinburg Cess Pools and Septic Tanks represented a family making a more than honest living cleaning sewer lines, septic tanks, and portable toilets. They were known as the best, boasting in every advertisement that they would leave your septic tank meticulously clean. Bill Falkinburg lowered himself into the tanks and sewers even late in life when his eyesight had gone from bad to worse to legally blind. The sons worked hard with their dad, hating every minute of the stench, filth, and ridicule.

"The work's dirty, but the money's clean," was Bill Falkinburg's business slogan. When family members were ridiculed or neighborhood kids teased the two sons, they retorted, "Your sh*t is our bread and butter."

Sally Falkinburg was far from the stay-at-home wife. Known as "Mimi" in her circles, she was a beauty who had many friends of her own. Her outgoing personality was endeared by the successful doctors, attorneys, and politicians in the area. She was rewarded for her womanly charms in many ways; and, although the family business was successful, Mimi had her own money and her own life.

Throughout her life, Mimi's controlling, manipulating personality and deceptive character was vented on her family, but rarely seen by her friends. Bill found refuge in the never-ending toils of his work.

Bill's hard work and Mimi's flamboyant personality shaped Page One's demeanor. By his early teens, his good looks and athletic skills made him quite popular. Outwardly, Mimi showed favoritism toward her oldest son, George, while emotionally and physically battering her rebellious son, Page. Page One's love for hot rods, beach cruisers, and Corvettes always kept him on the streets. By fourteen, he was drinking alcohol on a regular basis. As his mother became stricter and more bitter towards his antics, Page One worked, ran the streets, and drank a lot more. At the age of seventeen, his desire for manhood and freedom from Mimi's wrath pointed Page One to the U.S. Navy.

Little Page's mom, Sylvia Seigel, grew up in Pt. Pleasant, a beach suburb south of Asbury Park. A tall, slender, precocious blond, who developed early, she was always attractive. Her rebellious and independent nature was evident even in her early teens. An only child, Sylvia was never without the best. Her father, Fred, was a German immigrant builder who took government construction jobs out of town from time to time. In the early 1920s, when Fred first came to America as a young man, he worked as a professional wrestler touring the eastern seaboard as a jobber[1] for well-known European immigrant wrestlers. Fred Seigel married the former Doris Lipschultz. He was a craftsman who did fine woodworking, remodeling, and custom home building. Fred's independent character was inherited by his daughter, Sylvia, and throughout her early teens, they both tested Doris Seigel's fortitude. At fifteen, Sylvia ran away with an older teenage boyfriend in an act of rebellion. She returned only after her dad, Fred, had tracked her down and retrieved her from Texas, a far cry from the Jersey Shore.

Fred was a man's man. A tough, hard-nosed eastern European, he would tip the glass with the boys and occasionally entertain a lady on the side. From the beginning of their marriage, Fred and Doris were often separated. Most of the time it was the pursuit of employment, but there may have been incidences when he was away, but not on the road. With a love for burlesque girls and beachside honky-tonk saloons, Fred always had places to go.

The relationship of Page One Falkinburg and Sylvia Seigel began as adolescents in the neighborhood. Both had come from good homes with immigrant parents who had spoiled them with the rewards of the American dream. One summer, they discovered puppy love, backseat drinking, and sex. While her friends were enjoying sweet sixteen parties, Sylvia was soon pregnant and married.

Bill and Mimi Falkinburg welcomed Sylvia as the daughter they never had. They provided housing for the young couple as they awaited the arrival of the baby. Mimi kept Sylvia company while the men worked and played. Since Page One was a bit older and everyone knew his family, he was able to drink in a number of bars before he reached the legal drinking age.

---

[1]*jobber—An unrecognized opponent who typically loses to the favored opponent. Losing is often referred to as "doing the job."*

Sylvia Falkinburg
Mother:

I was pretty much barefoot and pregnant from sixteen to twenty-one. Page One was handsome, and really a good guy. All the girls liked him and his cars . . . but the drink always got the best of him. He never knew when to stop. His friends would drop him off all hours of the night after partying. Page One would try his best and do good for awhile, but it always seemed like it was just a matter of time before things went bad again. I was at his parents' home with his mom and dad while he was in the bars. It wasn't that I didn't want to be at the bars with him, I just wasn't old enough, and I was pregnant. He would come home drunk, wake up early for work, and do it all over again.

At sixteen, Sylvia had some new roles to play as wife, expectant mother, and live-in daughter-in-law. And, as the birth of their first child drew nearer, the frustration of staying at home and waiting for her husband mounted. There were arguments and split-ups, and soon after, make-ups. Within months after Little Page's arrival, his young parents found out that another child was on the way. As the family began to grow, the young couple grew further apart.

Page One Falkinburg
Father:

I started working at the age of nine, lying about my age to wash dishes in hotels. I was like my dad, working early and as much as I could so I didn't have to be around that mother of mine. Besides being a big bullsh*ter, she was a domineering con artist who bullied my father and me. I did everything possible to get away from her. Her daily routine of finding fault with me soon became a way to display her evil side. I took beatings from her at all angles. Kids at school teased me about Dad's work, calling me "shithead." They also said that I smelled and my father wore coke bottles for glasses. My older brother, George, always took advantage of my mother favoring him. I remember my mother whipping me with a coat hanger and me running from her, jumping off a high porch, and hauling a$$ into the woods. It was that same summer that I found another way, other than work, to get away from my mother Mimi Falkinburg . . . "kickin' a beer can."

As the pressures of parenthood taxed their relationship, Page One relied on working overtime and going overboard to deal with it. Sylvia's father had built them a home so that their growing family could be more comfortable. Interference from Mimi accelerated, and with his young wife unable to work and responsibilities mounting, Page One's obsession for long hours of work and play began to take its toll. His work ethic was compulsive, his love for cars a passion, and the temptation of beer and broads an escape.

SYLVIA FALKINBURG:

I spent a lot of that time with his mother, Mimi, who liked me a lot. She liked that I was young and beautiful. She was a female who knew what attracted men, and knew that my blond hair and figure would always be a plus. She had friends away from her husband, a more society-type crowd. Her husband, Bill, was always working, even though his eyesight was so bad that he may as well have been blind. Bill worked hard, and it was sh*t work; a good living, but sh*t work. Nothing was going to change there, and my husband, Page One, would come home late or not at all.

PAGE ONE FALKINBURG:

My mother, Mimi, and my wife, Sylvia, were two peas in a pod. They worried about themselves first. Sylvia's dad, Fred, was a playboy who took off for months at a time and was well-known around the bars. I don't think Sylvia trusted men, or ever will. I was no angel and probably made her dislike men even more.

Yeah, I was drinking and working on "muscle" cars, but I was working hard and late every day. The work was tough and dirty, but my truck was spotless and looked as white as a snowball all the time. But, I always loved my kids, and everyone knew it.

Only a young girl of nineteen who was a mother to three children under three years old could relate. Sylvia was quickly becoming more resentful of her lack of individually—the kind of individuality that women in the '90s seek with a vengeance. Although Sylvia had always had two in diapers, no one would have known it. Her figure bounced right back. Actually, it never really left, even during pregnancy. There was no doubt that she would not be able to control her rebellious personality and strong will.

There were lots of babysitters, especially for Little Page. By everyone's recollection, he could have been the poster boy for "the terrible twos" . . . only it lasted a lot longer than that.

SYLVIA FALKINBURG:

This kid was a handful. If the others had been like that I wouldn't have been able to handle it. I would take the three of them to the same sitter, and she would refuse to take them again. Finally, a super mom told me that she would be happy to take Rory and Sally again, but not Page. Just as she was saying this, I saw Page over her shoulder pulling himself up onto the table. In a flash, he grabbed the chandelier and started to swing. He was a giant of a kid, athletic and strong-willed. And, at a very young age, he refused to do it any other way but his.

"Little" Page . . . always ready to roll.

Doris Seigel was Gram, whose strength came from within and from her family. Page's other grandmother was Sally Falkinburg, or Mimi, and her strength came from her individuality and control.

Doris knew that Sylvia's rebellious and precocious nature was an inherited trait from her husband, Fred. Rory and Little Sally saw more of Gram's house than Page did in those early years. It was no different for Gram . . . the two younger grandkids were enough. Little Page was too much.

Doris "Gram" Seigel:

I loved it when I had those kids. Page had much more energy than the little ones. It was tough enough for me as it was, but he was so wild . . . climbing and riding his tricycle in the house. There was a lot of room for him, and he used all of it. He was big and fast, and I couldn't keep up with him.

Gram's house quickly became home for Rory and Sally, and a consistent drop-off place. However, Page was seldom at Gram's in the early years, and bounced from house to house, mostly with relatives.

Now that Sylvia had the kids covered, she began to refind her wings. She was ready to make up for lost time, and Page One's hard work and drinking caused their final split. By this time, Little Page was living with his Uncle George, Aunt Veronica, and their two sons, John and George, Jr.

Uncle George was Page One's older brother and had begun to control the family business. Aunt Veronica ran the accounting division and took more of a role in the family business, even though she had her children and Little Page to care for.

Page One began to have more problems dealing with the dynamics of work. He felt rejected and saw no future in Falkinburg Cess Pools and Septic Tanks. Feeling competitive pressure from George and intrusion from his mother, Page One threw in the towel and quit . . . several times.

Page One Falkinburg:

I was sick of George's brown-nosing and Mom's backstabbing, and hated going to work. I also hated going home to Sylvia, and we eventually split. I finally left the family business, but I never missed a beat, and began working my a$$ off as a commercial fisherman. I had every intention of working and keeping my kids together, but Sylvia was running her way and I was running mine.

During what proved to be their final split, Page One and Sylvia met other people, quietly went on dates, and eventually settled into a pattern of single life. Ultimately, an agreement was made which resulted in Sylvia getting custody of Rory and Sally (which meant that they would be at Gram's) and Page One getting his first son, Page, (who was living with George and Veronica). For the back child support that was owed to Sylvia, she received her ex-husband's prized possession—a sleek, new white convertible. The car was a head-turner, like Sylvia—clean, new, and ready to find a new road.

Not long into his single life, Page One met Elsie Hill, who may have seen a need to help this hard-working bad boy. They developed a relationship and soon married. It was a fresh start for Page One, another new home for Little Page, and a chance for Elsie to be a mother. Everyone seemed to like their new lives, but Page One couldn't break his desire to be out of the house.

ELSIE HILL FALKINBURG
STEPMOTHER:

I knew Page One as a good guy and a hard worker who was fun to be around, even when he had too much to drink. He was a great dad, and his intention was to get the kids back together. But he was getting frustrated over visitation rights with Rory and Sally. If it wasn't because of some scheduling problem, it was because he and Sylvia were at odds. This caused the kids not to see much of each other.

The marriage seemed to work well at first, but eventually the old pattern began to emerge. Page One was up and out early, and out late more and more. While Elsie was home helping Little Page with his homework, his father was out making new friends with his old friend, the nightlife.

Sylvia was enjoying her new life, working and dating. A striking, aggressive beauty, she had her own life Sunday through Friday, and the rewards of her efforts went to her kids on Saturdays. She quickly learned that by hustling and working hard, she could earn more, have nicer things, and get ahead faster.

Elsie's marriage certainly encountered the same hurdles as Sylvia's, but Elsie had a desire to be a mother to Page and to be a stay-at-home wife. At age four, it looked like Little Page would finally have some stability.

Elsie was a homemaker and was committed to her marriage. While Page One was out working and playing, she spent a lot more time with her stepchild. After nearly four years of marriage, Elsie

Reunited at "Gram's." Page, Sister Sally, and Brother Rory.

realized that Page One was going to do his thing and that maybe it was time that they went their separate ways.

That eight-month split-up was the first of many through a twenty-year marriage. However, it developed into still another change of scenery for Little Page.

PAGE ONE FALKINBURG:

I always wanted my kids to be together. I was hardly able to see Rory and Sally, so the kids didn't get to know each other. Sylvia's mother, Doris (Gram), was doing a good job, and I knew she could handle Little Page better now that all the kids were older.

Gram had taken the role of day-to-day mom to Rory and Sally. Her husband Fred (Pop) was generally supportive, but never really fathered the children. Sylvia was the financial head of household who provided the toys, clothes, and weekly cash support to Gram.

In those early years, Little Page would see his brother and sister only at birthday parties and around the holidays. He had lived away from them for six years.

I do remember that day when I left my dad's house. Elsie stood in the doorway crying as she waived goodbye, and Dad sobbed for most of the ride over to Gram's.I can't remember very much about my life before that day. It was much later that I realized I had been to Gram's house before by photos of me in her home. I had no idea that the kids I saw in those pictures were my brother and sister.

That's the yo-yo I don't remember.

CHAPTER TWO

LEARNING THE TURF. MY SECRET STRUGGLE, AND DODGING EVERYTHING BUT THE TRAFFIC

Life was different under Gram's roof after Page moved in. Doris Seigel's house was always a place that welcomed friends and neighborhood kids through the years, but for Page it became home, and a constant source of love, attention, and guidance. Page's arrival instantly added activity to Gram's home, and his outgoing personality resulted in Page being a leader in the neighborhood and with

Summers were spent hanging around the Falkinburg family business.

his classmates. As soon as school was out, Page was out too—
playing sports, making friends, and later, chasing girls.

Life was always different. Like a yo-yo . . . plenty of ups
and downs.

After my dad dropped me off, I don't think I saw him
again more than a couple times until I was eighteen. My
mother visited us on the weekends. She was there when she
really had to be.

It was Doris Siegal, my Gram, who did it all. She was my
family structure from that point on. In my early years, it was
the women in my life who were the steady ones; Gram, Elsie,
and Sylvia all contributed and did what had to be done. We
didn't have a normal family during those times, but we sure
didn't do without much.

I'm sure a therapist could explain how much damage could
be done to kids who grow up like I did. I could surely blame
any faults or personal problems on family members, but that
isn't me. It's not Diamond Dallas Page, and it's not Page
Joseph Falkinburg.

Looking back, I think that it was the beginning of taking
the negatives that surrounded me and turning them into
positives. I just didn't realize I was doing it.

My life didn't seem any better or worse than other kids
growing up in Pt. Pleasant, New Jersey. When I was eight
years old, one of the first friends I made was Stan Youcious.
He wanted to be a major league baseball player. His dad, Stosh,
said that Stan could make it to Yankee Stadium. I didn't have
a dad like Stan's. My dad couldn't be supportive because he
wasn't around and never knew that I had goals. He never
knew that I was going to be a professional wrestler.

Wrestling was a regularly scheduled program in Gram's
house. From a young age, I remember the matinee heroes of
professional wrestling coming into the living room. I liked
the showmen, the talkers, the villains, and the guys people
loved to hate.

RORY FALKINBURG
BROTHER:

Page and I watched wrestling with Pop (Gram's husband,

Fred). Pop had been a wrestler in Germany, won some belts, and was a big fan. We all had our favorites, but Page was the loudest and most passionate about his. He and Pop would disagree over most everything, and they got very vocal at times.

Although my siblings and I were close in age, we often attended different schools.

In the coastal towns surrounding Pt. Pleasant, Catholics generally attended parochial school. Rory and Sally were young enough to be enrolled in a new Catholic school named St. Dominic's, while I went to the nearby public elementary school.

Sally was the youngest, and although she and Rory had lived together all those years, it was apparent that Sally's personality was more like mine. I was athletic and competitive, and was accepted as a neighborhood buddy quickly. On the first day of school at the Ocean Road School in Pt. Pleasant, I made a lifelong friend in Bobby Hoy. Over the next two years, Bobby, Stan Youcious, and I were inseparable.

BOBBY HOY
FRIEND:

We grew up in a typical blue-collar neighborhood with different nationalities all getting along. When Page came to live with Gram, he fit in right away. Part of it was that everyone knew Gram, Rory, and Sally, but Page was easy to know. He was a good athlete and bigger than most kids, but his drive and intensity were what set him apart.

Stan Youcious was a natural athlete, and one of those guys who seemed to do everything better. When he walked onto the baseball field, he was the best in the area. His father, Stosh, was active in his son's life and was able to coach, instruct, and encourage Stan to stay focused academically and athletically.

Stosh Youcious had a presence in the neighborhood and especially in my life. He was Gram's ace in the hole. Since there was no father figure for me during that period, Gram would sometimes threaten me with discipline from Stosh.

This is not to say that Gram was a pushover. She ruled with firmness and always spoke her mind. When Pop was around, he'd sometimes yell and spank us a little if we were misbehaving. But for those times that a rambunctious nine- or ten-year-old was crossing the line, Stosh was the looming threat that Gram used.

STAN YOUCIOUS
FRIEND:

My dad was intimidating because of his size, plus the fact that he had been a Little League coach through the years. I knew that Gram would sometimes threaten Page with that call, but, for the most part, we were good kids concerned mostly with sports and, later, girls.

I remember the first time I saw fear in Page's eyes, though; it was the day that he forgot he was holding Dad's money.

It really was just a prank that I took a bit too far, but it was also a day that I'll never forget. I had gone over to Stan's house and saw a $20 bill on the kitchen counter that Stosh had left for Stan's mother. I made my usual grand entrance, and jokingly thanked Stosh for the twenty that he owed me, jamming the bill in my pocket.

It wasn't until we were at the basketball courts and I noticed Stosh's car pulling into the parking lot that I felt the bill burning in my pocket. While I was trying so hard to sell my performance at Stan's house, I accidentally left without returning the money to the kitchen counter. I struggled to get the money out of my pocket while I rushed to meet Stosh before he got to the courts. I hoped that I could somehow cool the heat that I knew I was going to get. He met me with an openhanded whack that was really more of an eyeopener than anything else, but it served as a reminder. From that day on, I was positively sure that I never wanted Gram to make that call to Stosh.

I learned many of life's lessons the way that most people do, but from an early age, I was observant of situations and people, and was able to read and react in a social and team environment.

Stan and I competed on the basketball courts with Stan's natural ability usually keeping the upper hand. He was supposed to win, especially when it came to finesse sports. He was the star pitcher, the leading basketball scorer, and the first one chosen on the sandlot teams.

I was more physical, preferring to play football and hockey. I became the dominant player because of my height and emotion. I didn't care much for basketball and was considered average at best.

STAN YOUCIOUS:

Page was the most intense player no matter what the game or activity. We would play game after game, and if Page lost, he'd want to play again. If he failed in any way, he'd try again, working harder each time. He didn't like to be beat in anything. Back then, we'd horse around and I would get him in this headlock that he just couldn't get out of. It was a wrestling move, and every time I put him in it, it made him madder. Determined never to be stuck in it again, he finally solved it.

With the talent that I was given, if I had worked as hard and been as persistent as Page, I could have made it to the major leagues.

In school, neither Stan nor I were admired as great students. Stan was average, but I barely got by, only excelling in class contribution. Sometimes my teachers did not welcome my contributions. I was too talkative and not focused, and my report cards reflected this. According to the research done since that time, specifically with learning disabilities, those early teacher evaluations proved to have had a hidden message.

F. PINDER
ELEMENTARY TEACHER:

Student Evaluation summary: Page is full of enthusiasm. However, he does not follow directions and must have constant teacher scrutiny. He acts as though he is the exception to every rule. His behavior is hampering his reading.

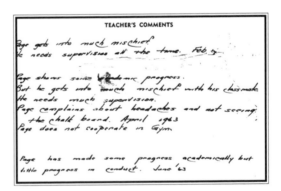

COMMENTS—1st Period   *October*   19

Page is full of enthusiasm. However he does not follow directions and does not work independently. If the teacher does not have him under constant scrutiny he misbehaves. Page acts as though he is the exception to every rule. If he would apply himself he undoubtedly would not be having the trouble he is having with Phonics. His behavior is hampering his reading etc.   Teacher

FRANCES RISNER
ELEMENTARY TEACHER:

Student Evaluation smmary: While Page shows some progress, academically he needs constant supervision. Page gets into much mischief. He complains about headaches, and says that he has trouble seeing the chalkboard.

TEACHER'S COMMENTS

Page gets into much mischief. He needs supervision all the time. Feb.

Page shows some academic progress. But he gets into much mischief with his classmate. He needs much supervision. Page complains about headaches and not seeing the chalk board. April 1963 Page does not cooperate in Gym

Page has made some progress academically but little progress in conduct. June '63

As early as I can remember, it was more of an effort for me to read than other kids. From the first time I was asked to read in front of the class, and every single time after that, my fear and embarrassment consumed me. I just didn't get it. At the time, I didn't know that I was seeing words and letters differently than other kids. All I knew was that I wasn't good at reading; I didn't like it and did whatever I could to get around it.

Although I was a popular kid who got the attention of my classmates, I wanted to disappear when called upon to read out loud. It was virtually a daily dose of the yo-yo.

(clockwise) Doris "Gram" Seigel seated in hat), Sally "Mimi" Falkinburg, Brother Rory, Page, and Sister Sally.

My communication skills were great, because I made sure that they were. Knowing how to talk and having my voice heard was always important, and it helped to hide my secret struggle.

I was always a hyper and extremely active kid. Today, I would definitely be a candidate for Ritalin. Hell, they could have made me their poster child. To get out of reading, I'd fake illness, go to the nurse's office, the bathroom, the guidance counselor, or play hooky. I was always attentive in class and participated in discussions, but not being able to read made it almost impossible to study. So when it was test time, I had no choice but to make cheat sheets to get by. I was the "king of the cheat sheets" and wasted time and energy trying to avoid my fear of not being able to read and comprehend like everyone else.

Today, I read very slowly. However, I enjoy the knowledge, power, and pleasure it gives me. I recognize now that the pain and effort of not reading was hardly a good trade-off. I cheated myself for many years, and I know it affected me in many ways.

I don't blame any of my teachers because I sure did a good job of kidding myself and fooling them. At that time, no one knew a great deal about learning disabilities and the individual struggles brought on by them. My teachers suggested tutors, but the tutors didn't really understand my problem either.

During those years, the guys I hung out with were making the transition from sandlot heroes to organized team sports like Little League baseball, Pop Warner football, CYO basketball, and youth hockey.

I was a jock who found a good place in which to hide my academic problems. I excelled in football and hockey, and those sports became an early arena for my physical ability. Organized team sports also became a place to demonstrate my hard work, determination, and desire.

I made new friends as a result of football and hockey, and when I was twelve, Gary Rossi and Mark Struncius became my closest friends.

GARY ROSSI
FRIEND:
We lived in the same neighborhood and liked the same things. We had nicknames, usually made up from our last names. I was Rosco, and Mark was either Strunko or Strunz. We gave other kids names too, even the girls . . . everybody had a nickname except Page.

Even when we were young, all we would have to say was "Page" and everybody knew who we were talking about. I could say that he didn't need a nickname because there wasn't anyone else named Page Falkinburg, but the fact is, there wasn't anybody like Page Falkinburg.

It didn't matter that he started later (seventh grade) at St. Peters' School than most of us. He was popular and well-liked, and he loved being in the middle of everything. Page always had big plans and good ideas, and insisted on telling us why his was the best idea of them all.

Following a successful season of Pop Warner football, Page turned his focus to hockey. He practiced hard, improved his skating, and was facing the biggest challenge of his young athletic career. The youth hockey bantam league team was for thirteen- to fifteen-year-olds, but Page was only twelve. It wasn't that twelve-year-olds weren't allowed to participate in the bantam leagues, it was just that it was rare that a twelve-year-old could play and contribute at that level.

Tryouts went incredibly well for Page, and he did everything that was expected of kids older than he. It was evident that his work ethic and passion for playing hockey were beginning to pay off. Hockey league officials were making their decisions, and the announcement was to come any day. Anticipation was great, and most of the players felt that he was not only going to make the team, but he was going to get lots of playing time too. Winter was approaching, it was hockey season, and Page was climbing up a rung on the ladder.

All school year, Stan and I saw lots of each other, especially every morning at the bus stop on Highway 88 in Pt. Pleasant. We had a daily ritual of flagging the bus down at a corner a couple blocks before its scheduled stop. It was closer to our homes, but best of all, it was across the street from a candy store. Some mornings we would go to the store together, and other times, one of us would wait at the pseudo bus stop, making sure that we didn't miss the bus.

There was snow on the ground, and as I was going out the door, Gram told me to put on my snow boots. As far as I was concerned, there was absolutely no way a kid could look "cool" wearing those snow boots. Some days, I could convince Gram to let me go without them, but not this day.

I didn't want to wear the boots. I was mad and late; not for the bus, but for the candy store. Stan stayed at the bus stop, and I started to rush across the street. I looked back at Stan to ask what he wanted, and I caught a glimpse of a car getting ready to hit me. For a split second, I thought about running, but instead I froze in my tracks.

STAN YOUCIOUS:

I was looking right at Page when the car hit him. Of course, it's a sight that I'll never forget. As quickly as the car hit him, his entire body was thrown high into the air. At one point, he was almost level with the telephone wires and looked like "Superman" flying through the air.

I didn't feel the car's impact until I woke up on the ground. But when I did, I realized that the car had hit my right leg, buckling my body and causing my face to bounce off of the hood of the car. My face hurt terribly, and the pain was excruciating.

As I lay there trying to focus, I realized I was cold and wet. The pain in my leg quickly spread to the rest of my body. People threw their coats over me, trying to warm me up. I was numb from the cold and knew I was hurt. The first words I heard as I was regaining my senses were from a girl who shrieked, "Look at his face . . . it looks so gross!"

STAN YOUCIOUS:

He was lying on the side of the road far away from where the accident actually happened, maybe over 40 feet. People were huddled around him. His swollen face was covered with blood, and he looked like Frankenstein.

From flying like Superman to looking like Frankenstein.

Page suddenly went from being the young Pop Warner football star with tremendous athletic potential to someone with tendon and cartilage damage to his right knee. His entire body had suffered trauma, bruises, and contusions, and he was lucky to be alive. Since he hadn't made it past the bus stop that day, he never heard the official news that he had made the hockey team. When he was informed, he was elated and devastated.

Although my hospital stay was short, the recovery took some time. I had a full cast on my right leg. I went from an overactive athletic kid out of the house all of the time to bedridden overnight.

I was no longer an aggressive, emotional kid releasing his hyper-energy by playing football and ice hockey. I was physically grounded; and the preliminary reports were not favorable. Not only was there no chance of playing hockey that season, but the doctors strongly advised that I never play contact sports again. No football. No hockey.

My mom got me an appointment with a top orthopedic surgeon, Dr. Nicholas. He had operated on Joe Namath's knees, and his client list included many national sports figures such as Willis Reed of the New York Knicks. If there was any doctor who could fix my knee and enable me to play sports again, it was Dr. Nicholas.

After he examined my knee, he fitted me with the first of several knee braces. Then he told me everything I didn't want to hear. He was very negative and said that I would never be able to play football or hockey again. Dr. Nicholas added that if I continued to play contact sports, I'd need a cane to walk with by the time I was forty. He said that I may have permanent aches and pains, and predicted that the weather would always affect my knee's condition.

I was angry and pissed to the point that I just snapped at Dr. Nicholas, "What do you expect me to do now . . . join the fu*king chess team?"

The x-rays and tests may have said one thing, but Page's heart and soul were saying something else. It was obvious to everyone at the time that he wasn't going to take the diagnosis lying down. The months of recovery were difficult and trying for everyone in the household.

Who knows how the new advances in sports medicine may have changed his athletic career, but Dr. Nicolas was right about Page eventually using a cane. However, Page's cane wouldn't be used to help him walk, rather it would be used to help his style and add a bit of flair to his swagger.

GARY ROSSI:

I remember the day Page returned to school following the accident, but what I recall was not so much that Page looked bad . . . but that his mom looked good. We'd never seen her before, and we were impressed. We were twelve or so, and Sylvia was young and good-looking. Nobody else's mom looked like she did.

I pushed myself to get back on my feet before the doctor's orders. As soon as I was able, I was at a basketball court

I swear . . . that's my mom, Sylvia.

shooting hoops, doing one-legged jumpers, and seeking an outlet for competition. Originally, basketball was the sport that I felt I had the least talent in, and even less desire to play.

I sucked at basketball. Stan Youcious had more natural ability, and Gary Rossi was the best overall athlete in the neighborhood. Rosco was taller and a lot better than I was even before the accident. Hell, everyone was better than I was before the accident.

I could stand on the court and shoot, and the better I got at shooting, the better chance I would have to play, even in this less mobile mode. I'd find someone to shoot around or play "horse" against, and tested my knee every chance I got.

GARY ROSSI:

We would play horse for hours. Page would lose and then insist on making it three out of five or five out of seven. Usu-

ally, we played till dark. One time, Gram was calling for him to come home. I was rushing home, already late. I stopped at the corner because I could still hear him dribbling the basketball. Looking back, I knew that he would never quit. He would practice his shot until he made it, no matter how dark or how late it got.

I was determined that I wasn't going to suck at basketball anymore, and although I didn't realize it, I was establishing the foundation of my work ethic. I practiced every day for three or four hours till dark. I went from a kid looking for a game to a kid who owned the courts. Someone looking for me could find me at St. Peter's Park bustin' my a$$ on the basketball court to play better every day. I could see the hard work paying off, and working hard on the basketball court became my new passion.

Page became known as a smart but physical basketball player with average speed, an average shot, and above-average size. There was little doubt that his aggressive play and tenacity made him a better basketball player, and his game was constantly improving.

Gary "Rosco" Rossi, Mom Sylvia, and Page.

Stan and Page were among the first boys their age to notice every girl they saw. They were also the first to have steady girlfriends, often double-dating as early as seventh grade. Page was more outgoing, charming, and sure of himself than most kids his age, and it became apparent that sports would always have to share his attention with the girls.

SALLY FALKINBURG SMITH:

Sylvia was my mother, but more like a sister. She worked all the time, coming down to Gram's house most every weekend. She brought Gram money to supplement the household expenses, and she brought us just about anything we needed. Sylvia made sure we always had the latest fashions and the most up-to-date clothes. But, we never saw Dad during that time.

Page had his own look and was definitely cool. He was tall and thin with lots of blond hair. All the girls, both younger and older than him, wanted to know Page. My girlfriends were very interested in what he was doing, who he was dating, and where he was going.

Like my mother, I always had a style of my own. I customized my jeans by adding metal studs, patches, or just the right amount of bleach. I also cut the sleeves off my shirts and made sure that everything was working from my shoes to my hats. I listened to rock and roll music, was a fan and member of *The KISS Army*, and had this long, thick, wild head of hair. I had so much hair that one time after making the high school team, I was faced with the dilemma of whether to cut my hair or sit on the bench. The hair lost, but not by much.

As Page grew older, his circle of friends expanded, and he was able to fit in with all the different cliques. By the time he got to St. Joseph's High School, Page Falkinburg was the outgoing center of attention. Not only was he fun and the life of the party, but Page was also a prankster whose curiosity, guts, and stubbornness kept him on the edge of trouble. Usually, Page had luck on his side, staying one step ahead of the school disciplinarian or Gram's threats to ground him or, worse yet, call Stosh.

He made great progress on the basketball court and went from bench-sitter in the eighth grade to a starter on the undefeated, 14-0, St. Joseph's freshman team. Page used the off-season to work towards making the Varsity team as a sophomore, but it wasn't his ability on the court that kept him away from the Varsity squad. It was because of his hair.

Apparently I was good enough to be a JV starter and was the leading scorer and rebounder, but it was made very clear that my hair was too long. When I finally gave in and got my hair cut, I was inserted in the varsity lineup the very next day, and from that point on, I contributed in a big way. By season's end, I had established myself as a starter, and I knew I was only going to get better. We couldn't wait until the next season, and our sights were set on the New Jersey State Championship.

One of the jock pranks around school during that time was to pull girls into the boys' locker room. The girls would not really see anything, and we would release them before anyone was offended. It was a ritual and something that happened all of the time without incident.

One afternoon following gym class, Stan Youcious and Mark Kashuda, both close friends and teammates, pulled this girl, let's call her Mary, into the locker room. The routine was that the girls would struggle a bit, put their hands over their eyes, and then run out. I decided to help the guys.

Once Mary was in the door, I said, "Let her go, it doesn't matter . . . no one is in here anyway." As Mary took her hands from her eyes, I popped my pants down, exposing my jock strap. She ran off, and we all cracked up laughing. But as she was coming out of the boys' locker room, one of the gym teachers saw her.

STAN YOUCIOUS:

As far as we were concerned, it was over, no big deal. But, the next morning, the school called and told my mom that she had to take me in to the principal's office. Even then, I didn't think that it was because of the locker room incident, but when I got to school, I knew right away that it was.

Prior to the start of the school day, they separated us and began their interrogation before we could get our stories straight. St. Joe's principal, Sister Carmella, was doing the questioning. This was way more attention than Mary wanted, and she cried as Sister Carmella asked her over and over again if she saw anything. Mary could barely squeak out, "I think I saw something." But that was enough for Sister Carmella. It didn't matter that it was my jock strap and it covered everything. The sentence was delivered and I was expelled.

Gram was behind me all the way, but it didn't matter. I had to attend Pt. Pleasant Boro High School. Youcious and Kashuda got the 49-demerit gimmick that kept them on probation, but they were still in school and were going to get to play basketball . . . together. I was crushed. Not only was I broken up from my bro's, but Pt. Pleasant Boro High was our archrival.

Even though a lot of the area kids had played Pop Warner football and other youth league sports together, once we got to high school, the typical rivalries ensued. Our jocks would get in scraps with their jocks. There were a lot of bad feelings and heavy heat between the schools. I never had any real enemies at Pt. Boro, but it wasn't like there was a welcoming committee waiting for me.

Page was accepted by the crosstown rivals, and he went on to be not only one of the starters at Pt. Pleasant Boro, but a star on the team. By the time he reached his senior year, he was averaging 18 points and 12 rebounds a game. Page played physical defense and was quick to hit the floor and dive for any loose balls. Basketball had surely proven to him that his hard work paid off, and the more he practiced, the better he became.

Although he couldn't really jump high, he could glide gracefully when he jumped. Page learned how to use his size to position himself, and covered lots of ground under the basket and near the ball. Though he was never the best shooter on the basketball court, he was usually the top scorer. His aggressive play sometimes limited him, and he fouled out from time to time, but Page never got out-hustled on the court.

I was now in the best games down at the town's basketball courts, and would often play with guys older than me. One of those guys was John Shipley, a great athlete. He was one of the first bodybuilders I ever met, and everyone had heard how tough he was when he played basketball.

During one game, I caught an elbow that bloodied my nose. I continued to play for at least another hour, using my shirt to sop up the blood. When my ride pulled in the parking lot, I ran to the sidelines, grabbed a shirt, and dashed to the car.

JOHN SHIPLEY:

Following the game, I went to the sidelines to get my keys and T-shirt. All I saw was a bloody rag of a shirt. I was really mad when I found out where my shirt was and that the bloody shirt belonged to Page Falkinburg. It was the first time I ever heard that name, and I remember the first words out of my mouth were: "What the hell is a Page Falkinburg?"

One of the guys who was in the car with me said, "That's not your shirt. It must be John Shipley's." I thought, *Aw man, now Shipley's pi$$ed and I'm gonna have some kind of confrontation with him.*

I did my best to make it right, but I also knew I wasn't backing down if he got in my face. It never happened, and a few years later, Shipley and I met again in a gym and laughed about that incident. Ironically, we would later discover that we shared a similar passion and dream, and had a lot more in common than just the bloodied shirt.

CHAPTER THREE

THE WAY TO PLAY, THE WILL TO WORK, AND A TASTE OF THINGS TO COME

I love my grandmother . . . she's truly an angel. Can you imagine going through menopause and trying to raise me at the same time?

Gram managed to weather the storm of the adolescent years of me, Rory, and Sally, and life settled down at home.

Mom was involved in a solid relationship with a great guy named Bob Widger. Although she lived nearly two hours away, Sylvia visited regularly, bringing gifts, clothes, and her free spirit.

Bob Widger was an established businessman with a thriving Chevrolet dealership in Livingston, New Jersey. Sylvia Falkinburg worked as his attractive and on-the-ball receptionist. Her natural sales ability and unforgettable looks were perfect for Widger Chevrolet. Bob was five years older and single, and he and Sylvia were very well-matched from the start.

They enjoyed 12 years of the best times together. There was plenty of jet-setting between New York City, a beach house, Las Vegas, and getaways to the Bahamas to develop a real estate venture. Sylvia and Bob became business partners, and later, retreated to a working farm in North Jersey.

Although there was no doubt that Sylvia had her own life and agenda, she was the financial stability who proved to be the security Gram needed. Sylvia's concern for her children was never questioned. From taking a day off to drive the kids to the best dermatologist in New York to dressing them in the latest fashions, Sylvia's influence and input were always there.

I never saw much of Bob Widger, but there was never any doubt that he was a major contributor to the structure of Sylvia's family and our household.

I really appreciated what Bob Widger did for all of us through the years, and he and my mom were a fun-loving, hot couple. They were hip, successful, and enjoyed great times together. Bob was very cool, and I knew he loved Sylvia. Although he was not a father figure, he was always there for me.

Gram was the day-to-day mom, dealing with the generation gap and the growing pains of teenagers. She did her best to prepare her three grandkids for the changes that life was sure to bring, while experiencing her own change of life. Gram helped instill fairness that many families, as well as our country, still wrestle with.

Like my brother, Rory, and sister, Sally, I didn't harbor prejudices. Our environment didn't promote hatred or bigotry, and our ability to make friends was never hampered by stereotypes or social barriers. Mom led a Bohemian lifestyle far more suited for the '90s, even though it was the '60s, and Sylvia never tolerated prejudices, name-calling, or judgmental attitudes.

Life for Page One and Elsie hadn't changed much with their move to Florida, and their on-and-off relationship was challenged by Page One just being . . . Page One. He was employed as a union ironworker, taking jobs on the road when they were especially challenging or when he needed a change of scenery.

It was obvious that he loved his children, and there were several feeble attempts by Page One to communicate with Page, Rory, and Sally over the years. He would call late at night when he was at a low point, sometimes drunk, sometimes guilty, but most times, both. The calls were ill-timed, and only served to increase the distance between a father and the teenagers he never knew.

My dad and Elsie had a family of their own and were living in Florida. We had a half-brother, Colin, and a half-sister, Jamie, who we seldom saw after they were babies. We just accepted the fact that there were plenty of birthdays and Christmas' when we never heard from our dad.

I always knew that my dad loved us, and I understood that everybody deals with their baggage differently. I look back at those years as one of life's greatest lessons rather than one of life's hardships. To this day, I strive to never judge anyone by the way they react to difficult situations.

Today, my family is closer than we have ever been, and my mom, my step-mom, my dad, and Gram each play a role in my life. Rory and Sally, along with Sally's husband, Paul, and my beautiful nieces, Sammi and Lexi, are as close to me as they can be as I travel across America. Whenever I get the chance to see my step-sister and step-brother, Jamie and Colin, we make the connection; even though we never lived under the same roof. The years have brought us together, and our family struggles have made us stronger individuals.

Summertime in Pt. Pleasant was a chance for all the young people who went to the area schools to get together. From the

backyard pool parties at Gram's to hanging on the boardwalk, Page had friends all along the Jersey Shore. He surfed with the hardcore surfers at Bayhead Beach or piled into a car to go see a rock concert; all the while spending hours at St. Peter's Park preparing for his senior year of basketball.

The Pt. Pleasant Boro team had a winning season, and, although they didn't challenge for the state championships, Page started every game and was amongst the team's leaders in several categories. Page was named to the All-Ocean County team, but more importantly, small colleges in the area were recruiting him.

Senior Prom with Denise Keating was the beginning of the walking sticks.

I really hadn't given college a whole lot of thought, but I knew that I wanted to play basketball. I didn't have the grades to be choosy. They were only good enough to keep me eligible to play high school ball, but I had reached a point where getting by in school wasn't good enough.

Like most teenage boys, I had a girlfriend, but unlike many kids my age, I had many girls who were friends. Denise Keating was my first love, and I dated her through my senior year and following high school, although my eyes often wandered. It was especially difficult for me and my bro's to maintain steady girls when the beaches were filled with female tourists.

In my world, we were the boys of summer. And the summer was for playing cards, listening to rock and roll, drinking beer, and watching and playing sports. We played cards all the time too. In fact, we gambled on everything—football, boxing, horse racing, and anything else we could think up. The girls were around when we wanted to include them, but there was always plenty to do without them.

Doris "Gram" Seigel:

Page liked the girls and the girls liked him, and sometimes it was hard for me to relate to the rapid changes in girlfriends and dating procedures. Page would come home some nights and ask questions about his date and other girls. Sometimes he'd get into areas where I knew I couldn't help him. I was aware that young girls could be aggressive, and I wanted to protect him from getting into a difficult situation, so I received an education on dating too.

Point Pleasant Boro High School Senior Class photo.

The only thing better than following girls was following sports, and I loved boxing, mainly because I loved Muhammad Ali. As a young kid, I was a fan, but Ali represents so much more to me now. He is and will always be "The Man." Thank God every sane person on the planet finally appreciates him, but when I was growing up, there were many people who judged him on his religious beliefs. He took plenty of heat. Sure, he was respected for his skills and ability, but too many people only saw his mouth back then. They never took the time to understand his personal commitment. I not only felt his self-confidence, but through the years, it motivated me. What better example of a man being held down, silenced, and stripped of his title and profession, only to turn every negative into a positive.

As time goes by, I look back and realize that I never knew what I was doing or why I was doing it, but I see that my desire helped me to become what I am today. I was turning negatives into positives in many situations. The yo-yo made sure I had a lot of practice.

There was plenty of action on the Jersey Shore, and summer was the best season to be a wild teenager, but it was also the

The first of many appearances as KISS. *DDP was a member of* The KISS Army *with Donnie Clark, Nick Keating, and Brother Rory.*

prime time to make money. People from everywhere flocked to the beaches, and working in the right place could make a kid a lot of money. Page always had nice things, and developed an appetite for the latest and coolest gadgets, clothes, and later, cars.

There was a great seafood place in Pt. Pleasant called Jack Baker's Lobster Shanty. I got a job there working as a dishwasher. The restaurant business has a ladder that often starts in the kitchen on the bottom rung washing dishes. I soon realized that I could climb the ladder by working hard, being dependable, and doing the best job I could.

From washing dishes, cleaning pots, and making salads to prep cook, I made the best of every opportunity to learn a new job in the kitchen. In a short time, I had worked nearly every station in the "back of the house." My enthusiasm overshadowed my youth, and I quickly moved up to line cook. Then a buddy told me that there was a busboy position opening.

Once I got out on the floor of the restaurant and could talk to people and see their faces, I knew that I would always love the hospitality business. And with the cash tips in my pocket, every night was like Christmas. This indoctrination into the hospitality industry instilled a love and understanding for that business that would remain a part of my life for years to come.

The State of New Jersey, like many states across the country, had just legislated lowering the legal drinking age to eighteen, and the bar business was getting ready to explode. I just happened to be turning eighteen as the new law came into effect. It was wild. We went from drinking in cars to drinking in bars . . . overnight. The Jersey Shore music scene was getting hotter by the minute, and bars, taverns, and nightclubs were popping up everywhere. I recognized early on that where there was booze, there was dancing, and where there was dancing, there were all kinds of girls—the chicks, the babes, and the broads.

A job at Jimmy's Sea Girt Inn was my first real taste of the bar business. As part of the day crew, I did whatever it took to clean the bar from the night before in time for that night's party. This included cleaning the mats the bartenders stood on to loading dozens of cases of beer into the coolers. I was mopping the floor one day when I accidentally nudged the office door open a crack, and saw the biggest pile of cash I had ever seen on the owner's desk. I figured out how much money was made on just the cases of beer I stocked each day, and I started liking the bar business even more.

Like any job, working in a bar surely has its drawbacks: the hours, the people, the constant party, and the loss of reality. But, like any job, there are also benefits, like the hours, the people, the constant party, and the loss of reality.

The manager approached me one night and asked if I wanted to work as a bouncer. I jumped at the chance, and within a few minutes of starting my job, I realized something very important. Girls acted differently towards me. The ones who would only tease me now wanted to please me. The very same girls who I had been looking for a reason to talk to were now approaching me, looking for something clever to say. It wasn't just me, though. Everyone in the bar business got babes—owners, managers, DJs, bartenders, barbacks, and even ice runners . . . go figure.

I liked it all, from the cash to the hours. And I really liked the booze, the broads, and the party that the bar business had to offer.

Since playing basketball was more of a goal for Page than receiving an education, he weighed the pros and cons of various small schools and junior colleges where he could see immediate action on the basketball court. Based on his level of play and its proximity to home, he chose Stockton State in Pomona, New Jersey.

Stockton State was probably a mistake since the school was so new. Academically, he made very little progress, but Page was able to become the leading scorer, both on the basketball court and socially.

Later, he transferred and became the hometown hero, playing for Ocean County Community College. He averaged 23 points and 13 rebounds per game, and was selected an honorable mention Junior College All-American. His success at Ocean County Community College captured the interest of other schools.

I was playing great. For a 6'5" white boy without a vertical jump, I could play against much taller guys. I played physically, wasn't intimidated, and learned to play well under the basket. I decided to attend Coastal Carolina College the following year. They had a good basketball program, and the school was located in Myrtle Beach, South Carolina—a beach town where I was sure I would be close to the bar business, the booze, the broads, and the party.

Once I started working in the nightclub business in Jersey, the summer months became part of my education. I was learning the bar business while learning about life, the streets, and girls. I worked in numerous bars like The Royal Manor in Wall Township, Casablanca in Briele, DJ's in Belmar, and many more. I even worked at the now defunct, but world-famous, Stone Pony in Asbury Park, the place Bruce Springsteen called home. The Jersey Shore was becoming famous for music, entertainment, and partying. Just as there were different types of bars, there were different types of operators. The managers and owners of the bars were like celebrities in their own way, and the ones who ran the best bars were like movie stars.

The bar business was booming. There were places popping up everywhere, and places that had been hot spots forever. There were also places where my father and grandfathers had gone when they were my age, and the bar owners knew my family tree. One of those guys was Jimmy Novarro who ran a bar that had been around for years called The Beach House. I used to go there just to watch the way Jimmy ran the place. Every place I ever worked was different, and there was always something new to learn and somebody new to learn from. Jimmy was like my godfather in the bar business, and was the kind of guy who would let me pick his brain to learn all I could.

I had just finished playing one of my best games ever at Ocean County College, scoring 38 points and delivering my first ever slam dunk, when I stopped by The Beach House to have a couple of cold ones with Jimmy. When I got there, I noticed a group of guys who had recently been in a fight with some friends of mine. Even though I hadn't been a part of that fight, they knew that I was the same big, blond-haired guy named Page who was part of the crowd that had roughed them up. They were ready to settle the score with me. It was a mismatch and a situation that I knew could get ugly, and Jimmy Novarro sensed it right away.

JIMMY NOVARRO
NIGHTCLUB MANAGER:

Page was a special kind of kid who stood out in a crowd. He never really started any trouble, but he wasn't afraid to stand up to a challenge. One night, there were six guys laying for him outside the bar. I took Page aside and warned him not to get involved. I knew he was a wild kid who wouldn't back down. He assured me that there wouldn't be any problems inside because he was going to go outside and get it over with. I couldn't believe how serious he was. He waited until I was distracted and slipped out a side door to confront his problem.

I knew that if I avoided the situation, it would continue, and the six guys would be in my face another time. I also knew that if I challenged them at all, they would beat me to a pulp. Sometimes it's better to take what's coming to resolve a no-win situation, even if it isn't right.

I walked out and let them know that even though I had no part of the last fight, I was ready to deal with whatever this was about. One of the guys approached me and told me to deliver the message to my buddies, and then whacked me with a solid right that split my face open. I flinched a bit, but never "sold it" as I waited for the next punch. I never raised my hands and had blood streaming down my face when the guy just stopped, looked at me, and said I must be crazy. He and the other guys walked away. Taking that one punch proved to be the end of a fight that could have produced a lot of physical punishment. It was over, and I never had a problem with them again.

I had found a niche. I was perfect for the bar business . . . and it was perfect for me. I was on top of the world. There was plenty of booze, broads, and parties. Every night was potentially more fun and exciting than the night before. It was the best summer I ever experienced, and the bar business was quickly becoming a big part of my life.

I was also looking forward to going to Coastal Carolina to play ball and be a big fish in a little pond . . . so I thought. A guy I knew from Jersey, Tommy Hickey, was also playing basketball there, and I was glad I would know someone. I left Jersey early, missing Labor Day, one of the biggest party weekends of the year, because I wanted to check out Myrtle Beach.

When I got there, the town was jacked up. The bar business was kickin' and the music scene was thriving. Cocaine was popular, and people were drinking damn near anything thrown in a shot glass.

I was there a couple of days and didn't see it coming, but the yo-yo was just around the corner. Within a few weeks, I was at the bottom of the string.

Shortly after Labor Day, the entire town of Myrtle Beach was shut down. I grew up in a resort town, but I never saw anything like this. The entire beach area closed completely down. At the time, there were few year-round residents in the beach community, and it became a ghost town . . . quickly.

It seemed that every hot girl I met was either sixteen or married, or both, and my social life was suffering. I was one of the few Yankees who went to school there, and a large majority of the students were from nearby, mostly the Carolinas.

There just wasn't anything to do except play basketball. I was healthy and in shape, and I was ready to play. But that too was about to change. Shortly after practices began, I caught the flu or a virus, and was bedridden for a week; sicker than I had ever been.

I tried to go back to practice a little too soon, and it only prolonged the illness. My wisdom teeth were also beginning to come in, and I went from not wanting to eat to not being able to. I lost 20 pounds within three weeks on a frame that was already lean and in basketball shape. I was at rock bottom, and I hadn't even been there for a month.

I was bored and frustrated with being sick, had missed weeks of practice, and I didn't know anybody besides my buddy, Tommy Hickey. I didn't have a girlfriend to play with, and was ready to make a change.

The Coastal Carolina team photo—includes Page (#32) with his ever-present knee brace; roommate, "Meryl" (#52); and Jersey hometown bro, Tommy Hickey (#40).

Tommy Hickey
Friend:

I knew Page from the Jersey Shore, and when I heard that he was coming to Coastal Carolina, I was excited. We were a couple of the only students from Jersey, and were looking forward to playing basketball together.

Page never really got acclimated to living in Myrtle Beach. Within a month, he disliked the scene and everything that was happening. We had a blast together, but I knew that Page was wrestling with the idea of going back to Jersey. He spent many nights on my couch since he really had very little in common with his roommate.

Page always had a plan and a couple of back-up plans, and one night, he took out a piece of paper and made two columns. One said: "reasons to stay," and the other said: "reasons to leave." When I looked at his completed analysis of the situation, I knew that Page wouldn't stay long enough to see the start of the basketball season.

His reasons to stay were short: play basketball and hang out with friends. But his reasons to leave totaled over 20. On the top of his list were Gram's home-cooked meals, cash flow, and girls.

Soon after that, Page placed a sign on the campus bulletin board that read: "Stuff for Sale." The list included a wet suit, a Cream surfboard, and some cassette tapes that he could live without. He made a few bucks, gave me his bicycle to square up the phone bill he owed me, and within a week, he was gone.

On the day I made my decision to leave school, I walked over to the gym to tell the coach that I was going back to Jersey. As I walked in the gym, I saw a sign that read: "Wrestling Tonight," with the only name I recognized being Ricky Steamboat. I went back to the gym that night and watched the action and the faces in the crowd. I remember thinking, *Man, would I like to be able to do this.* From that day on, that wrestling match was emblazoned in my mind.

Without any money, 20 pounds lighter, and at the bottom of the yo-yo, I headed home . . . to the Jersey Shore.

CHAPTER FOUR

PAINTING THE TOWN, THE MAT FOR A MINUTE, AND THE STAGES ALL HAVE BARS

I left Carolina knowing that my college days were probably over, and that I was going back to Jersey to face a totally new scene. Basketball would become a hobby and the bar business my new passion, but I wanted and needed money; so I looked for work that would give me the chance to do it all.

The Boys of Summer . . . Point Pleasant Beach, NJ. (left to right) Kenny Kleest, Jimmy Hart, Rory Falkinburg, Bigg Rick Kolster, and Page.

Although there were new bars and clubs because of the lower drinking age, it was still off-season, and there were fewer patrons to go around. Most places hired me for a night or two, but very few offered me full-time employment. However, it wound up being beneficial since the more places I worked, the more I learned about all facets of the bar business.

It didn't matter what night of the week or what kind of bar it was, there were lessons to be learned, people to meet, and money to be made. Being in the bar business on the Shore was attractive to everyone . . . from business people on Wall Street to the big-hair girls of Long Island. There was no better way to meet so many people from every walk of life. They were having a good time, letting loose, and, most of the time, spending money like it didn't matter.

A few summers before, I helped Pat Kane who owned a painting company. Pat was cool and loved to party, and I liked it that he made his own hours and only worked when he needed to. Once I returned to Pt. Pleasant and had picked up some nights in the bar biz, I received a few offers to paint for neighbors during the day. I needed help with a couple of those jobs, so I got a few friends who were not working and we banged them out.

Page's Painters were reliable— they just weren't early risers . . .

Painting was a perfect fit with the bar business. I bought some equipment and business cards, and registered the name "Page's

Painters." I owned my own painting business during the day and worked in nightclubs and bars at night.

Page's Painters never became a big business or made lots of money, but it always provided some extra bucks and extra action for Page and many of his old high school friends. They worked mostly by referral on residential jobs and had several repeat customers. The summer sun and winter winds took their toll on the beachside communities, and off and on over the next few years, Page's side business did very well.

J.R. CHARLEBOIS
FRIEND:

We were painting some condos and would drive there to-gether, stopping for lunch at the same place every day. We gambled constantly, all day, every day, and on anything we could think of. We'd bet on anything from the traffic lights changing to how long it would take someone to trim a room or paint a wall. We would bet lunch or five bucks here and there, but one day I lost a whole day's pay betting on which song would come on the radio. I was up on Page, which was rare, but when he bet me that he could name both the next song and the artist, I doubled the bet. He looked at me and said, "Chaka Kahn." I don't think there was ever another song where the title and artist were the same. To this day, when I hear the first two words of that song, which are "Chaka Kahn," I remember Page saying, "Cha Ching!"

We had a lot of fun making a little money, but the thing I learned about Page during that time was that he could make things happen. When we needed more work, he'd find a new job or call another painter who could use our services for a couple of days. Page always found some way or someone to help him make it happen.

KEN KLEEST
FRIEND:

The thing that I remember most about painting with Page was that he was the most fun to work with . . . and the best guy to work for. Page always found a spot for a guy who needed a few extra bucks. One of Page's close bro's had been burned in a terrible car accident and was very down. He was a good-looking, popular kid who was going through a long recovery and having problems with his self-esteem. Page made it a point to give the guy a job as soon as he was able to hold a paintbrush. The guy was still in rough shape and couldn't really do that much, but Page picked him up for work, and made him feel like he was as important and productive as the rest of us. Page always did the right thing, and was sincere whenever he would lend someone a helping hand.

By the time the summer rolled back around, Page had worked in various bars and clubs on the Shore, establishing himself as a nightclub guy and minor player in the bar business. He worked in some of the hottest places as a bouncer, doorman, and, sometimes, bartender who had a combination of energy and style that was not only successful, but remembered. However, with a few bucks saved and the tourist season ending, Page had a curious desire to follow the sun and see California.

I wanted to go to L.A., but wound up in San Francisco because of a contact that I had made there. California was way different than Jersey, and Frisco was not really what the word "California" usually brought to mind. I got a job the first day I was there, thanks to the bar business. After a few months, I decided to fly back home to Pt. Pleasant. It was Christmas, and I was anxious to be in Jersey at Gram's for the decorations, my friends, and the partying that went with it. Although I had every intention of going back to California, I never used my return ticket.

It was many years before I got back to San Francisco, but when I did, it was in the center of the ring at the famed "Cow Palace," and a sold-out crowd was chanting my name.

SALLY FALKINBURG SMITH:

It wouldn't be Christmas for me or my family without hearing Page roaring, "Ho ho ho." Our annual Christmas Eve

Surf's up on the Jersey Shore!

party started with a couple friends of each of ours stopping by Gram's house, but before we knew it, there were 40 guests, a line at the bathroom, and people looking for parking places. I can still see Page coming through the door with presents in his arms. The party would suddenly come alive.

I was a senior in high school when Page was flying in from California on Christmas Eve. Gram's house was packed, and we were all waiting for Page . . . like he was Santa Claus. We exchanged gifts, partied, and danced until the sun came up. Christmas has always been the perfect way for Page to express his imagination, creativity, and passion; and also the perfect time to show the people around him how much he cares for and appreciates them. He's always been a giver, especially with kids, and at a young age, he went out of his way to help the local Toys for Tots program. His spirit of celebrating Christmas and giving to kids has grown bigger every year.

I've always been "Mr. Christmas," and the holiday season is the perfect opportunity for me to be over the top with my outfits, decorations, and tree. I love to spread the holiday cheer.

From the first time I saw the movie *It's A Wonderful Life*, I have related to Jimmy Stewart's character, George Bailey. To me, it's the greatest feel-good movie of all time, and I have often described myself as a cross between George Bailey and the band *Motley Crue.*

The spirit of giving during the holidays creates the kind of energy that people can feed off of, and finding ways to help someone less fortunate can produce very positive effects.

A last minute decision to remain in New Jersey following the New Year brought Page back to where he was when he returned home from Coastal Carolina College. He was broke, in need of full-time work, and at the bottom of the yo-yo.

During the transition of getting into the bar business full time, I revived my painting business. But, I always found time to shoot some hoops and hang with my bro's. Working in bars assured me of seeing people I knew from all the schools I attended and had played against. One of those people I ran into again was John Shipley.

Shipley had been to college, but was now working much like me—as a bouncer, bartender, and at an odd job here or there. Although we had known each other before, Shipley was at least four years older, and we had never run with the same crowd. We had no idea that we shared a similar interest and dream.

JOHN SHIPLEY:

I heard of a guy named Tito Torres, a small-time wrestler who had a ring and a small gym in a storefront in Jersey City. I checked it out once when I was home from school, but after I ran into Page, I started thinking even more seriously about it.

Ever since I had seen that match in Myrtle Beach, I had the bug. The wrestling part was cool, but I especially loved the characters like "Handsome" Jimmy Valiant, Captain Lou Albano, "Classy" Freddie Blassie, and "Superstar Billy Graham." They were all talkers and showmen whose characters were entertaining to watch. I preferred the heels[1] or the babyfaces[2] with an edge like Dusty Rhodes, or later, Jake "The Snake" Roberts. I watched the interviews and hung on every word; but I also watched their expressions, outfits, and styles.

Shipley knew the wrestling moves by name and wanted to get on the mat. Right about the time we had been talking about finding an inside track to the ring, a wrestling show was announced for Asbury Park's Convention Center. It was right on the boardwalk, and Shipley and I got there early to hang around by the side door on the beach where we hoped to catch a glimpse of a real wrestler. After awhile, we spotted Greg "The Hammer" Valentine hanging over a railing, looking down at us.

It is a memory that I thought of thousands of times going in and out of arenas throughout my career, seeing kids and fans of all ages lined up along security rails. Sometimes the fans say or do things that aren't cool, but if there is one question that we hear most often, it is the same one we asked Valentine, "Hey, Hammer! How do we get into wrestling?"

His answer was short and to the point. "FU*K OFF!"

Greg and I have laughed about it many times since then, and, of course, he can't remember the circumstances. However, we've both agreed that he was probably having a bad day. That experience taught me not to answer questions that way, and to make sure that I never have a bad day in my life.

The live match at the Asbury Park Convention Center didn't provide any help in getting to the big time, but it did make us hungrier for a shot at the small time. Shipley decided to return to Jersey City to Tito Torres' storefront gym, and this time, he took me along.

JOHN SHIPLEY:

Tito's gym was like the embryonic stage of wrestling, not even the small time, but it gave us a place to learn some basics, bounce around, and work out. Page liked the flash of it all . . . but he was that way in the bars too. It was like he knew

[1]heels—The bad guys. A heel is doing his job when the fans dislike him.
[2]babyfaces—The good guys, typically the fan favorites.

he was going to be in the spotlight, and his confidence made everyone else believe. He worked very hard for it.

We progressed to the point where we were offered work in the Nashville circuit, but we needed our own money to get there, and there weren't any guarantees. With 400 bucks in my pocket and the name of "Buford Notice," I went on the road as a part-time jobber driving around Dixie in an old car. I was jerking the curtain[3] in the worst gyms, armories, and carnivals in the South while Page stayed with Tito.

Tito could only show us the bare basics, and anyone else we came across was not showing us the way, even if they knew it. Tito was a great guy, but he spoke broken English and was limited in his teaching and his contacts. I never went to Nashville, but when Tito asked me to go to Montreal for a weekend, I went to work a couple of independent shows as "Handsome Dallas Page."

There really weren't any highlights of that trip. A couple of tough, old ring veterans got a hold of me, a green kid, and worked me over pretty good. Those matches were more real than I was ready for, and I left with my knee pretty banged up. It sure made me reevaluate my dream of one day wrestling in my hometown at the Asbury Park Convention Center.

Although I never got to Asbury Park as "Handsome Dallas Page," I worked five or six independent shows, including one in Jersey City that Tito promoted, and a TV match for the veteran, "Crybaby" Cannon. I got a little taste of the ring before I hung up the boots and threw in the towel, but never forgot the dream.

John Shipley continued his quest for another year before accepting the reality that his dream of being a wrestling superstar was a long shot. During this time, Shipley saw action as a jobber in the independent circuit and with the WWF as "Buford Notice," and later, as "John Buford." After his brief career, he settled down and married.

Page maintained his love of the bar business, took an occasional painting job, and dabbled with wrestling until an offer by

---

[3]*jerking the curtai+n—The first match of the night. Often a bout featuring unknowns and little crowd response.*

Sylvia's longtime mate, Bob Widger, helped him make the decision to center all of his focus on the bar business.

Bob had bought a small local spot that he named "23 Valley Street," which was also the address. It was a three-level, two-story building with offices and an apartment on the top level, and bars on the first floor and in the basement. I could see the potential in this place. Even though I was only twenty-one, I already had a solid three years in the business.

Travolta's movie *Urban Cowboy* was just breaking, and I wanted to be one of the first places to feature western décor and a country theme. We called it the "Longhorn Saloon," and played rock and roll in the basement and country on the first floor. We did business from the jump with my sister, Sally, tending bar. Sylvia was there helping out too. Best of all, the place was packed with girls.

BOB WIDGER:

I felt that Page had lots of business potential. He was very mature for his age and had a great physical presence. He was able to be very aggressive without being offensive, and always had a new idea or a better way to accomplish things. It was the ideal situation because he had the management ability, was very promotion-minded, and the customers respected him.

Shortly after we opened, country music began to catch fire. I was listening to more country music than anything else. We had saddles for bar stools and lots of authentic western décor. I was wearing my first of dozens and dozens of pairs of cowboy boots that I would own.

I had to adjust to the fact that the Longhorn was about a third of the size of clubs and bars that I had worked in. It made it difficult for me to dodge certain girls when I wanted to.

I met many women during my years in the business, and knew that the more ladies who came to the Longhorn, the better the business would be. There were times when there may have been a half dozen girls there who I had entertained before and had invited to my new party.

Page's travels took him to Texas to further his education in the bar business. (left to right) Page, Steve Mathews, and Bigg Rick Kolster.

This was one of those times when I learned a lesson the hard way. I discovered that I couldn't hide from the truth; so from that day on, I had a new deal and a new program. Honesty.

"The truth will set you free," and it worked for me. From those days at the Longhorn, I realized that people, especially females, would rather have the truth, as cutting as it might be, than be misled or lied to. I told them what the deal was right off the bat; no stories, no lies, and no cover-ups.

The Longhorn and I had a good run, but the small bar became too confining and not enough of a challenge. For months, my sister's boyfriend, Bigg Rick Kolster, and I had talked about moving to Texas. The bar business was thriving there. Rick, who was a bartender, and my sister, Sally, had stopped dating, but by the time Rick made up his mind, I was already on my way to Houston.

I felt that if I could see more, do more, learn new turfs, and then return to Jersey with fresh ideas and promotions, I could turn my persona from cocky to confident and get my shot.

I took off for Texas with a girl I was dating. I knew that we could find work with our experience and bar presence.

When I got to Houston, I was a cocky club guy from the Jersey Shore. I thought Texas was going to be filled with cowboys and chubby redneck chicks, but I learned differently right away.

In many ways, Houston was a lot hipper than the Shore with well-dressed money guys partying their a$$es off, high-energy dance clubs with cutting edge promoters, and so many girls . . . the most gorgeous beauty queens and centerfolds I'd ever seen.

Bigg Rick came to Houston shortly after I settled in, and we tended bar and worked out together. For two guys from Jersey living in Texas, we fit in pretty well. Rick and I had been close friends for a long time, so when I needed a little help one night, I knew he'd be there for me.

BIGG RICK KOLSTER:

Let's just say that the girl from Jersey who Page was living with in Houston was very high-strung. They argued about everything and were on and off most of the time. I got a call at two in the morning just as I was finishing my shift at this bar where we worked, and Page said, "My car is fu*king broken down, and I got to get out of here. Come and get me now!" I jumped in my old, beat-up pickup truck and started across town.

It was about a 40-mile drive, and I didn't know what to expect. Hell, they could have kissed and made up by the time I got there. But, as I pulled down the street, I saw Page on the front lawn wearing only a pair of jeans and cowboy boots. He was very worked up, his hair was wild, and he had his hat rack, bicycle, and a couple of trash bags full of clothes laying beside him. Page threw his gear in the truck and instructed me to turn around in the driveway.

I put the truck in reverse, and the clutch went to the floor. It was locked in reverse. Page jumped in the truck, but sud-

denly realized that he forgot something and dashed back to the house. He came out of the house holding a bull-skull arti-fact and a box fan. He must have really wanted that bull skull, because going back into the house started the feud all over again. As he was running towards the truck, his highly-emo-tional girlfriend was right behind him whipping him with a belt and screaming at the top of her lungs. Page's head was bleeding as he jumped into the bed of the truck with his bull skull, fan, and other worldly possessions. It was four o'clock in the morning, and I was dead tired, 40 miles from home, and stuck in reverse.

A not-so-close, Navy-commander cousin of mine lived about five miles away from where we were, so I decided to call him for a couch to crash on till morning. It took us a little longer to get there than it should have, since we were driving in reverse and I wasn't sure where my cousin lived. Needless to say, it was an awkward introduction for my bro, Page. Now, when my cousin tells his kids that Diamond Dallas Page bled on his couch . . . well . . . no wonder they don't believe it.

Rick was right. It was a high-strung night, but I did get back together with that girl for a short time. She was a good lady, and we are still friends today. It was just a bad night for all of us.

The bottom line in Texas was that there was so much happening in the bar business that I couldn't wait to take what I learned to the Jersey Shore. The bartenders were showmen, flipping bottles and creating new cocktails and shooters every week.

The top guy in the biz was an owner-promoter named Bud Reynolds. This guy was a guru, a mentor, and a fu*kin' wizard, and was just the type of professor who a sponge like me was looking for. He knew his sh*t and was secure enough to share it with the next generation, provided they were ready to be committed and focused, and wanted to work to get it. That was me.

Before heading back to the Shore, I went to Ft. Lauder-dale to Grandmother Mimi Falkinburg's condo. Florida was great, but it wasn't time for me to stay there. I grabbed a few more gimmicks and promotional ideas, saw the biz as a tourist, and made long-term plans to one day return to Florida.

It was always great to return home to Pt. Pleasant, and this time I was especially anxious. I was jacked up and prepared to prove to any doubters that they were wrong. With my energy, the lessons I had learned, and my ability to detect and capitalize on trends, I searched for the right place to make my mark.

Rumor had it that a new club was projected for a spot in Asbury Park in one of the town's worst areas. Location was very important, but creating a new club from build-out to opening was the very best situation for a manager-promoter. With my new "diploma," I was chomping at the bit.

The man behind the new project, Club Xanadu, was Bruce Koenig. Koenig was a fast-lane type of guy who seemed to have everything going for him—good looks, a Jaguar, and a tricked-out beach house. But he wasn't a bar guy; he was more of a beachfront go-getter . . . and he was good at it. He hired me right away, and was sure that I'd be able to tend bar, manage, and do promotions from behind the bar. It was easy to tell that this place had more potential than planning. From the first day, I impressed him with what I knew and blew him away with what I could do.

I had the opportunity to put my signature on the project. I picked the staff, the format, and put all my promotional ideas in place. It was beautiful. We had a killer sound system, a great dance floor and stage for live bands, an exclusive Champagne Room, and VIP areas. Our staff was energetic and skilled. Despite a less than desired location and a dwindling budget, I had the makings of a winner from the start.

Club Xanadu had a very successful opening, but the beach bars did business seven days a week in the summer. I utilized a limited promo budget to keep the weekend business strong, offering a high-energy dance party that was starting to catch on. Overall, Club Xanadu was making some noise, and I was getting noticed, but the best days of this club were still right around the corner.

Many of the people I met I already knew or had heard of, but to many of them, this was the first time that I mattered.

Everyone wanted to be tight with the new guy in the new place, especially when the joint was jumping. The flip side is watching them disappear when it's not happening.

I vividly remember the night I met Tony Pallagrosi at Club Xanadu. He looked like the "Lord of Cool," dressed in black, wearing a pair of Wayfarer shades at night, and walking in a way that just oozed confidence. He reeked . . . hip.

TONY PALLAGROSI
FRIEND:

I was running a live music club called "The Fast Lane" that featured many local bands playing original music. It was typical to check out the new guy on the block, and when I walked into Club Xanadu, I got good vibes right away. There were plenty of girls, which meant a full dance floor. I liked the layout, noticed that they had a stage . . . and I met the guy who put it all together, Page.

I immediately felt the guy's contagious energy, and every word that came out of his mouth had passion and excitement.

Tony "Muff" Pallagrosi was an original member and trumpet player for one of the Jersey Shore's hottest bands, *Southside Johnny and the Asbury Jukes*. Pallagrosi was now out of the performance end of the business, and was booking entertainment and running nightclubs. He had always been respected for his ability to discover and show-case talent, and had successfully made the transition from entertainer to promoter.

Due to the success of guys like Bruce Springsteen, the music industry spotlight was aimed at the Jersey Shore; and the night-club and bar business benefited from that attention.

With the nation's eyes set on the Jersey Shore that sum-mer, it reinforced why the bar business was so attractive to me. How could playing college basketball, or working a straight gig, or finding some girl to settle down with contend with the booze, the broads, the party, and the spotlight that "The Boss" created?

I remember working at the now historic Stone Pony watch-ing Springsteen give it all he had for hours on end. His suc-cess came from his heart, his soul, and his work ethic.

But Club Xanadu was a different game. It was a dance club with a DJ and a dance-your-a$$-off theme. The season had been a great one for the beachside bars, and the live music clubs were battling each other. But with summer over, business had dropped. However, Page's staff and DJs were helping to create a high-energy atmosphere and promotions that were drawing new partygoers. Club Xanadu got hot early that fall, and by Halloween, the party kicked four nights a week.

Business was getting better, but I wanted to mix live music in with our format to be a more versatile club. I convinced the owner that Tony Pallagrosi was the guy to give us strong live music contacts. As Xanadu got ready to pop, Tony and I became partners, managing and promoting Club Xanadu.

Pallagrosi was a valuable addition to Club Xanadu. He assisted with the entire promotional campaign and was able to help me mature. He also sparked my natural marketing and promotional ability, and I had no problem sharing the spotlight with him. Although Tony and I were opposites in

Tony "The Muff" Pallagrosi became a lifelong friend while co-managing Club Xanadu. It would be the birth of Page's annual toy drive. Bill Peterson is Santa.

many ways, our personalities complimented each other. Bruce Koenig and I had developed creative differences, and Tony was the perfect buffer between us.

Tony P. made sure the bands were booked on time and at the right price. Since he knew the business from an entertainer's vantage point, Xanadu treated the bands better than any place else.

Xanadu was the place to dance, and was becoming the place to catch live music; but most of all, it became the place to see girls, lots of girls.

The dance floor at Xanadu was packed, and there were usually plenty of girls who dressed up in high heels with big hair and make-up that looked like war paint. Their attitude was much different than the girls who hung out at live music clubs who all looked like groupies and lived to tell the doormen that they were "with the band" . . . even if they were just "bangin'" the sound guy.

The Jersey Shore produced many nationally-known acts in the years to come. There were Springsteen and *Southside Johnny and the Jukes*, of course, but there was also *John Cafferty and The Beaver Brown Band* who were featured in the movie *Eddie and the Cruisers*. Page's buddy, Dave "Snake Boy" Sabo, and his band *Skid Row*, and Dee Schnider's band *Twisted Sister* came later. But there were other acts actually bigger on the local scene like *John Eaddy, Lance Larson, Holme*, and *Bystander*.

More and more bands wanted to play our stage, and there was one guy who was persistent and had asked me five or six times to see his band. Tony Pallagrosi had heard them and was impressed with the lead singer, but we were reluctant because this guy wanted to play all original songs. I finally went to see the band, and when I walked in, there were only 40 people in the room. The room was rocking the best it could with such a small crowd, but it was the kind of crowd that I liked. Of the 40 people, 25 were hot young girls going crazy for the lead singer, Jon Bongiovi.

I went to Club Xanadu's owner, Koenig, the next day, and said that we should give Jon Bongiovi a night he could build on. I wanted to book him for one night a week for a couple of months. I felt that he would hit it big nationally and that Xanadu could be Bongiovi's home, much like Spingsteen had put "The Pony" on the map.

Pallagrosi agreed with me about Bongiovi, and together we knew we could help push the young band. *Jon Bongiovi and The Wild Ones* was a bargain, and could take Club Xanadu to a different level in the live music scene. But, Koenig didn't see it quite the same way, and rather than commit to a series of nights, he agreed to only a one-night booking.

TONY PALLAGROSI:

Early on, Page and I knew that Jon was going places, and we wanted to be in the middle of it. I had booked Jon and his first bands at the Fast Lane, but a successful one-nighter for an original band in a dance club that featured cover bands was a difficult proposition. In many ways it was a no-win situation, but Club Xanadu booked the band on a Tuesday for $400.

We came far from knocking the town dead that night, but there were more than 40 people this time, and plenty of them were girls. Koenig was not overly impressed, and when Page went to get the band's pay, the owner complained of light revenues and wanted Page to offer the band only $200. They battled for a bit, and Page was finally able to get $300 from Koenig.

The band was breaking down, and we realized that, although it had been a fun night, it hadn't been an overwhelming success. It was evident that the night's receipts didn't warrant rebooking the band. Page told me of the plan to short-change the band, but before we decided on how to tell Jon, Page reached in his pocket, pulled out a hundred dollars, and paid the band the agreed-upon amount. Nothing was ever said about that night again, and neither Bongiovi nor the owner ever knew that Page was the one who made it right that night.

JON BON JOVI *(formerly Jon Bongiovi)*
MUSICIAN, WRITER, ACTOR:

It was summertime in the early '80s, and Asbury Park, New Jersey was alive with music seven days a week. Cover bands held regular nights at the premier bars, and original bands did showcase gigs, trying to capitalize on the successes of Southside Johnny and Bruce Springsteen.

I first met Page at Club Xanadu, primarily a cover band bar and the strip's main competition to the Stone Pony. For some reason, Page and his booking partner, Tony Pallagrosi, took an interest in my band. And against what their customers were paying for, they gave them my original music.

Page went to bat for me and our friendship was formed. Shortly after that, he moved to Florida, the scene dried up, and I got a record deal.

As Club Xanadu ended its second summer of business, I began to think more about Florida. I sensed a change in the air and in the attitude that I felt would affect the bar business on the Jersey Shore. To me, the writing was on the wall, and I planned to beat the yo-yo to the punch this time.

It was an election year, and by late summer, local municipalities had instituted random checks for drunk-driving offenders. As the November elections drew closer, the politicians saw the crusade as a way to gain headlines, and the roadblocks began to increase. Soon, many of the townships and boroughs began weekly militia-like checkpoints, setting them up only blocks away from the most popular local clubs, neighborhood bars, and restaurants.

It became increasingly evident that the fear being instilled by the roadblocks was causing people not to take that risk of meeting a cop on a mission, or a newspaper looking for a Sunday headline. It would eventually hurt the beaches, the music business, movie theaters, bars, retail outlets, and even real estate.

People who didn't even drink and drive didn't want to drive anywhere after dark because a roadblock could mean a 20-minute delay, and longer if it was raining.

Of course, I'm not advocating getting behind the wheel of a car when you are "fu*ked up," but this crusade was ridiculous.

One of the things that I learned about the bar business that relates to wrestling was that if success is in the cards, the rise to the top can happen somewhat quickly, but the fall can happen overnight.

I started getting itchy for a change. With the end of the season just ahead and the roadblocks beginning to hurt weekend business, I dreamt of the endless summer. I set my sights on Florida. I wasn't exactly sure how I was going to get there, or when I was going to leave, but from that time on, I knew I was going. And I wasn't going to wait for the yo-yo to force my hand.

Chapter Five

The Hot One And The Burn

Page was southbound and feeling good about his timing. Club Xanadu had been a success, despite a few speed bumps, and he had gained more experience and new respect in the bar business. His ability to find the right promotional formula was visible in the creation of Club Xanadu, and the format and image of the club reflected his style and high energy.

With the holiday season approaching, he began to make plans to head to Florida after the first of the year. The Ft. Lauderdale area seemed to be the obvious destination until another guy, who had the same desire to trade the bar life on the Jersey Shore for the opportunities that Florida had to offer, approached Page.

Tony "The Stallion" Coffaro was from nearby Belmar, New Jersey and had been around the beach and bar business for many years. He had been a lifeguard, bartender, and manager for some time, and had established himself as a great operations man.

"The Stallion" told me that there was a group of investors ready to back the right guys in a potentially major nightclub deal. The investment team was made up of a group of aging preppies from Pennsylvania. They were classic weekend warriors who had partied on the Jersey Shore for years, and who had dreamed of being in the bar business. Not only did they have the capital and desire to build a nightclub in Florida, but they wanted to put together three to six clubs in a span of a couple of years.

When Tony learned that I was headed to Florida, he became more excited and very animated. He was talking so fast that, for a minute, I wasn't sure if he was talking about the deal being in Florida or California. He kept saying that we could turn the West Coast on its ear, and at the time, I only knew of the West Coast as in California, and I had never heard of Ft. Myers.

I liked the sound of it all, and made plans to stay in touch with Coffaro. My first stop, however, would be the east coast of Florida where I was sure there was action. The most logical and economical place to start was in West Palm Beach where my grandmother, Mimi Falkinburg, had an empty condo where I could crash for awhile. With my experience and versatility, I knew that bartending would not only give me the fastest money, but would also give me the chance to see the most people, make the most contacts, and meet the most girls.

It was a long drive to my job in Ft. Lauderdale, but I was happy to have found work almost immediately at Shakers, one of the area's hottest dance clubs. I was able to get my foot in the door as a bartender, and was in the middle of the party from the jump. I adapted to the local scene while I took notes, made contacts, and absorbed information.

Although they had been divorced for a few years, Page One, Elsie, and their children, Jamie and Colin, had been living in Florida for several years by this time. With Page now living nearby, the opportunity to see each other enabled Page to bridge the gap that had existed with his father. Page was determined to write a new chapter in their relationship. It wasn't about closure or forgiveness—Page was just more compassionate and understanding of the struggles that had followed Page One throughout the years. Page was content to deal with the current dynamics, rather than to continue feeling rejected over the past. Unlike others, he realized that the past only mattered to those who allowed it to control their future.

Stallion called to let me know that everything was progressing on schedule for the new project. I worked poolside during the day planning the hype, concept, name, format, and promotions, while occasionally entertaining ladies and basking in the Florida sun. I was surely the topic for discussion around Mimi's retirement condo as I talked into a tape recorder while some chick applied tanning oil.

I asked people around me about Ft. Myers, and found that very few knew much about it. Within weeks, I had met most of the top guns in the Lauderdale bar scene, and within a month, there were many who wanted to join me in Ft. Myers.

The deal was becoming more of a reality when Stallion called to discuss a meeting in Ft. Myers with the investment group. I planned my first trip to see Ft. Myers and the selected location. Stallion had already moved there, and he and a representative from the investment group were negotiating a lease.

The shortest way from West Palm Beach to Ft. Myers was far from the most scenic. This was rural Florida, orange groves to the north and everglades to the south. The road cut through acres of cattle fields, dividing the state near Lake Okeechobe. All I had heard was that the west coast was different and not as crowded as Ft. Lauderdale.

I'll never forget that drive. I was with this leggy chick in a sports car. My hair was blonder and longer than hers, I had tattoos blasting from my cut-up T-shirt, and I was sporting a diamond earring. Although the map said I was going in the right direction, it didn't feel like it.

There wasn't one person on the street, in a passing car, at a gas station, or in a restaurant who looked like they would go to a high-energy dance club.

I began to have my doubts, figuring this was the fu*king yo-yo all over again. When I finally saw a sign saying that Ft. Myers was only eight miles away, the picture suddenly changed. The streets were lined with royal palm trees, and the homes and gardens became bigger and brighter . . . and I began to relax.

Coffaro had selected a defunct restaurant located on the main highway. Although the location appeared to be good, access to the building could be difficult during peak traffic hours, and the site had been unsuccessful for nine different restaurants over the years.

I got good vibes before I pulled into the parking lot, though. The building was visible from the highway, had a motel next door, and was located in front of the local airport . . . named Page Field.

The facility needed a lot of work, but I was jacked because I knew it had potential. I walked up to the sign near the building, and when I ripped it down, there was another sign underneath. Then I ripped that one down and saw still another sign. This one was familiar. Our future nightclub had once been a Jack Baker's Lobster Shanty, the same place I had worked at on the Jersey Shore when I was fourteen. It was where I had gotten the fever for the restaurant and bar business.

That day, I was introduced to Jerry, who was the mouth-piece for the investment group. Jerry was not what I expected, and looked liked the least likely person to be in the bar business. He was a low-key guy who was a now in our high-energy world. I always heard that we were to have complete control of the club, its layout, and format, but it became clear that this guy was the messenger-boy for corporate intervention.

Stallion and I had agreed on the name "Elationz" with a "z," and we intended to use the tag line, "The Hot One." I was planning to wrap the hype around the heat and the word "hot," using slogans like "Where Every Second Sizzles." The song "The Heat is On" was hitting the charts, *Miami Vice* was filming in the Florida sun, and there was no doubt in our minds that we were going to burn it up.

Jerry had submitted our plans to the rest of the investment group, which then hired three public relations and marketing consultants to evaluate our format and ideas. At that meeting, the investors decided that the name "Elations" with an "s" was fine, but that the letter "z" would be a detriment. They felt it was a connotation for sleep, and, as the last letter of the word, was unpleasing to the eye. Stallion and I were also informed that all three marketing pros had said that "The Hot One" had no promotional value and should be dropped.

I couldn't believe what I was hearing. As this nerdy-looking guy read from his folder, I tried to sell him on the fact that the word "hot" would work well as a tag line for a dance club. The number-one-rated dance station in New York City at the time was Z-103 and was called "The Hot One," and nobody was falling asleep to their high-energy dance music format. Chevy was also doing pretty good with the Z-28 sports car, and surely they had heard the word "hot" to describe a chick or a song . . . or a nightclub.

After battling over the "z" and "The Hot One" in what the corporate guys called negotiations . . . I gave in . . . sort of.

TONY "THE STALLION" COFFARO:

As we listened to this guy, Jerry, bringing us the news from the investment group, I figured Page was going to explode. All of a sudden, Page said, "Alright. We won't use the 'z,' and we'll drop 'The Hot One' from the sign."

I couldn't believe it . . . and I got pi$$ed. I couldn't figure out what made him give in. But later when I asked him, he half smiled and said, "I didn't give in . . . I said we wouldn't use it on the sign . . . but we will use it everywhere else."

That night, I planned to see what the nightlife in Ft. Myers had to offer and to begin my search for our staff. With a hot blond in stacked high heels on my arm, I went to a place called "Babaloo's." It wasn't hard to find the action, and as I located a piece of bar to hang on to, I spotted a guy in a wig behind the bar with 20 buttons on his shirt and props in a bag. He was showing a bit of flash, handling the volume pretty well, and the regulars knew his name.

That was me. And that was the first time I ever met Page J. Falkinburg.

It was unusual for a customer to extend his hand to a bartender, especially in a busy nightclub, but this was different. My cynical thoughts were interrupted by a warmness that isn't usually felt in that environment, especially from a club character like this guy. It was the weekend, and the crowd was diverse. Babaloo's was packed with varied partiers, from the transplanted Guidos and good ole boys who drove trucks to the Madonna wannabes and thirty-something divorcees ready to let their hair down.

He parted the crowd like Moses in rhinestones, and he owned the room from the jump. That's not to say that the blond on his arm wasn't getting looks of her own, but that night, it was his look, strut, and attitude that made it his room.

His first words surprised me. "That's a great look, bro . . . what's your name?"

I had a great look? This cat couldn't be serious. He was 6'5" with a broad chest and long blond curls, wearing the biggest diamond earring I'd ever seen on a guy. He quickly introduced himself.

"My name is Page. Page . . . like a book." He made sure to introduce his lady too, but it was his look and his charisma that made him different than anyone I had ever met.

I was the show behind the bar at Babaloo's. At the time, I owned the only bartending school within 150 miles, and although I was a master bartender and instructor, in this joint . . . I was playin' the room. I was carrying a bag with props, wigs, and hats at all times.

Although his date surely wasn't neglected, his attention was focused on the entire operation. He watched the bar, the dance floor, the front door, and me, and quickly had the entire room, music, staff, and pulse of the place . . . pegged.

"Bro, you're good," said Page. "I like the bag of tricks. You know, you're going to be working with me. We're putting together the hottest club this town has ever seen. Call me tomorrow morning at ten, 939-HOT 1."

Yeah, right . . . I was going to set my alarm on a day that I could sleep in. Sure, I was impressed with "Page . . . like a book," but I had heard this bullsh*t from assorted dreamers before. Babaloo's was smokin', I was making great money, and I was the top cat there. It was going to take more than this guy to convince me that the face of nightlife in Ft. Myers was about to change.

It was less than 24 hours after we first met that Page was back at the bar, and this time he was alone. He had a smirk on his face, and his tone was sarcastic. "What the fu*k, bro? You didn't call me! Tomorrow . . . Ten a.m. . . . . 939-HOT 1."

I hadn't forgotten the phone number. He turned his back on me to concentrate on the dance floor. After working the other side of the bar, I spun around and he was gone.

I set my alarm that night for 9:30 a.m.

I was sure that Larry Genta would have a place on the staff and would help lure some of the area's better employees. However, I wasn't convinced that anybody in Ft. Myers was really ready for Elations.

Some necessary help was on the way as far as the staff was concerned. Bigg Rick was coming from Houston to be our club manager, and there were a couple of guys and girls moving down from Jersey. Also, I had a flash bartender ready to move west, and another guy who was one of the first video jocks (and a technical wizard) joining us from Ft. Lauderdale.

Our DJ and his big-city attitude were from out of town, and I called him Johnny M. He was a 5'6" Jersey Shore kid with a chip on his shoulder that made him six feet tall. He worked for me first as a valet car parker, and later as an off-night DJ and weekend assistant in the booth. I knew Johnny was ready, and I was selling him as the top DJ in America.

Perception is reality, and the hype surrounding the players helped create the interest and curiosity of what was coming. The bigger the push[1] we gave the DJs, bartenders, and overall concept and format of the club, the more the town was with us. The staff helped to give a club its personality. A party could not be created if the hosts of the party were not ready to have fun . . . and help everyone around them have fun too.

TONY COFFARO
ELATIONS PARTNER:

When the local paper asked us what made Elations different at a location that had seen nine or ten unsuccessful business ventures, Page told the reporter that "we can create energy, the kind of energy that produces heat." He was rolling.

---

[1]*push—Planned and calculated publicity hype.*

Page warned that the heat would be so intense that when they drove by the club, they'd think there had been a nuclear meltdown. But, he told them not to be alarmed, and assured them that the heat would only be Elations . . . The Hot One. He emphasized that Elations would be the hottest thing to hit Florida since the sun.

Page was the "Prince of Promo," and he was holding court.

I made it clear to all of the employees I had hired that being a promoter was a huge part of their jobs. They were expected to hand out flyers, know all the promotions and specials, and do what was asked of them—from decorating the club for events to performing theatrics that would help gain the attention of the customers. Costumes, gimmicks, and dancing on the bar were not only encouraged . . . but required.

My dad and I had been getting together more often since my move to Florida, and he came to Ft. Myers to be part of the opening team. The building was in constant need of repair, and Dad could fix and clean anything. He joined the staff primarily to run the valet parking, but he was able to do so much more.

And so it was "Elations . . . The Hot One." On every radio ad, flyer, matchbook, billboard, T-shirt, hat, button, key chain, teddy bear, and, of course, all three levels of VIP cards, it was there. At the beach, there were parasails in the air, a party barge in the water, and plenty of beach towels and coolie cups to remind everyone that Elations was the place to party. The words "The Hot One" were everywhere and anywhere that the name "Elations" was . . . except for the sign in front of the building.

The Hot One caught on immediately. Weeks before the opening, people were already associating Elations with the new hot club in town. Elations was hot . . . and The Hot One was Elations.

With the opening approaching, I sensed that Stallion had been having minor troubles with the investors, and the contractors and craftsmen were not like the guys we were used to in Jersey. Ft. Myers was the land of mañana, and we were

Tony "The Stallion" Coffaro and Page brought a nonstop, high-energy, Jersey-style dance club to Ft. Myers, FL with the opening of "Elations . . . The Hot One."

"right now" guys. From the start, there were doubts that we would be open on our target date, and I could see the yo-yo every freakin' day. Some days I was welcomed like the new mayor, and others like a Yankee carpetbagger, and there was more than one occasion when I thought the deck may have been stacked against us.

There was a lady who became like a guardian angel for the project. Miss Dixie Lee was a colorful character and an over-the-top Southern belle who wore as much gold as Mr. T. She was a very confident and hip woman, and with her help, we were able to expedite the zoning and permit process. She liked both Stallion and I, and although her roots were in Ft. Myers, she was a big-city personality who fit in with the boys from Jersey.

Although Tony C. was quick to use me in the operations of the club and was preparing me to be the club manager, Page saw me as a promotion guy and an entertaining part of the show.

I ran errands and followed Page's agenda at a blistering pace, going from one topic to the next, mixing the promotion of the business into nearly every conversation. As I learned more about Page,

I learned more about self-promotion, hype, and the fact that he would never let anyone forget meeting him. He would kiss *every* girl's hand. He asked everyone their name too, even strangers passing by.

Page was easy to know and treated me like his equal most times. But at other times, I felt like his personal valet. There were lots of "get this," "do that," and "stop here, on your way to there." I would be halfway through my things-to-do list before I began to wonder: *Who the hell does this guy think he is?* Or better yet: *What does he think I am?*

I could tell early on that Page was evaluating my strengths and counting on me to handle whatever he threw my way. Like some Svengali, he got me and everyone else around him to react and respond. As a business, we were promotional monsters.

Every radio commercial was a big-city, high-energy production. Page interviewed and met every radio DJ, and listened to every voice that each station had to offer. He made them rewrite and recut the promos over and over again.

I wasn't just bustin' balls; I could sense that no one had ever used radio the way that I intended. I knew that both Tony C. and I had been accustomed to higher advertising costs in other areas and that nobody ever had a budget like ours—not in Ft. Myers, anyway. I went toe-to-toe with many of the media people, the account reps, and anyone who was selling us advertising to achieve the highest profile and the most promotional impressions.

On the day of our grand opening, the stress level was way over the top. And, for a major portion of that day, I had to do without Coffaro. The corporation wanted projections for the next club and had him in the office for hours. This didn't make sense, but because all of the partners were in Ft. Myers for the opening, they wanted updated projections based on a bigger club in a bigger town.

Stallion came out of that meeting pi$$ed that they had robbed him of some very precious time, but we were encouraged that the wheels were in motion for a project in Philadelphia.

There were so many delays that welders were still hanging the tail of a '59 Caddy in the Pink Cadillac Room while the staff was running around trying to learn the high-tech cash registers that the bean counters had rolled in at the last minute. Phone calls for more invitations were pouring in. I remember looking at my watch and realizing that it was still two hours away from the five p.m. cocktail party, and there were close to 50 people in line already.

Despite the inexperience of the staff, the time-consuming registers, and the mob of people which I never knew existed there, we opened with a *bang*! It was far bigger than I expected, and we were better prepared than I thought we would be, considering all that had gone on during the last week of construction.

We were in the zone from the very first day, and the roll we were on spilled over to even typically off-nights, like Monday and Tuesday.

Monday was our night for hospitality industry employees, and since we took good care of our own, we always had good crowds. They were like walking promos for us.

Every Tuesday night, we had a different theme using the current trends and radio spots to promote them. Wednesday was our famous "Hot Legs Contest," and Thursday was the "Lip Synch Contest."

On Friday night, we made sure there were lots of ladies present. We hooked up with a local jeweler and were giving away diamonds. They have always been a girl's best friend, and the lady who could locate "Diamond Jim" in the crowd would win. The ladies came out in force, and they danced and got crazier than they ever had before.

We made sure that they got even crazier every Saturday when we did our "$1,000 Champagne Dance Contest" that featured a bottle of Dom Perignon for the winner, and two cases of free house champagne poured and distributed to everyone on the dance floor.

I knew how important it was to get out of the blocks quickly. But, I understood this town, and if any club could get four busy nights a week, it was a big deal.

When Page told me that he would pack the place on Tuesdays, I told him there was no way. When he told me that we would have a new theme every single week, I laughed out loud.

It was the last time I ever thought that Page Falkinburg was full of sh*t.

On Sunday nights, a city ordinance forced us to close at midnight, which usually resulted in most nightclubs remaining closed, but we were prepared to be open and busy seven nights a week. While I was in Ft. Lauderdale, I met a guy named "Smittee" who was a visual comedian at a red-hot nightclub named "Confetti." He was very entertaining, and I wanted to feature him on Sundays. I convinced him to work for us on his only night off. It was unique, never-before-seen entertainment . . . on a never-busy-before night of the week.

SMITTEE
VISUAL COMEDIAN:

I first met Page at Shakers on my night off, where I would go with friends from the club where I was working at the time. Page was a crazy character and showman behind the bar. He had so much energy, and I sensed that he really knew the bar business. He always made me feel great, and told me how much he liked what I was doing. So when he offered to pick me up in Lauderdale and pay me to travel to the club he was opening, I took him up on it.

I didn't know why I traveled five hours roundtrip to Ft. Myers to work only three hours on Sunday, my only day off, but I did know that I wanted to work with Page.

Smittee provided a form of entertainment that was just being introduced, and Confetti's was a cutting-edge national chain. I wanted to promote him and his act nationwide, not just Sunday nights in Ft. Myers until midnight.

I also knew that if Smittee came on board, I'd have a better chance of recruiting the guy who ran Confetti's stage entertainment, Frank Ormstead. Frank could dance his a$$ off and had great promotional skills and stage presence. He knew nightclub music and entertainment well, and was the type of guy who could help our organization in so many ways.

Waiting lines to get into The Hot One were common most nights.

On the weekend, parking was a nice problem to have, and the lines stretched around the building. Babaloo's had been the place to go just weeks before, but was now closed and out of business.

The first month's sales at Elations far exceeded the projections, and with the added revenues, Page was able to offer Smittee full-time work and a plan for the future. We were also able to get Frank Ormstead to take over the entertainment staff at Elations and help with our promotional onslaught.

The entire town had jumped on the bandwagon, and we were preparing to grow. The business was booming, and the corporation was dangling future clubs within our reach.

On the operations side, Larry Genta had become Stallion's right-hand man, but at the same time, he could help me write the ads, help Frank produce a show, and help to lead and cheer on the staff. For me, he was my friend, my supporter, and a guy I could always count on.

When Page saw the visual comedy of "Smittee," he lured him to the west coast, a new future.

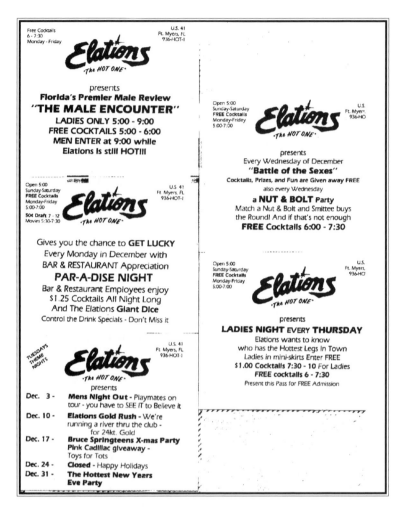

Elations was on a roll on December 18th . . . anticipating a record-breaking month before a visit from the yo-yo. Promotions were in full-swing for the holiday season.

SMITTEE:

I had just finished reading the book Wired *about John Belushi, and had learned about Smokey Wendell, who had been Belushi's protector and road manager during the best times of his career. Larry understood me better than anyone, so I began to call him* my *"Smokey."*

He never looked like a "Larry" to me in the first place, so from that day on, I made sure everyone called him "Smokey." The name just fit, and when it came to any bar challenges, I would warn his competition that "he'll smoke you!" Stallion would just walk by and say, "Where there's Smoke . . ."

Smittee had many talents to go with his comical and unique act, but occasionally, he was a handful to deal with. I took an active interest in helping Smittee expand his character, and asked Smokey to assist me with the management of Smittee's career.

At one point, Smittee qualified for a shot on Dick Clark's show *Puttin' on the Hits* in California, and "Smoke" was there to act as Smittee's road manager.

BOBBY SCARCELLO
ELATIONS BARTENDER:

Elations had it all. Not only was it one of the best dance clubs that I had ever seen, but we had fantastic entertainment. A dance troupe, a cast of lip synchers, or mimics and performers would constantly entertain. We had a staff magician, a photographer with an on-site darkroom, and a guy who did caricatures. We even performed a stage version of the cult classic The Rocky Horror Picture Show.

Springsteen was at his hottest, and Frank Ormstead had won the "National Air Band Look-Alike Contest." The Jump In The Saddle Band *had recorded the novelty song "The Curly Shuffle," and Smittee toured with them. Smokey and Richard Fresco were two of the best show-bartenders in the country, and the drink specials and contests made it fun every night.*

With Elations breaking all the projections, I planned the greatest "Christmas Extravaganza" ever. When people said it was too much, I said, "How can you have too much Christmas?"

We decorated for Christmas the day after Thanksgiving, and with all the promotions in place, I planned a quick ski getaway to Colorado with my old bro, Kenny Kleest.

FRANK ORMSTEAD:

Page's idea of decorating and promoting Christmas was outrageous. We had Santa in the club every night following Thanksgiving, and Page would trade free cover charges or free drink tickets for contributions to Toys for Tots. This wasn't the way nightclubs usually celebrated Christmas . . . and it wasn't the way a corporation treated their employees. Page and Stallion had too much heart. No one in the bar business ever treated us with that kind of respect. We were all drawn to him. He made us feel like a family.

While the staff continued collecting for Toys for Tots, Page bought gifts in Colorado for everyone: the managers, the bartenders, the bouncers . . . everybody. Even the bathroom attendants and the part-time girl in the coatroom received gifts.

With Smittee and I on our way to L.A. and Christmas just around the corner, we couldn't have been hotter. New Year's Eve was nearly sold out, and the tourist season was on the horizon. I had sold my interest in the Suncoast School of Bartending and was ready to do it all with my new bro's.

We were on top, and things were great. Smokey called from Hollywood to report that Smittee won $1,000 and the first round on *Puttin' on the Hits*, and was favored to advance to the next round for $5,000.

The club was hotter than ever at a typically slow time of year, and we had buried our December projections. We had a scheduled meeting with the investors to review our performance and to find out when the new project would begin.

Nobody thought we would do as well as we had. Stallion

Every Tuesday night, Elations featured a different theme. Back in September of '85, it was "Pro Wrestling Night" . . . Go figure. And don't forget—ladies in miniskirts were admitted free!

and I were feeling bold, and figured they'd be kissing our a$$es at that meeting.

TONY COFFARO:

We were anxious to sit down with Jerry and others from the investment group because we knew we had a hot hand. I agreed that we would pin the corporation down on the details of the Philadelphia club. We had heard very little besides promises to that point.

When Jerry slithered into the office, he had two cops and one yo-yo with him. Then he read a statement that said we were out. Basically, it stated that Stallion had not met the terms and projections of the contract, and that our bonuses, jobs, and dreams were null and void.

Obviously, Jerry had brought the cops with him for protection. I guess he feared our reaction. Maybe he was a little smarter than I thought.

TONY COFFARO:

When the investors saw the kind of numbers we were doing, they got greedy. With the sales that we had racked up, our bonuses were strong. We had crushed all the projections, and instead of being "elated" about it, they looked for a way to beat us out of our money.

We actually laughed when they claimed that we had fallen short of our projections, knowing that we had far exceeded them.

With their Philadelphia lawyers and the police standing by, they showed me the Elations-Ft. Myers contract with the Elations-Philadelphia sales projections incorporated into it. That was all it took to get us out of our club and into our lawyer's office in a matter of minutes.

Shocked, pi$$ed, and angry, we walked out of that meeting hoping that there was a way to win, and wondering what our next move would be. The bottom line was that Tony had a management contract and a non-compete clause, and I didn't. I never really knew what was in his contract, and he didn't know that he had left them a way out of the agreement.

What I did know was that we were fu*ked, and there was no way we were getting our jobs back. It was December 18th, just one week until Christmas, and we were unemployed. Smokey and Smittee were still in L.A., and they were out too.

A new manager was brought into Elations. The new guy would inherit a hot club with a great staff, and the corporation was convinced that they had an indestructible machine that anyone could operate—for a lot less money, with a lot more control.

I learned a big lesson that day—business has no conscience. This time, the yo-yo was back, pushing me way down, making me wonder if I should just shake off the Ft. Myers experience and move on.

No matter what, it was still Christmas, and I decided to go back to Jersey for the holidays, hoping that it would help clear the air.

CHAPTER SIX

TEMPTATION, REDEMPTION, AND MARILYN IS THE GIRL FOR ME

I couldn't believe how quickly everything changed. Elations was basically on autopilot during the busy holiday season, and I knew that as long as they were busy and the tips were flowing, all would be well with the staff. Page was in Jersey, and Tony was trying to celebrate his first Christmas in Florida with his young family. The faces who threw the party at Elations had disappeared overnight, and I wondered if I would ever get the chance to work with Page and Stallion again.

TONY COFFARO:

Getting legal advice during the holidays was impossible. During this same period, a local businessman named Walter approached me about reopening a place as soon as possible.

Walter presented himself as a retired dentist who owned a couple of dental labs. He was a New York transplant who loved the Florida lifestyle. Like so many people, he was fascinated with the bar business and the cash it could generate. Walter promised legal and financial backing to sue the Elations investors and to start a new project.

I had a non-compete clause in my contract with Elations, and that was going to be a problem. However, neither Page nor Smokey had ever been under contract, and I knew I could run the operations from behind the scenes.

Ft. Myers had always been a one-nightclub town, and the success of Elations had forced Babaloo's to close their doors. The owner of Babaloo's was very bitter over his club's demise, but when Walter approached him with a way to relieve some of his debt, he was willing to listen.

It was far from the ideal location, but we found out that we could take back Babaloo's building. The owner was trying to offset his lease requirements by selling fixtures and sound equipment. His lease term was only through April, but with four strong months of the tourist season ahead, we felt we might be able to make some money. It would be cheap to get in, and we knew we could do enough weekend business to at least challenge Elations and be a pain in Jerry's a$$. Walter was concerned that we may have trouble finding help, and suggested that we not tell any prospective employees that we would be out in April.

Tony phoned me at Gram's, and his first words were: "Dutch, are you ready to go back to work?" When Stallion called me "Dutch," it was usually when he was in a happy-go-lucky, loving-life mode.

I remembered Walter as an older guy who wore a Panama hat, driving around in his Mercedes ragtop with the license plate, "SPEND IT." He would occasionally visit Elations to check out the girls and scope out the nightlife, but when it came to business . . . Walter was a sharp son-of-a-bit*h.

The bottom line was that he was offering to help us get back in the game, but he also saw an opportunity to make some money and become part of our party.

Stallion, Walter, and I arranged a meeting as soon as I returned to southwest Florida. I called Smokey, and he left right away for the meeting in Cape Coral. We laid out plans to paint the walls, make a few minor changes, and open our new place as soon as we could.

The only thing that we disagreed on was the staff. I wanted no part of lying to our staff about the April closing date. I wanted to tell all prospective staff members the truth from the get-go. Walter disagreed, saying that no one would move from Elations to the old, tired Babaloo's location if they knew that they would be out of work after the season.

Walter asked me what percentage of the staff would leave Elations to work with us again.

I quickly answered, "All of them."

Walter thought I was dreaming. He told me that "all of them" was an unrealistic answer, and that it would be impossible to offer the same salaries, positions, and tip amounts in the interim location. Again, Walter asked me what percentage I thought we could recruit.

"Every single person we want and need will come with us," I said confidently.

Page didn't pull any punches about the deal being a four-month, Spring Break party bar, and he and I began to contact the staff by phone. When I walked into that meeting, I had no idea what to expect. But, within a few minutes, Page and I were like the *Blues Brothers* calling to say that we were "puttin' the band back together." We had the core of our staff ready to join us within a half-hour, and everyone we called was excited and ready to donate their time to help remodel, refurbish, and repaint the old Babaloo's. The purveyors, the radio reps, and the grapevine were all alerted, and the town was buzzing within hours.

We decided on the name of our new place right away. Since the people of Ft. Myers were elated with Elations, they would surely be tempted by "Temptations . . . The Hot One." Jerry and the investors had immediately dropped the words "The Hot One" from all Elations advertising, and that decision proved to be prophetic.

Temptations would have a scaled-down entertainment staff, making the bartenders more of the show. The Elations dancers who wanted to come with us would also serve as cocktail waitresses, shot girls, and hostesses. Smittee would be there, of course, and although we didn't want to lose Frank Ormstead, we knew we couldn't afford him.

The energy in the meeting room was great, and Walter was in euphoric shock. As a businessman, he knew that taking the staff with us insured that the crowd would be close behind.

The shake-up at Elations put some of the employees in better shape than they were when we were at the helm. Bobby Scarcello and Brad Maloney were middle-rung bartenders with us, but were offered assistant management positions at the new Elations. After we made a few calls, it was evident that the Elations staff would be depleted, but we also knew that Temptations had an expiration date.

There were two people we wanted to talk to in person, though. DJ Johnny M and Bobby Scarcello came right over.

We all loved Bobby "Scar," but we knew that he would be the hardest to convince. He was around our age, and was a veteran of the hospitality business. He had all the credentials to own, manage, and operate his own place. He had been offered a great deal as the assistant to the new manager of Elations, while we had only bar shifts to offer. With Smokey as the head bartender and the other top guns on their way, prime shifts for Bobby would be tough to come by. We knew that his best move was probably to stay at Elations, but we hoped that Bobby would join us and help in our plans for the future.

When Bobby Scarcello showed up, it got a bit emotional. He had started as our happy-hour bartender at Elations, and had been a fantastic addition to our team. He had come up the ranks and paid his dues. We all knew that Bobby would take a hit financially, but we also knew that he was one of us.

BOBBY SCARCELLO:

Elations made me a great offer to manage, but I felt that Jerry and the corporation had broken up our dream team. When Smokey called and I heard Page and Tony in the background, I rushed over to some dental office in Cape Coral to hear about Temptations.

They were honest about it being half the money, half the stature, and only a four-month deal, and I didn't want to compete against the guys in that room—they were my friends.

Surprised and happy to be back in business! Page, "Stallion" and "Walta" plan to create Temptations— a Spring Break party club.

Stallion and I drew up some changes on a piece of scrap paper. We would take down a wall, add a bar, and paint the whole place. We built a stage for Smittee next to the "Mad Hatter Bar" that featured Smokey and his dozens of hats and wigs. Our "Champagne Pit" was so casual that it was almost a parody of what we had created at Elations.

Johnny M was still at Elations, and when I spoke to him briefly on the phone, he was anxious to hear more about our new deal. He came right over to meet with us. When he walked in the door, he gave me bad vibes, and when he opened his mouth, he made me sick.

A nightclub DJ's ego typically tells him that he is the reason for the success of the club, and Johnny M was no different. He was not only living the hype that Page had created around "DJ Johnny M" . . . he believed it. I listened to Johnny M explain that even though Elations was just six months old, they were going to remodel the club to appeal to a more upscale clientele. They had discontinued the stage shows and were enforcing a dress code that would ban jeans. Johnny liked the new manager, and he also liked the direction in which Elations was headed. Johnny went on to say that Bobby Scar and anyone else who was leaving Elations would be making a mistake.

TONY COFFARO:

I wanted to strangle the kid before another word came out of his mouth. Here was a guy who got every break from Page, and now he was going to be the only one not to come over?

Although Johnny left that meeting leading me to believe that he would join us at Temptations, I knew he was going to stay at Elations. When he stopped by during the painting and decorating, it was obvious that he doubted the project at first sight.

Johnny M called the place "a dump," and warned that I was lowering myself by being associated with Temptations. He was sure that the crowds would never leave Elations, and predicted failure.

There was no doubt that Temptations was certainly not as attractive as Elations. In fact, there was no comparison when it came to the sound system, fixtures, and décor, but we knew that going in. I felt confident that we could create the kind of party atmosphere that would get people interested. I believed that we could shock the town once again, and flip the crowd back our way.

Page had brought Johnny M to Ft. Myers, and when he decided to stay at what was now our competition, it was a problem Page never thought he would have. While Elations could easily replace their bar staff, it would have been difficult for them to find a DJ had Johnny M rejoined our staff.

I was pi$$ed and felt betrayed, but I had a new focus. I needed a DJ. My only solution was to contact the old DJ from Babaloo's who we had forced into retirement. David Lee was a good guy, but he was self-taught and had little dance club DJ experience other than his time at Babaloo's. I called and offered him the chance to get back in the booth, and he was willing to listen to my plan. When I told him that I was flying DJ George in from Xanadu for two weeks to give him a crash course and help us open Temptations, he jumped at the chance to learn. George had been Johnny M's mentor and was on his way to Florida on vacation. He agreed to work and teach a couple of hours a night for $100 an hour.

The late-great DJ George was one of the greatest guys I had ever worked with, and I knew that if David Lee was willing to learn, George would be the perfect instructor. If the music was good the first two weeks and the place was a fun party spot, we had a chance. George could create it, and David Lee could maintain it.

We were pooling our resources to make the crowd follow us to Temptations while Elations' owners were trying to block Walter's efforts.

At the forefront was the fact that Tony had a non-compete clause, but Jerry and Elations' attorneys were attempting to make us cease the operation of Temptations for a multitude of reasons. We were in a war being fought tactically in the lawyers' offices and promotionally on the radio airwaves. And with Stallion on the sidelines, Page had the ball and was ready to march down the field with a great team behind him. Although most everyone believed that Stallion was active behind the scenes, it was Page who was making it happen. Tony Coffaro was known as a premier operations man, but Temptations' success was dependent on the promotion and hype, and Page was confident, cocky, and ready to take it to another level.

We began to use "The Hot One" tag line. Jerry decided to drop it from all Elations advertising immediately, but their next few decisions were all we needed to widen the gap right out of the gate.

As part of their desire to upgrade Elations' clientele, not only were jeans banned, but athletic shoes were no longer permitted. I knew that this was a great angle for us, but when

Elations tampered with the VIP cards, it was suicide. They abruptly stopped VIP privileges and made all cardholders reapply. The result was that all of the VIPs had to stand in a long line, waiting to fill out an application and be approved . . . so that they wouldn't have to stand in a long line.

With the confusion and confrontations at their front door and the changes resulting from Elations cutting their overhead to increase profits, we set out to light up the town.

With my game plan in hand, I went to the radio stations to deliver our new ad copy and promotions for opening week. Our theme line was: "The Entire Staff of the Hot One is Reunited." Temptations would have a grand opening party and accept all VIP cards and everyone who wanted to dance, have fun, and party at a new place.

Walter helped me add an element to the character I am today when he suggested that I become even *more* of a personality. On the day that I went to the radio station, he said, "You're the guy they see and hear when they come to the club, so your voice should be the only one they hear on the radio. They will hear your voice and see your face, and associate that with the fun they have had since you came to town."

From that day on, I was the voice on 90 percent of every spot we did. As the opening approached, I knew we were building momentum. Elations was on the run before we even opened.

The word was out that Elations was planning to close in three weeks for a bust-out, five-day period of extensive remodeling. They wanted a more upscale club like the ones that were popping up in Boca Raton and Palm Beach, and their plans included brass rails, ferns, and a stainless-steel dance floor.

"Temptations . . . The Hot One" had a grand opening party that was like New Year's Eve in Times Square. Meanwhile, Elations was open and had all the lights on, but there may as well have been police crime tape around the building.

With the promotions that were in place for the opening weeks, we stayed blistering hot. Free drinks flowed almost daily from eight to ten, and the dance floor raged. The music was great, the place was fun, and there was a party going on every night.

Elations was not the place to be. They still had our overflow on weekend nights, but their club was very sick. We smoked them the first month we were open, but the jury was still out. Everyone knew that they were going to remodel in time for the height of the tourist season. Spring Break was a month away, and that would be the deciding factor.

We were rockin' like never before with a crew who was having fun, getting laid, and gloating all the way to the bank. Having only four months became fun to them, like a constant party until their world came to an end.

We kicked Elations' a$$ for a solid month. I knew I was not only in the Elations owners' heads, but in their pockets too. They were cutting corners on promotions and staff, and spending it on lawyers. The legal situation had me worried a little since this was the first time I had ever had someone trying to legally hold me down. Walter's lawyer assured me that nothing would happen until our temporary lease expired, and by then, Temptations would be history.

Jerry had lawyers who had lawyers, and he and the corporate brain trust were trying every angle to stop us. They even went so far as to say that we stole the slogan "The Hot One." I laughed my a$$ off that Jerry was now fighting for the words "The Hot One." Go-o-o figure.

Major money was spent to change the look of Elations. They bought new fixtures, wall coverings, bar tops, and furniture, and even replaced the dance floor. The club was less than a year old, and they were rolling the dice on not only being new and improved, but being upscale and pompous.

Elations scheduled their grand opening from six to nine p.m. with free drinks, which was standard practice for a VIP party.

During this time, Page was making most of the decisions. Walter was wondering why he was paying Stallion not to work, and at the same time, Stallion couldn't see working with a wannabe like Walter. Three weeks into the opening, Walter had already changed. He would make grand entrances and order the staff around, and he truly believed that he was the reason for the success and money that were being generated.

Business was booming at Temptations, but I was getting hit from all angles. There were Elations' lawyers and Walter's misconceptions. To make matters worse, I didn't know what the hell I was going to do after my four months were up.

The final "extravaganza" at Temptations was a full house, even though the party was held on a Monday night. Within days, both Page and Smittee appeared on MTV. The "Prince of Promo" was taking "The Show" on the road.

Elations' reopening was scheduled for a Friday night, so Page countered with "The Hot One's First Annual Ft. Myers Appreciation Extravaganza" on the same night.

Our promotion was different than any other we had planned before because the free drinks included any type of drink or shot, and we extended our free drinks until 11 p.m.

Shortly after the free well drinks promotion at Elations ended at nine o'clock, there wasn't a soul in the place. But across town at Temptations, there was dancing on the bars, in the aisles, and on the stage. The new and improved Elations was being buried, and it stayed that way throughout the week.

During that week, Elations stepped up their pace promotionally. They made a point in their ads to mention their no jeans policy. I couldn't believe they were stupid enough to think that turning people away at the door was the way to go, especially when it seemed that *everybody* was wearing designer jeans and Reeboks *everywhere* they went.

After hearing David Bowie's song "Bluejeans" on the radio, I decided to make the coming weekend a "Mean Jean Scene." We promoted the party again with free drinks, but this time, the only people who would pay cover charges were the ones *not* wearing jeans.

That night, Temptations . . . The Hot One was packed, and I was jacked to the max. Elations was now "The Dead One," and had only been new and improved for barely a week.

The writing was on the wall, and the tune had changed for Elations' DJ, Johnny M. Now he was *begging* to join us at Temptations.

By the time we did the Mean Jean promotion, the ref was counting Elations down and out. The lines were formed outside of Temptations, and we had a faithful crowd who loved us. Spring Break was upon us, and I knew that in eight weeks it would all be over. Smittee was on fire, and the college kids were telling their friends at other schools to go to Temptations in Ft. Myers to see Smittee and be a part of our party.

The clock was ticking, and it was evident that there was little chance that any of us would continue in future ventures with Walter, and I was the first to jump. I went home to Naples to manage the hot club there, but this time we all parted ways from a much better place than we had just four months before. This time we were on top and going out as winners.

I learned some valuable lessons from the Elations-to-Temptations saga that will remain with me forever. I can easily make a connection between the bar business, as I knew it, and my life in professional wrestling. The struggles and feelings of exhilaration are similar. The bottom could seemingly drop out overnight. The life expectancy of a hot club could be just as fleeting as the careers of so many wrestlers. Those who are remembered are the ones who make the biggest splash and the ones who find the right gimmicks to withstand the changes in the industry.

I realized later that I never needed Walter. He only used me and my bro's for his personal gain. It really hadn't been profitable for me, and he never cut me in on the revenues at the end of our four-month blitz. But what he never knew was that I lived for the challenge and would have done it all for free. With a little help from my friends, I learned so much about myself and what I could accomplish.

Tony "Stallion" Coffaro and I were partners, but his Elations contract had taken him out of the picture. I was looking for options and felt confident that I could find an investor to front another new club in Ft. Myers, but in the last month of Temptations, my focus began to change. When I saw the impact that Smittee was having on the Spring Break crowd, I knew that if I could get him seen by the right people, we could sell it.

MTV was red hot and had scheduled a week-long "Spring Break Celebration" that was going to be shown live from Daytona Beach. There was no doubt that this was the perfect place to showcase Smittee, and I was determined to take him and his unusual style of comedy directly to them.

SMITTEE:

Page was the best manager anyone could ever have, and he was the first person to believe that I really could be in show business. Temptations had been great, and the Spring-Breakers loved my act, but we had no idea what was next. In just a few months, Page had been able to book me as the opening act for groups like Greg Allman, The Romantics, *Joe Walsh, and even my favorite, Weird Al Yankovic.*

Although I knew that he didn't really know how he would pull it off, Page boasted to everyone that he was going to get me on MTV, and told everyone to look for me at "Spring Break Live From Daytona."

Daytona was better than even I expected. Smittee was featured on the live telecast from the beach several times, doing his imitation of Curly from *The Three Stooges* and song parodies. MTV was cutting edge, and the hottest vehicle for music and entertainment in the history of television. Along with thousands of screaming college kids, the MTV management and crew "popped" for Smittee.

That weekend, I was introduced to some of the most creative men in the entertainment business. Through my pleasant persistence, I was honing my ability to promote myself outside of the bar business for the first time. That was the beginning of the confidence building that would later be necessary to pursue my dream of being in professional wrestling.

DOUG HERZOG
THEN MTV SENIOR VICE PRESIDENT OF PRODUCTION:

Page was a real hustler and go-getter who aggressively promoted Smittee and his crazy visual act. We liked them both right away, and Page was someone who could sense that he not only had the ears of the MTV guys, but that it could turn into a great opportunity.

His experience in the nightclub business and having had promotions on beaches and in bars gave him the edge and confidence that was necessary to get Smittee seen. But Page always had his own attention-getting look as well, and he walked with the swagger and style of a professional wrestler, even then.

I believed in Smittee, and I felt that I could assist MTV in finding successful ways to use his skills. That weekend, I found out that MTV was going to do a summer on-the-road series that would start in Asbury Park and center around the beach and the Stone Pony. It was ironic because I had been thinking about heading back to the Jersey Shore for the summer to promote Smittee full time, and to promote a bar or two while I was at it.

JOE DAVOLA
THEN MTV EXECUTIVE PRODUCER:

The first time we saw Smittee was when Page had set up a table on the beach for Smittee to do his "Eat It" bit.

We were blown away and in hysterics watching this guy with his hand stuffed up a chicken, pouring food into his mouth, doing a parody of Weird Al Yankovic's parody of Michael Jackson's song "Beat It."

That night, we were doing a promo in a bar, and Page had gone there with Smittee who was doing "The Curly Shuffle." The place was rockin'. I loved Smittee and Page, especially Page's energy. We wound up doing a bit with him called "Smittee In Training" where we had Smittee teach three Spring-Breakers how to do "Eat It."

Later that summer, we walked into a bar on the Jersey Shore, and there were Smittee and Page again.

At that time, we were doing an MTV on-the-road production called "Amuck in America," and later, Smittee played Nero on our live New Year's Eve show. We did a lot with Smittee over the next couple of years, and I developed a great friendship with Page.

I was sky-high when Smittee and I returned to Ft. Myers following our road trip to Daytona Beach. With the Temptations deal about to end, offers were suddenly on the table. Walter made me a lame offer that I paid little attention to, but Jerry wanted to talk, and that made me curious.

I met with Jerry and was half-a$$ thinking that he would offer me a job to relight the fire at Elations. I was ready to laugh in his face. But his offer was even better than that.

Elations barely held on through the season. They spent thousands on legal fees, while losing thousands in revenue after the opening of Temptations. Jerry realized that if Page put together another nightclub when Temptations closed, Elations would go under. His solution to stop losing money was to offer Page money *not* to do a deal in Ft. Myers.

It was perfect. I kicked their a$$, and they paid me to stop. Jerry offered me almost the same amount of money that Walter screwed me out of, and in return, I agreed that as long as Elations was in Ft. Myers, I wouldn't own or operate a nightclub there. It wound up being good money chasing bad because they had no idea that I was already making plans to leave with Smittee for the summer.

The financial beating that Elations had taken proved to be too much to recover from, and Elations closed for good within six months.

Page and Smittee drove out of Ft. Myers looking good and loving life in Page's recently-restored hot-pink 1962 Cadillac convertible. Encouraged by the response they had received from Smittee's appearance at Daytona, they were ready to see and be seen.

Once in Jersey, Page began promoting seven clubs for three different ownership groups. This enabled him to have seven different stages where he could book and promote Smittee. Even former partner, Tony Pallagrosi, helped add bookings, and most weeks,

Then an MTV producer, "Crazy" Joe Davola and Smittee enjoy a Spring Break beverage in Daytona, Florida.

Smittee worked seven days. Page and Smittee traveled together, lived together, and promoted . . . together.

We kept in contact with Joe Davola, and appeared at several of the MTV locations throughout the summer. Smittee's face kept popping up on the tube doing the Curley Shuffle, hitting a gong with his bald head, or smashing cymbals on his body. The exposure we received in such a short time was incredible.

MTV provided a tremendous angle to help secure bookings since club owners had a hard time understanding what Smittee was doing on stage sometimes. Video helped, but he really had to be seen live to appreciate what he could do to raise the energy and party level of a crowd.

The exposure had been great, and Smittee was seen around the world on MTV. However, even though his appearance schedule was full all summer, there was very little money associated with that exposure. Smittee didn't really work for MTV; they just liked him and his act, and plugged him in when he showed up at their events. Often times, it would be necessary for Page to sacrifice appearance fees for the opportunity to have Smittee perform on high-profile nightclub and comedy club stages. Prior to the summer in Jersey, Page had never taken a salary or commissions while he promoted Smittee, and often times, the money was used for expenses and channeled back into promotion and publicity efforts.

It was a great summer, overall, and I was able to keep Smittee busy the whole time, lining up enough work for him to squeak by. He had done a novelty TV advertising spot, and MTV was working on something for the holidays, but summer was over, and the beach bars were closing. This would be the first off-season experience on the Jersey Shore for Smittee and his wife, Dana, and at times, it was difficult for all of us. With fall turning to winter, business was dying fast.

TONY COFFARO:
From the day we were removed from Elations, I vowed to get back in that building. When they closed their doors in

September, I began to weed through the red tape, debts, and paperwork that lingered over the business.

I talked to Page, and we decided that if a deal could be worked out where we had protection and were actually partners with the investors, we would do it all over again.

As it became closer to reality, Page and I discussed it more. After he laid out the theme over the phone, I sharpened my pencil, redesigned the layout, and looked for financing. We had a winner if we could get a game—a cross between Elations and Temptations.

If and when the location became available, I wanted to be ready to go. Now that Elations was defunct, the non-compete contracts were null and void. Nothing could get in our way.

Stallion was possessed. I could hear it in his voice every time he called. He gave me blow-by-blow descriptions of the phone calls he was making to get back into the gutted building where, less than a year ago, we had been walking on water.

And Stallion made it happen. There were new investors who were actually the silent type, like most of them claim to be. We were on our way back, and this time it was going to be better than ever.

I have always been a huge Marilyn Monroe fan, and there was a time when Marilyn was not promoted nearly as much as she is now. The 25th anniversary of her death was less than a year away, and I had recently seen a TV documentary on her life which made me think about the era in which she lived when people enjoyed cocktails, dancing, and late-night fun.

I searched for books and magazines with pictures of Marilyn, and found that there were so many great shots of her, and so many possibilities for the décor of a club. Stallion loved my ideas, and we brainstormed over the phone. I knew that the timing was right to own the town again, but I wanted to make sure that this time we could make money.

We loved the potential and possibilities of our new theme, but we also liked the sound of her real name, Norma Jean. We decided that Norma Jean's looked better in print and on merchandise, and in a week, I was back in Florida. We knew we had our work cut out for us when we established a deadline that was going to be nearly impossible to hit; but December 18th was special. On that date, just one year earlier, Jerry and the Elations' owners had cut us loose . . . and ripped out our hearts.

"Norma Jean's Dance Club" did open on that night, and it was a grand celebration. Page and Stallion hugged and high-fived the entire night, while the champagne flowed and the registers rang. Many of the original crew were reunited, and were joined by a few energetic young studs and hot chicks who were always ready to throw a party. Smittee was back on stage, and even Johnny M was back in the DJ booth with a new attitude and the latest big-city dance music. Many of the successful promotions and contests were updated and brought back with even more prize money and more hype. Norma Jean's was hot out of the blocks and was steamrolling by the first of the year.

I had to pinch myself. Norma Jean's was open, and we were everything that we were before, and more. The people of Ft. Myers loved the club, the theme, and all that we had to offer. We sold out our New Year's Eve party before we had even opened, but for the second year in a row, I wouldn't be able to ring in the New Year with Stallion and our crew.

MTV planned to feature Smittee in their televised New Year's Eve special from New York City. We were ecstatic when we heard the angle, and the shot for Smittee to appear live was huge. MTV was calling the show "Nero's Eve," and they wanted Smittee to play the lead role as the Roman emperor, Nero.

I saw all the MTV people I had met the previous April during Spring Break, and it was evident that we were developing lifelong friendships. I was told that they wanted Smittee at Spring Break again, and I knew that this time I would be able to promote the hell out of him for the crowd at Norma Jean's as "MTV's Spring Break Mascot."

Norma's stayed red-hot, and many of the bar staff were getting burned-out from the incredible crowds that we had from the day we opened the doors. Smokey returned to give us a boost when we needed it. He was the most respected and fun guy to have on the staff, and was able to teach the rookies about "life behind bars." Best of all, he was a guy who knew how to contribute with ideas and energy, and he knew how to make money.

After work one night, Page and I had done a couple of shots of Cuervo and were ringing out the registers while the bartenders cleaned their bars. The Cyndi Lauper video for the song "Girls Just Wanna Have Fun" came on the big screen, and Page suddenly stopped to stare as if it were the first time he had seen it. I was confused since the song had been out awhile and was popular both on the radio and in the club. Page just shook his head and said, "I can't fu*kin' believe that wrestling and rock and roll got together without me!"

The video featured veteran wrestling personality, Captain Lou Albano, and had scenes that were shot in a wrestling ring. Seeing that video led Page to reveal his two childhood dreams to me.

It was that night when he first told me about his brief stint in wrestling, and his dream to be a professional wrestler. It was a bit of a shock, but when he told me that his other dream was to own and operate a year-round Christmas village, I just poured another shot. I knew that I'd never meet anyone who had those same two dreams in a million years.

Smoke looked at me like I had three heads, but watching that video made me think about my early dreams of being a

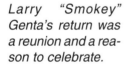

Larry "Smokey" Genta's return was a reunion and a reason to celebrate.

wrestler. Captain Lou was always one of my favorites, and as I stared at it, I remembered watching wrestling with Rory and Pop.

I knew that wrestling was hot, and I started watching it again, thanks to Jesse "The Body" Ventura, Bobby "The Brain" Heenan, and Jake "The Snake" Roberts. The bar business was good to me, and I was happy, but wrestling was one of those things that I wished I had pursued. There wasn't a time when I saw it on TV that I didn't think about what I might have been.

SMITTEE:

I was really looking forward to Spring Break this time, and I started believing that Page was right—I was going to be a star. I always wanted to make it big, and he had done so much to get me to that point. I knew that I wanted Page to be right by my side every step of the way.

But every once in awhile, Page threw out ideas that seemed totally off-the-wall. After we got back from Daytona, he sat down with my wife, Dana, and me, and told us how serious he was about getting us into professional wrestling.

It always amazed me how strong and athletic Smittee was, even though I never saw him work out or lift a weight. At 6'3" and 298 pounds, he was thick and strong.

The fact that the Cyndi Lauper video was so "over[1]," and that so many people were seeing Captain Lou for the first time, blew me away. My idea was that Smittee would train to work in the ring, with the angle that he would become the "MTV Wrestler."

While at Spring Break, it was easy to tell that the MTV execs liked Smittee, but they didn't know how else to use him. When I ran my initial idea by them, they liked it. They too could see Smittee as the MTV Wrestler and me as his manager. Since the Cyndi Lauper video was hot, and Andy Kaufman was wrestling and making waves on *Saturday Night Live*, it seemed like a natural. I told them that I needed to explain it all to Smittee, and that I would put the plans

---

[1]*over—A term for fan popularity, often used in the wrestling business.*

and the gimmick on paper.

I knew Smittee had so much untapped talent and the ability to entertain people, but he needed the right vehicle. MTV was the vehicle to get him seen, but wrestling was the vehicle to make him a star.

JOE DAVOLA
TELEVISION EXECUTIVE:

I was at Fox-TV by that time, but I kept in touch with Page. He was always pleasantly persistent, but never a pain-in-the-@$$.

I've loved wrestling since I was a kid, and I had done all the promo production work around the Cyndi Lauper video. Also, I had a close relationship with Vince McMahon dating back to Wrestlemania I, *and loved the idea of Smittee wrestling . . . with Page as his manager.*

I knew that Page had the ability and presence to get people to notice him. He's like the P.T. Barnum of the '90s, the ultimate showman. Nothing he has done, or will ever do, would surprise me.

DOUG HERZOG
CURRENT PRESIDENT FOX-TV:

While at MTV, we had done several things with the WWF, and were definitely considering Page's idea of making Smittee the MTV Wrestler. I think Page had done some initial talking with a contact that he had at WWF who may not have believed that he could deliver MTV. We were looking at the opportunities and had a few reservations about it, but I think that, ultimately, it was Smittee's "cold feet" that ended the discussions.

Smittee wouldn't hear of it. He said that he was a comedian, not a wrestler, and that he wanted to pursue his career the same way he always had. Page was more than bummed out that Smittee couldn't see the possibilities that we all saw. It had been a year since Page had been a soon-to-be-out-of-work nightclub manager who walked the beach looking for a camera to stick Smittee in front of. Now Page had developed an idea to promote himself, and had the major players at MTV considering Smittee as a lead character.

SMITTEE:

When I was younger, I wanted to be a wrestler too. I would imitate my favorite, Dusty Rhodes. I also wanted to be a football player, but now I was a comedian. I was still happy with what Page was doing, but money was getting tight, and I wanted only to be a visual comedian. I didn't think I was in good enough physical shape to wrestle because of back surgery I had as a result of a football injury.

But most of all, I was a comic. I didn't mind using my talents to make people laugh, but I didn't want to be a comic professional wrestler and have people laugh at me.

Yeah, I was pi$$ed. It was hard not to look at all those breaks that we had gotten and see that the best one was the one that Smittee didn't want.

This trip to the yo-yo was a bit different.

Norma's continued to break records, and was on its way to a long road of future success with the team we had. I was in the middle of the booze, the broads, and the party, and that was a comfortable place to be.

But I will always see Smittee's decision as a great opportunity that was missed. It was one that may have led to something much greater than it appeared on the surface. We had made an early connection with MTV, and it seemed that it had slipped away.

CHAPTER SEVEN

THE LOVES OF MY LIFE, SWEATIN' EVERYDAY, AND DIAMONDS ARE FOREVER

Diamond Dallas Page in a 1998 interview:
"People who I have known for years will come up to me and ask me what it feels like to be famous. I just laugh and say, 'C'mon . . . you know I've always thought I was famous.'"

And he was. Page acquired that fame in many different ways to the people who had crossed his path to that point. It may have been because of his unique name, or his determination to be a star basketball player. Some knew him because of his long hair, the fact that he was the kid who got hit by the car, or because he had been kicked out of St. Joe's High School. But growing up, Page always got noticed.

In the bar business, he was everything that they have said about him . . . The Prince of Promo and P.T. Barnum all rolled into one. His look and attitude were enough to get attention, but when he was at work, the sight of him in the DJ booth or on stage would light up the crowd.

His clothes were ridiculous. They consisted of zebra-print sport coats, airbrushed jackets, studded jeans, and cutup T-shirts; and his cowboy boots and matching belts were made from an assortment of reptiles. Ostentatious jewelry and oversized rings gleamed from the wireless mic, but when Page wore it . . . it just worked. Somehow, he looked slick, sharp, and showbiz in whatever he wore.

When Norma Jean's was packed with sunburned tourists, he loved to get in the DJ booth and give the temperatures from around the nation. Of course, they were "guesstimates," but they were close enough to jack up the crowd. Page would interrupt a song and yell, "In Boston today, it was 19 degrees, Philadelphia 22 degrees, Detroit 16, Chicago 24, and Ft. Myers . . . 86 degrees and SUNNY!" The crowd would go apesh*t.

Page served as emcee for all the various contests held at Norma Jean's. There were always wild promotions and his creative "gimmick-a-rama." There were contests to win pink Caddies, hot tubs, thousands of dollars in cash, tons of VIP cards, countless hours of limo time, trips to concerts, and Bahamas getaways. Businesses that hooked up with one of Page's promotions thrived, and he helped put many of them on the map. Since the Lani Kai Resort gave us weekends to give away, we brought our party to their beach. Hair stylists and swimsuit companies stood in line to be associated with a Norma Jean's Bikini Contest or our . . .

. . . often imitated, but nnnever duplicated . . . world-famous NNNorma Jean's Hot Legs Contest!

We did many varied promotions with sexual over- and undertones, but the Hot Legs Contests were the best. Each contest was memorable and always a little different. Sometimes, we gave them more of a pageant-like show; and other times, we strategically positioned a black curtain up to *there*, keeping the ladies behind the screen so that the crowd could see only their legs and their strut. It would get pretty wild some nights, especially when the crowd could see just a girl's attitude coming from her hot legs and black, high-heeled pumps. During Spring Break, the crowd usually voted for some college girl who was letting her hair down for the first time. But, Good Gawd!, if everyone thought the real show was in front of the curtain . . . forgettaboudit!

THOM "SKIPPY" POPPOLI
A NORMA JEAN'S BARTENDER:

Smokey was the man behind the bar, and Tony the Stallion was the "Godfather," but Page was the star of the show.

It didn't matter if he was on the stage getting everyone to vote for the best couple in the Erotic Banana Eating Contest or at the bar getting Smokey to build a pyramid of peach fuzz shooters . . . Page drew and held the crowd. I remember just days after the movie When Harry Met Sally *came out, Page had girls behind a curtain faking orgasms and screaming "Oh God!" for cash and prizes.*

The promotions and contests were outrageous, and, sometimes, even controversial. There were times when the male revues and girls wrestling in whipped cream got the ire of local right-wing groups and media, but Norma Jean's received national attention when the State of Florida banned dwarf-throwing contests.

Sometimes called "midget tossing," the contests were typically held at motorcycle rallies, but when a college bar in Florida began holding these contests, Page seized the opportunity and did his version on a grand scale.

Teddy Valentine was a customer, friend, and employee of Norma Jean's, and he was "special" like that. Although "The Little People of America" balked, Teddy was ready to become the star of

Teddy Valentine became a celebrity overnight as "Ted E. Bear," but he was a fixture at Norma Jean's. Teddy is pictured with other members of the security staff, "No-Neck" and "Big Man."

Page's newest promotion. Teddy stood his ground with the political groups that had objections, and once screamed at an overzealous representative of the "Little People's" organization, "Leave me alone! No one is exploiting me! Don't you know this is the most money I have ever made!"

Despite Teddy's willingness to be a part of the entertainment, the State of Florida banned the use of the words "midget" and "dwarf" from all advertising and promotions, so Page put his spin on it and found a way to make it work.

The promotion was certainly a big hit with the Spring-Breakers, and fun for everyone to be a part of, but with the state and local ordinances, it was difficult to advertise to the people who were coming in and out of town weekly. That's when Page changed Teddy Valentine's character to "Ted E. Bear." The promotion became the "Put the Bear in the Air" contest, and weekly, Teddy E. Bear, in full bear costume, got tossed onto layers of mattresses, which, of course, were on loan as part of the promotion.

I took a lot of heat about the contest, and the press tried to trump it up, but the bottom line was that Teddy had no problem with it, and he urged me not to give in to the pressure. We did it so it was legal. Teddy was physically protected and emotionally stable, and was making more money and having more fun than he ever had.

Most of all, Teddy is my friend. He was about nineteen years old when I first met him at one of our "Teen Night" promotions, and he was a cool kid who dressed sharp, was loved by the ladies, and danced to every song. The thing I liked most about him was that he never saw himself as being handicapped, and never felt like he was victimized by the situation.

Teddy helped make it fun, and looked and played the part like a pro. The club was able to get some "pub" (publicity), and Teddy made money and, at the same time, was a star. He was like me . . . he was having so much fun being a part of it; he would have done it for nothing.

KIRK TIPTON
FORMER ROOMMATE AND NORMA JEAN'S BARTENDER:

Page was always intense and demanding, and when he said he wanted something done, everyone made sure that it was done his way. As a roommate, his management skills sometimes spilled over from bar to home. The guys would break my balls and call me "Page's gopher" or "barback," but I owe so much to him for those times.

He taught me how to keep my head in the game, coached me with women, and not only showed me how to make money, but how to enjoy it. Yeah, he was tough and was like my a$$hole big brother at times, but at the same time, it was too much fun and a great education. There were plenty of good times, since we enjoyed the same things . . . girls, booze, sports, girls, working out, and more girls.

Ah, yes . . . there were always lovely ladies in the picture. The fact that chicks dig him has always been evident, but, let's just say, there were plenty of one-night stands, whirlwind weekends, live-in lovers, and broken engagements along the way. Almost every facet of Page's life has gone overboard at some point, and his romantic life was never an exception. Despite his travels, Page always seemed to be in pursuit of something that seemed elusive. The only thing that he could have added to his journey was a friend, lover, and partner to share the good times and the bad times that came with the yo-yo.

Through the years, there were some special ladies in my life—ladies I might have married and been happy with. I just didn't know if I could be happy and married to anyone for very long. I almost always had a girlfriend, and my relationship with each one had its own personalized yo-yo.

During those years, the women in my life knew that they had to share my attentions with a variety of my passions . . . the bar business, my friends, the gym, my dreams, and my whims. The lesson learned by the women during those single years was not to take it personally. I wasn't doing anything to intentionally hurt them.

I met a girl named Judy when I was running Club Xanadu in Jersey. I had been living with Roberta, the lady I backed away from in Texas. Roberta was a great lady, and we lived together off and on for a year or so. We broke up, and I moved out a dozen times, and that's not a jacked up number. I helped raise her son, Jimmy, who was sometimes like a son to me, and other times, like a little brother. Roberta and I dug each other, but we couldn't live together without constant battles.

Judy was different though, and we seemed compatible from the start. When I met her, she was working in New York City, getting up at five-thirty in the morning and putting in fourteen-hour days. We wanted to see more of each other, so Judy left her job to get on the same clock as I was on. We were tight, and Judy and I were falling for each other hard and fast. Within six months, we were talking marriage.

I knew that I wanted to be married, and Judy needed to know that, but I also knew that I wasn't really ready. We moved in together soon after we started dating, and as far as I was concerned, we were living like we were married. I would have been happy with a long engagement, but it was apparent that Judy didn't see it the same way. We had the ups and downs of most marriages, but were always close.

It was the move to Florida that separated us in more than just miles. I wanted Judy to relocate with me when I settled in Ft. Myers, but she wasn't leaving Jersey unless I set a wedding date. She wanted to start planning the ceremony, and gave me an ultimatum. She wasn't coming to Florida if there wasn't a definite date for our wedding. My response was blunt. "Well, I guess you're not moving to Florida."

Soon after arriving in Ft. Myers, I was distracted by a bartender on our opening staff at Elations named Tammy. She was a natural strawberry-blond beauty who was bright, laid-back, and unique. She was so unique that it was difficult not to notice that she had one blue eye and one brown eye.

I was immediately attracted to Tammy, and tried my best to resolve what was happening with Judy before I went any further. Tammy was great to be around, and while all my efforts were directed to the opening of Elations, we were in each other's company more and more.

Judy and I went days without speaking, and I finally called her and offered her an option. "Come to Florida now without us setting a date, or I won't be able to stay engaged."

Honesty is brutal at times, and no matter what, it's hard for anyone to deal with. It's the honorable way, for sure, even if that isn't always the motivation. The bottom line is that I'm a dead giveaway when I lie to anyone close to me. It's just easier to tell the truth than deal with the reaction and the drama of lying.

"Page J." was the Master of Ceremonies for the many contests and extravaganzas that took the stage. There were bikini contests and, of course, the weekly "World Famous Hot Legs Contests."

It bothered Tammy that I was honest about my strong feelings for Judy. It seemed to Tammy that I must not really love Judy if I was spending so much time with her. She didn't like it, but dealt with the fact that my relationship with Judy was left undecided. It was difficult for us to deal with the pain caused by my feeling that I had hurt the girl I intended to marry.

My relationship with Tammy had some rocky and emotional times, and it got tougher around the time I began to actively promote Smittee. We had grown apart a bit, but after I made up my mind to head to New Jersey with Smittee, Tammy expressed the desire to go with me.

I loved her and really wanted her to join me, but I didn't see how it could happen. I knew I could find work for Smittee and myself, but I couldn't imagine having my girlfriend by my side while booking Smittee and trying to make it all work. I wanted to get setup first, and then have her move during the summer after I was established.

While Page was operating the hottest clubs in southwest Florida, he was generally liked and endeared by everyone. The local celebrity status that he enjoyed was often enhanced by his ability to waive cover charges, buy drinks, and promote the various businesses in the area. But after Page left Ft. Myers, the contempt and jealousy that many of the local guys harbored reared its ugly head.

It's just a fact of life that a ladies' man like Page can legitimately pi$$ off other males during their pursuit of the opposite sex. It wasn't hard to find guys who attempted to sway Tammy's interest in Page. Even trusted friends played the game by telling Tammy of Page's improprieties and escapades. After all, he was gone and was no longer "the man" who could give a guy a job . . . or a VIP card.

They fu*kin' buried me. Some were close friends of mine who couldn't wait until I was gone so they could tell of my female conquests, acting as shoulders to cry on. The claims were exaggerated, but they really didn't have to be. I was up North in the middle of the booze, the broads, and the party. Tammy heard so much sh*t about me that it was no wonder she cut off our relationship.

It was hard to love someone who had a lifestyle like mine, and even though Tammy loved me madly, it was evident that she was not madly *in love* with me.

Back in Jersey, while I was working hard to promote Smittee, I was suffering over the yo-yo of my love life. Judy and I had gone full circle and were just friends. She was like family, and was very close to my sister, Sally, and my mom, Sylvia.

I actually cried on Judy's shoulder, and she helped me deal with the same kind of hurt that I had caused her. I was very down about losing Tammy, hurting Judy, and not having either one of them.

During that same time, I rekindled an old love of mine. This love would never leave me and would give back everything that I put into it. Imagine a satisfying, rewarding, and, most times, euphoric feeling that could be depended on everyday. My workouts at the gym with the weights, machines, sweat, and pain became my new passion.

I was determined that I was going to look better by the end of the first week. I made the same pact every week, and I saw results immediately.

Not that I was heavy or way out of shape when I started; I just lacked size and muscle tone. Working out also gave me focus and helped get my mind in shape. I began to feel better about myself, my decisions . . . and the loves I had lost.

Page was single and as free as he had been in years, and was returning to Ft. Myers with the spotlight at Norma Jean's turned on high. That Spring Break was incredible, and Page couldn't get his fill of fun. He was certainly living life to its fullest, and had rightfully earned his "player" status with the ladies.

I was playing hard and having a great time, but after being disappointed with Smittee's decision not to explore the possibilities of becoming the MTV wrestler, I decided to try it myself. I made a commitment to myself to pursue and chase my lifelong dream of wrestling—the dream I thought had slipped away.

I started watching pro wrestling regularly again, and it was hot. Bobby "The Brain" Heenan's commentary was always entertaining and made me smile, and I liked Jake "The Snake" Roberts' gimmick and ring persona.

Jesse "The Body" Ventura was o-v-e-r, and his flamboyant outfits and interviews made me a huge mark[1] for him. He personified the characters I had followed as a kid:—Classy Freddie Blassie, Captain Lou, Handsome Jimmy Valiant, and "Superstar" Billy Graham.

Ironically, it was around that same time that I met Jake "The Snake" Roberts.

Norma Jean's and Ft. Myers was a natural halfway point for the WWF road shows when they traveled between stops in Tampa and Miami. When any professional wrestling tour came to Florida, the biggest names in the sport would visit Norma's to party on their way through town.

At times, Page's ideas and intensity were hard to swallow for all of us around him. Sometimes, he would throw out concepts just to get a reaction. But when he told us that since he always wanted to be a wrestler . . . he was going to "go for it," we knew he meant every word. It was late, after a big night, and the after-work drinks were flowing when Page pitched the wrestling manager idea to us in the office at Norma Jean's.

I had made up my mind to do something about my dream, and was feeling out the boys to see what they thought. Not that their comments would have changed my mind, but those guys were some of the biggest "ball-breakers" on the planet. They were my friends and confidants, and I wanted their reactions and opinions. I knew I'd take some ribbing, but also knew that their criticism and skepticism would only help motivate me more.

It was in that backroom meeting at Norma Jean's that "Diamond Dallas Page" was born. We brainstormed the gimmick the same way we developed bar promotions. I knew that my wardrobe would work, but I wanted to have just the right name to go with my character . . . whatever it would be.

We all had nicknames, and I was called different names by

---

[1] *a mark—A fanatical follower, a super fan of an individual performer.*

different people. Coffaro and Scarcello often called me "Dutch," since I was the only guy whose name didn't end in a vowel. Smokey called me "The Prince of Promo" or "Dalli," shortened from the name that my dad, Page One, had called me.

"Page One" Falkinburg:

I started calling him "Dallas" right before he moved in with Gram because he loved the Dallas Cowboys. It was really a name between the two of us. Whenever I called him on the phone, he knew it was me when I asked, "What's happening, Dallas?"

In that meeting, the boys asked about my earlier days in wrestling. When I told them that I had a brief encounter in the ring as "Handsome Dallas Page," Smokey, the consummate quick-witted smart-@$$, replied, "Page, it's been awhile. You can forget about that gimmick now."

Everyone agreed that I had the look and attitude for wrestling. I had worn a diamond earring for years, and several promotions were targeted to "a girl's best friend." When I tried out "Diamond Dallas Page" on the boys, they liked it a lot. No matter what . . . "diamonds *are* forever."

As far as I was concerned, I was already living the life of Diamond Dallas Page. With the fame of running a hot nightclub came the limousines and all the perks, and, of course, there had always been the booze, the broads, and the party.

The ideas started flying. "DDP" would have to have a knockout babe for a valet . . . she could be called a "Diamond Doll," and there could be a different girl every time.

Tony Coffaro:

I knew Dutch was on to something, and it wouldn't be a stretch at all. It was already part of his real life. He would choose an outfit, stroll around the club checking out every girl, and then make his way to the stage or DJ booth. He was the master of ceremonies, starting and delivering the hype, and he was already like a professional wrestling manager.

It started sounding better and better. If Jimmy Hart had the "Hart Foundation," Diamond Dallas Page could have "The

Diamond Exchange." I could have two or three Diamond Dolls and a stable of wrestlers. I had convinced myself that I was too old to climb into the ring, but I knew I could be a great manager and mic man.

Too old? What the fu*k was I thinking? I was only in my late twenties. I guess I thought that I had gotten my one and only shot at the ring when Crybaby Cannon took me to Canada for a beating.

That night, with my bro's, Stallion, Smokey, and Bobby "Scar," I decided that I was going to do it. I was going to find out how to get there, and I wasn't going to stop. I was determined to tell the wrestling world that I was Diamond Dallas Page, and I was B-A-double-D-BADD.

For a few weeks following that, I made plans to produce, cast, direct, and, of course, star in a homemade video[2] announcing the coming of Diamond Dallas Page and The Diamond Exchange. It was easy. I would simply look at my life and find just the right characters to pull it off.

About the same time, a local cable access show in southwest Florida called *The Party News Network* did a story on Page entitled "The Voice."

It was a five-minute piece that showed him cruising in his pink '62 ragtop Caddy, and, ironically, he was wearing a *Wrestlemania* T-shirt. There were shots of Page enjoying the lifestyle that he had created. He was seen lounging by the pool surrounded by ladies talking about the nightclub scene, and as the shoot was ending, the host asked, "So, where does 'the voice' come from?"

Page popped right into character, threw on a pair of shades, and said, "The voice comes from Diamond Dallas Page . . . Daddy . . . I was born to be a professional wrestling manager!" Then, off came the glasses, and he went right back to being Page.

_____

[2] *You can see clips of that first video at* ddpbang.com

CHAPTER EIGHT

THE CALL, THE EDUCATION OF DDP (PART I), AND THANKING GOD FOR UNANSWERED PRAYERS

Doesn't everyone have two friends with the last name Smith who go by the name Smitty or Smitt*ee*?

Well . . . I do. Smittee is the visual comedian who became the MTV mascot, and Smitty is a guy who does a national sports talk radio show. Smitty was making a name for himself as a small-market radio personality in Ft. Myers. He was doing a call-in sports talk show on a local AM station that he was just starting to syndicate across the nation.

Within a day or two of my appearance as "The Voice" on *The Party News Network* piece, a call came in for Diamond Dallas Page while I was at Norma Jean's. I was surprised since I had only used the name with my buddies in the bar and on that one program which aired only one time at midnight on a local cable channel.

SMITTY OF "SMITTY'S SPORTS TALK":

I saw the feature segment on The Party News Network *and knew that Page would be an entertaining live guest for my weekly wrestling talk radio show. At first he was reluctant to come on the show because I was having Sargent Slaughter on with him. He asked me exactly what I thought he should say and when he should say it. I had to convince him to simply be himself. He was so entertaining from the second I turned on his mic that I knew he was destined. Ft. Myers was just the beginning for both of us.*

We never said that I was really *in* professional wrestling, and Sarge put me over as a knowledgeable wrestling mark. The fact that I had so much experience doing ads and other radio work made it easy for me to be comfortable and believable.

Smitty liked what he heard in his first introduction to Diamond Dallas Page, and suggested that Page make a tape to send to a contact that he had at the American Wrestling Association (AWA).

The AWA was a Minneapolis-based promotion that was run by the legendary wrestler-turned-promoter, Verne Gagne. It was one of the many regional wrestling promotions that were the foundation for all that is known as professional wrestling today. Verne Gagne was a legendary champion. He held title straps through the decades, and he was the owner of the AWA. His son, Greg, was the heir apparent to his dad's company, and was a featured wrestler in the AWA.

The Gagnes promoted wrestling from the Midwest to Los Angeles and even Canada. There was a time when Verne Gagne was one of wrestling's most influential names who trained wrestlers by the dozens in a boot-camp environment called "The Barn." Through the years, the AWA produced some of the biggest names in wrestling history, including Hulk Hogan, Ric "The Nature Boy" Flair, and Jesse Ventura.

By that time, it was evident that the AWA had begun to slide. Vince McMahon was in every home across America, thanks to cable TV. Not only had he depleted the talent at the AWA, he had killed, and then swallowed, smaller competitors around the nation. Gagne lost many superstars to McMahon and the National Wrestling Association (NWA). Despite its gloomy future, the AWA had time left on a contract with ESPN, and they were still taping shows to air weekdays at four p.m. on the relatively new cable sports network.

Smitty's AWA contact was a guy named Rob Russin,

who was a holdover from the glory days of the AWA. The AWA had just lost another talent, Paul E. Dangerously, who signed with the NWA, a company based in the South. Paul E. was not only a manager, but was one of the most gifted speakers in the business. Smitty said that Russin was willing to try anything that would help put a$$e$ back in arena seats. He was also convinced that if I sent the right tape, I could replace Paul E. Dangerously. I had my doubts, but I could see Smitty's point.

The AWA was lacking a talker after Paul E. left. I knew that I could dazzle them with all that Diamond Dallas Page had to offer. Smitty said that he thought I talked better than any of the managers who were still in the AWA, and he was probably right. I had a lot of radio experience, and had entertained crowds of nearly a thousand. Besides that, I was already being treated like a celebrity . . . in my world, anyway.

I went to the gym and recruited a few guys who wanted to be wrestlers. Then I grabbed a few girls who worked at Norma's, and The Diamond Exchange was formed . . . on videotape.

Diamond Dallas Page was the star of the video that he made for Rob Russin and the AWA. The would-be wrestlers were named The Ice Man, Big Badd John, and The Blue Knight. Even Teddy Valentine appeared as Ted E. Bear, which was now his wrestling persona. The Diamond Dolls looked like strippers, but acted like groupies, as they escorted Diamond Dallas Page in the shoot. The second most credible star of the video was regional broadcaster, Jack Bernstein.

Jack had deep pipes, a real broadcasting voice, and some wrestling experience that also helped. I thought the tape was great . . . and when I show it to anyone now, they are surprised at how good it is—good for someone who didn't have a fu*king clue, that is.

ROB RUSSIN
FORMER AWA VICE PRESIDENT:
We received dozens and dozens of tapes each week, and wrestler tapes usually outnumbered manager tapes fifteen to

one. Actually, Jack Bernstein called to tell me about how impressed he was with the taping and the guy who produced, directed, and starred in it. It surprised me that Jack was impressed enough to call me about it.

Jack was right. Page's tape was different in that it was more like a Hollywood production. He was as spitshined and polished as someone who had been in the business for ten years. He had so much charisma that I saw Jesse Ventura, Jr. in that tape. I thought he must have been buried in some independent territory somewhere. When I heard he was in the nightclub business, I was shocked. I really didn't have to look far to know that this guy was a natural for our business.

I showed it to Ray Stevens and Wahoo McDaniels, who were long-time veterans and the current bookers, and they agreed that he was better than anything we had, with the potential to be even better. Verne and Greg Gagne had been out of town for a few days, but by the time they returned to Minnesota, everybody in the office had seen the tape and were raving about Diamond Dallas Page and his Diamond Exchange, and, of course, his Diamond Dolls.

The first promo shots of Diamond Dallas Page and "The Diamond Exchange" were taken the day he taped his "homemade" video to send to the AWA (American Wrestling Association).

If Page had known how many tapes and how many dreams were sent to the dozens of regional wrestling promotions around the country, he might not have felt so good about his. A huge number of audition tapes were being submitted, since the AWA was on ESPN. And most of those tapes never got close to a tape machine. The odds were astronomical then, and they are intergalactic now. To think that anyone could get to the decision-makers with a single video promo tape is more than a dream. It's more like a hallucination.

When the call came, I was jacked to the f*ckin' moon. Rob Russin was on the phone telling me that they were impressed, and wanted me *and my boys* to do a local show in Minnesota. Then he said, "If it works out, and we like you . . . we'll take you and the boys to the ESPN show in Vegas."

Now, as the yo-yo was soaring to the top, the bottom fell out as I searched for the right way to tell him the bitter truth— I had no f*ckin' "boys."

"Rob, those guys, they can't work. They're just guys who want to learn how to be wrestlers." I made sure not to hesitate as I continued, "But, what about me? I'm ready to go . . . right now!"

He didn't act pi$$ed off, and he didn't dismiss me, but he couldn't stop the yo-yo that I was feeling. He answered, "Let me think about it, and I'll get back to you."

Rob Russin didn't call back that day, the next day, or even that week. Page began to wonder if he had made a mistake by casting "extras" in his tape, and as the second week of waiting began, Page beat himself up emotionally from all angles.

ROB RUSSIN:
Our product at the AWA had become stale, and the writing was on the wall to everyone except the Gagnes. They had to go with the consensus opinion that we had to have Diamond Dallas Page as soon as possible, even though they had become a little gun-shy.

They were afraid that Page would get too big, too fast, and become uncontrollable like some other guys who had started with the AWA. Verne Gagne had lost Ventura, Hogan, and announcer Gene Okerland to Vince McMahon; and now Paul E. Dangerously had left as well.

Rob Russin finally called back, and the message was short and to the point. He told me to contact Greg Gagne because the AWA wanted to take me to Las Vegas for a try-out. I knew Las Vegas was where they did the ESPN TV tapings, and I also knew that the AWA World Tag Team Championship was scheduled at the same time. That match was to feature a couple of young, up-and-coming superstars named Sean Michaels and Marty Jannetty, who called themselves "The Midnight Rockers," and they were scheduled to take on the team of Paul Diamond and Pat Tanaka, known as "Bad Company." It was fitting that my tryout would be held at the Showboat.

The call to Greg Gagne was one that I'll never forget. He said, "Okay, Diamond, we're gonna give you a shot. If we like you, we'll use you. If we don't, we won't." He didn't say anything that I didn't already know. It was just the way he said it. He went on to say, "Don't forget to bring all those fancy clothes and one or two of those girls from the video."

To make sure that he brought the right combinations of outfits, instead of packing two jackets, Page packed ten. Some had fringe or airbrushed art. Some had tassels or silver buttons. But, all had rhinestones and were emblazoned with "DDP" or "Diamond" or "Dallas" or "Page." He brought everything from neon to animal skin, and selected T-shirts that he had customized using scissors to strategically place rips and tears. He brought four or five pairs of boots, and his jewelry was a meld of glimmering diamonds, rhinestones, gold, and cubic zirconia. He even brought his walking stick, (and, no, Dr. Nicholas) not to help him walk . . . it just added to his strut.

I had it all, and I was bringing it. I believed that I needed *every* look and *every* gimmick with me. The one thing that I knew would wind up in the shoot was my favorite walking stick. The stick was completely covered in rattlesnake skin, and the head of the snake was curved to conform to the handle at the top. This thing was so over the top that the snake's eyes were red rhinestones.

As I narrowed my wardrobe down to fit into one garment bag, two oversized suitcases, a shoulder bag, my waist pouch, and a footlocker . . . I began to prepare Lee Ann for my try-out.

The AWA liked DDP, but they also liked the "Diamond Dolls," who were actually bartenders and waitresses from Norma Jean's nightclub. (Dolls left to right) Lee Ann, Wendy, and Tanya.

Lee Ann was a busty blond college student who was part of the opening staffs at Elations, Temptations, and Norma Jean's. She worked as a bartender and sampled the fast lane, but always seemed to keep in touch with her goal to get an education and graduate from college. Officially, she was the first Diamond Doll.

Lee Ann and I had been spending time together, so it seemed like a natural. I decided to make it a working vacation, and planned to arrive in Las Vegas a few days early and stay a couple days after the taping. Even though the AWA was covering my flight and the room, bringing Lee Ann, along with all the other expenses, was sure to exceed whatever they were offering.

I began to worry about Lee as we flew the second leg of the trip from Dallas. She was pale, ragged-out, and terrified. The whole idea of being on national TV made her physically sick.

Throughout the flight, I tried to comfort Lee. All she had to do was walk to the ring with me and let people look at her. I tried being nice and, later, tough . . . but nothing was working. I emphasized that all she had to do was be a sexy "bitch." Now, how hard is that?

I had plenty of outfits and gimmicks with me, but when I saw Lee's luggage, I had to laugh. It looked like we were touring the world on the Queen Mary. Others probably thought we were a band of homeless gypsies.

LEE MARSHALL
BROADCASTER:

I looked up from my lounge chair when I heard a man's voice say, "Lee, grab the bag!" I saw a stunning woman wearing a tube top and short-shorts. Standing near her was a big man with long blond hair. The Vegas sun reflected off what seemed like a dozen pieces of jewelry he was wearing. Looking closer, I noticed the guy had a walking stick.

This was not a cane . . . this was a fu*kin' walking stick . . . with a snake's head handle.

He growled again, "Lee, help out, we're late! Grab the bag and let's go."

Now I'm thinking: Who does this walking-stick a$$hole think he is? He doesn't know me, and he's ordering me around like I'm his personal bellboy. *As I got to my feet and took two determined steps toward Mr. Mouth, he said, "C'mon, Lee, we gotta go, babe!"*

That's when I realized that it wasn't me he was talking to, but rather the blond beauty who was blessed with the same first name as mine.

I extended my hand to introduce myself, and was met with the latest soulful handshake.

"I know, bro," he said, "I'm Diamond Dallas Page, and this is the Diamond Doll. Hey, bro . . . call me DDP."

Collectively, they had ten pieces of luggage and looked like rock stars, a transvestite circus, and the road company from Grease *all at the same time.*

I suggested that they get settled and join me for a drink later, but wasn't really looking forward to it. I wasn't sure I was going to like him.

Lee Ann was in the room still struggling with her fears, so I went over to the arena to check it out. The WWF was thumping the AWA, but seeing the logo, the bunting around the ring, and all the press milling around, I knew there was every reason to be in awe of it.

I recognized Verne Gagne as he leaned on the ring post, making notes on a yellow legal pad. I walked up to him and introduced myself. He never met my hand or said "hello." Instead, he sized me up and said, "My God! You have to be the tallest manager of all time."

Looking at his face, I knew that I was very lucky that the AWA needed a talker real bad at the time, because my size seemed to make Verne reluctant. For a split second, I wondered if I would even get my shot after all, so I responded with a barrage of trash-talk, and unleashed my trademark "Good Gawd" rap.

I was told that I was the new ring manager of Bad Company's Pat Tanaka and Paul Diamond. I knew that they used the song "Bad Company" as their intro music, and that they were to challenge for the tag straps, but now, with Diamond Dallas Page in their corner . . . they would be B-A-double-D BADD Company.

LEE MARSHALL:

The WWF and the NWA had picked the AWA talent apart, so there were fewer people to dress up. The Tag Team Championship belts belonged to "The Midnight Rockers," but the team of Sean Michaels and Marty Jannetty were on their way to New York, having lost their AWA titles while in Las Vegas. With Paul E. gone, and the Midnight Rockers on their way out, the AWA needed to replace that energy. They had always been known as a conservative promotion under Verne Gagne, and needed a bit of glitz and glamour while they were still hanging on.

In addition to Paul Diamond and Pat Tanaka becoming the new champs, they had a fresh face as their new manager. He came with a big rap and all the gimmicks. In fact, I don't think anyone expected that one guy could carry so many gimmicks.

Diamond Dallas Page was a walking carnival midway, complete with flashing lights and a Tilt-a-Whirl. He believed that he had to have it all going at once, and his rap rhymed and rambled and raised the tempo.

My first production meeting was surely one to remember. We were jammed in a musty, old room that had seen better days, but as I looked around the room, I was amazed at my surroundings.

It was the first time I met Ray "The Crippler" Stevens, who is truly one of the greats of wrestling. Ray was the road manager for the AWA, and was also on the booking committee[1]. During shows, he was in charge of the heel dressing room. While Ray was in charge of the bad guys, Verne Gagne and Wahoo McDaniels were in charge of the babyfaces. In those days, the two dressing rooms were usually as far apart

---

[1]*booking committee—Comprised of one or more bookers or matchmakers who help coordinate and set matches and feuds.*

Diamond Dallas Page made his debut as an obnoxious "heel" manager of the AWA tag team of Paul Diamond (center) and Pat Tanaka (right), who were known as Bad Company.

as possible, and, most of the time, the production meeting was the last time opponents saw each other before the ring.

Ray ran down the matches for the night, and Verne handled a few complaints from guys who felt they were being mishandled. Right before the meeting ended, Verne introduced me and announced that I would manage Bad Company.

The announcement was met with laughter from the back of the room. It was Sean Michaels. When Gagne asked what was so funny, Michaels replied, "Look at the size of this f*ckin' guy! Tanaka should be *his* manager."

My size wasn't the only issue; I'm sure that some of the boys didn't like my gimmick[2] either. No one had to tell me it was way over the top. I knew that . . . but I took pride in everything I said, everything I wore, and everything I did. I had a lot of cash invested in the gimmick too, but most of my stuff was from my nightclub days. I had always worn clothes like that, and always wanted a reason to dress the way that Diamond Dallas Page did.

---

[2]*gimmick—A wrestler's props, clothes, any other* attraction *that may be used to establish his character's persona.*

It went well for Page on that trip, and although he had lots of critics, it wasn't long before Diamond Dallas Page was working an angle for his first Pay-Per-View match. In a short time, Page had made it to TV, and not long after that, Chris "The Boomer" Berman mentioned Diamond Dallas Page on ESPN's SportsCenter.

While his critics struggled with his look, others saw it as a perfect fit for Vince McMahon, Jr. and "New York," which is what the boys of wrestling call the World Wrestling Federation.

McMahon was a visionary of cable television, and believed that the "show" should be more like traditional sports, offering

The friendship between Lee Marshall and Page Falkinburg began in the American Wrestling Association, at the first appearance of "DDP."

higher-quality production, sound, and marketing. As McMahon raised the technical level of the production, he also stockpiled talent—lots of talent. He made household names of professional wrestlers such as Hulk Hogan, Rowdy Roddy Piper, and Andre the Giant. For the hardcore fans, he added legendary announcer "Mean Gene" Okerlund and wrestler-turned-manager Bobby "The Brain" Heenan. It had become entertainment beyond a sporting event, and suddenly, its appeal and profile were at an all-time high.

LEE MARSHALL:

The Gagnes were holding firm on their style of presenting wrestling in a credible and competitive fashion. At the time, the ESPN contract was more valuable than McMahon's USA Network contract, and the Gagnes felt that the WWF was a passing fad. They thought the fans would tire of the lights, music, and outrageous wrestling personalities, and would want to see real wrestlers and wrestling—not a stage show. In fact, Verne Gagne would not allow the word "show" to be used to describe AWA . . . on the air, on the set, or even in the office.

However, the Gagnes were wrong. The fans no longer wanted the AWA. They wanted to be entertained, and there was no doubt that Vince was keeping an eye on the remaining talent in the AWA.

I was as "green" as they come, but I was *in* professional wrestling. Even though we only taped twice a month, I was on TV every week, and I knew I was being looked at. Like most everyone at the AWA, I wanted to go to New York where I knew my look would get noticed.

Although I received heat from some of the boys, there were others who thought it was just a matter of time before the WWF snapped me up. In fact, when Curt Hennig was planning his move to the WWF to become "Mr. Perfect," he asked me to consider being his manager.

CURT HENNIG:

It was obvious to me that Page had the gift when I first met him. It wasn't just the gift of gab, it was the gift to display the passion to learn and study something someone enjoys and respects doing.

I never cared about his size or aggressiveness, and felt he would be right for Mr. Perfect. He had great talent and charisma for doing interviews, and I had learned that it was the interviews that sold the seats.

We looked a lot like brothers too. When I looked at him closer, I noticed that his hair and moves were just like mine. Some guys would be angry or bitter, but when Page told me that he had studied my style, I took it as a compliment. It didn't make me mad at all because I also took stuff from other guys.

I saw that he respected what we did and was working hard to learn the business, and those are the guys that we want to help move up.

It seemed that everyone around Page at the time thought that he would wind up in New York—the boys at the AWA, the boys back at Norma Jean's, and the friends that he was making just because he was DDP.

His role was expanding with the AWA, and now, Diamond Dallas Page was also managing Colonel DeBeers and the female champion, Medusa. Even though he was gaining exposure in the AWA, there had been no call from McMahon, and no jump to New York.

I began to question myself, and wondered what I lacked, while I continued to wait for a call that never came. Lee Marshall finally cut through the bullsh*t and put the character, Diamond Dallas Page, under a microscope, dissecting DDP, gimmick by gimmick.

"Page," he said, "I can tell that you really want to make it big in this business, but you don't have a clue how to do it."

I was shocked because this was the first time that anyone had spoken about my future in wrestling at a time when I wondered if wrestling would ever have a place for me.

LEE MARSHALL:

I may have been a little cutting in my assessment of his character, but I always knew he could be a huge star if he took the time to figure out who Diamond Dallas Page was

Page and Curt Hennig first met in the AWA. Hennig (far right) considered taking "DDP" with him to the WWF to be the manager of "Mr. Perfect." Diamond Doll Tanya in center.

trying to be. To Page's credit, he always listened to what was being said, always worked hard, and had progressed in his days in the AWA. The DDP character was a major heel, a snob, and, most times, an a$$hole. While he wore fancy clothes, used a walking stick, and had Diamond Dolls on his arms, he mocked those who would never experience such pleasures. The put-down became his charm. He grabbed me for a drink or dinner periodically, and we had wonderful impromptu brainstorming sessions that often included thinking up new insults for opponents and their fans.

Lee has always been in my corner, and taught me so much about how to develop my wrestling character. It was Lee Marshall who said something that all of us in the wrestling game need to know and be reminded of. He taught me that whatever we did while we were on camera had to contribute to the overall product. He went on to say that no matter how hard we worked, the individual effort had to make sense to have value . . . and most of all, it had to make money.

I didn't believe it when Lee told me he had spoken to Classy Freddie Blassie about Diamond Dallas Page. I thought he was ribbing me, but Lee gave me Freddie's number, and I spoke to him for the first time.

I popped when Freddie Blassie told me to send a tape that he later forwarded to Pat Patterson of the WWF. Although Pat Patterson said he liked it, he, too, thought I was too big to be a manager. Freddie was very supportive of my efforts, and we have talked to each other through the years. He has always encouraged me to continue the journey with the same enthusiasm he saw on the tube and on those early tapes.

I was back at Norma's between monthly shoots, and I worked up a video to introduce the "Search for the Diamond Doll" gimmick that I wanted to incorporate into my character. Basically, I would go to a town, pick out girls who aspired to be Diamond Dolls, and run a contest in a nightclub. Not only did it look as if I had a stable of babes, but it saved me the money flying Lee Ann or anyone else from Florida to Minnesota.

The AWA didn't really have a creative staff to work up angles or gimmicks at that time, but they liked my Diamond Doll contest idea, and we ran with it.

It was at one of those nightclubs in Minnesota, following a Diamond Doll contest and an evening of partying hard, where I first met Eric Bischoff.

It had been a brutal day of travel, and after working the contest, drinking, and being way too tired, I approached Pat Tanaka, who was in conversation with a guy at the bar.

I had seen Bischoff around before, but didn't know him or what he did. I don't know if it was my beer or his beer that was doing the talking, but he and I just clashed.

Like that night, the story gets a little cloudy, depending on who you talk to, but both Page and Eric remember that tempers rose quickly. There had been a challenge, and neither was backing down. Pat Tanaka and whoever else was close by broke up the argument and intervened before Page could meet Eric in the parking lot.

In a split second, he was in my face, and I was rising to

the occasion. The boys managed to calm the situation, and with a late-night buzz, Pat and Paul took me to get some breakfast and cool down.

Paul Diamond and Pat Tanaka told me more about Eric Bishoff. They said he was a good guy who had just gotten carried away. They also informed me that he was a kickboxing champ and a former fighter with the PKA, Pro Karate Association. At the time, Eric was working in the office and doing some TV commentary for the AWA.

Following a late-night breakfast, Page was returning to his hotel room when his elevator door opened at the same time that the one across the hall opened. Ironically, Eric Bischoff was also returning to his room on the same floor. Tempers flared again, and the two had to be separated yet another time.

There was serious heat[3] between the two of us that night. Although I was a lot bigger than Bischoff, he was game, and talking trash. We were cutting promos[4] on each other, and the name-calling and taunting continued until Pat and Paul led me to my room.

I didn't sleep too well that night. Between having a hangover and being pissed off, I awoke at eight a.m., which was still like the middle of the night for me. Bischoff was on my mind, so I grabbed a pair of jeans and pulled on my boots, ready to confront him right then. I was prepared to find Bischoff and "get it on" when I heard a knock on the door.

It was Eric Bischoff. And, man, did he look rough. Looking that bad, he had to feel worse. He looked up into my eyes and said, "I heard I was a real a$$hole last night."

Before I got a chance to respond, he went on, "There are two ways we can handle this. Either you can accept my apology and shake my hand, or you can just punch me in the mouth . . . whatever you think is right."

It was one of the ballsiest calls I ever heard, and I told him so. It wasn't a back-down, and he didn't make excuses—

---

[3]*heat—Conflict that can vary in degree, bad blood between rivals.*
[4]*promo—A theatrical display of emotion.*

this was a solution. As far as I was concerned, I liked him for his guts from that minute on, and the hassle was history.

Back in Florida, Page was getting ready to put more irons in the fire. He and partner Tony Coffaro were planning to open an after-hours club called "Norma's Hideaway." Norma Jean's Dance Club was still booming and "The Hideaway" gave the hardcore dance partiers a place to go till six a.m. They were actively investigating the possibilities of more clubs and more concepts.

Page was still traveling to Minnesota for the AWA one weekend a month for tapings when he heard that Mike Graham was reviving Florida Championship Wrestling (FCW) in the Tampa area. The Graham family was a wrestling legend in the South, and despite the struggles that independent federations were having, FCW seemed to have a good chance of succeeding.

Things were more wide open then. Wrestlers were more like independent contractors who were able to work in other territories on "loan" to other federations. There were alliances and different versions of a good-ole-boy network that still remained. Many of the top guys who weren't in New York looked forward to the chance to work in Florida with Mike Graham.

Tampa was less than a two-hour drive, so I looked at it as a way to stay active in wrestling and have a bunch of fun too. With the situation looking bleak at the AWA, and the uncertainty that is in every phase of the wrestling business, I didn't know if I had a future as Diamond Dallas Page.

I sent Mike a tape to review, and he called me at Norma's to offer me a shot on an upcoming taping. Having Mike Graham like my work was a huge boost for me, but I still felt like the bar business was my life and wrestling was my love. Pursuing work at FCW certainly wasn't for money, but it was an alternative and a chance to prolong my "15 minutes of fame." Florida Championship Wrestling had some great guys on the card, including my buddies, Bad Company. There were fewer binding agreements back then, and just because I had appeared as Tanaka's and Paul Diamond's ring manager in the AWA didn't mean I was an automatic anywhere else.

The day of the match, I pulled out of Ft. Myers with two Diamond Dolls and a buddy who wanted to be a wrestler and was calling himself "Rock Hard Rick." It was late afternoon, and we were all dressed up for a wrestling show, cruising in my '62 pink Caddy with the top down, when thunderstorms began to roll in. We stopped, put the top up, and were cruising again and lovin' life when, suddenly, a red light on the dash came on. In a matter of minutes, we were on the side of the road going nowhere. By the looks we were getting, I wasn't so sure that we were great candidates to hitch a ride.

The clouds were over us, and time was ticking away. With at least an hour to go on the drive to Tampa, a tow truck and a pickup truck pulled over to lend a hand. After about 10 minutes of figuring a plan, the Dolls were on their way back to Ft. Myers in the tow truck, and I was in the back of the pickup, running from the rain on my way to Tampa for my introduction to FCW.

We barely made the show in time, and I was a little uptight. I had planned on being there with two Diamond Dolls, but showed up with "Rock Hard Rick" instead.

Mike Graham treated me great, and was more impressed that I had jumped in the back of a pickup and made the show than he was disappointed about the Dolls. It showed Mike that I was dependable and hungry, which are traits that are noticed and remembered in any business.

I loved being there, and when I was invited to hang with some of the boys after the show, I remembered the valuable advice that Curt Hennig had given me early on in the AWA. He told me that I would make more friends and contacts after the shows, in the bars, and at late-night diners than I would in the arenas or the studios. I give the same advice to the boys today, and give props (the credit) to Curt while I'm at it.

At that first Florida Championship Wrestling show, Page made an impression on Mike Graham, and made a friend and contact in wrestler, Johnny Ace. Despite careers on different continents, they have remained friends through the years, and, today, wrestling fans link the two wrestlers with their work *in* the ring.

While I pursued both the bar business and wrestling, my romantic life took a more freelance approach. Judy and I gave our relationship one final try, but parted as friends. Tammy was married now, and Lee Ann had always been more of a good friend than a steady.

The after-hours club had opened, and one night following work, I stopped by to check on Norma's Hideaway and, of course, to evaluate the female clientele.

I went right to the DJ booth and began to spin some *Whitesnake*, *Skid Row*, and *Bon Jovi*. Before long, two hot blonds approached me in the booth.

The taller of the two asked if I remembered them. Without missing a beat, I replied, "Remember you? I dreamed about you last night." We laughed as she reminded me that I had given her free passes. She also loved the music I was spinning.

Her name was Victoria, and having rock and roll music in common with her started me on yet another odyssey. Victoria was a distraction, a passion, and another one of the lessons of life I learned with the highs and lows of the ever-present yo-yo. She was visiting from Canada with her mother and her friend, Jennifer, and had only two more nights before returning home.

At the time, my roommate was Rico Costa, who was one of Norma's DJs. He was off that night, so I asked him to join my new blond friends and me. Like Victoria and I, he and Jennifer hit it off right away, and we all agreed to go out again the next night.

Rico Costa
Roommate:

No one would have ever guessed that we had only met the night before. It was a Monday night, and we were painting the town red. Page and Victoria made a good-looking couple, and Jennifer and I were hanging on each other all evening. We closed the club, and a limo took us back to our place where the driver waited outside till the sun came up.

I was digging her in a big way, and we talked and laughed the entire night. As we kissed goodbye, Victoria asked me how I could have such a wonderful night with her, say so many romantic things, and send her home with all the mementos of our first date . . . without even asking her for a phone number back home.

I told her that it was for all those reasons that I didn't want her phone number. Instead, I gave her all of *my* numbers: work, home, pager, cell phone, and fax. I told her that she could contact me on any of my numbers, but made one condition.

My last words to her that morning were: "Victoria, don't call me unless you are ready to fall madly in love with me."

About a week passed before Victoria called and left a message on the machine for Rico to call Jennifer. The message ended with, "Hi Page!" He never returned that call, but the next time Victoria called, Page was there to pick up the phone. The very next day, he was scheduled to fly to Toronto to see the girl who was ready to fall madly in love with him.

Every other weekend, we took turns flying between Ft. Myers and Canada. We were having a great time, growing closer with every trip. After six months, I planned to ask Victoria to marry me on her next trip to Florida.

CARLOS VELASQUEZ
MANAGER-NORMA'S HIDEAWAY:

Nothing could have been as big as the news that Page was going to ask Victoria to marry him. He had it all planned and scripted that he would dine waterside at the same restaurant where they had their first date, and that Rico and I would pass by on a boat as part of his proposal. He gave us a tape of the same songs that they first danced to, and told us the precise time that he wanted us to pass by with the boom box blaring. He had the route planned, and had figured out the exact time that he thought it would take us to get there . . . and, of course, everything had to be perfect.

What he didn't foresee were seas that were rough enough to soak us . . . and the boom box. I looked over my dripping-wet shoulder to hear Rico say, "Oh fu*k . . . Page is going to kill me . . . I'm dead."

Rico Costa:

I was nervous in the first place, and all I could think of was Page saying, "Don't fu*k this up, bro . . ."

I knew that a tidal wave wouldn't even have been a good enough excuse to mess up . . . so here we were, two guys out on the river, trying to remember the words to the songs on the tape. We decided to sing the songs ourselves, and to serenade the couple. I was so worried that Page would be mad about the boom box that I figured we'd better add some Temptations-style dance steps to at least make it funny.

It was very comical, but was really cool and the perfect improv. As someone might guess, the whole deal caused quite a commotion, and even though Victoria said "yes" right away, I realized that I had put her on the spot. I reproposed the next day, and we made immediate plans for her to move to Ft. Myers.

This time, I was the one who wanted to set a date. We were getting along so well on our weekends that I wanted a trial period of living together full-time before we married. I wanted to see how we would adapt to Victoria being away from her parents and both of us trying to live with the Diamond Dallas Page character.

Shortly after the proposal, Victoria moved in with Page. The next five or six months proved to be fun, and their engagement was still standing despite some unexpected hurdles that centered around Victoria's ability to find work. Being Canadian, she needed a green card to work in the States. This took time and patience, so an alternative was for Victoria to work "under the table" as a waitress, collecting nightly tips, and not worrying about a salary. Unfortunately, she lacked the patience and experience for the restaurant or bar business, and was unhappy with the work. It started to become a concern around the same time that Victoria was offered a modeling photo opportunity in Canada.

The modeling agency that she had signed with back home in Toronto wanted to send her to Vancouver for three weeks to shoot more photos for her portfolio. They promised to work with agencies in Florida that were already interested in her. It seemed like the trip would be good for everyone. Victoria could work on a future in modeling with opportunities in Florida, and she could see her family and friends while I got back to keeping my full plate spinning.

Everything seemed to be in order when Victoria left for Canada, even though there were some underlying family concerns. Behind the scenes, Victoria's parents were shuddering at the thought of their daughter marrying a nightclub manager who looked like a rock star and dreamed of a life in pro wrestling.

When Victoria and Page had been apart before, they had monstrous phone bills, and they talked nearly every day. However, during the middle of her three-week hiatus, it became difficult for Page to get in touch with her.

It was very frustrating. I would call her, page her, and leave messages for her in Vancouver. I even left messages in Toronto with Victoria's mother, and called Jennifer for reassurance that all was well. Although I had my doubts, Jennifer quickly changed my thought process. She told me that I was being ridiculous and that Victoria had said that she was deeply in love with me and was ready to set a wedding date.

It wasn't making sense, though. After four more days of not hearing from her, I called her mother again. She gave me every reason to have doubt when she told me that Victoria was confused and missed her friends. She also told me that she *thought* that Victoria loved me. By this time, I was frustrated and concerned enough to tell her mother that if I didn't hear from Victoria within a day, I would take the next flight to Vancouver.

Victoria finally called and professed her love to Page, promising that everything would be great again when she got back home to Florida. But first, she would be stopping home in Toronto. Victoria had been in Vancouver for the modeling shoot, and, as planned, she was staying with a girlfriend from Toronto who had just married a doctor in Vancouver.

I felt better right after speaking to her, but, once again, a few days passed with us playing phone tag and not talking. By this time, I had it bad. I was so uptight and frustrated that I wasn't acting normal. I was constantly second-guessing myself and remembered her mother's words. It got to the point that I was repeatedly listening to Victoria's phone messages to reevaluate her tone. I was getting crazier by the day. I spoke to Jennifer again, and my feelings of doubt became worse. Victoria had confided to her that she made a friend while in Vancouver who was really nice and a doctor too. Her tone bothered me, since I felt that if Victoria was going to tell anyone the truth, it would be Jennifer.

I remained positive, but doubts motivated me to settle this yo-yo once and for all. I was able to reach Victoria in Vancouver before she left, and told her that if she wanted to break or postpone the engagement, it would be okay. By this time, I just wanted some consistency. I felt like I was being lied to and deceived, even though she kept telling me that everything would work out when she returned to Florida.

Her tone and demeanor on the phone were less than convincing. Jennifer and I had become friendly from our phone conversations, and I was getting the feeling that Victoria may have played other guys in a similar way. Jennifer was due to pick up Victoria at the airport, and I made plans to be in Toronto to surprise her as she got off the plane.

Bottom line was that I lost trust and didn't think Victoria was telling the truth. This time, I knew the truth would set me free, and I was ready to confront her, get my ring back, and say "farewell." But in the back of my mind, I remembered how wonderful Victoria was when she was with me, and I hoped that this was only a speed bump in our relationship.

Page flew to Toronto on such short notice that the ticket was close to a thousand dollars. He met Jennifer at the airport, and as they waited for Victoria's flight to arrive, Jennifer received a voice mail message that added more drama to an already anticipated confrontation.

The new doctor friend Victoria had met while in Vancouver was less than an hour away from Toronto, and he also wanted to surprise Victoria at the airport. He was in the area to visit friends and attend a wedding, and he wanted his new friend, Victoria, to spend the weekend with him.

From this point on, let's just call him Dr. Biff.

The entire situation became comical to me. Victoria had no idea that the doctor and I were both in Toronto, and poor Jennifer was *fa-reaking* out.

Minutes before the plane was due, I spotted Dr. Biff. It was pretty easy . . . he looked like a Biff. He was preppy, cocky, and much more conservative than I ever was—not to mention my alter ego, Diamond Dallas Page. Dr. Biff was standing across the waiting area near the gate. I was beyond being mad, but I was feeling a bit devilish, so I decided to make this the most uncomfortable situation that either of them would ever encounter.

I grabbed a magazine and stood right next to Dr. Biff. Minutes later, when he went to the bathroom . . . I went to the bathroom. He stopped by the water fountain . . . so I did too. But never once did I make eye contact with him. By the time he took his place in front of the gate, I was nearby, and he knew it.

I was pi$$ed. I wanted to expose the lies, fix the problem, and move on. I was already starting to get over Victoria.

Over the phone, she had been reluctant to give the ring back, and I wanted it. And it wasn't because of the value. I was just determined not to let her have a piece of me, and that ring represented me.

Victoria got off the plane and was immediately immersed in the crossfire of glances and double takes. She saw me first. Then her eyes darted to the doctor who was standing between us. Then she looked at Jennifer, and then back to me. She quickly turned on the charm of an actress. "Page! Uh . . . honey . . . uh, what are you doing here?"

Dr. Biff was trying to be as cool as possible, and as I approached Victoria, he started to walk by us. He was ready to let her handle the situation, *her* way. As he continued by, I placed my elbow square in his chest, stopping him in his tracks.

"Hi, Victoria," I said. "Do you know him?"

"No, Page," she lied.

I couldn't believe she said that, so I asked her again, "Victoria, look closer . . . don't you recognize him?" She dropped her eyes and went over to the baggage carousel. I followed.

"He's just a friend, Page," she stammered.

Victoria got emotional, and I told her that I was there to settle our relationship. I explained that I didn't want the other guy to be involved in any way until we knew where we were heading. I didn't want to hurt her.

I've always tried not to carry grudges or negative energy with me on my journey, and I felt very strongly about it with Victoria. We both calmed down, and I told her that if we worked it out, it would be cool; but if not . . . it would just be another chapter of my life.

About that time, Jennifer approached us. She was very shaken up. "Victoria," she whispered, "Biff says that if you don't leave with him now . . . he never wants to talk to you again."

That pi$$ed me off. I spun around and walked up to him, making sure there were just inches between us. I cut a promo on him that he'd never forget.

Dr. Biff stuttered and denied giving Victoria an ultimatum through Jennifer, and boldly lied when I asked him what he had said. I repeatedly pressed my finger into his chest to emphasize every point, as I told him that I wasn't there to talk to *him* about anything. I reminded him that Victoria was my fiancée, that he was in my world now, and that I didn't like it. I think what I said next would be considered a threat. It was something about ripping his head off and using his neck as a toilet.

Then I told him that I thought that he and Victoria would be happy together since they were obviously two of a kind. They could lie to each other the rest of their lives, but all that was going to have to wait.

The night was mine. Victoria was going to leave with me, without speaking to Dr. Biff, and she and I would spend one last night together. I'd get my ring back, and it would all be over.

And that's just the way it happened. Victoria and I had dinner, an emotional yo-yo of a night, and I left with my ring and went back to my dream.

The careers of many people in professional wrestling are in constant limbo. Contracts are short and lack guarantees for most people in the ring, as well as behind the scenes. Many of the wrestlers who weren't signed to WWF contracts were hopeful that another federation would survive, giving them opportunities that seemed to be dwindling.

Mike Graham had gotten some good talent and had a shot at making Florida Championship Wrestling a profitable promotion. He was a second-generation wrestler and the son of one of the industry's heavyweights, Eddie Graham. Mike ran the Tampa offices of the NWA, and in the Sportatorium, he provided some of the biggest superstars in wrestling with their first opportunities. It was Graham who directed Terry Bolea to wrestling school and provided him with his first legitimate work in the business. Terry became Hulk Hogan. Randy "Macho Man" Savage, Lex Lugar, Scott Hall, Mick "Cactus Jack" Foley, and Steve Keirn were all seen in the early days of their careers in Graham-run promotions in Florida.

I was still technically a wrestling manager with the AWA, but the end was drawing near, and the shows that were being produced were often filled with pre-taped house shows and reruns of past matches. Mike Graham was known, and had worked in other federations, and I knew that if I made a good impression on him, there was a ray of hope that my dream would continue.

I waited for a call back from Mike Graham, knowing that I had to take advantage of any opportunity.

It was midnight, and I was in bed sick with strep throat. My head was pounding, and I had a stuffy nose. When the phone rang, I was hurting and needing sleep because I was due to fly to Minnesota for an AWA shoot at six a.m. It took me a second, but I recognized the voice on the answering machine. It was Mike Graham, and I could tell he had been "crushing a few cans."

I picked up the phone in time to catch him, and he jumped into the conversation.

"Dallas, I'm sitting here with Dusty Rhodes, 'The American Dream,' and we're working on our second case of beer." Mike was rolling, and I was listening.

"Dusty is going to be joining us here," Graham continued. "We've got some good things happening with Florida Championship Wrestling. We're going to pop this territory, and Dusty is talking about bringing in a couple of managers like Sir Oliver Humperdink, Babydoll, or Gary Hart. I was telling him about you, but I wasn't able to play your tape for him. I want you to get on the phone and show Dusty what Diamond Dallas Page can do."

My mouth dropped. It was a lot to take in so quickly, and before I even realized that this was my shot with Florida Championship Wrestling, I realized I was going to be talking to another idol of mine, Dusty Rhodes.

I begged Mike, in a whisper, not to put him on. My throat was raw, I was half asleep, and I didn't really know what to say. I wasn't prepared to talk to The American Dream. Then I heard Mike say, "Hang on . . . here's Dusty."

CHAPTER NINE

THE DREAM, AN ANGEL, AND THE FREEBIRDS

MIKE GRAHAM
LEGENDARY WRESTLING PROMOTER:

I thought Page had a great rap, a real good look, raw talent, and potential. But what impressed me the most was his desire to learn.

When I saw his tape, I knew that I wanted Dusty to meet him. "Let's get him on the phone," Dusty said.

A red light went on in my brain when I heard Dusty say, "Hello." I forgot all about my throat, and unleashed a promo that was a barrage of one-liners that began with, "Dusty Rhodes! Good Gawd! The American Dream, the man of the hour, the tower of power, much too sweet to be sour . . . "

I went on and on, ripping off every Dusty Rhodes line with sprinkles of Captain Lou and Classy Freddie Blassie, and, of course, my signature DDP lines that I would fire off to the "Copenhagen-dippin', coupon-clippin', draft-beer-drinkin'" rednecks. It was a montage of clichés that was a tribute to the great talkers I grew up watching. I knew I had nailed it when the lady with me sat straight up in bed with her eyes as big as saucers.

When I finished my rap, I went right back to whispering, "That's all I got, Dream. I'm sorry, but I'm really sick."

There was a long pause, and I thought he had hung up. I remember the exact words that Dusty said with his legendary tone somewhere between a lisp and a drawl. "Wazth ata rhecawdin, kid?" ("Was that a recording, kid?")

Dusty was going to Texas for the weekend and would take my tape with him. We arranged to meet the following week in Tampa.

Although I was still feeling the symptoms of strep throat on my trip to do the AWA shoot that weekend, I was jacked about the opportunity to meet Dusty Rhodes and the possibility that I would be working with him.

Dusty Rhodes has been a household name for nearly 30 years, and The American Dream has dropped his "Atomic Elbow" on opponents around the globe. Songs have been written about him, and movies have been made where the lead character was a blatant rip-off of his persona. He's met presidents and prime ministers, and partied at Studio 54 with the likes of Andy Warhol and Truman Capote. The legendary fashion designer, Halston, wanted to design robes for Dusty to wear in arenas and armories across Middle America.

Dusty Rhodes helped build the territory that was owned by Jim Crockett. When Crockett sold his promotion to Ted Turner's Atlanta-based broadcasting company, many people saw it as Crockett selling what Dusty had created. Dusty met with Jim Herd, the acting president of Turner's newly-formed World Championship Wrestling (WCW), but failed to come to an agreement. It was during that time that Mike Graham called Dusty to talk about Florida Championship Wrestling.

DUSTY RHODES
THE AMERICAN DREAM:

Jim Herd had the idea that The American Dream should become a bad guy. Turner's group made me a good financial offer, but I knew that I couldn't, and wouldn't, sell out or

DDP met Dusty "The American Dream" Rhodes through Florida Championship Wrestling (FCW) and Mike Graham. Page and Dusty have been friends ever since. (left to right) Tony Coffaro, Dusty, Page.

change my character. I was financially secure, and wasn't ready to tell my fans that I had turned on them.

Before Eddie Graham passed away, he told me that Florida was mine for the taking. The Graham family was like my own, and when Eddie's son, Mike, called, I headed to Tampa. In an old building, we started Florida Championship Wrestling.

Florida has always been a Mecca for professional wrestling, and even though I wanted to be a part of FCW, I wasn't going to leave my night job at Norma Jean's to do the wrestling thing as a hobby. On my way to that first meeting, I was determined not to have this opportunity cost me more than I could make.

I walked into the meeting and looked around the room. I saw Mike Graham, Steve Keirn, Dusty, and Gordon Solie, the dean of wrestling commentators. Dusty allowed me to pour it all out. I talked and talked, and these big-time players just sat back and listened.

When I finished my rant, Dusty dropped a compliment on me that stoked my fire. Now, just thinking about it jacks me up.

DUSTY RHODES:

I saw so much in this kid, Page. He pulled up in a Corvette, and I wasn't sure if it was borrowed, rented, or owned by him. He talked real good, but as far as his ring work went, he couldn't walk and chew gum at the same time. However, his energy and ideas about the business made me see many of the traits of Blassie, Ventura, and myself.

I wanted to take that raw emotion and energy and teach him the entire business. And, who better to teach him how to announce than Gordon Solie, who was like the Walter Cronkite of professional wrestling.

Dusty blew me away when he told me he saw me as the "Jesse Ventura of the '90s," and that, coupled with his offer to take me along and show me the business, made me want to work for nothing. It was Jesse Ventura and all his flamboyant gimmicks that helped raise my interest in wrestling again.

My first reaction was to tell Dusty that I wouldn't be good as a commentator, and didn't think I'd be able to speak intelligently about the action in the ring. At that point, I didn't know a wristlock from a wrist watch. Dusty assured me that anything I needed to know could be learned from Gordon Solie.

I wanted to learn the mat, and knew it would help me be a better "color man" and ring manager. The best way to know it was to do it, so I climbed in the ring and took the bumps. I had been working with Gordon, and soon began to drive to Tampa one day every other week to learn the moves, in and out of the ring, from Gordon, Mike Graham, Steve Keirn, and, of course, Dusty.

My trips to Tampa were never intended to start a career as a wrestler. Being in the ring and seeing, feeling, and learning the moves helped to add knowledge and credibility to my broadcasts. I know that it also helped with my confidence and ability to share the announcers table with Gordon.

GORDON SOLIE
LEGENDARY WRESTLING ANNOUNCER:

When I first met Dallas, I wondered what his angle was. He was an open book, full of confidence and opinions. I soon realized he had no angle at all, and he was just being himself—a straight-shooting, aggressive guy who was down-to-earth and sure of himself.

The thing that I liked the most about Diamond Dallas was that he was willing to do whatever had to be done to be successful. He always put himself in the position to accept and challenge every opportunity that came his way.

He started with us as a manager, but he displayed a tremendous gift of gab and natural ability on the mic. He studied and worked right into a color commentary position. Sure, he made some mistakes . . . but he listened, absorbed like a sponge, and then applied what he learned.

Working with Gordon Solie, "the dean of professional wrestling announcers," gave Page a solid foundation and credibility as an announcer. (left to right) "The Terminator," longtime friend "Johnny Ace," Gordon Solie, and DDP.

I knew that I had been given a special opportunity. The wrestling business has always been run by family ties and a tight-knit circle of guys who had paid their dues to get where they were. Many guys can tell stories of hanging around the business for years, doing everything and anything just to be a part of it, and most of the color commentators and managers had been wrestlers at one time. I didn't have any history and never did any of that, and was still given a shot to get in the middle of it all with FCW. With teachers like Dusty, Gordon, Mike Graham, and Steve Keirn, it was like going to Harvard.

For the next several months, Page continued to work hard, juggling his duties at Norma Jean's and Norma's Hideaway, and his career in wrestling. His time off from being a nightclub manager was used for a few final trips to Minnesota for AWA appearances, along with his weekly drives to Tampa for FCW.

Diamond Dallas Page had received notoriety and publicity as a result of his TV and PPV appearances with the AWA, and had also been featured and rated as a ring manager by some of the wrestling fan magazines.

I received my very first call from a fan at Norma Jean's one afternoon. It was a fluke that I even answered the phone, but when I did, I heard a little voice ask for Diamond Dallas Page.

The kid on the other end was from Cape Coral. He was ten or eleven at the time, and his name was John Buchanan. That call came around the same time that I had talked to Freddie Blassie the first time, and had wondered how excited I would have been if I had been eleven years old and gotten the same chance.

Besides my family and circle of friends, Johnny Buchanan was my first fan. I spoke with John about wrestling, and even found out a little about him. At first, he was a little scared, nervous, and out-of-his-mind excited, but he was pretty cool for a kid his age. After a few minutes on the phone, he got comfortable and asked me if he could have my home number so he could call me again.

JOHN BUCHANAN:

It was so cool. I had seen him on TV managing Bad Company, and now I was talking to him and asking a million questions. He stayed on the phone with me a lot longer than I thought he would, and spoke to me about wrestling like we were friends. DDP wouldn't give me his home phone number, but said that I could call him at Norma's again; but only about once a month.

Johnny called every month or so with plenty of questions and opinions about wrestling. I got to know him better over the next several months, but I found out more about him when his mother intercepted one of his phone calls and spoke to me herself.

Mrs. Buchanan told me that Johnny had lost his concentration in school, and that his grades had begun to slip. His focus had become wrestling. I asked her to put John back on the phone.

JOHN BUCHANAN:

Page was very direct when he told me not to call him again. He quickly explained that school came first, and that he wouldn't talk to me until my grades improved.

John Buchanan of Cape Coral, FL was the first official fan of DDP. From that first call to the nightclub till today, Page has been a "big brother" to John.

I was crushed. I had started out being his fan, then he became my idol, and by that time, he had become like a big brother.

Six months later, Page received a call from Mrs. Buchanan informing him that John had indeed brought his grades up to new heights, so Page reopened the lines of communication.

John Buchanan and Page have been friends for over 11 years, and have continued those monthly conversations. As John got older, Page was there for support and brotherly advice on every topic from dating to peer pressure, and John quickly became more of a friend than a fan. John Buchanan even attended Page's wedding, and would always know that DDP was in his corner.

JOHN BUCHANAN:

As I got older, Page was always there to give me encouragement and advice on so many topics. I really found out how important Page was to me about four years ago when I was diagnosed with Crohn's disease, an intestinal disorder. So many people were there to give me encouragement—my parents, doctors, and friends. But Page's pep talks made the greatest impression on me. He wouldn't allow me to waste time feeling sorry for myself, and made sure I remained positive and focused on getting better.

When Dusty Rhodes left the struggling efforts in Florida for the WWF and New York, it became evident that the smaller federations were no match for the larger companies that had TV money. FCW continued for awhile, but it was obvious that the sun was setting on Florida Championship Wrestling.

Life has always had the ups and downs of the yo-yo for me, and while there were new doubts about my life in wrestling, a bright light shined on my personal life. That light ultimately proved to be the end of a search and a beginning to a new life.

The days between Christmas and New Year's are a great time for the bar business in Florida. The hotels are packed, the beaches are mobbed, and tons of people are visiting from college or on vacation looking for a party.

It was a typical night for Page at Norma Jean's. He made the rounds, stopping by the bars and walking the club. He also checked out the ladies before heading to the DJ booth to grab the mic and officially bang the party into gear.

That night, my friend, Mr. Deke, brought in 10 girls from his aerobics class to dance and party. I immediately spotted a tanned goddess I wanted to know more about. She had such an exotic look that I couldn't tell what nationality she was, and I sure didn't think she was from Ft. Myers. I just had to know who she was.

Kimberly Lynn Bacon was in her hometown of Ft. Myers, Florida for Christmas Break. A senior at Auburn University, Kimberly had been filling in as an aerobics teacher at Mr. Deke's Workout, and was sampling the nightlife at Norma Jean's.

Kimberly Bacon is the oldest of four daughters raised in Ft. Myers by Dr. Bruce and Lynn Bacon. The Bacons are a tight-knit and respected family who raised their girls in an academic environment. Kim was a gifted student and a diligent reader who had completed accelerated courses at the Canterbury School, and was an honor student at Ft. Myers High School. She was far from your typical college senior, since she had not yet reached her twenty-first birthday, and was about to graduate from Auburn with a double major in journalism and public relations. Her 3.89 grade point average earned her the distinction of magna cum laude in her graduation class of 1990, and she was due to graduate earlier than June.

Although she maintained a high level of academic focus, Kim also showed athleticism, enjoying and playing both volleyball and softball. She had begun to especially enjoy physical conditioning and aerobics while at Auburn, and had started to teach classes.

KIMBERLY:

I was nearly finished at Auburn, and was home partying with friends. Norma Jean's was great because we could dance there before we were legally allowed to drink. Since we knew we'd never get "over-21" wristbands, and it was a festive time of the year, we had a few drinks before we got there. Even though I had a curfew, we just had to stop at Norma

Jean's. It was the place to go, and that night, the place was wild, and the dance floor was packed.

Deke introduced Page to me as the owner of Norma Jean's that night. We spoke for a few moments, but my curfew was earlier than most, and I left while the party was still going on.

The next time I saw Page was a couple nights later. I was in Norma Jean's again, but this time, I was with a date. As we were leaving the dance floor, Page came over and reacquainted himself with me. My date had started talking to someone, so Page and I went to a quieter bar where he offered me a drink, and we talked for several minutes.

Besides the fact that he asked for my phone number, I remember being worried that he'd discover that I wasn't wearing a wristband and had accepted his drink.

I noticed her as soon as she walked into the club a couple nights later, and waited for the opportunity to talk to her. When I noticed that she wasn't wearing a wristband, she quickly apologized and told me that she was just two days from her twenty-first birthday.

We only spoke briefly, but when I woke up the next morning, I called to invite Kimberly to the beach, and was jacked when she accepted on such short notice.

One of the very first questions I asked Kimberly that day was whether she liked adventure. I knew that life with me always had the potential for adventure, but I was really talking about my classic pink Cadillac. When times were good, it was the best car in the world, but it was a money pit, and at any given time, it could be on the side of the road. The car ran great that day, the weather was outstanding, and we were getting to know each other on a scenic drive to Sanibel and Captiva Islands. We had decided early in the day that we would go to dinner that night to celebrate her birthday since she was about to leave town.

KIMBERLY:

It was a nice day, and we enjoyed great interactive conversations from the start. Page was outspoken and opinion-

ated, and some of his views and preferences surprised me. Although it seemed that we had opposite views on almost everything, he was able to make me see his side of just about every issue, and may even have changed some of my opinions. I couldn't believe that this long-haired Jersey boy in a Bon Jovi *T-shirt was singing along to country music, and actually had me listening to the lyrics.*

We had lively discussions and kind of traded barbs throughout our first date. Even before we had lunch, he asked me how I felt about children, and declared that he didn't think I wasn't the girl for him based on my answer. I was barely twenty-one, and had no plans to marry young. I was ready to go on to graduate school at Northwestern, and certainly wasn't thinking about starting a family.

I really thought that we would finish our day at the beach and wouldn't see each other again, but the more I was around him, the more intrigued I became. I had never met anyone

From their first date in 1989, Page and Kimberly were a team.

quite like this guy. There had been dates with popular guys and a couple of bad-boy types before, but he was different. Page was older and more of a man than the boys at college, and he was animated and passionate about his work in the bar business and his dreams of wrestling.

When I tried to kiss her following our afternoon beach date, she ducked under me and jumped in her car. This was the second time that she had played "cat and mouse" with me. The first time was when she made me struggle to get her phone number. I looked down at her a little curiously confused and asked, "Are you f*ckin' with me?"

She put the car in reverse and replied, "Yep!"

Later that afternoon, Kimberly asked me if I wanted to change restaurants after discovering that her parents were dining in the same place. I thought she was embarrassed by me, but then she said that her mom intimidated most boys. I reminded her that I wasn't a boy, and explained that there had never been a woman who intimidated me. We went back and forth for a little while, but decided on Peter's LaCuisine as planned. When I first saw her parents' reaction, I wondered if they were expecting me to be Dr. Marcus Welby instead of Diamond Dallas Page.

KIMBERLY:

Dinner was wonderful. The owner knew Page, and the service and food couldn't have been better. Not only did Page send my parents a bottle of wine, but he walked over to introduce himself later in the evening. My parents were cordial, although taken aback by his look. Page was a true gentleman.

After I mentioned that I had a sweet tooth, he ordered one of every dessert and fed me a taste of each.

I was totally digging Kimberly, and could tell that she was having a great time. We had been together most of the day, but I still hadn't hugged or kissed her, and she had dashed every attempt.

Towards the end of the dinner, she asked, "What's wrong with you? You can't be so perfect." Then she quickly answered her own question by saying, "It's gotta be your feet."

KIMBERLY:

I noticed that he never took off his Reeboks when we went to the beach, so as our sparring continued, I showed my affinity for him, and, at the same time, saw the chance to rib him by saying that he probably had ugly feet. I even dared him to show me his feet later in the evening. And, by they way . . . they're beautiful!

I kept my shoes on at the beach because of all the seashells that Captiva is known for, but when Kimberly said that I could only have a kiss if I showed her my feet . . . Good Gawd! . . . my shoes were off in a heartbeat.

Page and Kimberly became an item after that, and it quickly turned into another airline and phone-line romance. Kimberly was finishing up her last semester at Auburn in Alabama, with plans to attend Northwestern in Chicago. They took turns traveling to see each other, and Kim would occasionally accompany Page to an FCW show. Other times, they would just spend a couple of days together in Ft. Myers, but every time they saw each other, their friendship and bond became stronger.

While their relationship thrived, Florida Championship Wrestling was having more and more problems. Dusty was long gone, and the WWF was nationwide. With Ted Turner's personal interest in professional wrestling and his new financial commitment, WCW in Atlanta was gaining in popularity, making it tough on the fledgling FCW.

In a matter of months, the AWA and Florida Championship Wrestling began to fade away, and that spelled uncertainty for the career of Diamond Dallas Page.

During that time, I had ill-fated tryouts with both the WWF and the WCW. The clock was ticking, and the yo-yo seemed to be looming.

I got a tryout in New York that was probably more to appease a request by Dusty than anything else. I wasn't ready, and they wanted me to modify my character, and that made the taping a little uncomfortable for me. The WWF was in need of a color commentator to replace Jesse Ventura, and I was in no way capable of filling those shoes . . . not at that time, anyway.

A couple of months later, I had a tryout with WCW, but I never thought that there was actually a position available. Paul E. Dangerously was in contract negotiations with WCW, and I may have been used for leverage to get Paul E. to sign. Shortly after my tryout, he did . . . and I didn't.

The AWA finally died, and Florida Championship Wrestling was in a coma that it wasn't coming out of. Norma Jean's was still my source of income, but my focus was changing, and my energy was directed in other places. It was different now . . . there was Kimberly . . . and I knew the times were changing.

I had been in love thousands of times before. Sometimes, it was for hours; sometimes, for days, but never like this. Hell, I had even been engaged twice!

With my yo-yo life, the stigma of the bar business, the kiss-and-tell girls, and the rumors that jealousy breeds, it was hard to imagine a lady like Kimberly coming into my life. I realized that Kimberly was brighter and smarter than anyone I had ever met, and someone who I knew I could love forever.

KIMBERLY:

Life with Page was so exciting, and his passion for everything he did was contagious. He was my constant emotional support and my confidence, especially when I entered graduate school at Northwestern. I had always excelled in school because I could study and learn anything, but graduate school was more of a lesson in ambiguity, and I lacked the competitive edge and the aggressiveness that it took.

Page provided the necessary passion and confidence, all the while pushing me to levels he knew I could achieve.

It seemed that everyone was constantly trying to influence and convince me that Page was not for me. This included my girlfriends, guys who wanted to date me, and random women who wanted me to hear their experiences with Page. They all suddenly knew what was best for me.

My parents knew that we were dating and growing closer, but I think my mother never thought it would last. While everyone else told me what I should be feeling, I knew that I was happy, secure, and very attracted to Page.

Many ladies had come and gone, but none had ever been able to deal with my yo-yo lifestyle for very long. I knew that the emotional roller coaster that came with my quest to be the very best was tough for them. There were my dreams of wrestling, the pressures of the bar business, and the spotlight and attention that was on me . . . and on us. But Kimberly was able to see it all—my value, my strengths, and my weaknesses.

I made the decision to walk away from the bar business while Kim waited to start graduate school. Stallion and the boys were still my close friends, but I felt it was time. I knew that I would have to change my way of life, most specifically the hours and intensity that came with nightclub life. As for professional wrestling, three weeks after I left Norma's, Florida Championship Wrestling closed its offices.

I needed a new venture in which to utilize my promotional and motivational abilities as I had done for years as a nightclub manager. Multilevel marketing seemed like a good idea.

The first year of dating was a long-distance relationship. But each trip home for Kim usually included the beach, a night out, and stealing a kiss in the DJ booth.

I had two friends from Jersey who had made a bunch of money in multilevel marketing, so I called them to find out where they saw the business heading. The government had just deregulated the telephone industry, and my friends had directed their investments to a new program that provided discount telephone service.

I jumped on board immediately, and poured my heart and soul into it. I put every ounce of energy, along with most of my savings, into NCN. But, NCN was about two years ahead of its time. It was a pioneer of the companies that popped up later, most notably Extel, one of the multilevel success stories.

I have learned that life is often about attitude and timing, and although my attitude may have been right, my timing was wrong. After about five months, my personal funds dried up. With the yo-yo now down around my ankles, I scrambled back to the arena I knew best—my old friend, the bar business.

I never considered doing a nightclub in Ft. Myers, since all my bro's were still kicking it at Norma Jean's, and I saw the future of the business going in another direction. Dance clubs were still hot around the country, but I knew that the sports bar concept with food and fun was the key to longevity. Port Charlotte was just 30 miles north of Ft. Myers, and was virgin turf. I felt that I could create a sports bar atmosphere with a late-night dance party.

The project was called "P.J. Bleachers," named partly by using the initials in my name—Page Joseph. I had been approached by three guys who expressed an interest in backing my sports bar-restaurant idea in Port Charlotte. A few of their friends were added, and before I knew it, there were eight or nine partners. Everyone had supported my idea to build this project, but getting the doors open was a living hell. All of a sudden, there were 10 opinions and too many silent partners who couldn't stop talking. This concept was also before its time, and really belonged in Atlanta, Chicago, or maybe even Tampa . . . but definitely not in Port Charlotte.

P.J. Bleachers caused Page much more aggravation than it was worth, and having a large group of investors created many philosophical and business differences. Within the first month, the partners had divided, and the tension had increased. Money had been spent on kitchen staff and a menu concept, but it became evident in the first few weeks that Bleachers was more like a dance club with busy weekends, rather than a restaurant that suggested reservations.

Page had always created a party atmosphere in all of the clubs that he was associated with over the years, and it was difficult to think of him in any other way. The locals were excited to have "the guy from Norma Jean's," and soon after opening, P.J. Bleachers became known as a bar with a sports theme, and a dance club that served food.

The investment group wasn't happy with the restaurant traffic, and tried to discourage the bar business, hoping to attract more diners. The more the partners intruded, the more damage was being done. The stress was hard on Page physically, and he dropped to less than 200 pounds before he issued an ultimatum to the investment group.

It wasn't the way I had intended it, but the place was doing big numbers, and the first month of business was good. We had exceeded our projections based on the added liquor sales, and although we were slowly building a lunch crowd, it was obvious that we were no competition for the major restaurant chains that were popping up. There were partners who were angry about the number of people who just wanted to party, dance, and make Bleachers their neighborhood bar, and they wanted to turn away business rather than build off of what we had.

Bottom line, P.J. Bleachers wasn't fun for me. And if it's not fun . . . I don't want to be a part it. Things had gotten out of hand, and I showed them how the place could work if theyallowed me to run it my way. The majority disagreed, and I walked away from the deal.

It really was a terrible time for me. I felt like my wrestling career was over. Plan A, multilevel marketing, had not worked out. And plan B, P.J. Bleachers, which seemed like a great idea, had also fallen apart. My only escape was my time spent with Kimberly.

It was a good thing that Delta loved to fly . . . because we made them prove it. We saw each other almost every weekend during our first year of dating. There were many flights between Ft. Myers and Chicago, and many hours of quality time spent with Kimberly. It was during that first year that I realized that Kim had far eclipsed any friend or lover who I had ever known.

It would have been very easy with all that had gone wrong for Kimberly and I to grow apart. Her resiliency and desire to weather the storm with me made me realize that she and I were . . . *foorrr rreeeal.*

Not only was she the key to my emotional and romantic future, but Kimberly helped me find the key to the biggest embarrassment of my life . . . my inability to read.

KIMBERLY:

From the early days of our relationship, I knew that Page had problems with spelling. He sent cards that had many mistakes, and transposed numbers frequently, but I really wasn't overly surprised since I knew athletes at college who had the same difficulties. The topic came up from time to time, and generally, I would gently kid him about his spelling or writing. But one time, I went too far and really hurt his feelings. I looked at his problems closer, and found that it wasn't as simple as him being a lazy student who hadn't studied his spelling. When he confided in me that reading had been a source of ridicule since elementary school, I couldn't help but wonder if I would have been the type of classmate who would have mocked him as he struggled to read in class.

It was part of getting to know each other, and I was amazed that this guy who gave me all the confidence in the world actually had these insecurities. It shocked me when he told me how much his fear of reading had affected him.

He had the classic symptoms of dyslexia, as I understood it, and I looked for ways to help. I would have him read to me, and I tried to make it fun as I constantly reminded him to slow down.

Kimberly helped me over the biggest hurdle—identifying the problem. I forced myself to read everything, but mostly in short spurts. At age 33, I accomplished a feat that I never thought I could.

The first book that I ever read from cover to cover was Lee Iacocca's biography. From that moment, I knew it wouldn't be the last. It was a great feeling to close that "chapter," and reading is one of the pleasures of life that I never thought I would be able to enjoy. Nowadays, I read all types of books and publications, and although I must still remind myself to slow down . . . I've improved to the point that what was fear is now fun.

Page and Kimberly were building the foundation of a lasting relationship with every weekend visit. There was little doubt that Kimberly had provided a bright ray of light on what was becoming a desperate situation, and during this part of the journey, Page's confidence was being tested. The most recent bounce of the yo-yo had drastically changed the scenery, and Page found himself in a place he had never been before.

Financially, he had reached his lowest point. His savings had been depleted following his career change, and the demise of P.J. Bleachers had compounded the problem. His expenses still included a condo on the water, a leased Mercedes, and a taste for the good life. His wrestling career had suddenly been interrupted, and the more he thought about Kimberly, the more he missed her.

Christmas was around the corner, and so was the first anniversary of his first date with Kimberly. He was unemployed, and it seemed that all his "irons in the fire" had been doused.

One of the friends I made in wrestling was "Cousin Luke" of the tag team "The Bushwhackers." Luke told me about a friend of his who wanted to build an American nightclub in his native country of New Zealand and needed help. The timing couldn't have been better, and within days, I was making plans to fly across the globe to spend a month consulting and creating the promotional and marketing plan for the project.

I saw the opportunity as the perfect way to help me get my head out of the water, and stave off financial ruin. It also gave me time to plan my next move. The project required me to be there through Christmas, but I made plans to return to the States in time to celebrate Kim's birthday, which, by the way, is New Year's Day.

With my travel plans set for New Zealand, I decided that it was time for a change. I planned to start the New Year with a move to either Chicago or Atlanta to try my hand in the bar business in a larger market.

Ironically, the grapevine had some interesting news. Dusty Rhodes was returning south to Atlanta to run World Championship Wrestling.

DUSTY RHODES:

I really couldn't direct Page, other than to tell him that if he truly wanted to resume his career as Diamond Dallas Page, he would have to be in Atlanta to do it.

New Zealand was more than just a financial boost for Page. It gave him assurance that his experience in the bar business had new value. It proved to him that consulting and creating concepts could take him beyond the day-to-day operation and promotion of the business. A move to a larger market made sense, and since both Chicago and Atlanta were convention destinations, it assured plenty of nightlife.

Kimberly was sure to be in Chicago for another year, but the news that Dusty would be joining WCW in Atlanta unlocked another door to Page's dream.

I stopped in Atlanta on both legs of the trip to New Zealand. While I was there, I cut some promos on video, and met with Dusty, who offered no guarantees, but did offer me an opportunity that would get Diamond Dallas Page back into wrestling.

"Dream" wanted me to continue my work as a color commentator, and also planned to make me the ring manager of "The Fabulous Freebirds." The Freebirds were one of the hottest tag teams at WCW, and were comprised of Michael P.S. Hayes and "Jimmy Jam" Garvin. I knew and liked both guys from my AWA days, and had kept in touch with P.S. after my trips to Minnesota had ended. There would be no contract, but I was excited about the chance to earn my place. And when The Freebirds told me that I would do *all* the talking, I was blown away. As far as I was concerned, they were two of the best talkers in the business, and they were giving me a shot to have the camera all to myself. They went as far as to start the promo with their backs to the audience and DDP delivering the rap.

MICHAEL P.S. HAYES
FABULOUS FREEBIRD:

Both Jimmy and I always liked Page, and in some ways, I thought he was a slight exaggeration of me. We were alike, in and out of wrestling . . . so I guess I liked his gimmick.

The WCW wanted to repackage The Freebirds by dressing us up a bit with Page, Humperdink, and, of course, a Diamond Doll. We were willing to give it a try, mainly because we liked Page and knew that he worked hard and always wanted to improve.

I was jacked as I headed to Chicago to see Kimberly. It looked like I was getting another chance to be Diamond Dallas Page, and the fact that I was breaking in as the mouthpiece for "The Birds" was huge.

On my way back to Ft. Myers from Chicago, I stopped in Atlanta to shoot more footage with The Freebirds. I also prepared for something bigger than a birthday or an anniversary, and much bigger than a New Year's Eve celebration.

KIMBERLY:

We had heard so much about a place in the middle of the state of Florida called Chalet Suzanne, an old, nostalgic, and very eclectic German hotel and restaurant. Our accommodations were right out of a storybook, with antiques and assorted artifacts, an oversized bed, and outdated décor that was gaudy and sort of funky at the same time.

I had made up my mind that on the anniversary of our first date, I would ask Kimberly Lynn Bacon to be my wife.

While Kim was settling into the room, I went to the dining area on the pretext that I was checking the menu selections and making a dinner reservation. But when I got there, I put a different plan into place.

It started with one rose . . .

Was it a birthday celebration or a New Year's Eve party?

Kim! Read the banner!

Kimberly's shock turns to "Elation."

The ring makes it official.

One year following their first date, Page and Kimberly were engaged at the Chalet Suzanne in Lake Wales, Florida.

I arranged for a dozen roses to be delivered to the restaurant, and also requested a banner that would be brought out as I was feeding her dessert, like I had done before, one year to the day.

KIMBERLY:

It was a seven-course meal, and we had just about the entire restaurant to ourselves. As the waiter filled our wine glasses and served each course, he presented me with a rose or two and a love note from Page. The notes were more loving with every course, and by the time dessert was served, there were a dozen beautiful roses on the table, and the entire staff had encircled us.

Page dropped to his knees, and while the restaurant staff was urging me to read a banner they had brought out, my shock swept to complete satisfaction. Despite what anyone had said, Page continued to show his total love and understanding for me. I knew from that first day at the beach that he was a good man with a sincere and sensitive side. Through my tears, I saw the most beautiful ring that he had designed, and knew that life with Page would always be exciting. He motivated me in so many ways, and his honesty and communication skills made me sure we would be perfect together.

Kimberly and I were engaged to be married that night, without setting a date. We knew that we wanted to be together, but we also knew there were changes ahead. While I saw Atlanta as my future, Kimberly had her mind focused on settling in Chicago after graduate school.

Once I returned to Ft. Myers, I packed my things in a U-Haul truck, attached my Mercedes to the tow hitch, and set my sights for Atlanta. And I was broke. In fact, I was three payments behind on the car, and there were no guarantees other than Dusty offering me a shot. I didn't have enough money to get my own place, so I made arrangements to stay with Kim Boggio, a friend of mine from Jersey who was living in Atlanta.

Boggio was a great guy, and extended his home to me without blinking an eye. I wanted Kimberly to fly to Atlanta immediately so I could show her all that it had to offer. I knew it would be a tough sell, but I also knew that Atlanta was my only option.

KIMBERLY:

Upon completing Northwestern's graduate program, I knew that I could have written my own ticket in the advertising field in Chicago. I had interned with one of the largest firms in the area, and I really liked Chicago much better than Atlanta. I loved Page dearly, but I felt that my education could provide the job that would create our foundation while Page was finding a new vocation.

I had made up my mind that Atlanta had nothing to offer me, but Page said that he would pick me up, and that our weekend together would be magical. I was excited to see Page, and I tried to remain positive about the possibility of a future in Atlanta.

I unhooked the Mercedes and discovered it wouldn't move. What I learned that day was that dragging a car on a trailer without disconnecting the drive shaft will strip the gears. That's strip the gears as in tearing up the transmission. With time running out and no vehicle to use to pick up Kimberly, I had to come up with an alternate plan.

I was so freaked-out at this point, and had less than an hour to empty the truck, set up and make the bed, shower, pick up flowers, and try to park a 24-foot truck. I knew that Kim wasn't so hot on moving to Atlanta, and I wanted everything to be perfect. But this was far from perfect. I was now going to have to use the last of my money to fix the car, and our weekend was going to be spent in a spare room full of boxes.

It was that kind of situation that looked like tragedy, but was really comedy. It became funny to me, and rather than concentrate on how bad things were going, I snapped out of it. I knew it would be difficult for Kimberly to see the humor in it all . . . but that was all I had to offer at that point.

When I picked up Kimberly, I had the 24-foot U-Haul truck outside waiting to whisk her away. Her mouth dropped open with a look of shock and disappointment.

I looked at her suitcases, then back at the truck, and all I could say was, "Gee, Kim, I thought you would have *a lot* more luggage."

It was our first weekend in Atlanta, and all I could think about was Kimberly telling me she liked adventure, and knowing I was doing a good job of providing it.

CHAPTER TEN

THE TALE OF TWO RINGS

Page's leased car needed a major transmission overhaul, but transportation wasn't the only hurdle that the move to Atlanta presented.

In the past, Page was never the one looking for a place to stay, but instead was the one who had always provided a place for someone to live while they were getting on their feet. And while he was in the bar business, there had always been another place he could manage or promote. Obviously, the bar business lacked security, but wrestling as an occupation was a roll of the dice. Money was tight, and Page was getting another lesson in budgeting.

Kimberly's visit certainly hadn't convinced her that life in Atlanta was the way to go. To her, Chicago seemed to offer a future that was more secure and more logical. With her master's degree from Northwestern's highly respected McDill School of Journalism, the Windy City looked like Kimberly's land of opportunity.

KIMBERLY:

The trip to Atlanta was very disheartening. The U-Haul story is a lot funnier now than it was then, and the weekend was a disappointment. I knew that Page was determined to live there, and he tried to convince me that Atlanta was where I wanted to be too.

I was six months from graduation, and Atlanta was not in my career plans. Because of the relationship that my graduate program had with the major companies in the Midwest, I felt that Chicago would be the best place to start our life together.

Page was excited about the opportunity that he had with World Championship Wrestling, but he had been excited about multilevel marketing and P.J. Bleachers too. It was just over a year since I met Page as the owner of Norma Jean's, and he was on his fourth career.

There were reasons to feel good about World Championship Wrestling, even though I was being paid by the appearance, rather than by the week. I had never been offered a contract or a regular work schedule before. In fact, I had never needed or expected to make money in wrestling before. For the first time, I had an opportunity to work with a company that was building something great, instead of one that was hanging on for dear life.

The first six months in Atlanta wasn't pretty at times. I'm so grateful to "Boge" for providing me with a place to live and helping me adjust to life in Atlanta during that time. Having all my worldly possessions in boxes in my bedroom was a long way from being "the man" in the bar business, and, often, it was hard to believe that I was in wrestling, engaged, and that this whole deal was going to work out. I was juggling whatever money I had to get out of the hole while, at the same time, trying to scrape up money for my next visit with Kimberly. I knew that the more they used me at WCW, the better the chances were for Kimberly and I to begin our married life together in "Turnerland."

There were lonely times and reasons to be depressed, but I refused to be negative and concentrated on working hard and staying focused. Sure, I knew that every time I worked, it helped me get closer to extending my dream, but a light WCW schedule would keep me from being able to see Kimberly. There were times when I had the time but not the money to see her, and during one of those times, I really got to know Terry Taylor.

Terry was an established superstar and proven pro, and was in a much better spot than I. Because guys come and go in wrestling, some guys who have been around awhile keep to themselves. Terry Taylor was a voice of experience, and he became a friend who helped me outside the ring. Both Terry and his wife, Trudy, knew what I was going through without me ever saying too much about it. Trudy would pack lunches for road trips, and Terry's encouragement was invaluable. Terry sensed that I wanted to visit Kim and that the only thing that was stopping me was the fare for the flight, and he offered and insisted on using his Skymiles to get Kim to Atlanta. It's that kind of thing that helps make the bond between the boys more of a reality, and Terry Taylor will always be aces in my book.

KIMBERLY:

We had great times when Page came to Chicago, but going to visit him in Atlanta was tough. His room was filled with boxes, clothes, and gimmicks. Consumed with establishing his wrestling career, I felt that his blind faith and positive direction weren't enough.

I was young, and my expectations for us were great. I knew that Page could be successful in business, but I didn't think that being married to a wrestling manager who was on the road and living in Atlanta was the best scenario. Having achieved the academic success that was necessary to find the right job, and with Page starting over, I felt that my degree and career would be our stability for awhile.

After the surprise, excitement, and congratulations of their engagement wore off, the doubters began to register their opinions. Page had been engaged before, and while Kimberly was at Auburn, it was obvious to her family and friends that her career and individualism were far more important to her than marriage. While Page's friends doubted his move to wrestling, Kim's friends doubted her move to Atlanta . . . with Page.

KIMBERLY:

Our engagement shocked many people, and there were doubts about my future with Page. Not only were my friends telling me to wait and to be careful, but when I visited Ft. Myers, I heard wild stories and innuendo from various girls who felt compelled to tell me that Page was not the marrying kind.

So much of the negative advice I received was spawned from jealousy or contempt for Page—for what he represented, his reputation, and his persona.

I understood my mother's concern because she and my dad had done so much for me and my sisters so that we could get our education and independence. And now, I had pretty much done a 180-degree turn from my single-career-girl goals. The whole idea of marrying a former nightclub guy who was trying to break into professional wrestling was hard for her to deal with.

The Atlanta problem was foremost on my mind, though. I wanted to be by Page's side and be his wife, but I didn't want that life to begin in Atlanta.

I thought for sure that Page would realize that it made more sense for us to live in Chicago. His future with World Championship Wrestling didn't seem nearly as bright as mine did as I neared graduation.

While I was being paid by the appearance, I knew that the more I could do, the better chance I had of working. The experience I gained while working with Gordon Solie put me in the position to be the color commentator on one of the WCW alternate broadcast teams. I couldn't help but relate my new career in the wrestling business with my old career in the bar business. As a bar manager and employer, it was the versatile guys who showed a willingness to learn who were always in the picture, and I was determined to be in the WCW picture. The short time I had spent in the AWA and FCW had given me newfound confidence and credibility. I knew that as long as retired wrestlers were managers and color men that they would have the edge that came with being in the business, but I wanted to be there . . . in Atlanta . . . and I wanted Kimberly with me.

The advertising business had slowed down majorly during the Gulf War. What normally would have been a fertile time for career placement and employment had almost dried up. Companies that usually hired Northwestern University McDill School of Journalism graduates and employment in Kimberly's chosen field were at a standstill. It now seemed that her degree was not better suited, so she decided that if she was going to wait it out, she wanted to be with Page.

No one had to tell me that I wasn't the ideal son-in-law for Bruce and Lynn Bacon. Although I believe they always liked me, there was little doubt that I had "mistake" written all over me as far as their oldest daughter was concerned. But I understood that. Kimberly's move to Atlanta and a firm wedding date probably calmed most of the critics.

KIMBERLY:

Ultimately, it was the communication skills that Page instilled in our relationship that proved to be the strength of our bond then, and even today. Eventually, everyone who mattered realized that Page and I were committed to each other, and that we were going through with that commitment. Of course, I wanted the support and blessing of my family, and I always understood their concerns. On the surface, it had been a whirlwind, long-distance romance that evolved quickly. Even though I was young, there was no doubt about my independence and desire for my parents to know that I was certain that Page was more special than any man I had ever known. He was honest and sincere, and I was not only proud, but lucky, to have someone like him. When my mother saw the confidence and assuredness that I had in my union with Page, we made plans for our future.

There was so much to do once I arrived in Atlanta. We decided on December 1st as our wedding date, and I had less than six months to set up our first apartment and plan for a wedding in Ft. Myers. Setting the date made it easier for my parents to accept that we were living together, and once we settled in, I started looking for a job in the advertising field.

Page with Kimberly's parents—Lynn and Dr. Bruce Bacon.

I found an entry-level position with one of the larger firms in the Atlanta area, but the position on the ladder for a fresh-out-of-college associate was the bottom rung. I was not content working in the copy room or doing clerical tasks. The salary was lower than I expected, and there was a long road ahead before my voice would be heard in the advertising business. I was busy and, fortunately, so was Page. His work schedule had increased, and he was earning more as a per-night employee than we thought he would the first year.

During the time that Page was the ring manager of The Fabulous Freebirds, he was also seeing limited action as an announcer. He was getting more work than he had expected, and he was positive that Atlanta had been the right choice. Ted Turner had purchased the NWA, and was building and televising World Championship Wrestling nationwide on his TBS Superstation. Many of the wrestlers, managers, referees, announcers, and office personnel from the defunct independent federations were seeking employment with the two companies that had cable TV exposure.

During that time, I heard that a guy from the AWA was coming in for a tryout to be a play-by-play man. They wanted me to do color for his test audition. I had heard the name, but I couldn't put a face to it.

Eric Bischoff
Friend formerly with WCW:

After the demise of the AWA, I was out of work for more than six months before I got the opportunity to audition for World Championship Wrestling. I was at the Omni Hotel, and had called to confirm my audition when I was informed that my broadcast partner would be Diamond Dallas Page—the same Diamond Dallas Page with whom I nearly came to blows. I really needed the job, and hoped that our past wouldn't affect my audition or my opportunity to get the job.

Neither of us said a word about our previous encounter prior to rolling tape for the audition. Page was doing the color commentary, and I was doing play-by-play, and the first few takes were a little awkward. The talent seldom knows what the producer or director is looking for in an audition, and that insight can be invaluable. Although Page wasn't a producer or a director, he coached me after those first couple takes, and helped increase my odds at that audition.

I knew that if he did remember me, he was putting that night behind him, but I looked a lot different, and I wasn't sure. I was curious, and finally turned to him after the last take and said, "Can I ask you a question? Do you remember me?"

The guy who I had met in Minnesota had long silver-gray hair. This guy had short black hair and looked more like a "Ken doll" than the guy I almost had it out with. But, as soon as Eric Bischoff sat down, I was sure he was the same guy.

I remembered him, and what I remembered, I liked. I hadn't forgotten what it was like needing a job and getting only one shot at it. Eric and I went on to become WCW's fourth-string broadcast team, travel partners, and, most importantly, close friends.

I'm often asked who designs or makes up the characters and gimmicks that a wrestler brings to the ring. It can happen in many ways, but most wrestlers create their own personas. Sometimes, the entire gimmick is created for him, and most times, a wrestler has been more than one character during his career. Some characters are a composite or a variation of another guy's gimmick, and once in awhile, there will be blatant rip-offs of other wrestlers. But most often, each guy has a distinguishing element that fans will hopefully remember.

The names chosen are very important. Whether a guy uses a variation of his own name or makes one up, the name can help create a look, just as a look can help create a character. Some of the looks are ideas from movies, television, music, or comic books. Sometimes, the boys think of them while on the road, in motel coffee shops, or on a layover in some dinky airport. They often ask each other about gimmicks, new angles, or hooks that can help get them over. It was one of those talks between the boys that led Scott Hall to call me in Atlanta.

SCOTT HALL
WCW SUPERSTAR:

I saw DDP working as the mouthpiece for The Freebirds, so I called him to find out how things were going with World Champi-onship Wrestling. I knew things were good for Page because his role as manager of The Freebirds was one of the top manager spots in the country. When we were in Florida Championship Wrestling,

I remembered talking to him about a character that he called "The Diamond Stud," and wondered if anyone had ever used it. He was jacked up when I mentioned it, and told me he had some ideas and would call me back soon. As he was hanging up, he said, "We gotta change your look, bro."

Scott Hall wrestled for years as "Gator" Scott Hall and "Big Scott" Hall in the AWA, the FCW, and the independent circuit. He had long blond hair and a walrus-like, Fu Manchu mustache. At 6'6" and 295 pounds, he not only had size, but he was, and still is, a good-looking guy who the ladies love. When he asked about becoming The Diamond Stud, I loved the idea. If I could get a push to promote an upcoming single wrestler in addition to being The Freebirds' ring manager, I knew that it would give me more appearances, more exposure, and a chance at a contract. There was no doubt that Scott Hall could work in the ring, but he needed to be *new*. The vision that I had for The Diamond Stud would mean that Scott would have to drastically change his look over the next couple of weeks, but I knew he might have trouble with all the changes, so I gave it to him in a couple of doses.

SCOTT HALL:
Page wanted me to dye my hair jet-black and cut it shorter. He felt that too many wrestlers had long blond hair at the time. We debated the point for awhile, and I compromised by dyeing it dark brown.

Those of us who know Page know that if he wants to talk or leave a message, he calls anytime, night or day. A few days after I had cut and colored my hair, Page called me at three a.m.. "Bro, you gotta shave the mustache too." I was half sleep, and before I knew it, he had hung up. That one was tough. I had that mustache since I was a kid, but Dallas was convinced it was the way to go. He is very strong-willed, and after we argued a bit, I decided to shave it off. I knew it would be easier to grow it back than it would be to change his mind. He told me to add a three-day stubble of a beard and come to Atlanta.

When I arrived in Atlanta, our first stop was at the hairdresser's. Dark brown wasn't good enough, so we put some temporary black hair color on my hair and beard, and went to the office.

Page hadn't told anyone who the guy under The Diamond Stud gimmick was, and I was anxious to see if anyone could figure it out. Page was right. They were completely fooled, and when they found out that "the new guy" was really a guy who had wrestled before and could work, I became The Diamond Stud. As a result of that phone call to Page, I signed a contract with World Championship Wrestling for the most money I ever made as a professional wrestler. More importantly, it gave me the security that I needed for my family that the independent circuit couldn't.

DIAMOND STUDD with
DIAMOND DALLAS PAGE

I wasn't setting the world on fire, but I was the manager of The Freebirds and The Diamond Stud, and was also announcing with Eric Bischoff. However, Scott Hall wasn't getting the push that he needed, and "Big Daddy Dink" was now appearing more and more with The Freebirds as another manager. Big Daddy Dink was probably best known for his Sir Oliver Humperdink character who had orange-red hair and wore a derby. "Hump" was 5'7" and had been around wrestling for years as an over-the-top heel manager. The corner was becoming very crowded when The Fabulous Freebirds went into the ring, since I always had a Diamond Doll on my arm. Hump is a great guy and remains a great friend to this day. He was always a supporter, and would visit me in the early days back at Norma Jean's.

I was still a ring manager which meant that there was always a possibility of physical involvement in matches. Usually, the managers are nothing more than mouthpieces for their wrestlers and a distraction to the opponents.

I'll never forget my first real exposure in the ring, and I doubt that the 5,672 people in the arena in Charleston, West Virginia will either.

Diamond Dallas Page was scheduled to participate in a Battle Royale match which featured dozens of participants, including other wrestling managers like Teddy Long and "Hump." In these types of matches, the managers are present to add to the gimmick, and are usually the first ones tossed from the ring. The match was scheduled for three consecutive nights of house shows, and would be DDP's first time in the ring in wrestling gear at WCW.

Arn "The Enforcer" Anderson
Legendary WCW Superstar:

Pranks and ribbing are a part of any locker room, but that match wound up being the damnedest thing I've ever seen in my years in the business. The Freebirds had cooked up something in the locker room with Rick Steiner. Rick and Scott Steiner were notorious for their pranks, and in the past, had taped guys to chairs, stuffed them into lockers, and even super-glued their gear to the ceiling. These guys were capable of anything.

No one needed to tell me that since it was my first Battle Royale match, I should be prepared. I picked out my favorite studded jeans to wear in the ring, and when Michael P.S. Hayes suggested that I wear tights so I wouldn't ruin my clothes, I figured something was up.

As soon as I got to the ring, my boys, The Freebirds, turned on me, and I was in a war before the battle had even begun. The crowd popped huge, and when I looked in the center of the ring, I knew why. Rick "The Dogface Gremlin" Steiner was waiting to wrap me up tight and take me down hard to the mat.

The boys do a shot. (left to right) Rick "The Dogface Gremlin" Steiner, Scott "Big Poppa Pump" Steiner, Marcus "Buff" Bagwell, and DDP.

RICK STEINER
WCW SUPERSTAR "THE DOGFACE GREMLIN":

I wasn't even scheduled in the match, so when The Freebirds asked me to join them in the prank, I knew Page would be surprised. I got Page in a hold called a "sugar" that can be pretty effective.

I didn't know what the fu*k I was doing out there, but I did know that I was fighting with everything I had. Within seconds, I heard Rick Steiner's sinister chuckle and was flat on my back with my tights around my ankles and Rick standing over me.

RICK STEINER:

*As planned, I held Page down while The Freebirds pulled down his tights, only to find another pair of shorts underneath them. I heard P.S. Hayes screaming, "He's got another fu*kin' pair! Get those too!" Page continued to struggle, but I held on as Garvin and Hayes grabbed the second pair and ripped them down too. I started to let him go, but saw that the SOB had yet another pair, and they were the most ridiculous little yellow running shorts I have ever seen.*

When Rick let me go, I was blown sky high[1]. I managed to wobble to the ropes, and, for a moment, I considered throwing *myself* out of the ring and making a run for it. I decided against it, figuring that since there were still two more nights that they could get me, I would just take whatever was coming. In seconds, Steiner spun me around, stepped on the pants that were around my ankles, and shoved me to the mat. He was standing above me again, and in one motion, Rick grabbed my shirt and shorts and snatched them right off my body.

Since those yellow shorts were more like underwear, there was no jock strap or anything else but me under that last pair. The crowd was going wild, and Steiner's eyes got real big when he realized I was naked. I just looked up at all the boys who were locked up and wrestling all around us, and they were frozen in time. It was like a freeze-frame of faces in disbelief.

ARN ANDERSON:

It was the most bizarre thing I have ever seen in wrestling. Page was lying there "buck naked" except for a pair of boots and a couple of pairs of pants around his ankles. If that wasn't shocking enough, Humperdink took off his shirt to give it to Dallas. Any other time, seeing Hump without a shirt would stop traffic, but this was an incredible scene, and Page was naked in front of all those people.

Page dropped the shirt at one point, and calmly bent down, picked it up, covered his crotch with it, and walked away. His a$$ was hanging out, and he was totally exhausted as he walked down the ramp like it was no big deal, business as usual, just another day at the office.

I wish I could say that was the only time I showed my a$$, but I know that sometimes my enthusiasm and my emotion have gotten the best of me. In my efforts to get everything just right . . . there have been times when I have gone about it all wrong.

Interviews and camera time are coveted opportunities and especially key for managers. I look at each interview as my most important one, and have given my input to the directors and producers, sometimes when they didn't ask for it. It's always been hard for me to keep my ideas to myself, and my passion can sometimes become aggravation.

DUSTY RHODES:

Dallas' emotion stems from his desire and genuine love of the business, and it's hard to discourage his passion. If he wanted to get his point across, he wouldn't care if Steven Spielberg were the director, he would try to help . . . and most times his ideas were

---

[1]*blown sky high—To be winded, out of breath, or exhausted.*

good, and sometimes, they were better.

He has always rubbed some guys wrong, but it's hard to fault him because of the demands he makes on himself. But there was a time that was far from one of his shining moments. He had this promo all laid out that he was doing with Scott Hall, The Diamond Stud. He had requested a hands-free mic like the ones that Bobby Brown and Madonna were using. He knew just how he wanted it to go off, and he was getting more hyper by the minute.

MICHAEL P.S. HAYES
A.K.A. WWF'S DOK HENDRICKS-FORMERLY WITH WCW:

Page was green enough at the time to think he could make a difference in the way they did things in the back and on camera. He would constantly ask, "Why do they do it this way?" or "Why wouldn't they want to do it a better way?" He was intense and always wanted to improve the product, but he didn't realize that sometimes there was no rhyme or reason why management was doing certain things.

That night, we were in St. Petersburg, Florida for a live Pay-Per-View, and Page was letting his enthusiasm get the best of him. He was all keyed up, and there were some technical problems. His amazement that the shoot was not going smoothly turned into frustration, and he copped a big-time attitude.

The entire shoot was a train wreck. It sucked. I had rehearsed the whole promo with everyone, and the more uncomfortable I became, the more I was showing my @$$. At one point, Dusty pulled me aside and came down on me pretty hard, telling me that it wasn't my Hollywood production, and that I should do it the way the producers and directors wanted it.

So we stumbled through the promo, and I was pi$$ed off about the way it went. As soon as the monitor went black, indicating that the taping had stopped, I looked at Scott and the Diamond Dolls and said, "Let's get the f*ck out of here."

But the tape had *not* stopped rolling, and there was no seven-second delay on the broadcast. I had said the F-word worldwide on Pay-Per-View.

When I got to the locker room, Michael Hayes and Jimmy Garvin were waiting for me, laughing and carrying on. They knew that I was really mad about the way the shoot went off, so when they told me that I had actually said "fu*k" on the air, I thought they were ribbing me.

A few days later, Michael Hayes told me that Dusty was getting a lot of serious heat over my on-air screw-up. I knew then that it was true, and huge. World Championship Wrestling and the Turner people were watching us closely, and I didn't have enough clout in the ratings or rankings for this not to be a major hassle.

DUSTY RHODES:
There was heat, and they overreacted upstairs. They wanted me to make Page an example, but I let them know that I wasn't going to buckle on this one. Fortunately, the corporate guys knew better than to force my hand, and, in due time, it settled down.

I couldn't tell this story without mentioning T.A. Magnum, a guy Dusty Rhodes first introduced me to. Magnum was one of those rare talents who had it all, and would have been a mega-star if his career hadn't been ended as a result of a terrible car accident. The accident, which would have killed anyone else, left Magnum partially paralyzed, ending his ring career instantly.

He miraculously recovered enough to get a job working in the WCW as a talent coordinator. He and Dusty agreed that for Scott Hall to get noticed, he would have to do it without a manager. So, while the powers-that-be had more or less decided to take The Diamond Stud away from me, Magnum made a sarcastic remark that I took very seriously. He joked that I should grab some boots, go to The Power Plant, put on a pair of tights, and climb into the ring.

I had been working out, and was in better shape than I had ever been. The thought of getting into the ring had crossed my mind many times, and I knew that the clock was ticking. My size was a definite drawback as a manager, and I felt that if I could just get on the bottom rung as a wrestler, it would keep me in the business. I decided to go for it.

I called to discuss the idea with Dusty Rhodes. The Dream has always been my mentor, and I wanted him to be the first to know. I expected, or at least hoped, that Dusty would encourage me, but I knew after talking to him that it was obvious that there were going to be more critics and disbelievers than I ever imagined.

DUSTY RHODES:
What Page wanted to do had never been done before . . . going from a manager and mouthpiece to wrestler, let alone a middle-card performer. The jokes, backstage chatter, and abuse that his body would go through would be rough on him. It just didn't seem worth it because of his talent as a voice and his natural ability to

be a creative force in the business.

Dusty's words were "Noooo, bay-bee, you're a fire breathin' dragon . . . you're gonna be the top manager one day. Don't do it. They will beat the sh*t out of you down there at The Power Plant."

But my mind was made up. Diamond Dallas Page was going to be a wrestler, and nothing was going to stop me. If I worked hard and stayed healthy, maybe I could make it to the middle of the card[2] .

MICHAEL P.S. HAYES:

I'll never forget it . . . Chattanooga, Tennessee was where Page told Jimmy Garvin and me. We thought it was the funniest thing we had ever heard.

We had this running joke about Page and his knees, his back, and any other ache or pain that he had. On road trips, he would be stretched out in the backseat with ice packs strapped to his body, telling us how bad he was hurting, and he was the damn manager! We're out there taking the bumps night after night, and the worst thing he ever really got was a sore throat. We rode him pretty hard, and he was the brunt of our jokes a lot of the time.

One time, Page was kicked back with his legs stretched out, and had just run down all his injuries. I had just asked him if he ever had any pain in his feet as Jimmy Garvin was lighting two packs of matches to give him a "hot foot." He was the most fun guy to give a hard time.

Actually, I thought it was a good move for him to try the ring. Page was smart enough to know that reaching a higher level as a manager wasn't in his future. I knew his age would be a deterrent, but I never saw it as his biggest obstacle. We all wondered how long his body could take the pounding, but there was no question about his work ethic or intensity.

It was difficult to find anyone who thought Page was making the right decision by entering the ring at the bottom of the ladder. The physical abuse, his age, and his lack of experience and dexterity in the ring were just some of the reasons for the skepticism. Some also thought that he didn't have the head for the business inside the ropes, and others wondered why he would want to jeopardize his present position in wrestling for one that was the longest shot of all.

---

[2] *the card—The roster of matches on any given night.*

Stone Cold Steve Austin
WWF Superstar-formerly with WCW:

Man, he was really getting good as an announcer, and had been a successful manager. I thought that he was turning away a secure job for a huge longshot. So often in this business, a person can get labeled and then overlooked—that was the biggest obstacle he faced.

Scott Hall:

When Dalli told me he was going to climb in the ring, my first question was, "Why do you want to step backwards?" He was a top guy as far as managers went, and even though he had an answer for every one of my objections, I thought he was making a mistake. There were a lot of guys at the bottom who wanted to move up.

Page agreed with Scott Hall. He had gone as far as he thought he could go as a manager, and he knew he would be starting back at the bottom. Diamond Dallas Page went to the official WCW training center known as "The Power Plant" to see Joseph "Jody" Hamilton.

Jody Hamilton was best known for his long and successful career as "The Assassin." In over 30 years as a professional wrestler, he drew heat with the best of them. Jody managed to remain one of the top heels in the business when wrestling played in high school auditoriums and county fair grounds on a weekly basis.

Following a career-ending spinal injury in the late '80s, Jody Hamilton opened an independent wrestling school in Lovejoy, Georgia. The professional wrestling industry didn't provide the next generation's superstars with enough training to reach the pinnacle in the industry. Jody had the foresight to see that the superstars of tomorrow needed an arena in which to learn and hone their craft.

In the years following Turner's formation of World Championship Wrestling, Jody signed a working agreement with the WCW. Soon after, he convinced the WCW to merge efforts, and The Power Plant was founded.

Today, "The Plant" maintains one of the best training facilities in the world. It is a primary source for the future talent of World Championship Wrestling. As many as four rings stay busy constantly with hopeful wrestlers and their dreams of stardom.

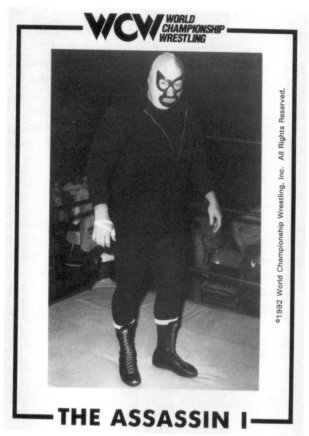

THE ASSASSIN I

Jody "The Assassin" Hamilton from his days in the ring, who became an important mentor for Page.

I was eager to climb in the ring and learn from every bump and toss that I knew I was going to get. The routine at The Plant was brutal. Learning how to fall was one of the most difficult things. Getting knocked to the ground seemed easy, but falling on my own was tough. I had arrived at camp in shape, and it was a good thing because it was a test every hour, every day. I quickly became a fixture there, and The Power Plant became the place where I learned, practiced, and experimented with the moves and techniques of professional wrestling.

Not a week goes by without people asking me the question, "Hey! How do I get into wrestling?"

First, get into the very best shape possible. Find out what a "Hindu squat" is, and be able to do 500 of them. When ready, contact World Championship Wrestling and try to get the three-day tryout at The Power Plant[3]. Make it the through the first day and immediately prepare for the next. After the second day, struggle through the final one. Most don't make it. In fact, only two or three out of the original twenty guys who try out usually make it to the next week.

Thick skin, a big heart, and an open mind are mandatory. And don't forget to check your ego at the door. Your desire must be unequaled, as the competition is fierce.

Jody "The Assassin" Hamilton
WCW Power Plant:

I really didn't know a whole lot about Page when he signed up for the school. What I did know was that his passion and desire were evident from the start, and he was willing to work hard. From what I had heard from Dusty and a few others, Page had a natural sense for the business, but was far from a natural in the ring.

Page was never satisfied with his role, and he was doing whatever it took to improve. He was the first one at The Plant in the morning, and we would have to run him out at night.

Everyone was against him, and were sure that he would never be able to work. The more I was around him, the more I realized he was a bit like me. He wasn't afraid of anything and was always ready to work. Every time he heard he couldn't do it, he worked that much harder to prove he could.

I pushed my body to the limit. For a guy who was the oldest rookie, I was relentless in my determination to be the first one at The Plant and make every day count. I was living, eating, and sleeping wrestling from my first day of training.

Kimberly:

Page was dragging when he got home. I would ask him if it was a three- or four-ice-bag night as he shuffled around the house. He was up early and back at The Plant only hours after he got home. It was during this time that I talked to Page about giving up wrestling for another occupation. I never doubted that Page could

---

[3]*The Power Plant—Call 404-603-3830 and ask for "Mr. Wonderful" Paul Orndorf.*

do it . . . I wondered if he should continue doing it. I knew that with the drive and motivation that he was putting into this dream, he could have done anything else and been way more successful.

Three weeks after my start at The Plant, I was given my first match. I was shocked. Gainesville, Georgia was the site, and when I heard that they were pairing me with Scott Hall in a tag match, I thought we would be a great team. Scott Hall wasn't quite as happy about the pairing of The Diamond Stud with Diamond Dallas Page.

In fact, he was hot about it. At that time, I had no idea why he was angry. Later, however, I realized that for Scott's career, it was like the kiss of death. He was on his way to becoming a semi-main-event guy with World Championship Wrestling, and now they were teaming him with a manager-commentator with only three weeks of school under his belt. Scott thought he was being misused, and he was right.

I knew that I would make lots of mistakes my first few matches, and I did. I remained positive, and really thought that my work wasn't as bad as it could have been, and I knew that I would improve.

But the events of my third match showed me that professional wrestling could get real *real* . . . real fast.

MICK FOLEY
A.K.A. "MANKIND," "DUDE LOVE," AND "CACTUS JACK"
WWF SUPERSTAR FORMERLY WITH WCW:

Dallas and Hall were the curtain jerker[4], and many of us wanted to see what Page looked like in the ring. Believe me, there were plenty of jokes and cutups before and during the match. Page made some typical rookie mistakes, but overall, I thought he did pretty well. However, when I saw him later in the locker room, he was hanging his head. I put my hand on his shoulder and told him not to worry. It was one of his first nights out there, and his mistakes were all correctable.

Page thanked me and said, "The match was alright, but I'm going to get heat over the fight." I had no idea what he meant, but within a few minutes, everyone was talking about Page's backstage skirmish after his match with "Firebreaker" Chip.

---

[4]*curtain jerker-The first match of the evening.*

[5]*receipts—Retaliation for an extra hard hit in the ring to an opponent; sometimes receipts are given at a later date.*

Curtis Thompson, a.k.a. "Firebreaker Chip," and Todd Champion, a.k.a. "The Patriot," were matched against Hall and me in the opening match. The match wasn't anything special, other than taking a few hits and each of us sending a few receipts[5].

After the match, Chip got in my face. He was hot about an incident in the ring. I knew that this was for real. Anyone who thinks that passion, ego, and determination do not get in the way in the ring is missing the reality of competition.

We were in the tunnel and butted chests like two angry friends would in a schoolyard. He pushed me, and I pushed back, before it escalated into Chip hitting me with a hard right hand. I began to bleed immediately, and retaliated with a kick to his stomach, followed by a front facelock.

It happened so fast that I just reacted and had him stopped, but he continued to struggle. My experience in the bar business was to stop a fight, calm the guy down, and get him out the door. So, I didn't know whether to continue fighting or what, as all of the top guys— "Sting," "Lex Lugar," and the "Steiners" gathered around us.

Chip and I were friends, and really hadn't had any heat between us before that match. I wanted it to end, but couldn't back down in this situation. At the same time, I knew that I didn't want to get the attention of the boys with a locker room fight.

SCOTT HALL:

It didn't take long for the boys to gather around to see what would develop. Dalli had the upper hand, and was able to control the situation before it got too crazy. It was a tough thing to do, but I feel that Page earned more respect from the boys that night than he could have earned in a year of being on the road.

MICK FOLEY:

Obviously, a fistfight in the back is not the way to start a life on the road. Page was able to get the immediate respect of the boys with the way he handled the situation. All eyes were on Page at that time, and everyone had an opinion on whether or not he would "make it." Many of us were a lot younger, but still had much more experience than Page. The way he would have to ice himself after each workout or match made many of the boys believe that he couldn't make it. They said he wouldn't last long, and waited for him to fail.

That back-room incident was the only time Chip and I ever had a problem with each other, and we were friends again the next day. Although back-room spats are a part of the business, usually the flareups between the boys are over as quickly as they start.

Kimberly Lynn Bacon and I were married on December 1, 1991. The wedding and reception were held at The Burroughs Home, a historical Southern home on the Caloosahatchee River in downtown Ft. Myers, Florida.

Many of my friends and relatives from New Jersey, Texas, and Florida attended the weekend extravaganza. The caterer put it best when he commented, "My, what an eclectic group."

The wedding party was large, and the rehearsal dinner was held at the restaurant where Kim and I first dined together, Peter's LaCuisine. Her bridesmaids included her three sisters, Jenny, Debbie, and Julie, and other friends. My groomsmen outnumbered the ladies, as asking me to narrow my bro's down to six proved impossible. The line was finally drawn at ten.

KEN KLEEST
FRIEND:

I was so flattered when Page asked me to be his best man. His circle of "solid" friends was large, and any of us could have had the honor. Many of the people at the wedding doubted if Page and Kimberly were ready for the hurdles of marriage. But as I left there, I knew that Page was ready and that he wanted Kimberly by his side, wherever his journey would take him. Since we were kids in high school, I saw Page's desire for all that life had to offer, and I knew that someday soon . . . they would have it all.

When Page and Kimberly had announced their engagement, Diamond Dallas Page was the over-the-top manager of The Fabulous Freebirds. Scott Hall was becoming The Diamond Stud, and Kimberly was sure that they would settle in Chicago.

Just six months later, they were together in Atlanta as newlyweds. Page was one of the oldest ring rookies in the history of wrestling, and with just three matches under his belt, he had shown promise. He knew that there would be hurdles, and he couldn't forget the yo-yo, but he was happier than he had ever been before. He was always that way around Christmastime, but 1992 was going to start off right . . . married to Kimberly and working his way up the ladder to his dream.

CHAPTER ELEVEN

THE ROAD, THE ROPES, THE KNIFE CUTS, AND THE AX FALLS

Page had a lot to be encouraged about as the New Year brought a whole new perspective. His marriage to Kimberly had clarified his personal life, and his decision to become a wrestler had given him an on-the-job taste of his boyhood dream. There were plenty of people who doubted that Page could get to this point in wrestling, and most anticipated his failure in the ring.

Page Falkinburg had already defied the odds. He had taken an idea to manage "The MTV Wrestler" to the creation of Diamond Dallas Page. He was "DDP the ring manager," "DDP the announcer," and now he could call himself "DDP . . . the wrestler."

In addition to his personal achievement, 1992 would bring a reward that provided as much financial security as was available . . . a one-year wrestling contract.

Signing my first contract with World Championship Wrestling was a great accomplishment, and having a year of financial security seemed like money in the bank. That contract was not for a lot of money. In fact, it was about the same as I had made as a per-night manager-announcer the year before. But nothing could have been better than signing a contract to wrestle.

Kip Frye was running the front office at World Championship Wrestling, and signed Diamond Dallas Page to his first contract. DDP was convincing as the arrogant, loudmouth heel manager turned bottom-of-the-card wrestler, and Frye proposed an interview segment and a push[1] for his character.

"Down With DDP" was intended to be the vehicle for the voice, and it looked like Diamond Dallas Page would get the TV exposure of a regular segment. Due to an injury to Scott Hall, Page had been named to replace The Diamond Stud on the wrestling traveling squad. The added airtime as a personality with his own weekly segment and the increased road schedule would give Diamond Dallas Page exposure. And his contract would help provide the time to capitalize on it.

I was now teamed with Kevin Nash, who has always been a talented and charismatic guy with potential. He had been known as "OZ," "The Master Blaster," and "Doctor X." without much success, and the booking committee wasn't sure what to do with him next. Nash had been off the road awhile before we became a new tag team combination.

WCW was in Las Vegas around that time, and Dusty and I were playing craps. We were winning and having a good time with a guy at the end of the table who was wearing a silk shirt, chains, a pinky ring, and shades. I was calling him "Johnny Vegas."

KEVIN NASH:

Page and I had both grown up in city-life situations, and would talk like "wise guys" sometimes. We saw the movie My Blue Heaven *and were mimicking Steve Martin's character, so we came up with an exaggerated version of the wise-guy gambler and called him "Vinnie Vega$." I had been given*

---

[1]*push—Management giving a wrestler's character a boost in promotion, TV time, and story-line involvement; a necessary tool in establishing fan base.*

a few different gimmicks that weren't interesting enough to get me a shot until Page and I hooked up and became "The Vega$ Connection."

As he was coming back from his injury, Scott Hall's WCW contract was ending, and he signed with the WWF. There is no doubt that Scott Hall's talent in the ring and charisma created what WWF's Vince McMahon later named "Razor Ramone." But the character was actually created in the WCW days when Scott did his *Scarface* voice. He would walk and talk the part, and had the mannerisms down pat. When he got to New York, it eventually got him to the main event and a title belt. As Razor Ramone, one of his best known gimmicks was his use of a toothpick.

SCOTT HALL:

One time when Page and I were on the road together, we were in a Waffle House and had both grabbed toothpicks. We were always looking for new gimmicks, and Page suggested we carry toothpicks while walking to the ring, and then flick them at the camera. On the way to the ring, he was "trash-talking," and his toothpick fell out before we got on camera. From that point on, it became my gimmick, and I've flicked toothpicks at cameras and opponents ever since.

I heard that Jake "The Snake" Roberts was coming to World Championship Wrestling, and I couldn't help but think back to those days at Norma Jean's when I had been so excited about meeting him. Jake always knew me as a night-club guy, and I had only seen him once outside of the bar business. Ironically, that was backstage at the WWF's *Wrestlemania VI*.

That night at *Wrestlemania VI*, Jake and I were on Vince McMahon's payroll, even though we weren't on the same side of the curtain. I was employed to drive my classic pink Caddy as chauffeur for the "Honky Tonk Man." So, technically, I've never actually worked for the WWF. It was really the car that got the gig.

Jake and I were both wrestlers by this time, but we were worlds apart in the ring. Very often, the main-event wrestlers never see the bottom guys, and certainly don't travel with them. But soon after "The Snake" joined WCW, I got the chance to be on the road and in the same car with him and Kevin Nash.

KEVIN NASH:

Page and I were tagging together, bottom guys on the road in Jacksonville, Florida, when Rick Rude offered us a hundred bucks to drive his car back to Atlanta. Jake Roberts joined us for the ride.

Rude had a classic '73 Chevy Caprice convertible that he bought with the first money he made in the business. Page offered to do all the driving, so Jake and I grabbed some beer and relaxed for the all-night cruise.

Page was explaining how great the car was running when, 30 miles outside of town on a pitch-black, two-lane highway, the engine light came on. Within a couple of minutes, the car's lights went completely dark as we coasted to a dead stop.

We were having a few cold ones, and wondered who would stop to help three guys ranging in size from 6'5" to 6'11" in the middle of nowhere. At about three in the morning, when the beer was gone, Jake got out and started walking. The Snake disappeared into the darkness, while Page and I wondered how we could get back to Jacksonville by morning to catch our original flight.

An hour later, an old tow truck pulled up, and Jake stepped out of the truck with a twelve-pack. The two guys in the truck looked like a couple of extras from the movie Deliverance, *but in minutes, we were being towed back. When we got to the service station, there were a dozen people who had gotten up in the middle of the night to pose for pictures and get autographs from "Jake the Snake" and the other "rasslers." After more and more pictures, we were on our way back to the airport by 6:30 a.m., and still had an hour to kill before our flight.*

I knew that things could change fast in the wrestling business, and I was always aware of how quickly things had changed for me through my life with the yo-yo. A month or

While they were both "bottom guys," Kevin Nash considered quitting. Later, both Nash and DDP became champions. (left to right) DDP, Kevin "Big Sexy" Nash, and Kimberly celebrate Christmas.

so after signing my contract, Kip Frye was out of the picture.

The new president of WCW was veteran wrestler-turned-promoter, "Cowboy" Bill Watts, the one-time boss of the Mid-South Wrestling Promotion. His reputation as an old-school dictator created immediate change for everyone at World Championship Wrestling.

Watts believed that there was plenty of talent who would work for less, and he quickly began across-the-board cost-cutting measures. Salaries were dropped, benefits dwindled, travel accommodations were less than ideal, and meals at the TV matches were eliminated.

Bill Watts was in, and my segment, "Down With DDP," was out—and cancelled after the first episode. I was still working and training daily, and I sure was relieved that I had signed a contract before he showed up.

The change to Watts made life miserable for the boys, and it seemed like nobody was spared. Announcers, managers, and the guys whose contracts were up for renewal were the first victims.

ARN ANDERSON:

Bill Watts came in and threw a wrench in WCW and the entire wrestling business. He tried to take us back to the '70s way of doing things. It was truly shocking. This was the type of thing that wrestlers feared from guys who didn't understand the business. Here was a guy who had been a wrestler, a good one, and no one could understand why someone who had come up through the trenches, like Watts, would degrade the sport and the guys who had made him his fortune. Watts was a bully, and when he owned Mid-South Wrestling, he had a reputation for strong-arm tactics.[2]

Arn Anderson later left World Championship Wrestling along with Bobby Eaton, Paul E. Dangerously, and many others. Kevin Nash continued to work, but was told that his contract wouldn't be renewed. Jake Roberts, who had a deal on the table when Watts took over, was told that his deal was off.

KEVIN NASH:

I was ready to hang 'em up and get out of wrestling even before my contract was up. I never felt like I had gotten an opportunity, and was ready to make a change. Page was "Mr. Positive," and kept saying, "Don't let 'em beat you, man." He was relentless, and I didn't quit. Instead, I worked harder and lasted longer than expected. Then I got the call from New York . . . and the rest is history.

Nash had gotten his pink slip, and had about 30 days left, when I told him he should "go out in a blaze of glory." Not only did he work past the end of that contract, but he later negotiated a deal to go to the WWF where he became "Diesel." Kevin was right when he said, "The rest is history."

---

[2] *This quote reprinted with permission from Arn Anderson, the author of the 1998 book,* A Look Behind The Curtain.

Jake was another story. He had agreed in principle with Frye on a contract, but never signed, and now The Snake was history. He left World Championship Wrestling as mysteriously as he had gotten there. Jake was another one of Watts' victims, and probably lost more money than anyone else as a result of the "Watts Regime."

JAKE "THE SNAKE" ROBERTS:

Let's just leave my opinion of Watts and that situation like this. I'd look forward to pi$$ing on Bill Watts' grave . . . but I hate long lines.

I continued to stay focused and live, eat, and sleep wrestling as I split my time off the road between The Power Plant and the gym. Nash and I continued to work together, and whenever I got in the ring, I was selling out the curtain[3]. I knew the boys were watching, and though I had friends who may have wanted me to make it, there were plenty of others who waited for me to give up or fall flat on my face. Staying healthy and in shape was my first focus, but I developed other rituals that I felt were helping me get better every time I stepped into the ring.

Probably, the most effective tool that contributed to my improvement was my video camera. I often taped matches to critique my broadcast when I was a commentator, but once I climbed into the ring, I taped every match.

"STONE COLD" STEVE AUSTIN:

Page had his camera with him all the time, watching his tapes over and over again. I never saw a guy who worked as hard and wanted to improve so much.

JIMMY "JAM" GARVIN
FORMER WCW SUPERSTAR:

We rode Page hard, teasing him about a lot of things, including his camera and tapes. He was the first one I had ever seen who watched and dissected his matches. Although

---

[3]*selling out the curtain—A match that gets the interest of the other wrestlers in the locker room; often times, they huddle in front of TV monitors or peer through stage curtains.*

I saw a few guys do it after him, I never saw anyone take advantage of it like Page did. Taping those matches was a great tool for him to learn from his mistakes, but, to us, it was just another thing for the boys to break Page's balls about. He was a good sport, though, and that was a good thing since there was always plenty to rib him about.

Page was also a one-of-a-kind guy on the road. He was like a bat, and always did everything to make the room the darkest it could be. On top of that, he wore a blindfold and taped the curtains shut so that not one drop of sunlight could peak through. He looked ridiculous lying in bed, bandaged up and blindfolded.

I had the latest and most compact camera equipment, but there were still extra bags to carry that took up extra space in the cars and motel rooms. When we got to the arena, I'd find a fan, friend, or member of the crew to tape my matches. Those tapes weren't filmed with audio, and were often taken with a shaky hand or an obscure camera angle. After my match, I'd go over and over the tapes, searching for clues on how to improve. The boys would rib about the hassle of carrying the camera, wires, and batteries, but there were plenty of times when I had company watching the replays. Sometimes, they would watch with me for their amusement, and I was a source of comic relief for Austin, Foley, and Scotty "Flamingo" Levy.

MICK FOLEY:

It was always more fun to rib Page because it was easy to get under his skin. Whether we were cutting on Page about his ice packs, tape machines, or moves in the ring, there was plenty of running commentary from the "gallery." "Stunning" Steve Austin had started adding voice-over for Page's tapes, and it was a riot.

STEVE AUSTIN:

We had fun with those tapes, doing play-by-play action, impersonating Gordon Solie, and finding other ways to cut up. But it was really just another chance to rib Page. We were all frustrated, and would cut on each other, but Page was always the most fun to mess with.

Although the times were lean, life on the road was full of laughs, pranks, and set-ups, and the pecking order determined who got the most attention. In many ways, the boys were like a fraternity, and the pranks were their equivalent of hazing. It broke up the boredom of living out of a suitcase and juggling travel, workouts, and dietary requirements.

MICK FOLEY:

We always found ways to mess with the inexperienced guys, and Page made it fun because of his many quirks and intensity. We were three guys, all trying to move up the ladder. The goal for many of us on the road was just to get to "156"[4].

Mick "Cactus Jack" Foley and DDP were frequent traveling partners while they worked together at WCW. Foley, a.k.a. "Mankind," is shown with wife, Collette.

[4]*"156"—A designated financial level desired by the majority of wrestlers; "156" meant three thousand a week, or an annual contract*

These days, it's hard to imagine Stone Cold, DDP, and Mankind splitting a $40 Days Inn motel room, but we did. Steve and I had the beds, and since Page was the rookie, he had a foldout cot. Steve was the top earner among us, and was the first to get to "156." In fact, Steve was at about "200" when I was reaching "156," and Page was at half of the number at that same time. We were still paying all the expenses out of that salary, and only had the security of one-year deals—and the insecurity of knowing that most guys would never get close to that magic number.

We were at the beginning of a seven-day road trip with Page just after he had started wrestling. Page, Steve Austin, and I would share rides and rooms, and we would bet on how many days it would take for us to get Page to lose his temper. Steve and I hid the towels when we knew he wanted to take a shower, forcing him to call the front desk. Then we'd hijack the towels in route, forcing another call, and then another. Finally, Page had to dry off with hand towels. He'd be standing there naked, dripping-wet, and screaming at the hotel operator. We'd do this in two or three different towns, making Page believe he was jinxed, and then we would find another way to crawl under his skin.

That same trip, we got a huge plate of chocolate chip cookies as a gift from a fan. Page was out late, so I lined his entire cot with the cookies, stuffing them between the mattress and the sheets. Steve and I were in our beds, faking sleep, while we waited for Page to get into bed.

I must tell the world that Page is far from modest. In fact, it was not unusual to see him nude, except for his ice bags rigged to various places, and just "hanging out" around the room. Of course, he slept in the nude, and when he slipped into bed, we heard him trying to get settled as the sound of cookies crumbled around him.

"Which one of you motherf*ckers put the f*cking cookies in my f*cking bed!?" he screamed.

In a rage, Page gathered up a handful of the crumbled cookies, threw back my sheets, spread the cookies around, and sat on me, grinding the cookies over me. While he jumped *all over me, he continued to scream over and over, "How do you f*cking like it!?" Calmly, I replied, "Page, I can deal with the cookies, but your naked a$$ is really going to cause you a problem."*

"Marvelous" Mark Mero
a.k.a. Johnny B. Badd-former WCW and WWF Superstar:

Page had every gimmick going when it came to fixing his body. He would use heat balms and ice, medical doctors, chiropractors, and physical therapists; and was willing to try anything new. He didn't care if someone was an herbalist, medicine man, or witch doctor. As long as Page thought he could use them, he would listen to anyone. When he started using a portable electrical "stem" unit, I thought I had seen it all. It would actually shock him as it was taped to his body. He had electricity and melting ice bags strapped up at the same time, and at any given moment, could have been a science project.

I never electrocuted myself by mixing my stem unit with the ice, but once I had it taped to my body while I was driving, and accidentally knocked the dial setting to "10." Since I usually kept it at about "3," it was shocking the sh*t out of me until I could pull the car over and find the control switch.

It's not like I didn't give it back to them, though. I could rib and rip with the best of them, and I look back on those times with fond memories. We were friends struggling to get to the top. Those friendships last forever. Hell, we had to be *really* close friends to rib each other the way we did.

One of those friends was Scott Levy, who wrestles as "Raven." Scott began wrestling in his early twenties, and we met briefly in Florida Championship Wrestling. Raven and I have remained close friends, and over the years, I've taken the roles of mentor, friend, and critic. Earlier, Levy was Scotty Flamingo, one of the guys who worked with and helped train me at The Power Plant. He was also a traveling partner in WCW.

SCOTT LEVY
FORMER WWF, WCW, AND PRESENT ECW SUPERSTAR
A.K.A. SCOTTY FLAMINGO, SCOTTY THE BODY, AND RAVEN:

Cactus Jack (Mick Foley), Page, and I were sharing a cheap motel room that had a small TV with only eight channels. Page was working the remote, and stopped for a second on the classic cartoon Droopy Dog. *He started flipping the channels again, and stopped when he saw a high school football game. Cactus and I ordered him to return to the cartoon, but Page refused. Jack and I reminded him that there were two votes for* Droopy Dog *and only one for football. Page replied, "We're watching football, not friggin' cartoons!"*

"The Emperor has spoken," I said to Jack, and from that point on, I have referred to him as "The Emperor." He's been a great friend who has gotten me the three biggest breaks in my career.

The road takes some getting used to; learning the tricks of travel, the art of packing, and the importance of making the most of a half a day in a town.

Packing is an area that we always look to improve, including more efficient ways to carry our gear. A lot of guys are real good at it, but it is universally acknowledged that Lex Lugar is the undisputed "King of the Road" in World Championship Wrestling.

Lex is an incredible human specimen, and his commitment to training is legendary in the business. For years, he has owned and operated The Main Event, Atlanta's premier total body fitness center.

Lex always has the best protein shakes and energy bars, and is one of the WCW's most respected authorities on diet, training, supplements, and bodybuilding. He was the first to utilize the zippered pockets in his luggage to store the shakes and protein bars which have become fixtures on the road today. Plenty of times, in the middle of nowhere, a supplement shake has held us over until we made it to a restaurant.

Lex Lugar
WCW Superstar:

The road can definitely take its toll on the new guys. After arriving in a town, finding the right restaurants and proper food can be hit or miss. Locating a gym, tanning bed, chiropractor, or massage therapist can be an all-day adventure when a rookie visits a town for the first time. Now, if one of those new guys has rubbed one of the boys wrong in some way, it can turn into a goose chase. It's fun to tell a guy that there is no gym to use in a town, and see his reaction when he finally does find a gym, and discovers that the walls are filled with autographs of all the boys.

Map reading and making flight arrangements is an art of its own, and finding the best travel route can save days on the road over the course of a year.

Learning about proper care and maintenance of the body is mandatory in the wrestling business. The best diet, the best workout, and the best training methods are all factors in preparing for the bumps of the ring and the road.

Additionally, one area that I made a point to spend time and money on was "rehabbing" after matches and road trips. Due to the constant physical abuse my body takes at my age, it needs all the help it can get in bouncing back, so it can take more punishment.

Smokey coined the phrase, "Humpty Dumpty Days," in reference to the time I spend rushing from medical doctor to massage therapist, to chiropractor, to applied kinesiologist when I'm home in Atlanta. As far back as 1991, I've had various doctors and physical therapists who have helped "put me back together again."

In the early days in Atlanta, my chiropractor was Pat Harvey. He adjusted my body for five years in the ring. The massage therapist who Kimberly and I have used since my start in wrestling is a woman named Marcy Joiner. She has also been a therapeutic ear and a friend to talk to through the years, and has seen me during the many dips, dives, and rises of the yo-yo.

To me, "icing" was, and is, crucial. I knew which muscles

responded to ice packs and when to apply heating pads because of the preventative care I had learned.

As time went on, more guys were strapping on ice packs after matches. However, since I was the first to do it on a grand scale, it provided yet another way to break my balls on the road.

STEVE AUSTIN:

We were on the damn road, standing in front of the motel ice machine. Page was "icing up," and I was getting ice for a couple of beers I had left over from the night before. I looked at him and told him that since he was strapping on ice bags, he might as well make himself useful and strap on my beers to save me from carrying a cooler.

The road has always been home to professional wrestlers. Traveling from small towns to metropolitan cities, and dining in top restaurants one night and greasy spoon diners the next, wrestlers are on the road every day of the year. As travel and routing improved, and salaries and revenues increased, the road became more tolerable for the top guys. But the sharing of expenses still exists on the road for many of the boys. There are wrestlers, referees, and announcers on the traveling squads in the WCW, WWF, and ECW who share rooms; and riding along with one or two guys is pretty much standard. This opportunity for the guys to spend a few hours with each other is often welcomed, more for the camaraderie and shoptalk than to save traveling expenses.

Some guys drive well and others ride well, while some can read maps and others can't. Some guys ask for directions and others barrel down the highway looking for signs. Some guys get better with experience and some guys never learn.

JAKE "THE SNAKE" ROBERTS:

Just for the record, Diamond Dallas Page is the worst navigator in the history of the wrestling business . . . and his driving isn't much better.

Paul Wight, who wrestled for WCW as "The Giant," and

I were frequent travel partners, and we became very close friends. I was able to give Paul some great direction early in his career in the ring, but on the road . . . that's another story.

PAUL WIGHT
WWF SUPERSTAR "THE BIG SHOW" AND FORMER WCW SUPERSTAR:

I didn't know a thing about the road. Growing up in a small town in South Carolina, I never saw traffic, and, at one time, was actually scared to drive in a city. Page always terrified me when he drove, and I began to overcome my fears of driving just so Dallas wouldn't be behind the wheel.

I had been in an especially grueling match with Scott Steiner, and had a knot the size of an apple on my head from a couple of chair shots[5]. I had a slight concussion, so "Mr. Icebag" insisted on tying an ice pack to my head. I looked like a cartoon character. At 7'2", I already didn't have much headroom in the car, and I didn't want to wear it, but rather than argue with him and lose . . . I wore it. I was slouched down in my seat with my head pounding and feeling miserable, but not in bad enough shape to let Page do the driving.

Page pointed me towards the expressway, and I took off like a bat out of hell. We had a three- or four-hour drive ahead of us. After an hour on the highway, my navigator, Diamond Dallas Page, asked me, "Are we going the right way?" I de-

DDP with his "Giant" little brother, Paul "The Big Show" Wight.

---
[5] *chair shot—Being hit with a metal chair*

veloped a bigger headache after hearing that, and then I saw a sign that said: "Welcome to West Virginia." After driving 97 miles out of the way, we had to turn around and drive for another five hours.

Page has helped me in many ways over the years, but when it comes to driving, he could get lost in a one-room sh*thouse.

Through the years, I traveled with many guys—from five or six of us "bottom" guys sharing a van to "splitting a car" with a friend that was more like a therapy session than a ride to work. One of the guys I rode with was my announcing partner, Eric Bischoff.

When it came to television production and creative ability, Eric was as sharp as anyone I ever met. Although we didn't always agree, he had a genuine love for the wrestling business, and the vision to see the potential that WCW had as an entertainment vehicle for Turner Cable.

Kimberly and I were renting an apartment, as were Eric, his wife, and two children. We had both been looking for the right home in the right area, far enough out of town, but not too far from the airport.

Dusty Rhodes' wife, Michele, was a realtor, and she showed us a few listings. Pretty soon, Kim and I decided on a split-level home in Mableton.

The next time Eric and I rode together, we both had news about our home search. The irony in our conversation was unbelievable.

Page: "Hey, we bought a house!"

Bischoff: "So did we!"

Page: "Really? We picked up a sweet house in Mableton."

Bischoff: "We did too!"

Page: "Bullsh*t. Are you ribbing me?"

Bischoff: "I'm not kidding. We bought a house in a real nice area of Mableton. It's on Main Street.[6]"

I was sure he was kidding, but I couldn't figure how he would know the street name, and wondered who had told him. So, I said, "Really? Our's is also on Main Street. What's your address?"

---

[6] *Yeah right . . . like there's really a Main Street.*

"I had to work with him . . . and now he's my neighbor?"
After a rocky introduction, Eric Bischoff and Page have
remained "tight" through the years.

Now Bischoff thought I was ribbing him, and he sarcastically said, "Our house is after the curve up the hill in the seven-hundred block."

No sh*t. Our house was before the curve at the bottom of the hill, and in 1992, we became neighbors.

Even though we recently moved, and we see less of them, Kim and I have been family friends of the Bischoffs and their children ever since.

That house in Mableton was the first one I had ever owned, and it was especially fun "lighting up the neighborhood" at Christmas the first time. I was decorating and needed way more lights, so I asked Eric to join me for the ride.

Eric Bischoff:

It was a rainy Saturday around Christmastime, and Page and I were on our way to the store. As usual, our conversation was about work, specifically where we stood with Bill Watts.

I was fed up with the way the guy was running the company, and it was obvious that more and more people feared and hated Watts. I thought that if this guy could run the company, then so could I. It really bothered me that Bill Watts had my future in his hands.

Eric got pretty emotional about Watts, and we were laundry-listing some of the fu*kups that Watts had made in so many areas. Suddenly, Eric said, "F*ck it. Someday I'm going to take that son-of-a-bi*ch's job."

ERIC BISCHOFF:

Page looked at me like I was crazy. I hadn't really thought about it before that day, and it wasn't really a goal. I just knew I could do a better job than Watts. Around the same time, I heard a rumor that Turner was considering creating an executive producer position and splitting management into departments.

Eric Bischoff was somewhat prophetic that day, even though it would be many months before the atmosphere changed at World Championship Wrestling's offices in the CNN Center in Atlanta. There are always changes in the world of sports and entertainment, but wrestling is in both worlds, and at times, the roots of change run deep. Although Bill Watts had begun to wear out his welcome, and had even alienated his old friends and supporters, he continued to control WCW and its talent.

JODY HAMILTON
WCW POWER PLANT:

Page was workin' his tail off and improving daily. He asked me to watch the hundreds of moves that he was working on, and did everything he could to refine his ring work. I stressed that he should focus on his timing because it was the one thing that all the great ones in the sport had in common. I told him it didn't matter how many things he had in his bag, but he had to know when and how to pull them out.

It was a shame, and it pi$$ed me off that he wasn't get-

While managing Norma Jean's Dance Club in Fort Myers, Florida. One of the vistors was one of Page's all-time favorites, Jesse "The Body" Ventura. Tony "Stallion Coffaro is on left.

Page used a "pank" Cadillac, a "pank" Harley, and even a "pank" school bus to help promote his nightclub. It was a natural for Diamond Dallas Page and his Diamond Dolls to travel in style. The Dolls (from left) Wendy, Leeann, and Tanya.

Diamond Dallas Page's entrance into WCW was as Ring Manager of The Fabulous Freebirds. Front: (left) Michael P. S. Hayes, (right) Jimmy "Jam" Garvin. Back (left) "Big Daddy Dink" and another Diamond Doll named Lea Anne.

DDP, "Stunning" Steve Austin, and Van Hammer take time on the road to visit Hammer's Dad, "Sledge."

Fellow Jersey boy and hometown friend, Jon Bon Jovi, takes time from a sold-out concert tour to visit Page in Florida.

Norma Jean's was the playground for wrestlers when they were on the road in Florida. The tag-team known as "The Nasty Boys," Brian Knobs (left) and Jerry Sags (right) were frequent visitors.

Photo by Bill Apter, *Pro Wrestling Illustrated*

Following his return to World Championship Wrestling, Diamond Dallas Page was named 1995's "Most Improved Wrestler of the Year" by Pro Wrestling Illustrated *magazine. DDP calls this "one of my proudest achievements." (Okay . . . I'm a mark!)*

The friendship with broadcaster Lee Marshall began while DDP was making his wrestling debut. It was Lee Marshall who helped to define the character—Diamond Dallas Page.

It was Jake "The Snake" Roberts who provided the Education of DDP Part II. Jake helped make Diamond Dallas Page a "Road Scholar" when he offered a shot on the independent circuit.

Photo by Ross Forman, *WCW Magazine*

Diamond Dallas Page and Kimberly celebrate following his victory over Curt Henning to win his first United States Heavyweight title on December 28, 1997.

The world knows Dusty Rhodes as "The American Dream," but "Dream" has been a friend, mentor. and confidant of Page's since their first late-night conversation.

*They love me . . . They hate me . . . They'll never forget me. The two-time, two-time Champion of the World, Diamond Dallas Page, with the man DDP calls "the most complete champion in history"—**14**-time World Champion, Ric "The Nature Boy" Flair.*

"I probably deserved this Diamond Cutter from Gram a long time ago . . ."

DDP's mom signals for a quick end to another "Main Event"

Kimberly and I always enjoy visiting my sister Sally and my bro-in-law, Paul Smith. But we especially love seeing my favorite girls—my nieces Sammi (left) and Lexi (right).

Two guys named Page Falkinburg. DDP's dad, "Page One," on a recent visit to Florida.

Kimberly Lynn Bacon and Page Joseph Falkinburg were married on December 1st, 1991 in Fort Myers, Florida. Yes! They're married in "real life!"

Diamond Dallas Page calls Randy "Macho Man" Savage his "most intense opponent," and the matches with Savage "the most brutal of his career." Their 1998 feud was called "the best of the year" by wrestling fans and critics.

When DDP and Kevin Nash ("Vinnie Vegas") were the "Vegas Connection" tag team, nobody thought either one would ever become a "Top Guy." Here, Diamond Dallas Page and "Big Sexy" Kevin Nash are seen in a World Championship Heavyweight match, making liars of their critics.

Page's "Circle of Friends" include his bro's from the bar business. This photo was taken at one of DDP's famous "29-again" birthday parties. (Left to Right) Bobby "Scarface" Scarcello, Tony "Muff" Pallagrossi, Tony "Stallion" Coffaro, Larry "Smokey" Genta, and Frank Ormstead. "Bigg" Rick Kolster is above and in back of everybody else.

"What was one of my fears . . . is now fun." When Page read to kids at his 1998 Secret Santa charity toy drive, it marked the first time in more than 30 years he had read aloud.

Page formed "Diamond Dallas Page's Bang It Out For Books—a grassroots charity to teach kids the benefits of reading. This bookmark acts as a reminder and souvenir that "reading is power."

DDP's two passions, his gorgeous wife and partner, Kimberly, and his custom bike. While this photo was being taken, both Page and Kim got poison ivy—so bad that DDP wrestled in bandages and Kim had trouble . . . er . . . sitting down.

Page celebrated his birthday, April 5, 1999 with Kimberly and other friends on the White House lawn as part of the Annual White House Easter Egg Roll. Page read "It's Not Easy Being A Bunny" to hundreds of children, then wrestled in Las Vegas later that day.

Photo by Ross Forman, *WCW Magazine*

"And, finally, I want to say thanks to all the skeptics who said I would never . . . or could never . . . Because nothing or nobody could have motivated me more."

DIAMOND DALLAS PAGE
— WCW Heavyweight Champion of the World —
— April 11, 1999 Tacoma, Washington —

*ting an opportunity to work much. He got passed over de-
spite my recommendations.*

After Bill Watts took over, Diamond Dallas Page saw some
action as both Scott Hall's and Kevin Nash's tag partner, but during that time, he continued his daily workouts at The Power Plant.
Also in training at The Plant at the time was Eric Watts.

Eric had been a collegiate quarterback at the University of Louisville who led his team to an upset Fiesta Bowl victory over Alabama in 1991. At 6'6" and 265 pounds, he had the size and athletic
ability to achieve stature in professional wrestling. Not only that,
Eric Watts had stroke[7]. He was Bill Watts' son.

JODY HAMILTON:

*Eric had been in the ring less than Page, and hadn't
reached Page's level, but both guys were making progress.
Bill Watts asked me if Eric was ready to make his debut, and
I was being honest when I told him he wasn't.*

*Hell, Bill Watts and I knew each other for years, and he
knew the type of program we were running. But he ignored
my opinion and started him too early, causing a lot of heat
for the kid that he didn't deserve.*

*He was too green to be put in that spot, and people turned
on Eric because of his father's decision. It was a shame because Eric was a good kid, and it hurt him bad in the long
run. Is it a good thing to be from a wrestling family? Most
times it is. But it all depends which tree you fall from.*

Eric was victimized. His career was buried for sh*t that
had happened years ago, and it really sucks. I love the guy, and
we've been friends for years, and I believe he still has what it
takes to be one of the superstars of the future. The problem has
always been the same for Eric—no one ever noticed what he
could do. They couldn't get past the name "Watts." Everyone
has their own stories of what Bill Watts had done . . . but they
get more and more exaggerated as time goes on.

Looking back, I thought I was ready and just as deserv-
ing of an opportunity to work in the spotlight or get the push
that included TV exposure. This was before *Monday Night*

[7]*stroke—Clout or influence.*

Nitro on TNT and *Thursday Thunder!* on TBS. A match or an interview on a Saturday night meant a notch or two up the card on house shows.

But, I know now that I wasn't ready for that push. Bottom line is that often times in a guy's career, he may not get an opportunity to showcase his character. If he does get that shot early, and it doesn't go well, it could be deadly.

I was "getting it" pretty well, and I thought I was good enough, but I had seen plenty of guys who I knew had plenty of talent who were still waiting for the "wrestling gods" to "push them through the roof."

Of course, I didn't know it then, but I had a lot more to learn, and it seemed that everything I had ever learned came from the ups and downs of the yo-yo.

MICHAEL P.S. HAYES:

Nash and Page were in a tag match in Florence, Alabama against Shanghai Pierce and Tex Slashinger. It was obvious that Page had taken a stiff bump and was favoring one shoulder. Page could sell[8] and oversell, but it was clear that he was in pain.

Cactus Jack asked me how bad the pain was, and whether I could lift my arm, which was hanging limply. I explained that the pain was shooting through me, and he knew what the problem was right away. He said, "You tore something, probably your rotator cuff."

The diagnosis was indeed a tear in his left shoulder, and rotator cuff surgery was scheduled. Life suddenly changed again for Page and for Kimberly as Diamond Dallas Page was officially on the shelf and unable to work.

It had been only about a year since it looked like DDP had a future in the ring, and with Bill Watts still at the helm and a sling on his arm, it seemed that the doubters were right. They had wondered if his body could hold up from all the physical abuse. They questioned if someone his age had the time and energy to start from the bottom rung.

---

[8] *sell—The art of dramatizing the "bumps" in the ring.*

But now, they wanted to see if he could come back in good enough shape after four to six months of rehabbing. And, more importantly, Page wondered if he did come back as good or better, would anybody care or even notice?

All of a sudden, the contract I had wasn't any security at all. I was going to be on the bubble at contract time, but, hell, so was everybody else at WCW. I remained positive, and since I could work with anybody, and my salary was lower than most, I thought I could dodge "Cowboy" Bill Watts' bullet.

It was less than a year before when Kip Frye had planned to use my announcing and wrestling to keep me in the picture at World Championship Wrestling. But now, I was home with six months of rehab ahead, and less than three months left on my contract. This time, the yo-yo was bigger than life, and the waiting would carry a lot of financial and emotional weight. Kim and I were still newlyweds in our first home . . . with our first mortgage.

Kimberly started working while trying to get more involved in modeling. I was home on the friggin' couch, unable to work out. I watched tapes of my matches over and over.

It was miserable watching the mistakes that I had made, and not being able to go to The Plant and improve. Let's just say the bottom line was agonized limbo.

I had no idea what to expect when my contract ended, so with my arm still in a sling, I went to see Bill Watts. As I left Watts' office that day, I knew that there was not going to be another contract offer after mine expired. Bill Watts and his regime had no plans for Diamond Dallas Page.

The yo-yo had nearly hit bottom again. I was sitting on the couch, soon to be officially unemployed and out of wrestling. I rehabbed, and anxiously waited to get back to the gym.

There was only one thing I was sure of . . . I wasn't quitting.

CHAPTER TWELVE

THE EDUCATION OF DDP (PART II)

Page had been at the bottom of the yo-yo before, but never like this. His schedule, his regimen, and his daily routine had drastically changed. His arm was in a sling that made it difficult to do any of things that he had taken for granted. It wasn't unusual for a wrestler to be injured and unable to work, but for Page, it was a roadblock on his journey that he hoped wouldn't come. We'll never know if Bill Watts would have offered Diamond Dallas Page a renewal of that first contract to wrestle, but the injury sealed his fate at WCW, and, suddenly, the future looked bleak.

I was a caged lion, on the couch, with a remote in one hand and my mind on what was ahead. Watching movies and replaying old wrestling matches became my standard day, and I was itching to get back in the gym and down to The Plant.

I remained focused on my dream, but my positive attitude was tested. At times, I had a hard time seeing the light at the end of the tunnel.

KIMBERLY:

It was tough to be out working while Page was home with his dream in a sling. When it became apparent that Page wouldn't be offered another WCW contract after his shoulder healed, I wondered if this was an indication that the end to his wrestling career was looming. I wanted him to quit. He was so driven that I thought that his motivation and positive attitude were blinding him to the reality of the situation.

I saw things differently than Page. I never stopped believing in him or his quest to chase his dream, but I didn't trust the business of wrestling. The entire world was out there for Page, and I wanted him to see that it might be time to move on.

Kim had some valid points about starting over. My return from an injury would add doubt that might be hard to overcome for any federation. I was a bottom guy with little experience who wasn't being resigned by the company that *thought* Diamond Dallas Page had a future in the ring. Money was another issue as soon as that first contract ended, and my workmen's comp disability check of $250 a week was only compounding the problem. All I had to go on was the hope that I could come back, and that I could create a break if I couldn't find one. There were plenty of reasons not to go on, but I was stuck on positive.

As soon as I was able, I started back in the gym doing cardiovascular conditioning and some light training, but I was still almost a month away from being able to bump around the ring. I was keeping my head up, even though I was being fueled on knowing that I was going to give it my all, but I also knew that this time it would be different.

Since I wasn't with the WCW, I wouldn't be able to return to The Power Plant. My comeback would have to start in a ring in some warehouse where guys without contracts and other independent wrestlers went to train.

I began searching for one of those rings, and was only about two weeks away from being able to wrestle again, when

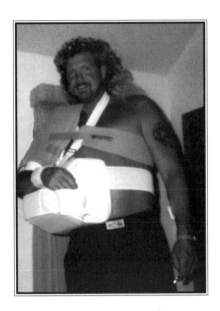

Page was off the couch, bulking up, and repackaging Diamond Dallas Page.

I received a call out of nowhere from Jake "The Snake" Roberts.

Jake Roberts is one of those gypsy road warriors who defy the laws of nature. Jake has been able to walk through the rubble of his life, conquer himself, and remain standing, while others would have faded away. He is arguably one of the biggest names ever associated with wrestling, even though he has not had the TV exposure that either World Championship Wrestling or the WWF offers for several years. To this day, he continues to travel with his 12- to 15-foot cobra as one of the top performers on the independent circuit, and Jake "The Snake" is known worldwide for his ring work and persona.

The Snake has burned a few bridges and blown some up too. He has fought personal demons his whole life, but Jake *knows* wrestling. It's ironic that someone as entertaining as Jake Roberts is left to toil on independent cards around the globe, and after meeting him, I decided that big-time wrestling misses Jake more than Jake misses the big time. His personal story is a complex one, and will be told in his upcoming autobiography sarcastically entitled *The Life and Death of Jake "The Snake" Roberts.*

JAKE ROBERTS:

It wasn't a very good time for "Jake" when I called Page. I had just split from that wife, and was living in a hotel while waiting to start an independent tour. I called him just to shoot the sh*t and find out about his injury and rehab.

I was more shocked that Jake was calling *me* than I was to hear that he was living at The Marriott in Atlanta. I've always had a tremendous amount of respect for Jake in and out of the ring, and knew it had been a tough year for him. After leaving the WWF and being screwed at WCW by Bill Watts, he was now involved in *another* bitter breakup with his wife. I knew that living in a hotel had to be a drag, and since we had a room with a private entrance and bath, I asked Kimberly if Jake could stay at our house while he got a new place and waited for his indie tour to start.

JAKE ROBERTS:

I was very touched when Page extended his home to me, since, in this business, it is fashionable to give a guy a beating when he's down. But I could hear the guy's guts in his voice when he insisted that I stay with him and Kimberly. He convinced me that it was cool with her, and that he was looking forward to hanging out together while we were both off the road.

KIMBERLY:

I knew that Page always had tremendous respect for Jake's knowledge of the business. He was a colorful character who I always found to be a great guy, and since he would only be staying a few weeks, I welcomed the opportunity for Page to spend time with Jake while he prepared a plan to continue in wrestling.

Jake and I were fast friends, and we clicked in a way outside of wrestling. I knew guys like him from my days in the nightclub business who could be their own worst enemies, and at the same time, be superstars at the top of their game. The Snake was a walking contradiction at times, and many people misunderstood him. A lot of the heat that Jake had in the wrestling industry came legitimately, and most times, I saw Jake as the ultimate "example." Sometimes, he was the best example of what to do, and other times, he was the poster boy of what *not* to do in this business. I liked him, and knew that just hanging with Jake could help me to learn what to do with Diamond Dallas Page and my comeback.

Jake settled into the downstairs bedroom, and we began to talk more about wrestling. I told him that I couldn't wait to get in the ring with him so he could show me how to refine my moves and work on a few new ones.

His reply wasn't what I expected. "Brother, you are going to learn more from me sitting on this couch for the next two weeks than I can teach you in the ring. You've got the moves down. In fact, you've got too many. You just don't know how to get over."

JAKE ROBERTS:

I had a lot of the same opinions on Page's idiosyncrasies and habits as some of the other guys. Through the years on the road, I have shown little regard for my body and well-being, so when I saw Page iced up, it doubled me over laughing. In the ring, he wore more pads and braces than a crash dummy, and at first, I thought his tapes were just "Page marking out for Page." At times, I thought he was an idiot with his 14 bags of gimmicks, his video equipment, a blender, and all those pads.

But as I observed Page and got to know him, it impressed me that he was a student of the business. His love for the game was similar to mine, but his approach was completely different. Page was a new breed of student, and he was his own breed of man. He was all-real, all the time.

It wasn't hard to hear the backstabbing and trash-talking that was going on behind his back. So many guys were making fun of him and his work that I became a supporter of his from afar. The more they tried to hold him down, the more I wanted for him to prove all of them wrong. I have always felt that Page and I are the type of guys who will be underdogs in one way or another.

I knew that Page would get better once he trimmed down his bag of moves. The answer was right in front of his eyes . . . on all those tapes he had been watching over and over again. He just wasn't seeing them, and had to hear how to make it work for him.

Jake pointed out something on one of my tapes and said, "What if you had gone into that hold this way?" He showed me how my timing was wrong for the crowd to get the full effect of the action.

He explained by using Muhammad Ali as an example. I wondered if he knew that Ali was my all-time idol, but I should have guessed that Jake had followed his career, and was also a huge fan of Ali.

He referred to the "Ali Shuffle" and the patented wind-up punches that would get the crowd to sit up and take notice before "The Champ" would deliver the pop the crowd had come to see.

The light began to come on again. Jake's advice wasn't that much different from Dusty Rhodes' and Jody Hamilton's. I just related to Jake better, a road warrior who had created his own problems, and someone who learned how to fix them along the way.

Within a couple of weeks, Jake had taught me so much. He was a composite of some of the fiercest competitors who I admired, like Terry Funk and Randy "Macho Man" Savage. Jake was a renegade and a chameleon who could make a change and take the crowd with him.

It is my nature to want to learn, and then do it my way, but it was Jake "The Snake" Roberts who told me to always take advice and coaching when it was offered, and to only pass it on to those who prove they want it. I've always tried to show others the way, but the thing I like the most that I adopted from Jake Roberts will always be that stand-alone-guy attitude when I got in the ring.

JAKE ROBERTS:

For christsakes, I didn't think he was going to make me watch all those tapes over and over again . . . but when he did, he saw them differently. He took it all in, and then went to work. Once I told him that every match begins at the back door to the arena, he began to get the big picture. I always believed that you couldn't sell anymore seats once you got into the ring, and if the ones that were in the seats were entertained, then we were successful. By the time we got in the ring, he was a sponge who couldn't take a drop more. He had seen where he needed improvement, and he was making changes. Diamond Dallas Page was getting good. Real good.

Jake said so much in so few words. He told me that in his first few years in the business, he had 5,000 moves in the ring. A few years later, he had trimmed it to about 1000 moves, and a year after that, he had cut that number to only a hundred. But now, while he was still one of the hottest superstars in the business, he had narrowed it down to 50 great moves, and he really only needed half of those.

When Jake explained, "It ain't what you do, it's how you're doing it," I began to see it all.

Jake had a short independent trip scheduled, and then a break before a long tour overseas. He was still staying at our house, but had hooked up with a girl and was spending time with her at her place and ours between trips.

KIMBERLY:

When Jake first moved in, he was leaving a relationship, but within a week, he had a girlfriend. By the second week, his new girlfriend and a 15-foot cobra that he was taking on the road were also staying with us.

It was cool at first. Jake let me touch the snake as he demonstrated how the snake would plunge its fangs into a glove on his hand.

His girlfriend was okay, but when a rare blizzard hit Atlanta, the four of us were thrown closely together for nearly three days. By the time we dug ourselves out, cabin fever had gotten to all of us.

It was cabin fever and Jake Robert's desire for "bar food" that motivated "The Snake" to shovel out of the snow.

JAKE ROBERTS:

We were trapped in the house for a couple of days without any normal food. There were plenty of skinless chicken breasts and vegetables, and lots of no-fat and low-fat sh*t, but we were snowed in, and I was drinking. And when I'm drinking, I need chips and sandwiches—food that goes with being snowed in. By the end of the second day, I was shoveling out, and couldn't wait to get to a bar that had wings, burgers, and other fried foods.

KIMBERLY:

We dug out, and the four of us drove to a restaurant and nightclub called "American Pie." The roads were icy, and we slid all the way there and back, but we really had an unforgettably fun time.

The next morning when I woke up, I noticed that Page had a bunch of pillows propped up against our bedroom door.

After Kim went to bed, Jake said that he had something very important to tell me. He had put the snake in the bathtub downstairs to absorb some moisture, and it had disappeared. There was a 15-foot cobra lost in the house. I didn't want to tell Kimberly, but I had to, since Jake left the house shortly after the snake left the bathtub.

KIMBERLY:

Page tried to be calm when he informed me of the missing cobra. I knew that it could have been in a wall, in the plumbing, or anywhere. I wondered how well Jake knew his snake, and I was concerned about whether it was a male snake or, perhaps, a pregnant female snake. Realizing that Jake never addressed the venom issue increased my concerns, to say the least.

I had lots of questions, especially the whereabouts of my cats, Spooky and Sophie. Page was confident that they were in our bedroom, since he'd put the pillows in front of the door to stop the cats from getting out through their cat door. I just wondered if the snake could get in through the cat door.

When Page told me that Jake wasn't going to be able to assist in charming the snake out of its hiding place because he had left, I was livid. With a cat under each arm, I informed Page that I was checking into the Ritz-Carlton and wasn't coming back until the snake and Jake were found—and were both out of the house.

Hitting the independent circuit with Jake "The Snake" Roberts was The Education of DDP, Part II.

Page called around and found a snake trapper who thought that the snake was probably behind the vanity in the bathroom, but I wasn't convinced.

The snake trapper was right, and we eventually captured the snake. I got it back to Jake just as he was preparing to go on the independent tour. It sure was comical looking back, but it was strange to have a snake that big on the loose in a bathroom that small.

JAKE ROBERTS:

Aw sh*t, I still think Page hid that snake to be a hero with Kimberly, and he was doing some kind of "here I come to save the day" thing. I think he was feeling guilty and wanted to get back in her good graces after he had spent so much time with me, forcing me to watch those fu*kin' tapes of his.

The whole ordeal was a curable crisis, and really made us all closer. We are still close, and Kim would welcome Jake again, but no snakes are allowed . . . unless they are a pair of boots, a belt, or a *very small* suitcase. His visit was memorable in many ways, but it was time for all of us to move on . . . the snake, Jake, and the career of DDP.

As Jake was being offered independent shows around the country, he strongly suggested that promoters use me on the under-card. If the promoter balked, he demanded that I be included.

He was promoting me and giving me a personalized push by arranging to add me to as many of the independent events as possible. I was looking forward to any opportunity to show what I had learned. Jake was in my corner, but I didn't know just how strongly until he told me of an upcoming tour to Asia.

Jake was finalizing plans for a tour that included trips to Singapore and the Philippines. One day, I overheard a phone conversation he was having with the tour promoter, putting me over like I was the next superstar of the sport.

It blew me away, and, at the same time, made me a little uncomfortable. I wasn't sure if he was doing the right thing by raising the expectations of these independent promoters.

JAKE ROBERTS:

I knew it would be good for Page to go on a few independent tours, especially the one overseas. He also needed to be away from the WCW until Watts was gone.

He earned his shot, as far as I was concerned, and I touted him. But believe me, I was sure that he had everything that it took to be a part of those cards, or he would never have gone on the road with me. I looked forward to seeing DDP silence his critics himself.

Before we left, I told Page, "You've got the talent. If you continue to work hard and keep listening, learning, and staying focused on your goal, you will be a top guy. In two or three years, Diamond Dallas Page will be one of the biggest names in the sport."

Those words were like throwing dynamite on my fire, and it was Jake's assessment and confidence in me that kept me going for years after he first said them. Jake unlocked a few doors for me, and I was ready to *bang* through them.

See no evil, speak no evil, hear no evil . . . me and Jake? Yeah, right!

For the first time, I was on the international road with Jake and a bunch of other great guys. Many of them are still current superstars in our sport, like The Barbarian, Paul Dangerously, Konan, and Public Enemy, as well as legendary wrestlers like Bob Orton and Kevin Sullivan.

One of the first shows I worked was in Mexico's AAA promotion where I appeared as Jake's ringside "bodyguard." The "Triple A" was, at one time, Mexico's top wrestling federation, and current WCW superstar, Konan, was way over. The crowd cheered there the same way they did for Hulk or "Macho Man" here in the States. I still hadn't wrestled again, but had started taking a few bumps as I got more involved in Jake's matches.

When I did start in the ring, we were scheduled to wrestle in San Diego, before heading overseas. I was to meet up with Terry Funk in Los Angeles and share a ride down the coast with him. It had been a long time since I had seen Terry Funk, and I was excited to have the opportunity to talk to one of my all-time favorite guys in the ring. I also wanted to hear about the match he had just had with Mick "Cactus Jack" Foley.

The wrestling historians will know which match I'm talking about, but without having to exaggerate, Foley and Funk had one of the most physically brutal matches in history. Those two crazy bastards battled on thumbtacks, a bed of nails, and even had barbed wire in the ring with them. They used explosives like they were land mines, and sh*t was blowing up everywhere. They use the word "hardcore" when they refer to those types of matches today, but as far as I'm concerned, Funk and Foley are in a category all by themselves. Neither one is more hardcore than the other, but they are way ahead of whoever is second in that poll.

When the van door opened, I saw Terry Funk's swollen, bruised, and battered face. He was bandaged like a mummy, and whatever skin was exposed had visible gunpowder-type burns. I was speechless as I looked at him from head to toe, and he broke the ice by saying, "How ya doin', Diamond?"

Terry Funk was "walking wounded" and completely jet-lagged coming back from overseas. He was burned-out, and burned up . . . literally. I am often reminded of that scene and the commitment that the *real* pros in our business make to the fans night in and night out. I was still relatively new to the mat, and as I was looking forward to continuing my life as a wrestler on the independent circuit, I was witnessing a true gladiator.

Let's never forget that what we do is sports entertainment, and the attitude is the same as it is in Hollywood . . . "the show must go on." The difference is that our show is unmatched when it comes to physical endurance and travel requirements. There was nothing fake about Terry Funk that day.

When professional wrestling comes to town, fans don't care what happened in the matches the night before. The promotion of each show usually advertises the matches in advance, especially the main-event match. It is understood that if someone is scheduled to appear, then they do whatever it takes to drag themself to the ring.

I know plenty of guys play hurt in other sports, and no matter what we do for a living, we all go to work on days when we are sick. But when an entire arena, the promoters, and the bookers are expecting someone like Terry Funk, a pro like Terry Funk shows up and gives it his all. I know many guys who have withheld injuries to doctors and the booking committee so that the fans were satisfied, and so that the injury didn't wind up becoming a missed opportunity.

There have been plenty of nights when I wondered how my body could take another night of abuse, but the memory of seeing Terry Funk helped dull whatever pains I was having.

I was headed to Singapore and the Philippines, and, later, Austria and Germany, all places I never imagined seeing while growing up in Jersey.

My first night of the tour was spent in Malaysia, and the hotel we stayed in was just incredible—a friggin' palace in the middle of a poor, Third-World country. It had been a favorite stopover of General MacArthur's during World War II, and had been a famous resort getaway ever since.

Halfway through the next day, I got food poisoning and was in bed for three days. By our first scheduled match, I was weak, but feeling better, and one guy after another started getting sick. At one point, seven guys were sick during the first week of the tour.

Not every hotel was as luxurious as the first, but who could complain after seeing some unimaginable poverty and living conditions. I was also exposed to a rigorous schedule and the physical demands that came with wrestling overseas. Add to the mix the language barriers, exchanging money, foreign customs, and change of time zones, and it was a huge learning experience.

But we were treated like superheroes by the fans who cheered us on in the smallest gyms and buildings. We wrestled in some of the most backward, underdeveloped places, but this was my schooling, my graduate degree, and my internship all at once. I heeded Jake's words of advice and stayed focused. My work seemed to pay off, as I got smoother and more fluid every time I climbed into the ring.

My shoulder was responding well too. It still needed ice and constant attention, but I hadn't lost anything as a result of the surgery.

Meanwhile, back at WCW, Bill Watts had reached the end of his rope. His departure caused Turner officials to shake up the structure of management. The operational duties were split, creating a separation between the wrestling and production departments.

An executive producer position was created, and the competition for that high-profile spot was fierce. The longshot candidate and final selection was Eric Bischoff. This decision shaped the future of wrestling on TV for Turner executives and millions of new viewers.

While I was working independently, I kept in touch with many of my friends still at WCW, including Eric Bischoff.

Eric was ready to take the executive producer job on with intensity, and I knew that this was his shot to show everyone else the creative force that I saw on those rides to the next show.

I was close to being ready to come back to the States and

get back into wrestling with either the WWF or with the "new deal" at World Championship Wrestling. My look was changing, and my work in the ring was better, but I wanted to have it *all* together when I made my return.

A lot of times, my neighbor, Eric Bischoff, and I had long talks in my garage, crushing a few Coors Lights and sharing Cuban cigars. One of those times, Eric asked me if I wanted him to drop my name around the wrestling department and booking committee. I told him, "Not yet."

Making my way back to World Championship Wrestling was about timing, and that entrance had to have the right look and the right feel. My look was just about ready, and I had begun to feel it. I knew that it wouldn't be long before I was ready for another shot at Atlanta or New York.

CHAPTER THIRTEEN

THE NEW LOOK GETS A NEW LOOK

While I was working as an independent, I made up my mind to keep my options open when I felt ready to seek a new contract. I fully intended to make contact with the WWF, but decided to talk to World Championship Wrestling first. There was a new direction for the entire company, and the beginning of a commitment by Turner Broadcasting to give World Championship Wrestling the funding necessary to compete with New York.

I felt like I had unfinished business at WCW, and that there had been too abrupt of an end to what I had started at The Power Plant. I wanted the opportunity to show whomever that they had been wrong. I had progressed with my ring work, revamped my look and my gimmick, and was anxious to be back.

There was no doubt that DDP was different. I had gained weight, gotten bigger, and changed my appearance in a more artistic way. Long before body art became as mainstream as it is today, I created the part of my character that I am asked about most frequently.

It was a guy named "Worldwind Walt" who did my artwork at a place called "Tornado Tattoos" in Atlanta, and as it is in most cases, every picture tells a story. My tattoos incorporate everything I wanted to say, and really are a reflection of my life in many ways.

They were done in stages, and the left arm took 11 hours to complete. That side represents the gambles of life and some of the superstitions that revolve around them: the black cat that everyone dreads, the "Dead Man's Hand" known by card players as aces and eights, and a pair of flaming dice rolling seven. The unlucky number "13" is present, but so is my symbol of good luck—in the middle of the numeral "one" are the initials "KLF," which are the same as the letters on my wife's stationary.

My right arm took a little longer, about 13 hours of work. The main character is a bad@$$ cat modeled after *The Stray Cats* album cover. The "wild cat" just may be me since he has the same dead man's hand tattoo on his left arm. The cat also has the last one of the tattoos that I got as a kid, the star on the right side of my chest.

There's no yo-yo, but the wild cat is positioned "behind the eight ball," which is a place that I have come to relate to

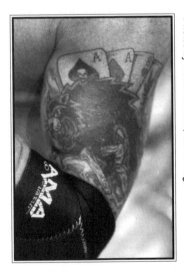

DDP's right arm.   *. . . and the left one*

from time to time. An oversized martini glass is present as a tribute to where it all began in the bar business.

I knew that the "tats" and the fresh look would get some attention, but I wanted a shot to earn a spot. No one had to tell me that there wasn't any security, and the concerns about my age and durability were ever present, but I just wanted an opportunity for the fans to get a good look at the new and improved Diamond Dallas Page.

By the time Page made the decision to leave the independent circuit and return to a more steady existence in the world of professional wrestling, Eric Bischoff was calling the shots at World Championship Wrestling.

Bischoff technically replaced Bill Watts, but the administrative roles had been redefined, and Bischoff's presence changed the focus of the company. WCW was now making a greater effort in the production of a "show" rather than just the televising of wrestling events. Eric Bischoff would concentrate on building a television audience and the rebuilding of the arena fan base that had steadily declined. He utilized the talents of many of the superstars and creators of wrestling history that remained at World Championship Wrestling to take care of the day-to-day wrestling operations.

The timing couldn't have been better for me to test the waters at World Championship Wrestling. Dusty Rhodes was very active in the wrestling operations and was doing the booking, and Eric Bischoff would be representing WCW with a contract offer.

I honestly never looked at Eric or Dusty or anyone as my ticket to anywhere. Even though I knew I was as good or better than many of the wrestlers on the roster at the time, I only wanted to be measured on my value to the company. At the very least, I was better than I was when I left WCW the first time, and I had been under contract and on the traveling squad at the time of my injury.

The realization that being Eric's friend might not necessarily be a good thing was evident as soon as we sat down to talk money. There was never a doubt in my mind that Eric wasn't going to establish himself as someone who greased his friends through the system, and I never wanted anything handed to me.

Professional wrestling, like Hollywood, Washington, and most businesses, has a good-ole-boy network that still exists in some form. There have always been behind-the-scenes foes, as well as back-room allies, in wrestling, and a change of power in the administration can elevate or decimate a career overnight. Diamond Dallas Page had worked his way back into the picture at WCW, and had earned this opportunity for a new contract. But Eric Bischoff wouldn't be accused of overpaying his neighbor when it came to that first contract between the two overachievers.

I was seeking something around that "156" that Cactus spoke about, and I felt I deserved it. With a push, I knew I could earn that much and bring even more to the company. But it was immediately obvious that this figure was far more than WCW was offering. I agreed to take less money, but wanted a one-year deal so that I could prove myself and earn the chance to renegotiate.

Bischoff promised that a push would come in the first few months of my contract. He insisted, however, that I sign a two-year deal at the lower rate, and offered the opportunity to move up financially after the first year. I understood that the front office wanted to wrap a guy up for two years, rather than push him and promote him only to see him leave for a better offer after his character was successful.

The number and the contract sucked. It was the same money I had made in my last contract with WCW, and that was nearly two years earlier when I had less than a dozen matches under my belt. I was making slightly less than half of that magic 156.

For a professional wrestler, a promise of a push is sometimes enough to sweeten the deal. Often times, the fans took that first push and catapulted a wrestler into the feature matches, the Pay-Per-Views, and the chance at one of the several belts and titles. In present-day professional wrestling, merchandising follows the path of the athlete as he works his way up the card to the main event. The more TV time and PPV exposure, the more dolls, T-shirts, key chains, and even bowling balls are marketed. That push could turn to gold if the wrestler developed a fan base that created TV ratings or merchandise sales.

I was being economically underestimated, and it bothered me. This was the contract that I thought was going to be different, and I really believed that I could work as a mid-card wrestler. I rationalized it all, with the thought of taking full advantage of the promise of a push and turning it into real money the next time I sat down to talk contracts with Bischoff.

It had been over a year since Jody Hamilton said that I had the ring knowledge and work ethic to be a top guy someday. Then Jake Roberts told me the same thing after noticing my improvement from the training that I had received from Jody. I wanted to prove them right.

Within days of signing a two-year deal with World Championship Wrestling, I made plans to sit down with Dusty Rhodes to talk about my ring life.

DUSTY RHODES:

In many ways, Page was still the same guy who had driven to Tampa because he wanted to learn the wrestling business. His hard work was paying off. I was surprised at how much he had developed.

Page always saw himself as a main-event guy, and although I loved his spirit and energy, I didn't agree. I saw him as an entertainer and character, even an announcer; but I never saw him as a wrestling star or top guy.

He still had a long road ahead, but convinced me that he had the talent and ring smarts to back it all up. I had seen plenty of guys who I thought had what it took to succeed never make it as far as Page had. He had worked himself into a position to move up.

I was so of damned proud of him, and I wanted to tell him so.

If my lowball contract was the bottom side of the latest bounce of the yo-yo, hearing the words of The Dream was enough to bring it back to the top.

I was jacked up knowing that the progress and accomplishments I had made since the injury were noticed by someone like Dusty, but more blown away with him being so straight up with me. He looked me in the eyes and told me that I had surprised him and proved him wrong.

KIMBERLY:

Page was down over the negotiations and the contract, but at least our finances were getting off of his yo-yo for a couple years.

He worked so hard, and I was proud of him for not giving up. He clawed his way back into the picture, and maintained his positive attitude through the injury and all the negativity under the old regime at World Championship Wrestling. And it paid off.

A booking committee comprised of several members generally governed the wrestling end of WCW. There were several combinations of members on that committee, and various factions within that ever-changing branch of management that was "the product." Usually, one guy is the leader or "head booker," and other committee members contributed in the areas of evaluating talent and determining the matches. In a way, it's like a small government with branches of expertise and power, and those branches often have factions or party affiliations. And sometimes, there is a sway of power, creative differences, or moves in different directions.

I had been back in WCW for only six weeks, slowly working into a regular role, when Dusty suddenly left. The creative direction went from one booker to a committee, and Dusty went back to being a color commentator. With Dream gone from that spot, so was my little push. I started working less, and my schedule was more erratic than it had been as an independent.

I was on TV matches once every eight weeks, then off for six weeks. After that, I was on for two weeks in a row, and then off again for another five weeks. I was basically being paid to sit home. But this is not unusual when under contract. Some guys learn to like it, and even get comfortable with the process, but it was driving me crazy. I was frustrated at being in limbo because if I couldn't work, I couldn't get better. All I knew was to go back to my old formula. I resumed my work at The Power Plant.

The tide had changed once again, and it was tough to swallow. But I wasn't selling it.

JODY HAMILTON:

The Plant had always been a training facility where guys came to learn. Once they got contracts or TV matches, we normally wouldn't see them. Guys always tried new moves on each other while on the road, but the ones who lived in the area would seldom come back when they were home.

Dallas changed that. He continued to come down almost daily, working with the new guys like it was his first month there. He didn't care if anyone else had done it before or not; he was relentless in his work ethic. Page made the training center his home, and set a precedent for work ethic at The Power Plant.

It wasn't a popular thing for me to be going to The Plant and working so hard without a steady spot in which to display it. It didn't really matter to me, but others felt that it was a waste of time. What it boiled down to, though, was that it wasn't my time yet, according to the booking committee. And beneath it all, there were still plenty of insiders who thought my time would never come.

I felt that the harder I worked, the luckier I would get. If I continued my plan and worked my formula, someone would notice. Like Jake had said, if I worked to learn how to give the fans something to remember me by, eventually the matchmakers and bookers would have to respond.

The persona of Diamond Dallas Page had an obnoxious ring presence, and his character always had plenty of gimmicks intended to draw attention: jewelry, shades, gum, cigars, and, of course, Diamond Dolls.

There were many Diamond Dolls over the years, and they were usually blond and very "hot." Even though his match schedule was sporadic, when DDP did make appearances, he typically had a female valet on his arm. His verbal mistreatment and condescending attitude toward his scantily-clad Doll would draw instant heat for the loudmouth heel, Diamond Dallas Page.

The Diamond Dolls were always a part of me, and some were better than others. Sometimes it was difficult to coach them, and other times, the fans got under their skin. The abuse that we got was pretty ugly at times, and it was tough for some of them to handle.

It was becoming more difficult to find a Diamond Doll who looked hot and could be on call and ready to go on short notice. So I got the girl who knew what it was like being DDP's all-time, one-and-only Diamond Doll—my wife, Kimberly.

The development of Diamond Dallas Page had undergone some changes, but when Kimberly became the last Diamond Doll, it was a positive move in many ways. No one understood the character or the real guy better than Kim, and it allowed Page and Kimberly more time together on road trips, and more opportunities to become a team.

Since The Power Plant and World Championship Wrestling is based in Atlanta, the majority of the boys have always lived, worked, and played in that arena.

Buckhead has been the trendy, hip area for restaurants and nightlife for sometime, but Atlanta is also the home of dozens of gentleman's clubs. It has always been a place to which male athletes tend to gravitate. Not only do players from the major Atlanta sports teams frequent the clubs, but visiting players, corporate leaders, and most red-blooded American males do too.

I enjoy going to gentleman's clubs from time to time. It's a place where guys like the boys and I can go and not be the center of attention. In clubs that feature beautiful women, patrons *should* be looking at the other bodies in the place instead of ours. And yes, I am allowed to go. My wife knows.

It was at one of those clubs back in 1994 that I first met Bill Goldberg. Although he wasn't a well-known player, he was a member of the Atlanta Falcons, and was a hometown boy who had attended the University of Georgia. After five minutes of standing next to one another, we started a conversation. Within 10 minutes, we were doing shooters together. Twenty minutes later, I knew Bill Goldberg had that something that would translate in the wrestling business.

BILL GOLDBERG
WCW SUPERSTAR:

The night I met Page, we had a friendly relationship right off. We had been talking awhile when he said that he could see me in the ring following my football career.

He really caught me off guard, and I still don't know what he saw that night. I never watched wrestling growing up, and didn't really respect what they did. I thought: Yeah right . . . wrestling?

I know Goldberg was surprised that I saw him as a potential superstar in our world of wrestling. After all, he was a member of the Atlanta Falcons in the NFL, and the masses will always rate and respect that above our business.

I saw "Goldie" as much more than a linebacker on a mediocre team that played 16 weeks a year. His quest to wear a Super Bowl ring had his focus, and I didn't blame him for pursuing it. But he was also in a place that I could relate to, rehabbing from an injury and stuck in the obscurity of a pack of guys who wanted the same dream.

I planted the seed in Bill's head the night we met. Over the next several years, we bumped into one another, traded phone numbers, and kept loosely in touch. Often, Goldberg and I would trade training methods and dietary tips. But almost every time I saw him, I replanted the seed of him becoming a wrestler. Little did I know that the seed had begun to take root.

BILL GOLDBERG
WCW SUPERSTAR:

I ran into Page from time to time in restaurants or around town. He was always persistent, and coaxed me about wrestling. I liked him and his commitment to physical training, and began to appreciate what these guys did all year long to stay in shape. I met and became friendly with more WCW wrestlers, and went to a match with Sting (Steve Borden) and Lex Lugar. I had a new respect for the business, and over time, I began to consider wrestling. Following my football career, it crossed my mind again.

Change is constant in professional wrestling, but during the mid-'90s, there was a brisk amount of activity between the WWF and World Championship Wrestling.

Bischoff and Turner Broadcasting were seeking marquee names and had the financial backing. Within a couple years, some of the biggest names in wrestling were headed to Atlanta. Randy "Macho Man" Savage and, eventually, Hulk Hogan would join the ranks at WCW. Superstars were being added to the mix in droves, while many guys who had been in the middle of the pack saw their futures reaching a dead end.

Sometimes when a guy made the jump from one company to another, it created tension in the back and new competition for exposure. The thought that the new guy was there to challenge their spots produced anxiety for a lot of guys. Other times, when guys would leave, it appeared that a door might open that wasn't anticipated. However, I can honestly say that I never looked at a guy leaving as my break, nor did I feel that the addition of a new superstar would break me.

There have been many guys who I was sorry to see leave the WCW, but the nature of the business is that there will always be more who come and go.

We travel together and laugh together, and we develop tight friendships and positive working relationships with each other. Although there is no "wrestler union," there is a common bond among the members of this industry. It has happened to all of us. A guy who we may have seen 250 times last year and drove thousands of miles with, and came to respect and trust, may be gone, sometimes without warning or fanfare.

Since the companies route their tours differently and usually opposite each other, it becomes not only an effort to see one another, but a virtual impossibility. We play phone tag and keep an eye on each other's angles and matches, and maybe see each other at an airport, but it is never the same. We really get to know someone when we are in a car, pouring our hearts out, overhearing phone calls to wives or girlfriends, sick moms and dads, and to kids whose dads and moms live on the road.

There is bonafide, legitimate, and real-as-real-can-be dislike between the WWF and WCW. Enough lawsuits have been filed between the two companies to fill a huge closet. And while both companies do basically the same thing, the approach is very different at times.

It's kind of like a Coke vs. Pepsi thing. It has been proven that there is enough room and money for both of them to prosper. At times, the Turner front office and McMahon's organization may even have mutual respect for each other, but they definitely don't like each other. Most of their anger and bitterness stems from the intensely competitive nature of the business and the desire for the lion's share of the advertising dollar. As long as there are TV ratings and PPV buy rates, it will get worse before it gets better.

The heat between the companies pretty much stops there. As wrestlers, we are glad there is an option for us to be seen on a national level, to earn great salaries, and, most of all, to entertain in front of thousands of people. No matter how many issues our companies have, the boys don't let that come between the real friendships we have made over the years.

WWF's Michael P.S. Hayes, Mick "Cactus Jack" Foley, "Stone Cold" Steve Austin, Hunter Hearst Helmsley, and Paul "The Giant" Wight are guys who I consider the closest of friends. But we are rivals every Monday night when we battle for TV viewers. I know their wives, their kids, and their goals.

I feel confident that after it's all over, we'll get together in some out-of-the-way bar and split a bucket of beers like we did when we stayed in those $40 hotel rooms.

Guys have left one federation for another for many reasons. I remember when Steve Williams, who was known as "Stunning" Steve Austin, was let go by WCW while recovering from an injury. At the time, no one could ever imagine that "Stone Cold" Steve Austin would become a mega-star. Based on the popularity of wrestling back then, none of us ever thought *anyone* could be that big.

"STONE COLD" STEVE AUSTIN:

Page was always a positive guy, but it was a difficult time for all of us. One by one, we realized that WCW was buying stars, not building them. We were looking for opportunities that just weren't there. I thought Page had the toughest time getting over since he was perceived as a manager, not a wrestler. The fact that Page had the talent and was more serious about improving every match didn't matter. Nobody saw it. Hell, WCW let some of the biggest stars in the business get away in their prime. They didn't realize what they had.

Steve and I had somewhat similar situations at different points in our career. While I was let go by Watts, Steve was let go by Eric Bischoff, and it happened when we were both rehabbing. I prefer "let go" to being fired, because the latter sounds like we weren't doing our jobs when the decisions were made not to renew our contracts.

Both moves were wrong, but Bill Watts and Eric Bischoff probably never figured it would play out as it did for either one of us.

Steve left WCW while I was being paid not to work. "Stone Cold" was created much later, and his success was far from overnight. Steve possessed the skills and knowledge of the business necessary to attract the fans, but there are two things that can't be thrown on a scale when evaluating talent—heart and charisma.

We all notice and embrace it in all forms of entertainment and sports. The biggest superstars have the ability to get attention and then hold the crowd. It is not something that is usually acquired. Charisma has to be discovered within an individual's persona.

Charisma is obviously a great tool in life, love, and business. And if someone is trying to get over in the public eye, it is a necessary attribute. It's not on a resume, and there aren't charisma coaches in the yellow pages; but when someone's got it, they've got something.

My schedule was so unpredictable that it made absolutely no sense. Not getting more steady work was killing me. I didn't know if the booking committee was holding me back because they still didn't believe, or if it was purely political.

No one had to tell me that life wasn't always fair. I knew the score. There would always be politics, grudges, misunderstandings, and heat. Prejudices and miscalculations were a part of life, but defining the reasoning of the wrestling gods will always be a curiosity.

Greg Gagne was a member of the booking committee. Page had worked for his father in the AWA. Greg was the son of a legendary world champion, and had also been a champion while the AWA was still in business. When his ring career ended, he was brought into WCW based on his upbringing and knowledge of the business. Greg Gagne was now on the other side of the curtain, and helped determine the direction of the matches, the feuds, and the involvement of the wrestlers. His role was limited at WCW, and his stay was short.

Greg knew I was working hard at The Plant and improving, and I wanted his input. After all, he was there when I started in the business. I wanted to know what I still needed to get a shot, or any push at all.

I hadn't been getting good vibes from Greg. Once, when I saw him socially in a bar, and after talking for awhile, I just asked him, "So, Greg . . . why do you hate me?" He simply replied, "I don't hate you."

I reminded him that he was one of the first people to see something in me when I was a ring manager, and asked him why he thought I couldn't get a break and what he thought I was lacking.

He put his head down and took a sip of his drink, pausing as if he was searching for a reason or explanation. Finally, he said, "What you're lacking is . . . charisma."

Now, this guy could have said almost anything else, like I didn't know how to bump, how to sell, how to look, or even how to work.

I burst out laughing, and with a smile, said, "Now I know you hate me, bro . . . because there are two things that you can't tell me that I don't have. One of them is my ability to talk, and the other thing I *do* know I was born with is . . . charisma. "

Yeah, Greg . . . whatever.

The first half of my two-year deal with World Championship Wrestling was coming to a close with no real end in sight to the bullsh*t position I was in. Confusion and frustration were becoming disenchantment and bitterness. I seriously considered asking for my release. I was ready to pursue the WWF in New York or go back to the independent circuit. Anything was better than the spot I was in.

KIMBERLY:

Even though the circumstances were different, I wanted him to get away from the situation he was in. If it meant asking for his release, then I was all for him quitting. I wasn't quite sure if the WWF was the way to go at the time, but I never saw him getting a chance at World Championship Wrestling.

He would go to The Plant and the gym, and hang out with the guys, and they would commiserate on their situations. The only problem was that Page was trying to evaluate it, understand it, deal with it, and get through it when there didn't seem to be any light in that tunnel.

From the moment he was given the opportunity, Eric Bischoff worked hard to change the complexion and image of World Championship Wrestling. He was creating the company that would later challenge the long-time, well-established leader, the WWF.

When Bischoff took the reins, the WWF had it way over Turner's WCW— better TV ratings and PPV buy rates, larger crowds at arenas, bigger superstars, more endorsements, and greater concession sales.

Eric Bischoff set his sights on WWF's Vince McMahon, Jr., the undisputed king of the wrestling world.

The WWF had WCW beat through years of national exposure and live appearances across America. Eric Bischoff had a plan to give World Championship Wrestling higher visibility and positive exposure. He proposed a working relationship with Disney World that would bring WCW's original southern regional wrestling promotion to millions of visitors to the Orlando, Florida attraction.

Bischoff put his a$$ on the line when he proposed the deal with Disney. The behind-the-scenes chatter was full of doubt, and nearly everyone thought he was setting himself up for a fall. At that time, the thought of Disney World embracing wrestling was mind-boggling. While Bischoff strolled to the plate with everyone thinking he would strike out, he hit a home run.

World Championship Wrestling signed a 13-week contract to broadcast live and tape weekly shows, as well as to provide personal appearances and autograph sessions. The combination of the Disney contract and the addition of Randy Savage and Hulk Hogan put WCW in the position to challenge the overwhelming popularity of the WWF. It proved to be grueling for everyone—the wrestlers, the front office, and the production staff—but the fruits of the effort were sweet.

Everyone thought Bischoff was a dreamer, and were convinced that he couldn't challenge Vince McMahon, Jr. While I was waiting for any opportunity, Eric was making the best of his.

We had spoken often, and he knew of my frustration. It wasn't his call whether to give me a shot, even though, by now, he was the vice president of the company. He knew that I had been promised a push, but when the deck was shuffled, I got buried, and the answer remained with the booking committee. Eric had already said that there was nothing else I could do except wait, but it was a hard pill to swallow. We were close enough that I spoke to him about my thoughts of trying out for Vince in New York. I was shocked with his take on the situation, and his solution.

ERIC BISCHOFF:

I offered to buy him a plane ticket with my own money. I saw the guy in agony over the situation, but I had my doubts that Page was ready for the type of push that he wanted. Sometimes, it seemed he was trying to do too much to overcome whatever it was that was keeping him from taking the next step.

I actually thought that maybe there would always be road-blocks for Page in World Championship Wrestling, and that he should go to New York. It would be a change in scenery and a new start.

Page is my friend, and I've always wanted the best for him and Kimberly, but it wasn't happening for him at that time in WCW.

I've got to laugh now, because he was right. It did not look good for me. I was beginning to notice that people around me were realizing what I had felt before. Eric Bischoff being my friend was actually making it harder to climb up the ladder than easier.

The fact that we were former announcing partners and neighbors kept us close, but I knew that it was the thing that made me work three times harder.

While I started getting more comfortable with the idea of walking away from the second year of my guaranteed contract, I was selected as one of the wrestlers to make the trip overseas to wrestle for WCW in Europe.

I was shocked because I couldn't believe that after not working me for weeks, suddenly they were going to send Diamond Dallas Page and the Diamond Doll, Kimberly, to Europe.

Then I got paranoid. I figured they were trying to expose my faults and set me up for failure.

Little did anyone know . . . I was ready to work. Regardless of what happened overseas, I was going to make my move after the European tour. Once I returned, I planned to pursue every opportunity and call every contact in the business. It was time for me to take it on myself. Failure was not a fear of mine, but not having the opportunity to work meant I could never win.

I felt like I could always jump back in the nightclub business. There's a part of me that will always feel that way.

During that time, I visited Page in Atlanta, and could see that he was a little unnerved by the politics of wrestling. He was in great shape, and looked younger than I had ever seen him. I could tell that married life was great for him, but I could also tell that his job was wearing on him. It was not the pounding that he was taking in the ring that was taking its toll, it was the constant beating of his head against the wall.

He spoke seriously to me about coming to Atlanta to start a consulting firm for the hospitality industry. He was prepared to establish an alternate plan, and was getting itchy for something other than the yo-yo life of a bottom-of-the-card wrestler.

He told me about how most of the 70 or more gentleman's clubs really didn't know how to promote and sell drinks and beverages, and he thought we could show them how to increase production and lower their bar costs. It never became much more than a backup plan, but he was ready.

The European tour coincided with the arrival of Terry Bolea to WCW. Better known as Hulk Hogan, he has generated the most money in wrestling history. And when he is surpassed, it will only be because he paved the way. With Vince McMahon's guidance, Hulk Hogan became a household name in the '80s.

At that time, there were two historical and political traditions that radically changed. The Berlin Wall came down, and democracy was brought to communist East Germany. Of almost equal magnitude in the world of TV wrestling was Hulk Hogan cutting his ties with McMahon and the WWF and joining Randy Savage at World Championship Wrestling. Hulk Hogan was not only leading the American wrestlers into East Germany, but "Hulkamania" was doing it with WCW and Ted Turner.

Something happened outside of the ring on the tour that changed my mind about pursuing an option other than World Championship Wrestling. I was in the back of an arena in Berlin, Germany when Hulk Hogan approached me for the first time. I had met him in other circumstances, but this was the first time that we hooked up just to talk.

I'll totally "mark out" and tell you that I was in awe of him . . . without selling it. The fact that he was speaking to me was huge at the time. In some strange way, that alone made me feel like I was in the business that much more.

I'll never forget the first words out of his mouth: "Dallas, how are you getting so much better?"

HULK HOGAN:

I watched Dallas on that trip to Europe, and I had to know what made this guy tick. He was a dark horse who didn't fit the equation. The opinion was that a guy like him wasn't supposed to be a wrestler, and he had everything going against him.

The European tour put us in different towns every night, and, most of the time, we worked with the same wrestler night after night. The road can make a guy weary or stale, but I saw Dallas working and digging, and trying different moves

DDP and Kimberly traveled to Europe as part of the WCW "Hulkmania" tour.)left to right) Jimmy "The Mouth of the South" Hart, Kimberly, Hulk Hogan, and Page.

every night. He didn't care if anyone was watching, but it was hard not to notice how much better he was getting.

It was easy to tell from talking to Diamond Dallas Page that he sincerely loved the business. He was far past most guys when it came to having a sense for it.

Hulk Hogan had always been a class act and a gentleman, but this was too much. At one point, I was thinking: *Is he talking to me?* The fact that Hogan noticed my effort gave me even more confidence.

Jody Hamilton, Jake Roberts, Dusty Rhodes, and, now, Hulk Hogan all saw more in me than the booking committee ever had. That was enough for me to decide that I wasn't going to give in, and I wasn't going to go away.

Once back in Atlanta, I continued my daily regimen of working out at The Power Plant, eating right, and staying positive. I was determined to use the last year of my contract to work even harder. I looked for any angle to make something stick that the bookers and matchmakers wouldn't sh*t on.

Creating a character, "getting over," and becoming a top guy is like looking for the pieces of a difficult puzzle and solving it with a million people watching. I was on my way, but I knew that the big-picture puzzle still needed a few more pieces.

CHAPTER FOURTEEN

A YO-YO BUILT FOR TWO

For several months, Diamond Dallas Page's planet revolved around working out as a substitute for being out working. During that time, the yo-yo was still looming as part of both Page and Kimberly's world.

The Falkinburgs were far from the couple-next-door type, but they were not immune to the typical issues and hurdles that newly-married couples have. Money woes, family concerns, and career struggles were present in those early years, and could have been enough reason for a negative outlook; but sometimes the commitment of love conquers all.

Money had become a major issue quickly as a result of the setbacks following Page's decision to leave the bar business behind. Kimberly had found out that the advertising business was not the answer to their finances, and the insecurity of a new profession made budgeting even more difficult. But there were more than just household bills and expenses that caused concern. Problems were compounded by the reality of an outstanding debt to the Internal Revenue Service.

I was horrible when it came to that part of it, and had never really kept track of how much I was earning, let alone my expenses. I would justify it all by saying that I was a creative guy who knew how to make money, but wasn't good at keeping track of it. The bottom line was that it always cost me big money to make bigger money. However, it took the fear of the IRS and Kimberly's smarts and spirit to help teach me a huge lesson.

KIMBERLY:

As far as his recordkeeping skills were concerned, Page was organizationally challenged. He's much better now, but he never kept receipts, had a budget, or realized that his bag of gimmicks were actually business expenses. Whether it was his wardrobe from the bar days, the money he spent promoting Smittee, or his travel expenses, he threw receipts away like gum wrappers. Obviously, he owed tax money, but now we owed money. And I was going to make sure that the IRS got every cent that was due, but not a penny more . . . as soon as possible.

After Kim showed me how to do it, and made me realize why I had to be better with the financial end of my work, I became good at it. Probably the best lesson I learned was, sadly, watching some of wrestling's biggest names walk away from the business penniless. Johnny Ace, who later helped me in the ring, also enlightened me about dealing with the dollar. Jake Roberts, who was my mentor in the ring was, on the other hand, always the example of how *not* to handle money.

That's no knock against Jake, and in his defense, he has had plenty of bad breaks; but the difference was that Jake broke Jake, too often. If cats have nine lives . . . then Snakes have a dozen.

Page became better with money as a necessity, since his on-and-off salary was on its own yo-yo. While this money-crunch was evolving, Kimberly worked in various jobs in the Atlanta area, but it was her love for physical fitness that eventually unlocked the door for her exposure on runways, in magazines, and while accompanying her husband ringside.

KIMBERLY:

I had taught aerobics as a student, and found that there was plenty of work in this field in Atlanta. Lex Lugar's Main Event Fitness Center, The Sporting Club of Atlanta, and Corporate Sports utilized my services to teach aerobics. I loved it since fitness had always been a part of my life, and, from there, I signed with a local modeling agency.

Atlanta is one of the top cities in the country for conventions and trade shows, and I also picked up work as a hostess at numerous trade-show booths. Since I had modeling experience, my new agency gave me some catalog and runway modeling work.

I still searched for a more permanent job that would suit me personally, as well as financially. I felt that as long as Page was in wrestling, it was important for me to have steady employment.

Kim's love for aerobics and sports training, combined with her tall, exotic look, began to attract more attention, and she appeared in several foreign fashion magazines. This led her to a meeting with Cynthia Kaye, the Southeast producer for *Playboy* magazine's newsstand editions. These issues

Kimberly glows in the evening gown phase of a fitness competition.

are different because they are more like theme-oriented pictorials that are distributed throughout the year for retail-only sales.

KIMBERLY:

Cynthia and I hit it off from the start, and she suggested that I try out for inclusion in Playboy's 40th *Anniversary Edition. She saw a bright future for me in show business, and also thought that Page and I would be a great combination.*

I never thought that much of anything would develop, but soon after the first photo shoot, I was introduced to Jeff Cohen, the editor and publisher of Newsstand Playboy, *and it quickly became a reality.*

Kimberly's photo shoot was immediately accepted. Shortly after posing for her nude photos, she appeared in the first of several newsstand editions. Those issues have included features in *Playboy's Book of Lingerie, Playboy's Wet and Wild, Playboy Nudes, Playboy's Girls of Summer,* and, most recently, *Hardbodies.*

It happened so quickly that there wasn't enough time for family and friends to make judgements and register their opinions before the first copies hit the newsstands. And, naturally, there were varied comments about Kim's exposure.

Imagine my gorgeous wife and her master's degree in *Playboy*! I was proud of her, and I always knew she had what it took. The camera loves Kimberly.

We discussed her options with the nude photos, but it was always her final decision. It's a good thing too, because Kim has always been a decisive independent and, sometimes, fanatical woman. Without a doubt, we are alike in that respect. Once we decide on something, we chase it with the same intensity.

I was still chasing and training hard at the time, hoping for and anticipating a break at World Championship Wrestling. Kimberly was training along with me, and she began to appear as the Diamond Doll on occasion, but I wasn't working enough for either one of us to get noticed. I loved having er with me for the ride, and we would get a little pop[1] whenever we walked together to the ring.

---

[1]*pop—The reaction of the crowd.*

Kimberly maintains a rigorous training regime. She began daily workouts in high school, and remains committed to physical conditioning.

KIMBERLY:

I had never walked down a ramp to a wrestling ring before, although I had seen enough matches on video to qualify me for the part. It started mainly because it was convenient. Too often, Page would get called the day before a match, and it was difficult to get the girls he had used before to drop everything and be ready to go.

Besides, it was extra money and fun to road-trip with Page. It wasn't glamorous travel, however, since it was mostly one- or two-day motor trips through the Deep South—Huntsville, Birmingham, Chattanooga, and places like that.

In January of 1994, Kimberly signed her first contract with World Championship Wrestling as the Diamond Doll. She would accompany Diamond Dallas Page exclusively, and would act as his valet, taking his cigar and then waiting for him to remove his jewelry and various robes and jackets before the start of each match.

The modest contract gave Kim and the household some added financial security, but since Diamond Dallas Page was still positioned on the lower half of the wrestling ladder, it also gave her time for one of her passions.

KIMBERLY:

While working out with Page more regularly, I added some weight training to my aerobics and decided to enter a local fitness contest. That led to entering a few more, including The Ms. Fitness USA *and* The Fitness America Competition *that were televised by ESPN. I did pretty well in the six contests that I entered, and I enjoyed the struggle and preparation it took to reach that level of competition. I was fortunate that I was under contract with WCW and could still compete, but it looked like that was going to change.*

After months of inconsistent scheduling, DDP was being included on more house-show cards, which led to occasional TV appearances, and my role began to expand a bit.

After Kimberly became DDP's permanent ring valet and Diamond Doll, she began to be featured both with and without Page on the pages of various wrestling publications. Kimberly began to have her own identity as a ring valet, and was rated and compared to the other women of wrestling. What had begun as a convenience, a little extra money, and a chance to spend more time with her husband was developing into something more.

Any wrestler who had a female valet at the time was hoping to be mentioned in the same breath with Randy "Macho Man" Savage and his valet, "Miss Elizabeth."

For years, the "Macho Man" has been one of the most recognizable names in wrestling, and he and his former real-life wife were the premiere couple around the ring. While in the WWF, Macho Man and Miss Elizabeth parlayed their popularity into one of the business' greatest media events, an in-ring marriage on TV.

KIMBERLY:

Fans always wondered if Page and I were really married, even though we always answered the question truthfully in interviews. I'm still amazed that not a week goes by before both Page and I are asked, "Are you two really . . . ?"

Page was finally getting more TV time, which was an opportunity to become more of a fixture on the undercard. This increased our exposure to the media, and it also increased the opportunity for Cynthia Kaye to bring up her idea of featuring Page and me together in a photo project.

Just as my television appearances began to consistently increase, we were asked to do a photo shoot for the upcoming newsstand issue of *Playboy's Nude Celebrities.* The shoot went great and was much more fun than I thought it would be. At that time, my position on the card was far from what could be called celebrity status, but we had fun doing the shoot and just hoped for the best.

Neither Kimberly nor I realized that these photos would figure into the angle that would help take me to the big time and Diamond Dallas Page to the "Main Event."

CHAPTER FIFTEEN

THE FINISH, THE GIMMICKS,
AND THE SEARCH FOR AN ANGLE

A wrestler's character is certainly a composite of several factors in and out of the ring. His persona starts with his size, name, costume, and gimmicks. This helps the booking committee include that character in an "angle." An angle with another wrestler can establish fan appeal, a following by the wrestling media, and smart marks[1].

In the ring, a wrestler must be able to work. Usually that work is a combination of showmanship and the physical display of wrestling moves. Those moves and their names are often deep-rooted in collegiate or Olympic Greco-Roman-style wrestling. Arm drags, wristlocks, arm bars, and leg sweeps can all be seen in the nearly empty field houses where collegiate and high school wrestling matches are held.

In professional wrestling, the conventional moves are still a part of every match, but the names that aren't heard in amateur wrestling are much more imaginative and vivid, and sell a lot more

---

[1]*smart marks—Fans who believe they are insiders or know more than average marks; often the source of Internet rumors. Many believe the term is an oxymoron.*

admission tickets. "The Mule Kick," "The Torture Rack," "The Tornado Lariat," and "The Scorpion Death Lock" are moves that are seen weekly in televised professional matches. There are no judges or scoring systems that allow a wrestler to win on points. A disqualification, which is rare in Olympic or collegiate grappling, is an all too frequent ending to a TV match. In pro wrestling, the pin is often elementary, while the "finish" creates the intensity and the pop.

A wrestler's finishing moves become his signature, and help promote an identity that creates the entertainment value. Fans remember wrestlers by their finish. How the wrestler sets up and executes his moves can be more exciting than any costume, gimmick, or angle.

When I returned to Atlanta following the European tour and my encouraging talk with Hulk Hogan, I decided to turn it up a notch. I had made the decision to stay with World Championship Wrestling, and was determined to come up with something that would get me noticed even more.

I was working out religiously at The Power Plant, mostly with new guys, and I was experimenting with different moves. Hoping to discover the bridge to the Main Event, I contacted an old friend and found an important piece of the puzzle.

JOHNNY ACE
INTERNATIONAL JAPANESE WRESTLING SUPERSTAR:

I met Page while working with Florida Championship Wrestling. I liked his flamboyant nature from the start, but I also saw another side of him. He was sincere, genuinely wanted to learn it all, and was willing to work hard to get it.

He had a lot going against him from the start—too big for a manager, no experience around the ring, and most of all, no connections.

Page and I kept in touch through the years, and I was home from one of my first trips to Japan when we hooked up. I was driving back to Florida through Atlanta when Page invited me to stay a couple of days, and asked me if I would work out in the ring with him.

Even before we got in the ring, I watched Page's tapes and his live work. When I knew him in the past, he was a manager and announcer who had a ton of charisma and enough mic skills to last in the business. He had come a long way physically, and I quickly saw that he had a new focus, and that he wanted to be known for his work in the ring.

Page always took advice and suggestions in stride. We both learned from other guys in this business because we showed genuine interest to learn. I saw that his work was good, but I explained to him why some moves and finishes looked good, but would never get over.

The first thing was to find a move that could be done on any opponent, from the 7-footers to the luchadores[2]*, and from the 150-pounders to the 400-pound giants. Some of the best-looking moves are limited because of the difficulty with the various sizes of the guys.*

It's important for a wrestler to have a finish that does damage to his opponent, but not to him. Too often, both guys feel the finish. I always warned Page about the wear and tear on the body that each move would make. For example, the splashes from the top rope look really good, but tear up knees and elbows, which doesn't help with a guy's longevity. Page was in great shape, and knew his body very well. He would take it to the limit, but he had learned to be controlled in the ring.

Johnny Ace is not a household name to fans who recently discovered wrestling on Monday night's prime-time TV listings. But mention his name to other wrestlers, and they speak well of his work and his long international and independent career. Wrestling purists and marks remember Johnny from the old NWA and his successes in Japan. But the smarts speak in awe of his finishing move. The move and its variations may be the most over moves in professional wrestling history.

I had been working out frequently with Eric Watts, Chris "Kanyon" Klucsarits, and Paul Levesque at The Power Plant at that time. Paul Levesque is known to wrestling fans as Hunter Hearst Helmsley ("Triple H"). Hunter has become a

---

[2]*luchadores-Spanish name given to smaller, more acrobatic wrestlers.*

huge superstar in the WWF, but was with WCW at the time. Terry Taylor and I had both noticed Paul's ability in the ring, but it was Terry who said that "he's got a work ethic like yours, Page." I agreed and remembered commenting back that "he has something I never had—a future in this business at *his* age." Hunter Hearst Helmsley will be another one of those names that wrestling fans will hear for years to come.

Johnny Ace and I went to The Plant, and he observed several things I had been working on. He liked some of the moves, but when he climbed in the ring, he showed me the move that had gotten him over in Japan.

JOHNNY ACE:

Kendall Windam first showed the move to me, and it was a variation of the "neckbreaker." I used it in my first match in Japan after Tom Zenk suggested that I establish a finish for the Japanese fans. While by my opponent's side, I'd grab him with a one-armed neck-lock and drop straight down and flat out.

The Japanese crowd went crazy because they had never seen me, or that move, before. I didn't even have a name for it when the Japanese media were interviewing me. Hell, I was just happy to be getting a paycheck. Actually, it was a member of the Japanese press who named it the "Ace Crusher."

I showed Page the move by grabbing Eric Watts' head with one arm and taking him right down. Page said, "Wow! I like that."

I liked Johnny's move a lot because it happened so quickly, looked so devastating, and ended with both guys on the mat. No one was using it here in the States, and I immediately asked Ace if he minded if I used the move or a variation of it.

JOHNNY ACE:

I certainly had no problem with Page using it. Some guys believe that a certain hold or move belongs to them, but all moves are really a variation of others. I laugh when people say that any move was stolen, let alone the Ace Crusher.

I began to work with the move, trying several ways to execute the hold. Out of respect, I would never take a guy's finishing maneuver and do it exactly the same . . . without asking, anyway. So even with Johnny's approval, I looked for a way to personalize it.

Steven Regal, the veteran British wrestler, showed me a hold called a "cravat" that, when applied correctly, was virtually impossible to break. I would begin the move with a headlock, using both hands locked at the fingers, and then I would kick my legs and body out. This took my opponent headfirst to the mat, as I went flat to my back. From that point, it was easy to roll out and over my victim for a pin.

I practiced numerous variations of the move until I liked what I saw. By grabbing my opponent with the cravat, I was able to secure and take down anyone with my version of the Ace Crusher, from the high-flyers to the biggest in the business.

That was proven at *WCW Starcade 1998* when I executed the move on the 7'2", 500-pound "Giant," Paul Wight. It was a Diamond Cutter that the world never saw coming. (Thanks G.)

Around the time of Ace's visit, Jake Roberts had moved to Athens, Georgia, just over an hour from Atlanta. I drove there from time to time to show Jake my latest matches and talk strategies.

After my time with Jake on the independent circuit, he became the source for much of my ring psychology, and was always there for me with constructive criticism. Jake and I have so much in common. We are built the same, and our movements in the ring are similar. A lot of Jake has rubbed off on me, and I have adopted his ideology about timing and changing the pace of a match.

I never felt *anyone* could duplicate Jake's devastating, show-stopping finishing maneuver known as the DDT[3].

---

[3]*DDT-The name of a deadly pesticide that was eventually taken off the market. There is a generation of wrestling fans who know only of DDT as Jake "The Snake" Roberts' finishing move.*

The DDT was, and still is, the most imitated move on the planet. Many of the finishing moves used in wrestling today are variations of Jake's DDT. For my money, the only other memorable DDTs are the versions of Michael P.S. Hayes' (Dok Holiday), and, most recently, Scott "Raven" Levy's. Raven's version, "The Evenflow," is the best and most effective version of the DDT used in pro wrestling today.

JAKE "THE SNAKE" ROBERTS:

Page always knew the "Total Snake" and treated me unconditionally. Once, he was talking to a future "ex" of mine, and told her, "You say you love Jake, but you only love one of the Jakes. You act like you don't even know Jake the Party Boy, Jake the Excessive, or Jake the Playboy. Until you realize that there are many sides to Jake Roberts, you two will always be at each other's throats."

No one had ever summed it all up in so few words. Page and I will always be like brothers.

Jody Hamilton had given me the solid foundation beginning at The Power Plant, and has always been there for me, but Jake and I had developed a different kind of friendship. Once I got a taste of what it was like to experience life in the ring and on the road, I understood a whole lot more . . . and Jake and I became solid.

Whenever I got a match, I used the new finish, but matches were hard to come by at the time. I was still waiting for my shot, but I wanted to be prepared if the fans or the powers-that-be saw something they liked. The move was quick and devastating, but wasn't getting the reaction that I thought it would. It appeared that the move had a lot of potential, but it still came down to timing. It had to be seen in the right situation, and still needed something more.

Bobby "The Brain" Heenan is a most colorful and comical guy, and one who made the traditional transition from ring superstar to ring manager to announcer and commentator. Bobby "The Brain" has always been one of the most entertaining performers of wrestling from either side of the ropes.

After one of the matches where I used my version of the Ace Crusher on my opponent, Bobby met me backstage. He had been the commentator for the match, and he made it a point to tell me that he liked my new finish.

Just mentioning that he liked the move was a cool enough stroke, but when "Brain" asked me what I called it, I didn't have an answer. He said, "It's quick and it's clean . . . and it cuts the guy right down. You should call it the 'Diamond Cutter.'"

And I did. The Brain was right. It was quick, sharp, and decisive. However, for any move to be successful, it would have to get a reaction and a pop when it was applied. For the Diamond Cutter to sparkle, it would have to get the attention and reaction of the fans.

JAKE ROBERTS:

When I first saw the Diamond Cutter, I knew that Page had added an element to his game that could elevate him. The move had many of the characteristics of the DDT, and if he applied some ring psychology to get the crowd involved, it could be the vehicle to creating his own following and break.

Jake and I were watching the training tape that included the Diamond Cutter, and were dissecting it from all angles.

"I was thinking that if a guy was getting ready to 'souplex' me," I said, "I could give him a quick shot to the ribs, grab him in the lock, and, out of nowhere, I'd just *bang* him right there."

Jake began to laugh. Then he smiled. "Congratulations . . . now you're getting it."

It was the first time I used the word "*bang,*" but it seemed like the perfect word. I thought of a shot that no one sees coming, like a gunshot. Not a pop, but a *bang*!

In the summer of 1998, the publication *Inside Wrestling* rated the finishing moves used in professional wrestling. Not only did the Ace Crusher rank in the top three, it was called "the most imitated

As the crowd signals for the "Diamond Cutter," DDP executes his finish, and "Mortis" feels the bang! Mortis is actually DDP's bro, Chris "Kanyon" Klucsarits.

move of the last five years." The magazine reported that at least a half dozen variations of the move were presently being used, most notably the Diamond Cutter and Steve Austin's Stone Cold Stunner.

"STONE COLD" STEVE AUSTIN:

The move I use, called the "Stone Cold Stunner," was shown to me by Dok Hendricks (Michael P.S. Hayes) when he got to the WWF. When Dok showed it to me, he told me that Page was using it. But the difference was that he was locking up with two hands, and going flat to his back. My variation had me using one hand and dropping down to my @$$, finishing in a sitting position. It accomplished the same effect, but looked different than the Diamond Cutter.

I hadn't really seen the Ace Crusher, since it was used primarily overseas, and it wasn't until later that I heard that Page's move had come from it. They are all different . . . but they all work.

So, how are all three moves different?

The Ace Crusher is applied with one hand, as is the Stone Cold Stunner. Only the Diamond Cutter uses the two-handed cravat, but ends with DDP flat on his back like Johnny Ace's Ace Crusher. Steve Austin's Stone Cold Stunner ends with Steve in a seated position.

And, how are they similar? They are all *over* with the fans, and are responsible for some of the most exciting finishes in professional wrestling today. Johnny Ace continues to dominate opponents in Japan, while Steve Austin has used his version to rule the WWF for the past few years.

Since my opportunities to display my new move in the ring had been slim, I continued to work at The Power Plant, but with a new twist. Instead of searching for the right finishing move, I was finding new ways to apply the Diamond Cutter.

Within the first few weeks, I came up with a dozen ways to get into the hold that would create the *bang*! The move incorporated so much of what I had learned, and it was exciting to discover and work out all the possibilities. While the hold can be dangerous to my opponent, the bump isn't too bad on my body (and that's a *good* thing).

The Diamond Cutter can be effective on anyone, and can be applied from almost anywhere . . . but most importantly, it is impressive and exciting to watch. It was at The Power Plant that I added the very last piece of the puzzle. I had been trying the move in different situations on different sized guys when I met Ron Reece.

Reece was fresh out of college and had recently begun his WCW training at The Plant. He's a huge, burly seven-footer who played collegiate basketball at Santa Clara State University. It was his basketball experience that created the sign that would get the fans even more involved. It would help Diamond Dallas Page and his Diamond Cutter etch a place in professional wrestling history.

RON REECE:

It was rare to see a guy who had been in wrestling as long as Dallas at The Power Plant working out with us rookies. He was working on his new move when I remembered a play that we used in college. We called it "Diamond." Our coach would raise his hands and put them together to form a diamond shape when he wanted to use the formation.

When I showed it to Dallas, he looked a little confused. I told him it might work if he used it before or after putting the Diamond Cutter on his opponent.

A diamond wasn't the first thing I thought of when Reece put his hands together like that. Later, though, I became more comfortable with it. I threw my hands up to form the diamond sign right before I executed the move at a few house shows, and the fans started to get with it. After I used it, I began seeing a few fans making diamond signs in the crowd, so I answered them back with the same sign. It became so natural that I began flashing the diamond sign as I emerged from behind the curtain. Every time I got a new match, there were more and more hands raised in the air signaling for the Diamond Cutter.

Despite the hours of training and the encouraging words of legendary wrestling superstars like "The Assassin," "The American Dream," "The Snake," and "Hulk," Diamond Dallas Page was still searching for a break, and a way to consistently be on the card.

The fans still generally hated DDP, and even though he had begun to trim down his many gimmicks, his heel status was firmly set with his interviews and ring antics.

All I ever wanted was a chance to get out there on a regular basis. I never forgot the words of Jake Roberts when he had told me that "if the people were entertained, the wrestling gods would have to take notice." But without steady involvement of an angle or program[4], it was impossible to get a reaction.

I attempted to gain fan interest when I came up with the gimmick of picking the name of a wrestler out of a fishbowl and challenging him. The gimmick didn't last long, and I was still seeking an angle that could develop into a running feud.

The setup for such a feud began when I started challenging other wrestlers to arm-wrestling competitions. One of those challenges was against David Sullivan, who had a similar place in the eyes of the matchmakers. Like me, David was never seen as much more than a lower mid-card guy with limited potential. But when he defeated me in an arm-wrestling match, it led to a Pay-Per-View appearance at the 1995 *Great American Bash*.

Every wrestler, and most fans for that matter, likes to concoct story lines and angles that they believe will get over, and, periodically, the boys can have varying degrees of input in the development of a program.

A wrestling feud and angle are similar to a television drama miniseries, which occasionally includes a bit of comedy to accompany the nonstop action. The physicality walks a fine line between acrobatics, stunt work, and street-fighting.

This particular angle centered on Sullivan, the good guy who had a romantic crush on the bad guy's girl.

---

[4]*program—A series of matches with the same opponent; a running feud.*

David's desire to be with my Diamond Doll became the source for our confrontations in the ring. Kimberly was now my full-time ring valet, and it seemed natural to incorporate her into the program. The angle was one of the first that I ever laid out, and it had some potential, even though everyone pretty much sh*t on it.

The angle began with Sullivan bringing her flowers and gifts, and when that didn't meet with my approval . . . he wound up in a hospital bed. Kimberly began to feel sorry for him, and was seen in disguise visiting him in the hospital. She brought him a pet rabbit as a gift.

The angle went back and forth. I'd steal the rabbit, and he'd get it back. It ended when I put the Diamond Doll up and David bet the rabbit in a "winner takes all" match. If he

The matches with "Johnny B. Badd" proved to be an important mid-card feud for both Diamond Dallas Page and Mark Mero.

Photo by Rick Diamond, *Pro Wrestling Illustrated*

won, he got a date with the Doll, and if I won . . . I was going to make rabbit stew.

My work with David Sullivan was really the start of everything that would establish me as someone who could fit in the right angle. I think the angle accomplished as much as it could, and, at the least, showed my versatility and ability to work with a different style of wrestler.

On the negative side, the rabbit gimmick certainly had its limitations, and may have been a bit corny. In fact, almost everyone thought it absolutely sucked, and they may have been right.

But the positive spin was that the angle achieved our goal. We got some fan interest, and made people talk about us . . . even if it was just bottom-of-the-card small talk.

KIMBERLY:

I was excited and encouraged by the David Sullivan angle because it had been Page's idea and the first in which we actually had a story line to follow. It happens too often that an angle will be abandoned before it has a chance, especially at the bottom of the card.

Coming off the program with Sullivan, Diamond Dallas Page began to build more heel heat, and when he pinned Alex Wright at *Clash of the Champions XXXI*, he moved into the WCW rankings for the first time.

Those "magazine rankings" and his PPV victory set up a bout for the WCW TV Title Belt. While this title is the least coveted by established performers, it was the first of many championship steps. This first title match also meant another Pay-Per-View appearance.

Beating the Renegade for my first "strap" at *Fall Brawl 1995* was a big step, but only a prelude to what I considered my first real climb up the ladder.

Following the victory, it was decided that I would enter a featured angle with "Marvelous" Mark Mero, who wrestled at World Championship Wrestling as Johnny B. Badd.

Mero was an upper middle-card guy, definitely a few steps higher in the pecking order, and it presented an opportunity to get more TV exposure. His character, Johnny B. Badd, was exciting, flamboyant, and more visible than David Sullivan would ever become.

Johnny B. Badd resembled the classic rock and roll musician, Little Richard, except he wore a loincloth. His good looks and charisma gave him a recognizable gimmick for the fans. He threw Frisbees on his way down the ramp, and had a confetti cannon that he brought to the ring.

I was jacked to be working an angle in the middle of the card, but was more excited about working with Mark Mero. Mero was a guy who I really respected for his hard work, both in and out of the ring. He was always as enthusiastic as I was, and there was no doubt that it was the biggest break I had gotten to that point.

We were both determined to make our matches as entertaining as they could be, and Mark Mero gave 100 percent every time we entered the ring. He wasn't afraid to hit hard

Mark "Johnny B. Badd" Mero was one of several WCW "bro's" who looked to New York and the WWF for an opportunity.

and take the stiff bumps[5] in order to give the fans the best matches and entertainment possible. We were two guys who weren't afraid to knock the hell out of each other if the end result was positive.

MARK MERO
FORMER WCW SUPERSTAR JOHNNY B. BADD:

We just clicked. Page and I developed a friendship that I never knew existed in the business.

The Johnny B. Badd vs. Diamond Dallas Page angle was my favorite, and was probably the best angle I was ever in because of the mutual respect and friendship that we built. It started in the gym. I had this grueling "ab" (stomach muscles) workout that I developed in my days of boxing, and it pi$$ed me off that Page was the only guy who could endure the workout and follow it exactly.

Not many people know that it was Page who coaxed me into talking to the woman who became my wife and partner for life.

Buff Bagwell, Page, and I were on the road in Jacksonville at a restaurant called "Quincy's" when the most beautiful girl I ever saw walked in. Every head turned, and after I commented on her looks, Page said, "Go ahead . . . give her your best line, bro." He was giving me his best bar advice when he said that "to make an impact on the really beautiful ladies, you have to use your very best line, because you might not get another chance." I laughed it off, but Page pushed me . . . a couple of times.

Finally, I grabbed a cocktail napkin and wrote:

Do you like me?

Yes   No

Circle one

Page just looked at it a little puzzled, and said: "If you're sure that's your best line, then go with it."

---

[5]*stiff bumps—Harder hitting to sometimes close to full contact moves.*

I had a waitress take it over to the lady. She didn't sell it at all, and had absolutely no reaction. So, of course, Page and Buff began to ride me, with Page asking me over and over again if I was sure about that being my best line. A half-hour after I sent the note, and just before we got ready to leave, the waitress dropped my note back. The lady who would become my wife replied with . . . "MAYBE."

Well, the boys changed their tune and rallied behind my best line. After she and I spoke, Page, Buff, and I left, but I had Rena's phone number. I wouldn't have talked to her if Page hadn't prompted me.

Rena Mero, no doubt, is beautiful, and besides being a wife and mother, she also became one of the biggest super-stars in the WWF. The world was introduced to her as the character, "Sable," but Rena Mero has an even brighter future since leaving the world of wrestling. She has graced the cover of *Playboy* . . . twice, and has merchandising items and acting opportunities to accompany the mega-star celebrity status she received as a result of professional wrestling.

The angle between me and Johnny B. Badd was more elaborate, and had been built around intensifying me as the obnoxious heel and establishing Johnny B.Badd as a "knight in shining armor."

It was also an opportunity to increase Kimberly's visibility. There was little doubt that her good looks and natural stage presence were a positive addition to Diamond Dallas Page and World Championship Wrestling.

The angle began with me supposedly winning 13 million dollars while gambling in Las Vegas. After that, it was all about the money. It was a perfect way for me to be a complete @$$hole who cared only about wealth, jewelry, and ego. This spun into my on-camera mistreatment and lack of regard for Kimberly.

I held the TV title for a little over a month before losing the belt, and I also lost Kimberly's services as my ring valet to Johnny B. Badd. For the next several months,

I lost every match against Badd, including a rematch at *World War III*.

Kimberly gained even more presence when she assisted Johnny B. Badd in another victory over me. One time, while I prepared to defeat Johnny, Kimberly threw a chain into the ring. It went through my legs, enabling him to use it on me . . . and beat me yet another time.

KIMBERLY:

Page was great as the big heel who constantly berated me. His uncivil treatment and browbeating caused Johnny B. Badd to feel empathetic. Johnny was the consummate gentleman in his role, and the meaner DDP was, the more charming Johnny became.

Once I became Johnny B. Badd's valet and ringside partner, the angle turned toward the demise of Diamond Dallas Page.

I had introduced the Diamond Cutter, but hadn't used it regularly. With the string of losses, there was no place for a finishing move, and I couldn't showcase the Cutter unless I was going to get my hand raised in victory. It was all about timing.

Outside the ring, Diamond Dallas Page was named "Most Improved Wrestler" in a 1995 readers' poll of *Pro Wrestling Illustrated*. It seemed that the fans had started seeing DDP as a rising superstar.

Despite repeated loses to Johnny B. Badd, the angle was building steam, and Diamond Dallas Page was getting noticed.

That award will always be one of the highlights and proudest honors of my career. The list of past winners was a "Who's Who" of professional wrestling, and included the former WWF champions, "Razor Ramone" (Scott Hall) and "Diesel" (Kevin Nash). It was especially gratifying to have the entire wrestling community see me in a different light.

But it sure went sour for DDP on TV during that phase of the program. In a matter of months, I was broke. I had lost every penny that I supposedly won in Las Vegas to Kimberly. Then I lost still another match to Johnny B. Badd on Pay-Per-View at *Superbrawl* in February of '96. Following that loss, the angle focused on DDP's personal and financial demise. At one point, I was seen in a TV tape selling a pair of my wrestling tights to raise money for bills.

Kimberly continued to accompany Johnny B. Badd to the ring. She was now dressing more athletic, and had become more of a cheerleader than a valet. She would help get the fans involved in the matches, and with her good looks and ring presence, Kimberly began to build her own fan base.

The payoff was supposed to come after I underhandedly helped Lex Lugar defeat Johnny B. Badd for the TV Championship Title.

We were setting up for a showdown at the next Pay-Per-View called *Uncensored*. The loser was to retire from wrestling, while the winner would keep Kimberly as his valet.

The showdown never happened.

The timing appeared to be right for the underdog, DDP, to finally gain a victory after he had lost virtually everything to Johnny B. Badd. But before all that happened, the uncertainty of the wrestling business created new dynamics and an aborted conclusion to the nearly four-month angle.

MARK MERO
FORMER WCW SUPERSTAR JOHNNY B. BADD:

The months that I spent in the angle with Page were the best times in my career. It was the first angle where my over-the-top character had put down his confetti cannon and Frisbee gimmicks and actually wrestled. Page's intensity had added that dimension, and it worked in its own way for both of us. Going to work was fun, productive, and rewarding for me, and I was making a real friend. Page was the first guy in the business who I trusted as a friend and also respected as a wrestler.

I was coming to the end of my contract, and it was no secret that World Championship Wrestling and Eric Bischoff had a different opinion than I did about my future.

**THE BOOTY MAN
WITH
THE BOOTY GIRL**

"The Booty Man" with Kimberly—"The Booty Girl."

I would have loved to have finished the angle and stayed with WCW, but Vince McMahon offered me the first guaranteed contract in the history of the WWF. It was the biggest contract that I had ever signed, and I was the first of many WCW wrestlers to make the move to New York. I don't think anyone had jumped for just the money, though. At the time,

*the WWF offered the hope of a bigger and better opportunity
to climb to the top.*

*I'm sure that the intensity of the angle with Page added
to McMahon's determination to sign me, but it also made a
lot of people in "the back" finally believe that Page wasn't
going to go away. He had overcome what people had said
about him, and had taken his love for wrestling and made it
into his career.*

The Johnny B. Badd angle was the first solid step that I
had taken to be a guy who could work at another level. Each
match with Mero was better than the one before, and the angle
had gotten pretty damn good. I had heat, and was getting the
crowd reaction that made the boys in the back notice. And
Kimberly was getting over as her own entity . . . and *bang!*—
it was all over.

Mark Mero was suddenly on his way to New York, and
Johnny B. Badd disappeared. The wrestling gods at WCW
were forced to scramble to plug in a new opponent for the
upcoming *Uncensored* Pay-Per-View match. It was going to
be difficult, if not impossible, to build the heat that quickly
with a totally new character. We just relied on trying to be
entertaining, and hoped that there was still the chance that
the fans would buy it.

My new opponent was Ed Leslie, better known as Brutes
"The Barber" Beefcake, from the WWF. Ed Leslie had been
one of wrestling's top performers prior to a severe accident
that nearly killed him. His comeback to the sport was now at
WCW with a new character named "The Booty Man."

The retirement angle was still in effect, although the match
lost most of its buildup since Johnny B. Badd had disappeared
without much of an explanation. And Kimberly had suddenly
become "The Booty Babe."

I lost to The Booty Man, and I lost Kimberly. And I now
had a new environment for my wrestling persona . . . the
gutter.

Chapter Sixteen

Hitting The Highway And
A New Road Is Just Around The Corner

Page Falkinburg has been called both a pioneer and a plagiarist. He was a pioneer in evaluating his work by using video, and his intense training and unique methods of healthcare and rehab are like no other.

His way of doing things is no secret to anyone. He is constantly selling and touting his favorites, whether it is the skills of a doctor or who has the best low-fat burrito. Having Page Falkinburg on someone's sales force takes "word of mouth" to warp level. He can't help it. He's a promoter.

Page is a spokesperson personified. Everything and anything that Page likes, he endorses, and it becomes his new passion. Does he plagiarize? Is he a bandit who takes ideas of others to a higher visibility? Can he take someone else's concept and retool it into a fundamental practice or accepted procedure?

Yes, yes, and yes, again. The sponge and the yo-yo have been with him for so long that he has learned how to take the negatives of most situations and spin them into positive weapons for his arsenal. Page's work ethic and optimistic attitude helped make the yo-yo a source of self-esteem and confidence.

Mark Mero always spent time and money to promote his character and to enlarge his fan base. Whether it was buying Frisbees to throw to the crowd or actually making his own confetti cannon, Mark believed that everything he did would eventually reap benefits. He was also one of the first people (and the first wrestler) I knew who had a computer and was actually having fun learning about it. Kimberly had one that she used in college, but it was already a "dinosaur," and seemed less user-friendly than Mero's.

At the time, computers were still fairly new to the masses. They were way more cost prohibitive than today, and certainly weren't looked upon as something that might add anything to the wrestling business. Mark had just spent a lot of money on a new computer, and it seemed that he was spending more and more every month updating and buying new software. He thought that one day the computer, the Internet, and the Web would mean more exposure and bigger salaries for the wrestlers.

I thought Mero was crazy to spend so much money on a computer, but I quickly saw potential and benefits that this new source of information and communication had to offer.

MARK MERO:

Like anyone, I couldn't pull myself away from the keyboard after I got my first computer, and Page even began looking over my shoulder while I was using it.

After I showed him some of the Internet comments from the fans regarding our Johnny B. Badd-Diamond Dallas Page feud, it became one of the funniest days we ever spent together.

Page was fascinated by the whole thing. He watched what people were "saying" and joined in the dialogue. Somebody wrote a few derogatory comments about DDP that upset Page, and he asked for the keyboard. Slowly, he pecked out a reply, actually going off on the guy with just one short sentence.

I replied with two words: "BLOW ME!"
I reacted, not only to what the guy had "written," but I

was excited that I had found an immediate way to know how the fans were reacting without being in the arenas. Wrestling fans are created and encouraged to be vocal, rabid, and opinionated; and now, potentially, every fan, mark, and critic from anywhere in the world had a voice . . . even if they didn't know what they were talking about.

I wanted to "talk" on the Internet and see what the fans knew about wrestling and Diamond Dallas Page. I rushed home and told Kimberly that we were getting a computer, and it wasn't long before we were hooked up. Soon after, Kimberly established a bulletin board called *Kimberly's Korner* that she used to talk to fans.

I watched Mero pecking away and saw Kimberly typing quickly, and I knew I had to learn how to type properly. So, as soon as we got the computer, I bought my first program called "Mario Teaches Typing."

There was a wrestling fan in the chat rooms named "Maddog" who set up bulletin boards for Mero and Kimberly. Soon after, they could post messages and information, as well as receive letters and comments from fans.

KIMBERLY

Page wanted me to be there for him to navigate his every move. Finally, I showed him how to turn the computer on and "threw him in the pool." He got frustrated, but persevered. I couldn't believe it, and was so proud of him when I saw him teaching himself to type and finding his way around the World Wide Web (WWW).

Learning how to type helped, and I became obsessed with the thing. I went through the typical frustrations of connecting to the Internet and communicating with people by typing a few lines at a time.

During this time, I was playing the heel hard, and almost everything written was negative to my character, and even to me personally. The comments and name-calling didn't bother me at first, but when I saw lies, rumors, and innuendo . . . now that pi$$ed me off! I lashed back with my usual statement: "Blow Me!"

Originally, I felt the Internet would work for Mero, but not for me. I immediately thought that a babyface could better use it to chat with fans. Heels had it worse since we wanted a negative reaction from fans, but I soon realized that it was all about interaction. Of course, people always doubted it was really me after I sent them a letter or message. When they finally realized it was the real DDP, they changed their tune and wanted to be on my "buddy list" . . . yeah, right.

Page and Kimberly's involvement with the Internet wasn't spared the drama or the financial drops that came with the yo-yo. They were having fun, and they were both hooked on their computer as they began to spend hours on-line talking to friends and surfing the Web. Until . . .

KIMBERLY:

We were home a lot of the time, but since we used our computer on the road, we had programmed our modem with the "800" number to access our server. It was easier to use that phone number than it was to get the local access numbers in each city.

Kim was at her desk writing out the bills one night when she started laughing about a charge on our credit card for over $1,000 in extra Internet server fees. We knew it had to be a mistake, so Kim wrote a letter and sent it in with the bill, explaining that the charges couldn't be ours.

KIMBERLY:

We never heard anything until we got our next credit card bill, and that's when it wasn't funny anymore. There was another charge, this time for $800, and now our server charges totaled $1,800.

After what seemed to be hours of hold time and electronic messages, I finally got through, and was told that every time we used the "800" number, we were being charged for connection time. They were apologetic, but firm, and told me the charges would stand.

I couldn't believe what I was hearing. Was I fu*ked up, or doesn't 800 mean toll-free? I didn't flip out (at first), and thought that if I made a call to the supervisor explaining this situation, they would surely understand.

It was all still pretty funny to me until I found out that it would take most of the afternoon on hold, and I'd have to tell my story a couple of times before I got to a supervisor. The supervisor was no help, and he told me that the charges were "accurate and past due."

Kimberly and I had been using that server exclusively, and had gotten people to sign on just so they could read our postings. We were using what everyone on the planet would think is a toll-free "800" number, and now my server was laying us away with a bill for $1,800?

It was hard for me to take "no" for an answer, and I asked the supervisor if there was any way we could reduce or adjust the bill, and he flatly said, "No." I then asked him if he wanted to lose us as customers and have me tell everyone that I came in contact with how much their company sucked. Apparently, that's what he wanted because we had to pay the entire bill.

The principle of the thing mattered, but the money mattered more. Eighteen hundred dollars was like eighteen thousand to us at the time. I tell this story every chance I get, and if my readers ever see me in person, maybe I'll tell them which server it was. It still pi$$es me off to this day. I think I am charged twenty bucks a month for unlimited access these days, so I figure I am owed about seven and a half years of free hookup time.

Slow as hell, what the hell . . . whatever . . . there is still time to make it right. The server company can call me, or they can just . . . go to hell.

KIMBERLY:

Finding out that our postings and surfing had cost us so much took a lot of the fun out of it, that's for sure. While we were hoping for the server charges to be resolved, we met a guy who has become a real friend to both of us.

Mark Mero told me of a guy he had met on-line who was not only very witty, but knew the wrestling game. "RichInKC" had visited Kimberly's Korner *and left some interesting and funny letters with his take on our Johnny B. Badd angle, along with other comedic wrestling observations. From time to time, I replied to his letters.*

Kim laughed out loud at what RichInKC was writing, and I dug it too. Most of the stuff I had read before about wrestling on the Net had been negative bullsh*t, but this guy was entertaining, and had some very interesting ideas. I liked what he said, and, via Kimberly, I asked Rich to write to me.

RICH SCHMICK
"RICHINKC":

I really couldn't believe that Mero, let alone Kimberly, was answering my e-mails. A wrestling fan for years, I posted an article that I had written with my reflections on the current wrestling angles after I received e-mail from Johnny B. Badd. I didn't believe that it was actually Mero who was writing, but after I did everything, including insulting him on-line, I was convinced it was really him. We communicated back and forth, and when I heard he was jumping to the WWF, I half-joked that he should call me to hear some ideas I had for him.

I was shocked when Mero called. During our conversation, he told me to check out the new bulletin board that Kimberly had set up. Within a few weeks, Kimberly and I were writing fairly regularly, and I soon began to e-mail Page too. Now, I wasn't a DDP fan, and I didn't follow WCW as much as WWF. Page and Johnny B. Badd's angle was the first time that I had seen very much of Page. I never went for the cigar-smoking-while-chewing-gum gimmick, and thought of him for what he was: a bottom- or barely middle-of-the-card guy. Besides that, I think he lost 40 or 50 matches in a row once.

Of course, Kimberly was another story . . . and if I had to get DDP as part of the deal for a glimpse of Kimberly . . . so be it.

There was no doubt that Rich was a huge wrestling fan, but I was, and still am, leery of meeting people on the Net. So it took awhile before I gave him our phone number. In fact, I missed his first few calls on purpose just to make sure I hadn't made a mistake by giving him my number. Once Rich and I did hook up, I liked him, and enjoyed hearing his take on wrestling and, more specifically, what I was doing in the ring.

During those first few months when Rich and Page were communicating via e-mail and telephone, Diamond Dallas Page's character went through some drastic changes. DDP went through his in-the-gutter period, and, months later, a mysterious benefactor put him back in the money. While the wrestling world wondered who the benefactor was, Rich and DDP were becoming on-line and phone friends fast.

Rich was always cool to talk to. I'd bounce ideas off of him, and he would tell me exactly what he thought—even if it wasn't necessarily what I wanted to hear. He was traveling a lot in his job with Gateway, the computer firm, and I would call him while he was on the road.

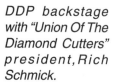

DDP backstage with "Union Of The Diamond Cutters" president, Rich Schmick.

RichInKC:

I was writing to a few friends who I had made on-line, and I could see that there was a lot of curiosity and confusion about Page and his career, so I asked if I could interview him as a freelance writer.

He was shooting[1] from the start, and the interview rolled on and on. If someone didn't know Page before that interview, they sure knew him after.

Although the popularity of wrestling on the Internet was still in its infancy, RichInKC forwarded his five-page, in-depth interview with Diamond Dallas Page to the largest Web sites dedicated to professional wrestling. Within days, it was posted by Al Issacs of *Scoopswrestling.com*, Blake Norton of the *Bagpipe Report*, Ricky Geary of the *Wrestling Gazette*, and Bob Ryder of *1Wrestling.com*.

The interview was a great way for me to clear up so many of the rumors and misconceptions about me. I felt at ease with Rich as the interviewer, and I answered questions for him that I wouldn't have answered for others.

Although Rich and I were both on the road a lot, we never crossed paths. I live on the phone as it is, but I had added Rich to my list. He was just a guy who I dug talking wrestling with. Both Kim and I felt like we knew him, but we still hadn't met, so we invited him to an upcoming Pay-Per-View in Las Vegas.

RichInKC:

It was during the Diamond Dallas Page and Eddie Guerrero feud that Page first used one of my ideas on camera. We had been talking, and he told me that there would be an upcoming confrontation with Eddie's nephew, Chavo.

I suggested that he use the name "Chavo" in a parody of "Copa," the Barry Manilow song. I sung a few bars over the phone, and Page was rolling on the floor.

I was home watching TV when I saw DDP doing an interview, singing, "His name was Chavo . . . he was a showgirl . . . ." I just lost it. I was blown away. DDP actually used my

---

[1] *shoot or shooting—Refers to accuracy; telling the true story.*

idea. As far as I was concerned, it was like scribbling a play on paper and having Jimmy Johnson use it in the Super Bowl.

And it got over. It seemed that Diamond Dallas Page was getting over, one day and one fan at a time.

We made arrangements to meet in Las Vegas at the next PPV called Halloween Havoc. In the back of my mind, I wondered if it was all real, and if I was really going to Las Vegas to meet my on-line friends who were in professional wrestling. I thought: Yeah, right . . . this is just a prank that wrestlers play on their mark fans. *Page never made me feel that way, but after all, it was professional wrestling, and maybe it was just a work[2].*

Page and I met up as he was walking through the lobby of the MGM to a cab that was waiting for us. Before we got into the cab, Page stopped to say hello and introduce me to wrestlers Kevin Nash and Sean Waltham as his buddy, Rich (which was pretty cool).

I was taking it all in, and couldn't help but think that I had talked to Page enough to know him, but the anonymity of the Internet made it different. Usually, when a person first meets someone, they have plenty to talk about, but anyone who has met someone in person after conversing on-line knows it can be awkward.

When Rich first called me in my room in Vegas, I could tell he might have a bit of, let's say, nervous anticipation. But after we were in the cab for a few minutes, I couldn't believe that he was the same guy who had written all that funny sh*t and had been so cool on the phone. He was so quiet, and I didn't know why.

RICH SCHMICK:

Like I said, I was taking it all in. Besides that, I never heard what he said to the cabdriver, and we were hauling a$$ on a desert road. I began to wonder if this was some kind of frat stunt where the wrestler gives the Internet geek a quarter and a compass, or maybe . . . just maybe . . . we

---

[2]*a work—The unreal story; opposite of a shoot.*

*DDP and "RichInKC" Schmick "in the pits" at Richard Petty's
Driving Experience outside of Las Vegas*

*were going to "live the gimmick" and go to the Mustang
Ranch.*

*Page really made me feel comfortable and like an old
friend while he told me that he had us hooked up to drive
racecars at Richard Petty's Driving Experience, which was
about 20 minutes out of town.*

*Doug Dillinger, the head of WCW security, and other
WCW officials met us, and for the next couple hours, I was
driving at "a buck twenty." When we were climbing into our
coveralls in the pit area, Page pretty much summed it up when
he said, "Rich, you just never know what to expect when you
hang out with me."*

*I couldn't stop thinking about what an unbelievable guy
he was to include me with some of the top brass from his
company.*

*There were so many truly memorable things that happened
in Las Vegas that weekend—hanging out with Page and Kimberly, being backstage, and meeting almost everybody I felt I
knew from seeing them on* Monday Night Nitro. *I came away
from the experience with a new respect for these guys, and*

saw more of what the people in the wrestling business endure than I could have ever imagined.

Rich and I had a great time that afternoon at Richard Petty's driving school, and as far as I was concerned, we were solid friends, even though we hadn't met until that trip. A few days after the trip, RichInKC asked me if he could post his second freelance report, this time telling about his trip to *Havoc*. It was that posting that led us to Brian Bentley, and soon after, we were on our way to forming a "union."

RICHINKC:

I couldn't wait to tell the world about my trip to Las Vegas at Halloween Havoc 1996. *And again, the top wrestling sites posted it. That article was more of a recap of the weekend, but I got a bunch of e-mail asking for more information about the guy who used his Diamond Cutter to beat Eddie Guerrero.*

The e-mails kept coming, and DDP was the main topic of discussion as I opened more e-mail than I thought possible.

During the early days of Page's Internet activity, he started another e-mail friendship with a young computer programmer and Web site creator. Brian Bentley had only been out of college for a couple of years, and found his current employment limiting. He left his job to start his own company, and was working out of his bedroom when he joined DDP's ever-growing circle of friends.

Brian Bentley is a whiz kid, and he can bridge the technical bullsh*t with the reality of the average computer user. We had an opportunity to create business for him, and we had a team to develop Web traffic for wrestling fans. It reminded me of some of the opportunities that were created in the bar business with cross-promotions and trade-outs. Rich, Brian, and I had chatted on-line, and the more we kicked around ideas, the more I wanted to put a site together. After our first conference call, we had a plan.

BRIAN BENTLEY
MISSING LINK MEDIA:

*After reading the posting by RichInKC of his trip, we be-
gan to communicate. My business was just two and a half
weeks old when I first got in touch with Page, and I briefly
mentioned to both Rich and Page the idea of a DDP Web site.*

*From the first time I talked with Page, I knew he had a
passion for the Internet. Rich Schmick gave us spirit and commitment from the start, and we had the right combination to
build and maintain a site. I was experimenting with a lot of
different graphic and server technology, and the creation of
DDP's site gave me an opportunity to grow.*

After speaking with Rich and Brian, we decided to create
a free Web site and call it *The Diamond Mine.* As far as we
knew, there weren't any wrestlers who had their own site.
Mark Mero and a couple of others had bulletin boards, but no
one had a site dedicated to giving Internet fans a way to stay
in touch on a regular basis. I really didn't know what to expect, and was depending on Rich and Brian to fill me in as
we went along.

I was jacked about my site, and I can recall a few of the
boys commenting that "not too many people have computers,
and if they do, they aren't wrestling fans." What I found out
quickly was that there were a lot more people in "cyberland"
than I ever imagined, and there were more on the way.

I realized that the Internet provided something for wrestling fans and for wrestlers at the same time. The "closet" fans,
as well as the die-hard marks, now had a forum where they
could chat, read gossip, look up the history, and also bitch about
wrestling to each other. On the flip side, it provided a voice for
someone other than a handful of top guys. It was an avenue for
any wrestler, even the bottom guys, to have a voice. Suddenly,
I wanted the site to be more than just the world according to
DDP, and saw it as an avenue for interaction.

RICHINKC:

We called the fans the Union Of The Diamond Cutters
(UDC), *and with that first e-mail "State of the Union" ad-*

---

[3]*Many of those "State of the Union" addresses are archived at ddpbang.com.*

dress[3] from Page, the UDC was officially born.

The response was overwhelming. We received over 200,000 hits the first month. It was incredible.

BRIAN BENTLEY
MISSING LINK MEDIA:

Collectively, we had the vision to build the site www.thediamondmine.com *into more than a personal Web page. By doing that, we established what became the model for all other wrestling superstar sites. And, remember, Page wasn't even a superstar. He was just a middle-guy who worked harder than I ever imagined anyone could. With the site up and running, Page led the way in making it more than something that was by DDP and about DDP.*

It became an outlet for wrestlers to speak candidly. For the first time, someone like Page could give his real name, admit that he and Kim were really married, or speak openly about an angle that sucked.

Rich Schmick, Brian Bentley, and I were partners in the truest sense. Each gave the other an unlimited avenue for creative release. Although Mark Mero really spawned the part-

UDC members are "in the house" for Monday Night Nitro shows.

---

[4]*hits-Internet term for the number of times a Web site is visited.*

nership with his early Internet involvement, *thediamondmine.com* was getting hits[4] that kept on coming.

RICHINKC
RICH SCHMICK:

Brian was doing some really cutting-edge stuff, using animation to enhance the look of the site. The entire thing would have never happened without him. He and his young company were doing it all for free, and it was snowballing daily.

Page was gaining fan appeal and, as the number of hits increased, so were Page's ideas. He wanted the site to be more of an alternative to what was out there.

From the start, the Union Of The Diamond Cutters *was much more than a fan club because it was the first wrestling site that actually gave the true stories of the pro wrestlers. Early* UDC *members were the first to see an exclusive interview with Bill Goldberg.*

It was during the same time that I was asked to be a contributing writer to Al Issac's Scoopwrestling.com *wrestling site. It was an honor that I could have never imagined just a few months before. I was a fan who had an opinion, and through Page, I was now making friends around the world who had read my work on both* The Diamond Mine *and* Scoops.

I knew early on that the Internet would have an impact on the wrestling business. Everyone thought I was crazy. I didn't know how much of an influence it would be, but I knew that it had no boundaries. One night, I saw a sign at a match proclaiming that a member of the *UDC* was "in the house." That's when I realized that the Internet was the way to get fans to react anytime and anywhere.

BRIAN BENTLEY:

Page wanted the site to be a forum for both the wrestlers and their fans, and it was. I really think that it was our site that created access to the talent. Goldberg had never talked before, and Page got Rich to interview him. Page also set up interviews with longtime wrestling announcer Mean Gene Okerland and veteran superstars like Steve Keirn and Harley

Race. These quickly developed into a "Q and A" forum for the average-to-rabid fan who was on-line.

Page came up with an idea to post up-to-date photos of anyone who had taken a picture with him, and invited fans to send in copies.

Rich and I knew that it would be a logistical nightmare, but Page insisted. We opened a photo gallery on the site that began to grow weekly. That move generated more traffic than I ever imagined. As a photo went up, fans told their friends to check it out.

I've heard people say that Page over-promotes, and I've heard Page admit he's a shameless self-promoter, and both may be true. The fact is that he instinctively knows how to do it better than anyone else. The thing that makes Page different is that he promotes everyone around him too, better than they can promote themselves.

The site was cooking, and I was on a mission to tell everybody I came in contact with about the impact the whole *www.com* thing was having. At the same time, people were approaching me and telling me that they had seen the site. They would ask me questions about the Net and the site, and suggest wrestlers for Rich to interview.

I knew that we had made it when World Championship Wrestling decided that I couldn't have my own Web site separate from theirs. They wanted me to kill my site or run it through their *www.wcw.com* Web site.

Other wrestlers had begun to establish Web sites, and World Championship Wrestling was enlarging theirs to accommodate the amount of traffic that sites like mine could generate. Now, this was at a time when the masses were still intimidated by "the information highway," and some huge companies were still without sites . . . and it wasn't that long ago. I looked at the situation as an opportunity, based on what we had built with our site, and I saw it as a positive tool for everyone in the company. I went to WCW's Mike Weber with the intention of becoming partners on the Internet. Also, with Brian and Rich, I had the guys who could help develop and grow other wrestler sites within WCW's site.

More importantly, I was very concerned that we would lose our editorial and creative control if we just handed the site over to WCW. It was Rich and Brian who had built and maintained this communication machine, and they were going wherever the site was going.

I was ready to go to the mats to fight for this one.

BRIAN BENTLEY:

Page was like my agent at that meeting. He was not going to let the site get away without Rich and I getting something for our efforts. At one point, Page got up and was ready to leave the meeting and site behind.

He said, "Fu*k this! They can have it . . . we'll go off and start another official Web site!"

There was no doubt that he was serious, even if he was bluffing. The end result was that we leased the site to World Championship Wrestling for a nominal fee for the length of Page's contract. Today, both Rich and I are contracted and paid to maintain and recreate the site weekly.

I knew from that visit to Atlanta that he was a rare guy. While we were out at a famous Atlanta nightclub, one wrestler after another complimented me for what we had done for Page. He constantly gave Rich and I the spotlight when, clearly, Page was the reason for it all.

RICH SCHMICK:

So many doors were opening as a result of the site. There has always been a lot of work and hundreds of late-night calls from Page, but in addition to my column at Scoops, *I was on the WCW payroll. As Page climbed the ladder in the ring, so did our number of hits. Being linked through WCW slowed the process slightly, but our membership grew, and our* UDC *members were now discovering the WCW site, as well as others. At the same time, we made a few adjustments and came up with ways to separate the* Union Of The Diamond Cutters *and to create new interest.*

It has always been free to link to the site, but we created another free "members-only" group where, periodically, registered members would receive exclusive mail.

ddpbang.com *was created by Brian Bentley and his company, missinglinkmedia.net. Here, DDP is pictured with Brian and his wife, Melinda.*

Obviously, there were many factors that contributed to the crowd getting with me. My work ethic, The Diamond Cutter, the hand sign, and my new intro music were just a few reasons that the tide turned. But the Internet was huge. Sure, I could hear the fan reactions in the arenas, but the Web was a way to find out what people were thinking

The www.thediamondmine.com site is now located at *www.ddpbang*.com, and it has matured into the prototype for many Web sites. DDP's site was nearing an unheard-of one million hits a month before the site was even a year old. By current standards, a million hits, while still impressive, is not nearly as lofty a number as it was in 1996.

The popularity of Diamond Dallas Page was increasing with every match and every e-mail to the *Union Of The Diamond Cut-*

ters. While DDP was entrenched in a solid middle-card feud with Eddie Guerrero, the road was taking a quick turn, and the obnoxious, loudmouth heel, who got booed from coast to coast in three different wrestling federations, was building a grass-roots union on the World Wide Web. As of this writing, there are over 24,000 members (and growing) of DDP's e-group who receive the weekly "State of the Union" address.

It's great to be able to look back at the role that *The Diamond Mine* played in making the steps up the ladder so sweet. Currently on our site, there are enough pages to keep any fan entertained and informed about the week-to-week happenings of this yo-yo journey and those who have joined us for the ride.

To pinpoint the creation of *The Diamond Mine* as the turning point for the fans wouldn't be fair. It wouldn't be fair to The Diamond Cutter, The Diamond Sign, The Self-High Five, or The Bang!

As DDP the wrestler was coming out of the gutter, thanks to my unknown benefactor, I could feel the reaction and the interpretation of the planet changing.

CHAPTER SEVENTEEN

THE GUTTER, THE MIDDLE, AND THE nWo

When Diamond Dallas Page decided that a life in the ring was his future in wrestling, his goal was to be able to consistently work at the middle of the card. The feud with Johnny B. Badd helped establish that position for DDP, and it put him in a place that most thought was unreachable. That aborted program made more fans and foes realize that he would continue to work hard and make the best of his shot.

Mero and I would have blown the roof off had we had the chance to finish the program, but, more importantly, I had made it to the middle of the card. The next few months were going to be important, just as every feud and every program would be from that point on.

I remember going to Dusty's house right after Mark Mero left the company. At the time, Dusty was far removed from the business, but that night he furthered my education by not being able to give the answer to the equation.

"Page, you got yourself to the middle," he said. "And to tell you the truth, I don't know how you were able to fight your way this far. I wish I could tell you where to go from here, but I can't.

The only thing I do know is that the next jump is the hardest. The next spot is the key spot."

Did someone say . . . gutter? They wrote the yo-yo into the angle, and they never knew they were doing it.

DUSTY RHODES:

Persistence got him to where he was, and, on that alone, I knew he could get to that next spot. I just didn't know how to tell him to get there. There is no formula or secret to that puzzle. All I knew was that everybody who had ever gotten there had done it their own way.

In our business, there is an upper tier of guys, and until a wrestler can reach up and touch someone at that level, he'll remain in that crowded pack. Sometimes the company just determines that it is time to reach up, and sometimes it just comes down to being in the right place at the right time.

Page was determined to entertain the crowd with his flair and style until his time came, because there was never a plan to put him there.

"The Booty Man" beat me and took Kimberly as his ring valet, and the story line continued with DDP looking for work. It was revealed that it was actually Kimberly who was rich, not me. Apparently, I didn't own those diamond mines in South Africa after all. No more limos, jewelry, and glitter . . . and no more glitz. My beard and hair grew longer . . . and, I guess, I even lost my comb.

As the angle played out, I lost everything. Diamond Dallas Page had hit rock bottom; busted, disgusted, and could hardly be . . . Good Gawd . . . trusted. I was living on the streets of Las Vegas, and was penniless. Go figure . . .

KIMBERLY:

I was now appearing as "The Booty Girl," getting somewhat of a push and developing new fans. They were happy to see me rid myself of that DDP character who was now a bum on the streets selling his possessions.

Of course, the angle produced even more doubt that Page

and I were married . . . but then again, some people were convinced that Page really had been living in the lap of luxury and was now panhandling.

The Booty Man had ended DDP's ring career according to the stipulations of the final match at *Uncensored.* That marked the end of DDP as he was known; a wealthy, egotistical heal. He had been stripped of his wealth and possessions, and the cameras now focused on his plight as a homeless former wrestler. Diamond Dallas Page had lost the girl and his lavish lifestyle, and was now a social outcast. His skyrocketing debt forced him into a series of comical situations that played out on TV for nearly three months.

The angle had a film student capture a man resembling DDP on an amateur video documentary he was making on the plight of the homeless. The student would sell the video to the WCW, rather than the tabloids that wanted to present the shocking turn of events.

Of course, World Championship Wrestling outbid the TV tabloids for the video, and aired it on a telecast. From that point on, we were rolling tape as the camera followed me to the dregs of the earth.

I was seen scalping day-old tickets to a rodeo at half price, only to get away before my victim found out that the tickets were worthless. I sold my wrestling gear, hocked my rings, and worked a street corner as a windshield washer. And, for more drama, I was doing it in the rain. When I demanded payment, the driver noticed who I used to be, and refused to pay.

The segments were pretty funny, and included scenes reinforcing that I was actually down and out in Vegas. I did it all—76rummaged through trash cans, scammed, begged, and peddled.

In reality, I was home with an Atlanta-based Turner film crew shooting scenes downtown, a few blocks from the CNN building.

One of my favorite scams happened while I was working in the middle of a median strip in what was thought to be Las

Vegas. I was one of those homeless guys who holds a sign, but my sign had a twist. Diamond Dallas Page had resorted to: "WILL WRESTLE FOR FOOD." Now, that's not hilarious, but it is funny.

What was hilarious was what happened during the taping.

"STAGGER" LEE MARSHALL
FORMER WCW ANNOUNCER:

Page's vignettes had been airing during telecasts, but I hadn't seen him in several weeks. I was staying at the Omni Hotel in Atlanta, as I always did when my WCW duties were at the home offices.

The town was jammed with several conventions, including a surgeons' conference. Most of the doctors were staying at the Omni, and taxicabs were difficult to find.

I finally got into a taxi with four surgeons who were talking about the latest pulmonary breakthroughs. Our travel route took us through the busiest downtown streets of Atlanta, where it was not unusual to see a half dozen homeless people huddled on a corner. As we paused for traffic, I spotted a taller-than-normal homeless man rising from a seated position.

I was totally in character with scruffy, worn, ill-fitting clothes. My sign and I were baking in the "Las Vegas" sun as the tape rolled, showing me approaching various cars. A taxi was slowing at the corner to make a turn, when the window went down, and I saw a familiar face.

LEE MARSHALL:

Opening a window in the city heat and humidity of the Deep South is crazy. So when I began to roll it down, the surgeons, who thought I was one of them, looked my way.

The tall homeless guy started jumping up and down and screaming, "Marshall! Hey, Lee Marshall! Over here! Lee, it's me . . . Page!"

I've known Page a long time, so seeing him stripped of his gimmicks, without the jewelry and the animal skins, was shocking enough, but Page looked every bit the part of a homeless person. His pants were too short, his shirt was in shreds, his beard was grown out, his shoes were tattered, and his hair was dirty looking. Even the sign was beat up.

It quickly became evident to me that it was part of the angle. So, I yelled back, "Page! . . . Page! . . . How ya doin'?"

The taxi began to move on. Before I closed the window, I looked into the back of the car, only to see my surgeon buddies with their mouths wide open.

"You know him?" one of them asked.

I answered confidently and matter-of-factly, "Yep."

They seemed shocked and a bit uncomfortable about the experience. I could tell there was an obvious difference in their opinions of a human life on an operating table and a human life on a street corner; especially one who proclaimed his wrestling prowess as a way to get food.

Yes indeed, Diamond Dallas Page was at work and living the gimmick within the angle.

The angle was intended to make some sort of sense of the riches-to-rags story of DDP. The scripts and vignettes were, at times, humorous; and at other times, ridiculous. And they never received critical acclaim. In fact, far from it.

The demise of DDP and his road to the gutter lasted over three months, so, during that time, Page went back to his regimen of daily workouts at The Power Plant and the gym, and weekly physical therapy.

Even the casual fan compares the on-screen battles of professional wrestling with the drama of a soap opera, and the changes and swerves within the story are actually anticipated and expected. The in-the-gutter angle took a drastic turn when it was revealed that a mysterious benefactor had offered a hand to the skid-row version of Diamond Dallas Page.

I owe it all to the benefactor, I guess, since he, or was it she, financed my comeback. More significantly, the benefactor hired a team of lawyers to find loopholes in the contract that erroneously terminated my career with World Championship Wrestling.

We won the case, and I was reinstated and ready to climb out of the gutter, all thanks to the benefactor.

So, who was the benefactor? Trivia fans know that it remains an unanswered question, but here's the answer. I was sleeping with her then . . . and I'm sleeping with her now . . . yes, it was Kimberly the whole time.

KIMBERLY:

The Booty Man character was not working, and the gimmick was scrapped. Although I still had time on my contract, this was an end to my ring involvement for awhile. We completed the Playboy *reshoots, which had increased from two to six pages around the same time.*

The *Playboy* shoot for the *Nude Celebrities Edition* evolved into something larger than life, and, ironically, had its own little built-in yo-yo.

Kimberly had appeared in other newsstand editions as "Kimberly Page," but never as the Diamond Doll or Mrs. Diamond Dallas Page, the wrestler's wife.

There had been talk of including a shot of me in the ring, as well as a couple of shots of me with Kimberly. This was the first time that I ever came anywhere close to being called a celebrity, and it was exciting. We were even more jacked when we heard that Cindy Crawford, Pamela Anderson, and Jenny McCarthy were also going to be featured. After *Playboy* saw the test sheets, they decided to reshoot with the possibility of increasing the number of pages.

KIMBERLY:

The shoot went better than we hoped, and Jeff Cohen and Cynthia Kaye thought Page was a terrific addition. It's certainly worth ordering a back issue just to see my husband, the over-the-top DDP, helping me with the womanly chore of polishing my toenails. The photos of us together were classy, very entertaining, and, at times, amusing.

And we were hot too. I was proud of every one of Kim's modeling sessions, including everything that she had done with *Playboy*, but the increased "ink" in the magazine made me a bit paranoid.

The magazine did indeed have some top female celebrities who posed nude for *Playboy* photographers, but there were also women who were linked to their celebrity mates. Along with Diamond Dallas Page, actors Kelsey Grammer and Lorenzo Lamas appeared (clothed, of course) with their lovely ladies. The list of stars was impressive, and also included Samantha Fox, Anna Nicole Smith, Nancy Sinatra, and many of the *Baywatch* babes.

The magazine was projected to break all sales records with the upcoming newsstand edition of *Playboy's Nude Celebrities*.

I was ecstatic and proud that we, as a couple, were featured in *Playboy*. But, somehow, I appeared in *Playboy* a lot more than I originally expected. Instead of just an inset photo or something similar, I wound up on a lot of pages—so many that I was on almost every one. The spread tied a slim and sexy version of Anna Nicole Smith for "most pages" in the magazine.

In my excited state, I told Eric Bischoff, who gave me a strange stare and asked if the Turner people had "okayed" the added exposure.

My heart sank. It was a potential problem since the added associations with Disney and Time Warner had caused a more conservative attitude that neither old-school wrestling nor Vince McMahon ever had to worry about before.

It was known, but never flaunted, within the company that Kimberly had done some work for *Playboy*. But now I was in the magazine with her, and the increased number of pages would also increase the amount of publicity to more than was originally expected. I was worried about how "corporate" would interpret the whole deal, and how it would affect my job. Fortunately, Bischoff and I never discussed it again, and I decided to stay as low-key as possible and see how it all played out.

With both real and perceived drama, on and off TV for Diamond Dallas Page, he also used his time at home to develop a passion that even he might have thought impossible at one time.

With Rich and Bentley maintaining the Web site, I cut down my time on-line; although I was still giving DDP's weekly "State of the Union" addresses. Since I was home a lot, I *slooowly* began to enjoy reading.

No kidding. The same kid who became stressed when he had to read in front of people was actually enjoying it. It was tough for me, though. I still had to slow way down so that I could see all the words.

Kim and I each had a book going. Usually, I was reading something that she had suggested to me, but I was also searching for various topics that interested me. It was something we could do together, and we both looked forward to our reading time.

KIMBERLY:

I tried to choose books that I had already read and knew Page would find interesting. Then I would ask him what was going on in the story to make sure that he understood what he read. He took his time, and after he finished a book, he'd look forward to starting another.

It is difficult to keep me from being on the telephone, and it is even more difficult for me to stop living, breathing, and sleeping wrestling; but I found reading, once my biggest fear, to be fun. Author Carl Hiaasen, who often writes intriguing stories that originate in south Florida, became my favorite.

Reading became an enjoyable and entertaining part of my life later than for most, and I know that almost everyone takes reading for granted. With audio and video so expansive in our society, it seems that people have forgotten the importance and rewards of reading.

I know from my own experience that it opened doors that I never knew about, and it has given me knowledge, a sense of power, and confidence that is part of my present life.

I had always heard people say that they "liked the movie ... but the book was better," so after seeing a film about the life of Satchel Paige, I read the book.

Satchel was one of the greatest baseball players ever. He was a man of little education, but one of tremendous endurance and perseverance. For years, Paige was a dominating force in the Negro baseball leagues, and not only did he have to deal with the social prejudices of the times, but he was kept from competing at a level that allowed him to show his talents to the masses. Satchel was a great communicator who was outspoken about the years that were lost before Jackie Robinson finally shattered the racial barriers in professional baseball.

He pitched for years, and, through it all, his drive and tenacity were unmatched. His love of baseball became more of an obsession, and, by all rights, it should have been Satchel Paige who got the shot to end segregation in baseball.

There was always the question of his age . . . and everyone wondered just how old he was. Hell, people had heard of him for years in his obscurity with the Negro leagues. They figured he must have been 50 or more when he finally got to the "show," and the topic of his age obsessed people. They said he couldn't belong because of his race, and once he did, they wanted to show why he wouldn't last. They questioned his records, his level of competition, and, most of all, his age.

Until the day I walk away from regular competition, people will probably speculate about my age too. It has always been a way for all of my critics to attack me, to underestimate me, and to devalue me in some way.

The more I read about Satchel, the more I could relate, and I drew from him for my motivation and a new sense of assurance. I was in the best shape of my career, mentally and physically, and I was ready to tell the world.

It was Satchel Paige's famous quote, but now, "Dallas Page" was using it every chance I got. When anyone asked my age, I answered in the same way that Satchel did—by answering with another question. "Let me ask you a question . . . If you didn't know how old you was . . . how old would you be?"

Think about it. If there wasn't a system for measuring the aging of our minds and bodies, and there was no way to know what a certain age was supposed to be like . . . then how old would someone be? How old would someone feel? Me? . . . I'm 29 again.

It was no secret that I started late, but I wondered why no one was talking about why I did deserve a shot. I had worked hard, trained in and out the ring, and paid my dues. And I had something to offer. I began to tell it like it was, and I was shooting every chance I got. I wasn't the heel manager who was the walking gimmick who would make loud and wild claims about what he could do in the ring.

But, it was the way I felt.

When Diamond Dallas Page returned to the ring, he came back to an unusual debut, thanks to the benefactor. He had returned to the over-the-top DDP, but this time, the gimmick was pumped up to include $75 cigars, high-fashion clothing from Versace, and more jewelry than ever. The benefactor angle placed DDP in the middle of "The Battle Bowl" at the PPV known as *Slamboree 1996*, where the winner would walk away with the title, World Championship Wrestling's "Lord of the Rings."

Diamond Dallas Page was an upset winner at that PPV, using a series of Diamond Cutters to walk away with a victory in his first match back.

"STAGGER" LEE MARSHALL:

The title "Lord of the Rings" was not nearly the coveted title that it appeared to be. There was no belt associated with it, and it was a promo angle that never took off. Page may have been the last one to hold that distinction.

The thing I remember most about Page winning was that he did a better job promoting the honor after he won it. He was proud of the title, and used it in his interviews to warn the world that with the Diamond Cutter as his finishing move, he would be a force to reckon with.

People started to talk about the move more, and from an announcer's standpoint, the Diamond Cutter was something that we could build up to in each of his matches. I marveled at how he was getting his finishing move over, when most guys in that spot didn't even have a finish . . . and if they did, no one cared.

It was crazy. People began to pop for me, like I was a babyface. The whole underdog, hard-work ethic angle that was the real story started playing out to the fans. Internet subscribers and average fans began to anticipate the Diamond Cutter, and interviewers asked me about it all the time.

I figured, *Fu*k it.* If the bookers were going to listen to the fans, then I was ready to put it into full gear. It was time to tell my story in more interviews. I pretty much said, "Look at me, I'm not supposed to be here . . . but I worked hard to be in this spot."

I took Reece's advice and started using the hand signal every time. Lee Marshall and I came up with the "self-high-five" hand-slap. It was a way to tell the world that I stood alone, and only needed myself to celebrate my new place in the world of wrestling.

The fans dug it, and by the time I entered into my next program with Eddie Guerrero, the "good-guy-bad-guy" reaction of the crowd was mixed. The cool part was that they were getting louder.

LEE MARSHALL:

From my vantage point, it was pretty astonishing that Page was able to continue to turn the crowd when the very basics of the angle pitted a big man against a smaller, more tactful wrestler like Eddie Guerrero. The Guerrero family was legendary in the business, and Eddie was the top mid-card guy, just a notch below the big men in the top tier.

Typically, one of the easiest ways for a guy to get heat is to fight and beat a smaller opponent. Page stands at least 6'5", and Guerrero is, at the most, 5'10".

The angle wasn't the big story; it was the fact that working with a professional like Eddie Guerrero made it exciting for the fans. Eddie is one of the top highflyers in the game, and the threat of the Diamond Cutter was beginning to take hold. I never planned or imagined that the fans would start getting with me as quickly as they did.

The feud continued when DDP was defeated by Guerrero at *The Clash of the Champions* PPV, only to come back to sideline

Eddie with a series of Diamond Cutters in ensuing matches. The angle was altered when Chavo Guerrero, Eddie's nephew, took his injured uncle's place. By the time Chavo took a devastating Cutter at *Fall Brawl*, the finish, the sign, the Web site, and Diamond Dallas Page were getting more over.

The world of professional wrestling was about to go through a rebirth. It had been nearly a year since Turner Broadcasting, with Eric Bischoff at the helm of WCW, had begun to televise one hour of *Monday Night Nitro* on live TV. The popularity was building quickly, and *Monday Night Nitro* was increased to three prime-time hours. It was the upstart for Bischoff, who was ready to go head-to-head with Vince McMahon and his *WWF Monday Raw!* program on the USA cable network.

There had been some changes at both federations. The most significant was when two of the sport's newest and biggest super-stars decided to return to World Championship Wrestling. Kevin Nash, known as "Diesel," and Scott Hall, known as "Razor Ramon," had left WWF.

Hall and Nash fought and lost the legal battle to WWF to keep

The formation of the nWo had Eric Bischoff and World Championship Wrestling flying high atop the TV ratings.

their Diesel and Razor Ramon identities after leaving. Their long-time friendship and natural bond resulted in their teaming up as a tag team known as "The Outsiders." Together, they eventually distanced themselves from the rest of the WCW talent, calling themselves the "New World Order."

The formation of the New World Order not only rocked World Championship Wrestling, but it rocked the entire world of wrestling. Eric Bischoff was the originator and creator of the idea to form a new alliance of wrestlers within World Championship Wrestling. He called it the "nWo," and the idea may have been spawned in my garage on one of those nights when Eric and I would grab a beer and shoot the sh*t. We would literally throw hundreds of ideas at one another, and even though the "uprising of rebels" really wasn't a new idea, it had never been done the way Eric had it planned.

The New World Order was formed as a new federation. It had its own select members, set of rules, look, attitude, and agenda. The nWo was Eric Bischoff's baby, and he was committed to establishing a unit that would work cohesively, on and off camera. It was important to assemble the right combination of talent so that the New World Order was feared and hated from the start. It was an exclusive bunch, and, in its early days, Bischoff's role was strictly behind-the-scenes. Soon after, the nWo had their own referees, announcer (Bischoff), and, more importantly, an all-star lineup.

It was apparent that the New World Order led by Nash and Hall would be a formidable team, but the biggest surprise came when Hulk Hogan joined the group. Hogan, who had been the most over babyface in history, announced to the world that he would be known as "Hollywood" Hogan, and that he didn't care about his fans or the WCW. The switchboards at WCW were flooded with phone calls hoping that the news about Hulk becoming the bad guy, Hollywood Hogan, wasn't true. But Hogan, Hall, and Nash were now the nWo, which had set its sights on controlling the world of wrestling.

The team boasted three of the biggest names in the industry, and, from week to week, wrestling fans around the world wondered who would be next to defect to the New World Order.

Monday night TV changed, and Turner's WCW began a long stretch of dominating ratings over the WWF. The combined ratings of the two televised wrestling shows proved to be more than a formidable challenge for prime-time ratings. Even the NFL's twenty-some-year tradition of *Monday Night Football* was losing their fan base to wrestling.

World Championship Wrestling as a company had what seemed like all the top names in professional wrestling, past and present. Hogan, Savage, Ric Flair, and Roddy Piper were wildly popular legends. Lex Lugar and Sting were longtime WCW main-event mainstays. Now, with Nash and Hall back in Atlanta as part of the nWo, WCW formed a huge nationwide fan base. And, of course, there were plenty of guys with enormous potential, like Paul "The Giant" Wight, The Steiner Brothers, Chris Benoit, Marcus "Buff" Bagwell, and Bill Goldberg who was fresh out of The Plant. There were also guys who should have moved up, but couldn't, and plenty of would-be superstars who had already bailed out.

Emotions, at that time, were pretty much a shoot. Hall and Nash were not happy with the situation at WCW. To them, it was reminiscent of our early days in the business.

That night, in Macon, when Scott Hall returned to a thunderous pop, he teased the crowd that he was bringing "the big man" with him next week, and "The Outsiders" were born. It was huge for our company to have these guys back after they had become so popular while in the WWF. As they added members, the fans began to see the New World Order as an alternative force in pro wrestling.

KEVIN NASH
WCW SUPERSTAR:

When Bischoff first presented the idea, I didn't like it. But Scott Hall and I had reunited in the ring, and had formed The Outsiders, and that felt good.

We had been back for awhile, and were disenchanted with the whole deal. We had one-year deals, but within the first few months, I was considering going back to New York. It was the same as it had been before, too crowed at the top. Hall and I were really The Outsiders in more ways than one. Scott and I were more like city guys, considerably different than the other guys and the overall atmosphere in Atlanta.

It started to get good when we added Sean "The Kid" Waltham as the sixth member of the New World Order when he came to WCW from New York. All of a sudden, I was running with three of the five guys who I had hung out and traveled with for the last few years in the WWF.

Ted DiBiase, who was known as "The Million Dollar Man," was added as manager and mouthpiece for the group, and the New World Order gained steam. With the upcoming additions of "Sixx Pac" Sean Waltham and Paul "The Giant" Wight, everyone wondered who would be next to join this group.

Scott Hall and Kevin Nash created what seemed to be an immovable force. Hogan was lashing back at his fans, and whenever the New World Order showed up, they would create havoc. They disrupted matches or rushed the ring to make sure that they finished opponents by surrounding them with two, three, or more nWo henchmen.

The nWo was running wild and taking control of the matches and the crowd, but, at the same time, fans were reacting more positively to me. I never expected or wanted the fans to cheer me. I hadn't been the clear-cut fan choice as the good guy in the Guerrero feud, but it was the Diamond Cutter that was moving people to the edge of their seats. When I first heard the crowds begin the chant of "DDP! DDP!", I thought of Jake.

I knew that my initials sounded like "DDT," which was the chant that filled arenas every time Jake Roberts entered the ring. His DDT finishing maneuver had been so over for so long that the chants would begin as soon as he climbed in the ring. DDP had a finish like Jake's DDT, and it was natural to react in anticipation of the Diamond Cutter.

It was always about timing, and, although I tried to be patient, my timing never seemed to be right when it came to contract time. I wanted to stay at World Championship Wrestling, not because I didn't want to go to New York, but because I had hung in and lasted longer than they thought I would.

Some said I was too old, too green, too loud, or too whatever. Then there were others who threw enough dirt to "bury" five guys. There were plenty of guys who admired my work ethic and intensity, but even they never believed that I would make it to the top.

One of my most vocal doubters in the beginning wound up being a close friend, supporter, and motivator. Brian Pillman was one of those "guys in the middle" who I first met during the early WCW years, while I was a bottom-guy rookie. When I came back to WCW following the independent circuit, I was lucky enough to really get to know him.

They were tough times for the guys in the middle at WCW, and eventually, Austin, Cactus Jack (Mick Foley), Mero, and Pillman all left for what they thought would be greener pastures.

Brian had been critical of my gimmick and my ring work in the beginning, but he was a student too, and he had noticed my improvement and told me so. Brian Pillman was a tough sell, and a guy who I never thought would see me as a legitimate wrestler. Changing his opinion of me meant something.

Pillman and I became close, and we also became each other's motivation at times. When times were bad, we found ways to help each other. Whether it was when my future looked even more dismal than the futures of the guys around me, or when Brian's demons and desires began to tempt him, we had developed a tight bond. We would talk by phone when we were both in different states of depression and frustration, and whoever needed it the most seemed to get pulled out of it after a good talk.

Many times in my career, I thought I was ready to make the next step, but I remember Brian calling me and saying, "Dallas, you are a big star waiting to happen. If you were in New York, you would be a top guy." Hearing that gave me a surge of energy and a boost of confidence. Anyone who knew him knows that Brian wasn't the type to "candy-coat" his statements.

After Brian was injured in a car accident, the pain and the pressure began to mount for him. He wasn't working much,

Brian Pillman was one of DDP's biggest critics. He later suggested that Page make the move to New York.

and when he did, he was in constant pain. I had been working on the road more, and had lost touch with him for a brief time when the world heard about his sudden death.

It was so sad, and it is still sad when I think back or see photos of Brian Pillman. He was a great guy, a good friend, and a charismatic worker, who had even more talent than we, unfortunately, never got to see. Brian was a straight shooter and the kind of guy who would tell it like it is. When he was critical, we knew it was the way he really felt, and he was going to shoot on his opinions on any selected topic. At the same time, he was one sarcastic son-of-a-bitch, and, like Austin, he could be brutal. Austin and Pillman have to be the all-time ball-breaking backroom tag team champions of the world.

Inside the ring and in front of the camera, Brian had it, and I know that he would have been one of the biggest draws in wrestling today. His injury and tragic death came right before wrestling had its resurgence, and I wish Brian could have been there to enjoy it with us.

I've got to agree with Brian's widow, Melanie, who reminded me that Brian probably had a hand in our success from above. She's right . . . I can see him working his way into that big booking committee in the sky . . . infiltrating the wrestling gods and shining a bright light into the ring below.

I'll never forget the look on Brian's face the night that "the loose cannon" worked the world when he slapped Kevin Sullivan, and delivered the now classic line, "I quit, Mister Booker Man!"

Miss you, bro.

Once I had reached mid-card, the tide began to turn, and guys who thought I would never last felt that the longer I stayed at WCW, the less chance I would have to see the top tier. They were encouraged by their new starts in New York, and thought I should look north at contract time.

Maybe I was just stubborn, but I saw it differently.

Even with all those perennial and potential superstars, I saw myself as someone who could contribute to the company. Not that I think anyone at the top felt the same way, but coming off the Mero and Guerrero feuds, I felt like I was starting to get it as the fans hinted that they were getting with me.

To all the "rag sheet" writers and finger-pointers out there, I can say that my contract meeting with Eric Bischoff didn't take place in my garage. There was no special treatment and no stroke[1] when it came to money or benefits.

I reluctantly signed a two-year contract that took me into 1999, and wasn't happy about it. We agreed on the first-year salary based on my middle-card status coming out of the Guerrero feud, but Bischoff and I disagreed on the second year of the deal. There was to be a slight increase, but the figure was still very average. I never asked for anything that wasn't due me, and there were plenty of guys working less and making more. I knew that the payroll was up, and that the card would be as hard or harder to climb, but I wanted to be treated the same as everyone else. My perception and Bischoff's reality of the situation left me wanting to prove myself all over again.

Page had watched three of the guys who he had come up with, along with two of the biggest names in wrestling history, create an organization that was arguably responsible for the overwhelming

---

[1] *stroke—Clout or special consideration.*

mainstream success of wrestling in the late '90s. He had shared rides, hard times, and his innermost thoughts with Bischoff, Hall, and Nash, and had gained the respect of Hulk Hogan. The nWo was the feature and the franchise, and seemed like the future of World Championship Wrestling.

With the addition of Randy "Macho Man" Savage, the New World Order had not only taken control of World Championship Wrestling, but it catapulted the ratings of *Monday Night Nitro!*

After so many years of being the "other" promotion, WCW was not only competing and winning, they were trouncing the WWF week after week. It was like the upstarts in the South had lanced the giant in the North. The battle was being fought over TV ratings and PPV buy-rates, and also went into the courtrooms. The competition between professional wrestling promotions rages on to this day. But, the battle that changed the entire war was the formation of the nWo.

I watched my bro's, Nash and Hall, and wondered if and when they would ask me to join them in the New World Order. I knew them from the Diamond Stud and Vinnie Vegas days, and if anyone wanted to help change the order of the world of wrestling at that time, it was Diamond Dallas Page.

For a brief time, I thought about what it would have been like to be there when they formed the nWo, but as time went on and other members were added, the invitation began to lose its value to me.

SCOTT HALL
THE NEW WORLD ORDER:

Dalli was finally becoming more like the guy we all knew behind the scenes. He was becoming popular with the fans for being the type of guy he really was. He is the most positively motivated and hardest worker in wrestling, although his character and persona can sometimes become overbearing. I remember unwinding with Bischoff after a show and suggesting that the fans get the chance to see Page the way he really was.

ERIC BISCHOFF:

I knew Page thought he was ready, and there were many times in his career when I had seen his frustration and really felt for him. He had obstacles that others didn't, and, in some ways, he needed to go through all of those things to get to where he really needed to be. I believed it was time to show the real Diamond Dallas Page.

As part of the story, Hall and Nash finally extended an offer to me, but it just didn't work. They wanted me to be their eighth or ninth member, not knowing that once they got to their fourth or fifth member, my mind was pretty much made up. DDP was prepared to stand alone.

The nWo became more of a factor, and during the end of my feud with Guerrero, they made their presence felt in our matches. They were running wild in WCW, and had added "Buff" Bagwell and Scott Norton, among others. They interfered, and cost me a victory over Guerrero that created a match between Norton and Guerrero at *Clash of the Champions XXXIV*.

But, on that night, I avenged my loss by coming to Eddie's aid. With my Diamond Cutter, I grabbed Norton and bang!, he went down. Eddie covered him for the victory.

My interference put more nWo heat on me, and a match was set up between me and Norton at the *Souled Out* PPV.

I was one of the few remaining members of World Championship Wrestling who had successfully retaliated against the nWo and refused the offer to join them. Nash and Hall wanted to see if their old friend would refuse the offer in person. Bischoff was heading them up by now, and it seemed everything was going the way the New World Order wanted it to.

KEVIN "BIG SEXY" NASH:

Scott and I decided that we would confront Page in New Orleans at the Superdome on Monday Night Nitro! *There had been some trouble convincing him, but we felt that he was ready to join us for life. We knew that Page wanted to be asked by Scott and me, and in New Orleans, we both entered the ring as he was preparing to tell the world his decision.*

The fans liked that I was taking a stand against the nWo.

The threat of the Diamond Cutter had given me a weapon that I could use against anyone. I knew they had strength with their growing numbers, but I refused to give in to them.

Hall and Nash asked me to join the nWo that night, and they offered me a shirt as an invitation. When I took the shirt, the crowd seemed disappointed, but both Hall and Nash were ecstatic. Nash climbed up to the second rope with his arms raised in victory as Scott Hall extended his hand to me.

KEVIN NASH:

When I turned around, I saw Scott sprawled out on the canvas as a result of a Diamond Cutter. I attacked Page, but he ducked me and fled the ring before the rest of the nWo could get him. We got our answer, and planned revenge against Diamond Dallas Page.

Hall never saw it coming as I grabbed his hand and pulled him into the cravat, and, bang!, he was cut down. The world heard me refuse the New World Order for the last time.

Scott Hall taking a Diamond Cutter was huge. At that point, he was, by far, the biggest name to feel the bang!, and, at the same time, was a friend who was putting the move and me over. (Thanks, Chico.) I was in a full-fledged feud with the nWo, and was becoming even more the crowd favorite.

I had all the reasons for fans to boo me back then . . . which, at the time, was good. But that changed drastically after I rejected my old bro's, Hall and Nash.

World Championship Wrestling was dominating the cable TV ratings wars, and there was no doubt that the success of the New World Order was a major factor. Bischoff was taking more of an on-air role as the heel leader, but, behind the scenes, he had turned WCW into a ratings monster and, more importantly, a moneymaker.

The commitment by Turner Broadcasting began to pay off as arenas across the country were selling out. Merchandising was exploding, and wrestling fans around the world started to recognize the nWo as wrestling's future.

When Bischoff made an on-air decree for all WCW wrestlers to sign nWo contracts within 30 days, I became the first to deny the New World Order.

For the most part, all of the top guys had gone to the nWo. As wrestlers announced their allegiance for one side or the other, there was one guy who remained a mystery.

Steve Borden, better known to wrestling fans as "Sting," is one of the cornerstones of World Championship Wrestling. Along with Lex Lugar, he goes back to the early days of Turner's involvement. Although his character always had the same name, Sting became a silent, mysterious man who resembled the character in the movie *The Crow*. He wore face paint and a long black jacket, and carried a baseball bat. But, it was Sting's entrances that were the most anticipated, as he dropped from the rafters from heights of over 70 feet in the air.

As I was writing this book, the wrestling community lost one of its own using a similar entrance. Owen Hart died tragically when his character, "The Blue Blazer," fell while attempting to ride a cable into the ring at a WWF Pay-Per-View.

The actual details are still unclear, but whatever happened that night in Kansas City is a reminder to the world of how precious life can be. Wrestlers, past and present, know that any bump, stunt, or fall can end a career, but the loss of Owen Hart was especially difficult for the boys. The history of the Hart family has been well-documented, and Stu, Brett, Owen, and the entire family have made a lasting and positive impression on the business. What we do as entertainers and athletes is often times very dangerous. I know that the fact that the outcome of a match is part of a program or story line makes what we do seem unbelievable, but each of us has certain fears and thresholds when it comes to stunts. It's always tough to lose a contemporary, but the loss of Owen Hart was especially devastating for many of us. The fans and members of the wrestling community can't feel or absorb the loss of a son, a brother, a father, and a daddy.

Sting's entrances caused major reactions, and were truly spec-
tacular. Every appearance by Sting was dramatic, and he was
cheered wildly by the crowds. He was feared by the New World
Order, although he seldom wrestled them. For months, Sting intimidated the nWo with the threat of his intervention in their matches.

Sting was clearly kryptonite to the mighty New World Order,
and the eyes of thousands looked to the rafters when the New
World Order appeared. Often, the nWo showed up in force at the
conclusion of matches to ambush the contestants. They were ren-
egades in every sense of the word until Sting would appear.

To be on the same side of the nWo issue as Sting was like
climbing another rung to the main event. I was jacked up by
it all, but at the same time, I knew I was still on the fringe of
something big. As always, I watched the replays, and hearing Diamond Dallas Page mentioned in the same promos as
Sting, Hall, Nash, Lugar, Savage, and even Hogan gave me
goosebumps. Living a dream? You bet your a$$!

While DDP refused to side with the New World Order, his ring
career was making victorious strides. His entrance music was met
with standing approval, and the diamond sign was being raised
above the heads of more fans every night. But, it was the Dia-
mond Cutter that everyone was waiting to see.

*Having the endorsement of "Sting" and Rowdy Roddy Piper
firmly established DDP, and the trio battled the rival nWo.*

My confrontation with the nWo put me into the main story line, and while that was happening, I was winning with the Diamond Cutter. Normally, two scenarios would take place, with the end result usually putting me facedown in the ring.

The nWo was famous for their run-ins at the end of matches. Whenever I was matched against another opponent, they would get involved at the end of a match. After winning a match with a Diamond Cutter, various members of the New World Order ran in and blasted me from all angles, leaving me in a heap in the middle of the ring.

MARK MADDEN
WRESTLING JOURNALIST:

Even though the fans loved the New World Order, Page won them over since they wanted to see someone stand up to the nWo. As more superstars jumped on the nWo bandwagon, it was DDP and, of course, Sting who clearly sided against them.

My stand against the nWo got Sting's endorsement when he dropped from the rafters wielding his bat to stop their assaults on me. Often times, the fans watched me win with a Diamond Cutter, only to see me attacked by members of the nWo before they looked to the skies in hopes of seeing Sting.

STEVE BORDEN
WCW SUPERSTAR "STING":

It was an incredible time for us. Creatively, we were all clicking, and it was probably the most exciting time of my career. The crow-like gimmick came out of those creative times. In fact, it was Scott Hall who came up with my look and gimmick. Collectively, guys like Hall, Hogan, Bischoff, and myself, along with others, were contributing to the success of the entire nWo program.

My character developed to the point where just my presence and the flip of a bat elevated the energy and signaled the crowd to expect a confrontation.

There were actually two key appearances by Sting that set the table for the future.

One time, Sting came to my aid before the nWo could get to me. As they approached the ring, Sting threw a second bat my way. The crowd popped huge as Sting and I were side by side and back to back, each holding bats against the New World Order . . . as the TV screen faded to black on that episode of *Nitro*.

Steve "Sting" Borden:

Through my years in wrestling, I never saw anyone who wanted it as bad as Page. There is no doubt that he had earned the title "the hardest working man in wrestling," but, to many of us, it was evident that he was trying too hard. His intentions were always good, but it takes time to figure out how to get there and when the timing is right.

I think that most wrestlers will say that there is an amount of risk involved whenever there is an opportunity to elevate anyone, and it wasn't until that point that I felt good about the timing. There had been other opportunities for me and other guys to help elevate Diamond Dallas Page, but that night in Baltimore was exactly the right time for Page, World Championship Wrestling . . . and me.

On a couple different occasions prior to then, Eric Bischoff had presented a few ways in which DDP could get the opportunity to move up, but it wasn't until I entered the ring carrying two bats that a clear-cut opportunity became the way to do it.

DDP was in trouble, and as I ran down the ramp, I had two bats for the first time. Entering the ring, I just tossed the bat high into the air and turned my back away from Page, who grabbed it in midair. The pop was huge, and we all knew the magnitude of the event, not only for Page, but for the entire angle. It was awesome.

It was now clear to the fans that Sting and I were comrades against the nWo, and the next time Sting dropped in, he didn't leave alone.

---

[2]*ring apron—Padded area around the ring itself.*

I ran in and crashed the ring during one of Savage's matches, blindsiding him, and within minutes, I was attacked by the nWo outside the ring on the apron[2]. I was out cold on the mat, and in what seemed to be a helpless situation. Sting didn't disappoint the fans, and dropped next to me, chasing the nWo and getting them to retreat a bit. As he stood over me, they began to circle us and close in on Sting. It looked like they were finally going to get to Sting as they had him and his passed-out ally surrounded.

There was only one way out, and we took it. Sting reached down and attached a hook and cable to me. The two of us, over 500 pounds of combined weight, were lifted to the rafters, 120 feet in the air.

This great escape was perfectly timed as the credits rolled on yet another highly-rated *Monday Night Nitro*. The fuse was lit and the fire stoked; and Diamond Dallas Page was ready to explode into a main event program.

Photo by Bill Apter, Pro Wrestling Illustrated.

Diamond Dallas Page began to enter and exit the ring through the crowd while fans chanted, "DDP! DDP!"

I'm not afraid to say that I was scared and more than concerned when the angle was discussed to have Sting and I airlifted 12 stories out of Boston's Fleet Center. I can't really say I'm afraid of heights anymore since I did it . . .but I was freaked out at the time. The fact that there would be two of us on that cable and that it was going to be a first just added to my anxiety.

On the other hand, the production people, stunt coordinators, and, especially, Sting were prepared, cautious, and confident. That certainly made me more comfortable with the idea.

It was strange sitting in that meeting knowing how huge of a push it was for DDP the character to be airlifted 120 feet in the air, and, at the same time, thinking that it might not be so easy for the real-life Page.

Fortunately, there was not an extended period of time for Page to mull over the consequences of the stunt within the angle, and

How over was the nWo angle? Even my Dad (far left) wore their colors. The guy in the middle is ion the wrong place . . .

his focus would have to center around the match leading up to the escape. This was yet another stepping-stone, a rung in the ladder, and an additional appearance in the *Monday Night Nitro* main event.

To say that any one event was a turning point would be difficult, but there was little doubt that Diamond Dallas Page's rejection of the nWo would certainly be a definitive move into the spotlight. Initially, the fact that Scott Hall had been the recipient of a Diamond Cutter added credibility, and the endorsement by Sting signaled an arrival to still another level. It was evident that the fans and the media had taken more interest, and the magnitude of being in the featured angle was certainly apparent. But, like so many occupations or vocations, the real measures of success are the acknowledgments of one's peers.

I could feel the difference in the locker room, but when I returned to Atlanta, my answering machine would be the greatest motivator and more significant indicator of what was happening. There were messages from friends and family, but when I would hear the voices of my bro's in the business, it would blow me away. So many people realized what a big step DDP was making, but to hear it from the guys who knew where I had been made it so much sweeter.

I got calls of congratulations from several people, but when Mark Mero, Mick Foley, and Michael P.S. Hayes left messages, I played them over again.

"Marvelous" Mark Mero:

I called to congratulate Page because I was genuinely happy that he had proven us all wrong, defied the odds, and managed to work himself into that spot. I was now a mark for my friend, DDP the wrestler, when at one time, I thought that his character and ring career were only a gimmick.

The first time I ever worked in the ring with Page was a tag match with P.N. News against Page and Teddy Long in a "managers" match, and it was horrible. I remember actually going to the bookers and telling them that I thought it made us all look ridiculous, and that it was wrong to put me in a match with two guys who would never be "wrestlers."

I was never happier for anybody who I ever worked with when I saw Page in the middle of the nWo angle. I knew that he had made it to a place that was virtually impossible to get to from where he started.

Perseverance and work ethic were Page's visible strengths, but the way he dealt with the mental aspect was incredible. His energy and business smarts were feared by many and misunderstood by most.

MICK FOLEY:

To see Page in that spot was terrific. I had to call him because I knew how tough it was for him all along. He had a tougher road the whole way because he was the only one who believed he could make it, and he had to change the opinions of everyone around him, one at a time.

I never told Page this, and, at the time, I thought it was just an offhanded remark, but after only the second match of his career, he got an endorsement from one of the all-time "greats" of the business.

Abdullah the Butcher is a 35-year veteran of this business, and is probably the oldest working professional in wrestling.

Abby and I were in a rental car shuttle when we looked out and saw Page strutting through the parking lot. As he walked by, Abdullah looked at me, and said, "He's gonna make it, champ." When I asked him what he meant and why he thought so, Abdullah said, "Because he lives the gimmick, champ . . . he lives the gimmick."

I never thought too much about what Abdullah said that day so many years ago, but seeing Page reaching the top made me smile, and I had to tell him how proud of him I was.

MICHAEL P.S. HAYES
WWF SUPERSTAR DOK HOLIDAY:

I had never been so happy in my life to eat crow. I had to call with congratulations because I knew what Diamond Dallas Page had gone through. He battled impossible odds, and wouldn't let them beat him. This business has a way of breaking a guy's spirit, and it has crushed the drive and the dreams of many, but Page wouldn't let it happen. He used all the negative vibes to get something better.

DDP was on a different kind of bubble, and it appeared that he might get the shot they said would never come. There was just one more hurdle to get over\

Dusty Rhodes had prophetically remarked that it would take someone at the very top to lift DDP to the last rung of the ladder. It seemed like the time, the opportunity, and that shot had finally become reality.

"STAGGER" LEE MARSHALL:

What most people will never realize about Page Falkinburg is that it was never about success or money or fame or bright lights that got him to the position to have all of those things. Page had already achieved that in the nightclub business, and I think he always knew that he could return to public life and reach whatever goals he would set for himself.

All Page ever wanted was to be accepted and substantiated as someone who had something to give to the sport and business that he loved so much.

Even at that point in his career, I think it was the last crossroad for him. There was no doubt in my mind that he had been labeled, but if he was held down, it went on behind closed doors. I never saw it as Page being held down by the system.

It was worse than that. He had been ignored.

Diamond Dallas Page had reached the point in his career where everything was right for him to show that he belonged.

CHAPTER EIGHTEEN

MACHO IS "THE MAN"
AND THE MAIN EVENT IS THE PLACE

RANDY "MACHO MAN" SAVAGE:

No matter what I thought or what anyone said about Page, his work ethic and desire could no longer be denied. I watched Page for awhile, and believed it was time for his shot.

DDP was firmly set in his rejection of the New World Order, and it was time for a more definitive direction for the new Diamond Dallas Page. He was now being wildly cheered, and every one of his matches became an opportunity for the fans to register their support for the WCW establishment.

In a span of a few months, DDP went from the middle of the pack to one of the superstars who had taken a stand against the revolutionary force that was changing the shape of wrestling.

Being on the same side of the issue with Sting and Lex Lugar gave Page a new presence. But it wasn't until Randy Savage ambushed him that Diamond Dallas Page rocketed into the spotlight.

When Macho Man attacked me after a match, it was my stairway to the place that I never believed I would see.

Randy Savage is without a doubt one of the biggest and most recognizable names in the history of professional wrestling. Besides being a second-generation pro wrestler, he is a tremendous athletic specimen who played professional baseball before dedicating his efforts to the ring. He is a consummate professional, and one of the greatest showmen who ever performed. Randy Savage is one of very few guys who successfully made the transition to the consciousness of the mainstream public, and his long-running ad campaign as a spokesman for "Slim Jim's" has been seen worldwide.

Behind the curtain, "Mach" is known and respected as an intense performer and one of the most physical athletes who ever wrestled. Working a program with Randy Savage was not only the opportunity of a lifetime, it was the biggest challenge of my career.

When it became evident that we would "lock up" in an extended program, I knew I would have to be ready for anything, both in and out of the ring. There were no boundaries or guidelines, and Savage was not cutting me any slack when it came to our feud. His attacks were well-planned, and when Savage ambushed me and spray-painted the letters "nWo" on my back, the program was defined. The New World Order had a vendetta against me, and it was the Macho Man's mission to enforce it.

Over the next several months, Diamond Dallas Page and Randy Savage engaged in one of the most action-packed, entertaining feuds of the '90s. Although Savage was a key member of the New World Order, he didn't need the assistance of the nWo to help fight his battles. This feud was a one-on-one battle between an established former heavyweight champion and a guy who was not supposed to be much more than "The Lord of the Rings."

In addition, the program saw a reunion of sorts between Macho Man and his former wife, "Miss Elizabeth." Their marital split was documented and well-publicized, so when they appeared together, it created still another opportunity for fan curiosity.

KIMBERLY:

Page had been working without a valet for several months, and I hadn't been seen since I had left "The Booty Man" angle. But, when it became clear that Elizabeth was going to be by

Randy "Macho Man" Savage spray-paints DDP and Kimberly. "Miss Elizabeth" exposes the Playboy Celebrity Nudes *photos while "Mean Gene" Okerlund reports the action.*

Randy's side, I knew it would be necessary for me to be in Page's corner. I had no idea how visible I would be, and while the battle was just getting started, it elevated to a war very quickly.

Savage and Elizabeth came busting in on an interview I was doing with Kimberly by my side. I've said that wrestling can get really real . . . real fast, and that night, Randy Savage crossed the line and entered into our life outside the ring.

By this time, the *Playboy* nude celebrity issue had hit newsstands across the country. Rabid fans of wrestling who lived on the Internet were made aware of the issue, and had posted some of the photos, while others discovered the nudes of Page and Kimberly after purchasing the magazine. And now, a nation of viewers of the number-one, cable-rated, prime-time TV show at the time were being let in on the secret.

One of the shots of Kim was spread over two pages, and when Savage and Elizabeth came out showing the photo with "nWo" strategically painted across her body, it shocked many people. They had not only confirmed that Kim and I were married, but had exposed her nude appearance in Playboy. After publicly confronting us with the photos, Savage questioned how anyone could allow his wife to appear nude in a magazine. Then he verbally attacked Kimberly.

LEE MARSHALL:

Page totally won the fans over that night, and defined himself as a superstar in professional wrestling. Savage's actions established "heel heat" and the potential of the program when Diamond Dallas Page stood tall, with his lovely wife on his arm, and faced his accuser. I believe that it only took five words to change the public opinion of DDP. He won them over when he flatly and vigorously told Savage, Elizabeth, and the world, "We're proud of those pictures."

Not only did the nude photos clarify the union of Page and Kimberly, they established The Macho Man as the heel; making Page, Kimberly, and the Playboy appearance the babyface. By Randy Savage being the first to comment on the nude photos, it turned a potentially off-camera negative into an on-screen positive for the program, the fans, and everyone involved.

The events around the ring made the program more intense. Kimberly was in a different role than before, and at times, I was not comfortable with it.

Kimberly had been the Diamond Doll, and was never very close to live action. Savage's tactics kicked it up another notch, and when he dragged her by her hair, it leaped to another level. I was willing to let the angle go as far as it had to, but I never wanted it to be that physical for Kimberly. Sometimes it gets too real out there.

My dream of becoming a main-event wrestler was all over me, and it was up to me to give and take in every way. Sometimes, the physicality in the ring goes beyond the point of showmanship, and the bumps and punches get pretty heavy. The line was extended with Savage, and when he landed hard,

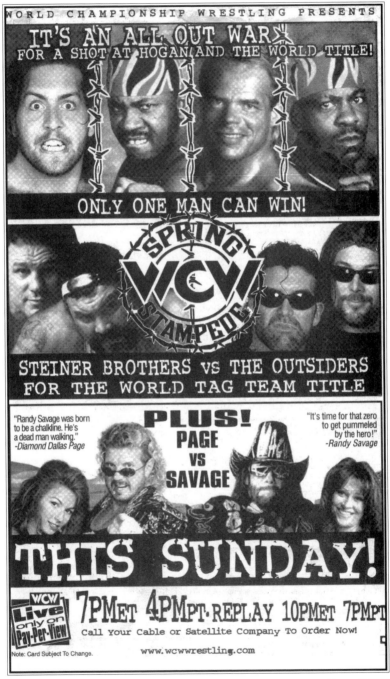

The Savage-Page feud placed DDP in his first "Main Event" PPV match. Over the next year, he would be featured in nine more PPV

my reflexes, emotions, and ego caused a stiff retaliation and heavier receipts from me. But Savage was different—he welcomed my best shot. It was like a poker game—he would see my bump and raise me two.

RANDY "MACHO MAN" SAVAGE:

For the program to work, Page had to trust me. This wasn't about him working with me or me working with him, and it wasn't about me winning or losing or him winning or losing.

I wanted him to trust me and know that I wasn't trying to screw him. We had to be committed only to getting the feud over and bringing it to new heights.

We couldn't go out there and try to scam each other, or it would wind up being a cluster-f*ck. When that happens, there is very little entertainment, and the fans end up getting screwed. There was none of that during our feud, and we went at it knowing we were going to max out.

After Page was repeatedly spray-painted by Savage and the nWo, Kimberly was ambushed and also spray-painted. Actually, spray-painting the letters "nWo" on Kimberly bolted the program from the starting blocks to the top levels. Elizabeth became instrumental in the attacks with Savage, and, at one point, offered to stop the assaults on Kimberly if she left Page and sided with the New World Order.

RICH SCHMICK
UDC PRESIDENT RICHINKC:

Brian Bentley called me right after another spray-painting, wondering what would happen if Macho Man tried to hack into DDP's Web site. Before we knew it, Savage somehow got in and spray-painted "nWo" over Page's home page, crashing the rest of the site. Over the next few days leading up to the Pay-Per-View, more and more people anticipated the next turn in the Page-Savage feud.

In the early part of the program, Randy Savage had an injury that put him on crutches. When I confronted Randy in an interview, Hollywood Hogan came to the aid of his fellow New World Order member, and together they began beating me with the crutches. When I reflect on that moment, I am completely blown away that the two biggest and most recognizable names in the industry were beating (actually, whipping the fu*k out of) me on national TV. It was a physically painful spotlight and one of the sweetest highlights at the same time.

Hogan's entrance into the program became another shining and defining moment. If Savage's brutal attacks weren't enough for DDP to digest, the involvement of "Hollywood" Hogan created still another opportunity. Having these two legendary showmen siding against him would be all the attention Diamond Dallas Page would need from that point on.

During this time, my body was being tested beyond belief. Besides working on nearly every live performance and road trip, I had never endured the kind of beatings that the nWo and Randy Savage were laying on me night after night. That top rope elbow of The Macho Man crushed my ribs, chest, and stomach on and off for nine months. I had torn cartilage, and my rib cage was so banged up that it was hard for me to laugh. My kidneys were so bruised that I pi$$ed blood for 13 out of 16 weeks. Those injuries, along with the crutches, belts, and metal chairs, became a regular occurrence. My physical rehab routine and hunger to work were the only things keeping me on my feet.

I never once thought of missing a match, though, no matter how much pain I was in. Downplaying the pain and hiding injuries from trainers was part of my mental conditioning. I was working at the top, and wasn't going to miss any of it.

"HOLLYWOOD" HOGAN:

It got to the point that guys wanted to work with Page just because he was so committed and was adding to the angle with his energy and motivation. The ones who have lasted the longest had to have that passion—an inner drive that is almost a sickness to make every angle, program, and feud the best that they can be.

"LaParka" is a character best known to wrestling viewers as a Mexican "luchadore." A luchadore often wears a colorful masked costume that is ornate and flamboyant, and the Mexican style of highflying acrobatic moves creates great drama for these typically mid-card performers.

LaParka is even more entertaining than the average luchadore since he is the tallest and biggest of the Mexican superstars. His black costume and hooded mask have the white outline of a skeleton, and LaParka typically strums a metal chair to simulate playing a guitar prior to using it as a weapon to assault his opponent. Although LaParka was, and still is, an obscure fan favorite, it was easy to predict that his antics could never defeat Randy Savage.

RANDY SAVAGE:

Page's idea was an all-time classic. It worked so well that I knew it was the perfect way for me to give back so that we could both take it to another level.

Actually, I think it had been Terry Taylor's idea, but together, we made it work. Mach is right about it—it's a classic.

The match started in the usual fashion with the challenger, LaParka, making his entrance to babyface-like cheers. Macho came down to a typical mix of nWo cheers and conventional heel boos. He immediately stopped LaParka and his strut, and was getting the upper hand early in the match. La Parka was flat on the mat as Savage climbed to the top rope to deliver his classic flying elbow drop.

Suddenly, LaParka lifted his leg to meet the diving Savage. It caught Savage in the chin and staggered him. Startled and stumbling, he tried to recover. LaParka jumped to his feet, spun Savage around, and had him set up for . . . bang! . . . the Diamond Cutter. And no one saw it coming.

Surprised, I came out of my chair and found myself cheering for LaParka. For a moment, I thought he had stolen DDP's finishing move, but like the rest of the world, I was swerved. When LaParka's mask came off to reveal Diamond Dallas Page, I knew that Page Falkinburg had made the big time. The fans went ape-sh*t crazy.

DDP as "LaParka" swerved Savage and the world. Backstage with UDC *members (left to right) Adam, Mark (in Cutter), and Johnny "Delta" Moreno.*

That match[1] was one of my favorites and one that I am still asked about. There wasn't anyone, not my friends, the fans, the smarts, the rags, or any of the "experts," who saw it coming.

Savage was the one who helped make the entire swerve and angle possible. Working with him increased my confidence and reassured me of what I always knew—I could entertain, and only needed the opportunity to show it.

There was no better way or time for Diamond Dallas Page to come out. According to *Pro Wrestling Illustrated*, matching creative ideas with maximum efforts was the reason Randy and I became "Feud of Year" in 1997.

[1]*That match, along with others, can been seen in the WCW video* DDP Feel the Bang!.

RANDY "MACHO MAN" SAVAGE:

Once we both determined that we trusted each other, I didn't look at him as anything but a top guy. We had made our deal, decided to "rock," and were committed to making it the best. Page answered every challenge, and held up his end of our agreement in every way. That's what makes guys different from one another.

On paper, this business is not that hard. If both guys have trust, the cooperation of each other, a little "smarts," and a flair for the dramatic, then the fans will be entertained. Without all of that, the fans are disappointed, and the feud falls apart.

It does get difficult because we are often working day to day and week to week, and plans must be made in pencil. Things can change quickly, and guys must have confidence in each other. Sometimes, it's hard to have that trust in your fellow workers, but it's that way in every walk of life. And, occasionally, that suspicion is well-founded and deserved.

Page and Savage tangled over the next several months, and each had their moments of triumph. The program was, by far, the most popular with the fans, and played out in grand fashion. Page saw his name on a series of PPV matches, and, although the Savage-Page match wasn't always the final match, it was getting the most attention on every monthly PPV card. From *Spring Stampede* to *The Great American Bash*, and all the other PPVs along the way, DDP was in the middle of a feud with Savage and the rest of the nWo.

Even when Savage was injured for a time, the nWo, led by Hogan and his henchmen, made it clear that DDP's self-high-five attitude was no match for the New World Order. Whenever Page delivered the Diamond Cutter on a member of the nWo, he was surrounded and pummeled after the match. Sting, Lugar, and even "The Giant" were there to help at times.

At *The Bash at the Beach* PPV, Page's old friend from the AWA, Curt Hennig, was announced as a partner against the New World Order. The match was another chance for the nWo to continue their domination over the WCW as Hennig turned on Page that night, and became a member of the New World Order.

The score with Savage was left unsettled, and as the season's biggest Pay-Per-View, known as *Halloween Havoc*, approached, the rematch was set. Each had been victorious in past PPVs, and this time, the world would be watching the main event from the MGM Grand in Las Vegas.

Halloween Havoc was the third PPV match between Savage and me, and the biggest match of my career to that point. I was in Vegas as a featured main-event wrestler in a WCW Pay-Per-View match against Randy Savage with my beautiful wife, Kimberly, watching from backstage. Toto, this sure wasn't Point Pleasant.

The match was another classic battle of brutality and intensity. Savage and I kicked it up a notch, although things went bad for DDP when I was knocked out of the ring to the floor below. As I pulled myself up to reenter the ring, I noticed Sting coming down the ramp towards me. I sensed that he was there to protect me from the nWo when he came ringside wielding his bat.

This time, the bang! came from the bat, and I was down and out. The match was over, and I was left lying in the middle of the ring.

It was Hollywood Hogan under the Sting face paint, and his bat had my name on it.

Savage won the match at *Havoc*, and although we continued to battle, I was determined that Hogan and I had plenty to settle. I was intent on tracking down Hennig, Hall, and any other members of the nWo who wanted to tangle.

The feud took me to another level, and my career had a different perspective. And Diamond Dallas Page had a fan base that even I could never have imagined.

Professional wrestling was catching fire, and so was I. And, while World Championship Wrestling and the New World Order were dominating the ratings, my old buddy, Steve Austin, was making big-time waves in the WWF.

Steve had come off an injury and left for New York about the same time I returned from my injury and re-signed with WCW. While Steve became WWF's "King of the Rings" following a battle royale match, I won a similar type of battle and the title "The Lord of the Rings." Neither of us ever got world title shots that were supposed to come with winning those titles, though.

Steve and I were on the phone talking about the direction our careers were headed in when he said, "Dallas, it's time for us to eat some deer and drink some beer." It didn't sound like "The Ringmaster" (Austin's first WWF persona). It sounded more like my bro, Steve (Austin) Williams. It wasn't until then, when we both stripped our characters down to the core, that we started to climb our different ladders.

Steve Austin's rough-around-the-edges character was now "Stone Cold," and he was in a feud with long-time fan favorite, Brett "The Hitman" Hart. As I was settling into my feud with Randy "Macho Man" Savage, both Hart and Savage had injuries that not only interrupted our feuds, but put both our opponents on crutches.

Hart beat Austin with crutches, and Savage beat me with crutches. We retaliated against our opponents with those same crutches, and, even though Stone Cold and DDP started out as heels, the fans got with us and put us over. They began to follow us as a result of our finishing moves, and the similarities of the Diamond Cutter and the Stone Cold Stunner have been well-documented.

Steve Austin became the mega-star of the WWF, and eclipsed and shattered earnings and merchandising records. At one point, he appeared on the cover of the monthly WWF magazine with then heavyweight boxing champion, Mike Tyson. Ironically, I was on the cover of World Championship Wrestling's magazine with my idol, the greatest boxing champion in history, Muhammad Ali, the same month.

It sure was a long way from Steve and I sharing a $40 motel room with Foley in Johnson City, Tennessee.

"STONE COLD" STEVE AUSTIN:

I don't usually compare things like this, but I know that our careers are similar in some ways. The one thing I'm sure of is that neither Page nor I ever tried to get the fans to like us. Like Page, it didn't matter to me one way or the other, but the fans got with us, and the rest just happened.

The end of the Savage feud saw Kimberly grabbing her own spotlight—a spotlight big enough for her and some talented friends.

In the months prior to the involvement with The Macho Man and Miss Elizabeth angle, WCW president, Eric Bischoff, began to develop an idea to fill a void that he saw in the production of *Monday Night Nitro*. In the next few months, Kimberly played a major role in making that concept a reality.

ERIC BISCHOFF
WORLD CHAMPIONSHIP WRESTLING PRESIDENT:
The idea of the "Nitro Girls" developed during dinner with my wife at a Mexican restaurant in our neighborhood. We knew how skilled Kimberly was, and with her ability to organize and

Diamond Dallas Page calls his matches with Savage "my most brutal." Here, DDP uses crutches to retaliate against the "Macho Man."

*evaluate talent, I believed that the Nitro Girls could become a
reality. I saw them as an entertainment alternative during commercial breaks for the fans who attended the* Nitro *matches.
My wife, Lori, and I were convinced that the talented Kimberly could not only handle the challenge and responsibility,
but that she would be a key asset from the start.*

KIMBERLY:

*I loved the idea, and when Eric assured me that the Nitro
Girls would be more than just a dance troupe, I was even
more excited. Eric explained that he wanted the Nitro Girls
to be not only entertainers, but, more importantly, goodwill
ambassadors for World Championship Wrestling.*

The Nitro Girls were a welcome addition to the world of professional wrestling, and have been more than just pretty faces
and great dancers. When the selection process began, the key
was to find attractive, talented ladies who were also individuals of
good quality and nature. Kimberly's input, along with Bischoff's
vision, helped develop marketable characters who the growing
legions of fans could get to know.

Kimberly auditioned and screened hundreds of applicants, and
her selections became familiar with millions of viewers. The Nitro
Girls are better known as Chae, Tygress, Storm, Spice, and Fire.

KIMBERLY:

*I knew we would be successful, but the team far exceeded
my expectations. Most of the girls have stayed grounded,
and our roles have expanded to include charity and promotional work. Each girl brings different talents and back-
grounds to the table, and we are all about fun and friendship. The fans have been so very responsive, and we have
added new merchandising, a Pay-Per-View video, and a millennium calendar. Also planned is a national search for a
new Nitro Girl that will ensure the fans of the best talent
available from around the country. I've enjoyed my time with
the Nitro Girls, but I'll always be available to accompany
DDP to the ring.*

Following the 1997 *Halloween Havoc,* Page appeared

in the *Fall Brawl* PPV match teamed up with Lex Lugar against Savage and Scott Hall.

DDP and Lugar were victorious. At the same time, Curt Hennig won the title of "U.S. Heavyweight Champion," and he was wearing the belt for the nWo.

When Hennig won the U.S. strap, I wanted to get it back from nWo control. Of course, I hadn't forgotten Hennig turning his back on WCW when he joined the New World Order, or his betrayal of me. When we met at the *Starcade* PPV, I left wearing the "United States Heavyweight Championship" belt.

As 1997 ended, I started the last year of my contract, but this time as "Champion." The way my ups and downs had gone, I knew the yo-yo was ever present. I was cautious not to forget how my dedication to my dream had projected me to where I was able to make a difference and work myself into that spot. I will always be thankful and proud that Randy Savage reached down and allowed me to grab a lightening bolt.

I was now ready to contribute to World Championship Wrestling from a different vantage point, and I had gained more respect and security in my new role and position on the card.

RANDY SAVAGE:

Page did what he said he would do all along, and he filled his part of the bill. It was a good, long feud, and he worked hard and he worked hurt. He was entertaining for the fans, and was a professional to work with. At the same time, Page and I laid it on the line, and that feud brought both of us up. Of all the programs and matches I've had over the years, the feud with DDP is one that fans ask about all the time.

He deserves everything he has accomplished. He learned, he worked hard, he didn't quit . . . and when it was his time, he knew what to do. We worked our deal, and we stayed close after it, which is rare.

Page has a passion for this business, and that is an asset. But most of all . . . he always keeps up his end of the deal.

CHAPTER NINETEEN

THE MAIN LINE TO THE MAINSTREAM

It goes with the territory that the more someone is seen, the more they are recognized, and I was being noticed by more people every day. I'd see people raise their hands, yell "Bang!" or chant "DDP . . . DDP" while walking through airports, malls, or even at the movies. Not only were there a lot more people recognizing me, but the stereotype of the wrestling fan was changing more and more.

I was signing an autograph once, and a distinguished-looking guy caught my eye. "I don't want an autograph," he said. "I just want to shake your hand." He continued, "Every Monday night, you're my hero."

I said, "Thanks, bro . . . What's your name?"

"I'm Doctor so and so," he replied.

I never caught his name, but I heard the doctor part. It cracked me up. Imagine that. I was his hero . . . and he was a doctor saving lives for a living.

It hit me hard that day that it wasn't just "rasslin'" anymore.

Following my feud with Savage, and prior to winning the U.S. title, Smokey called me one Sunday from Florida. He told

Hey, Einstein, . . . That's a pair of "Diamond Cutters."

me that Herschel Walker of the Dallas Cowboys had thrown up the Diamond Cutter sign following a long touchdown run.

After watching the replay, I had to call Page, at least to leave a message for him to try to catch *SportsCenter*. I wasn't positive, but it looked like a Diamond Cutter to me.

Later that evening, Kim and I were watching TV when we saw the replay on ESPN's *SportsCenter*. There was former Olympian and Heisman trophy winner, Herschel Walker, using my sign on national TV. I knew it meant that Diamond Dallas Page was beginning to find a more secure place in professional wrestling, and in the hearts of Americans.

HERSCHEL WALKER
FORMER HEISMAN TROPHY WINNER:

I had watched pro wrestling with my father since I was a kid, way back to the NWA days. And I had watched Nitro *from the start on Monday nights, since by the time Monday rolled around, I'd had my fill of football. The only sports I ever watch on TV with any regularity are track and field events and pro wrestling. I follow my buddy from the University of Georgia, Bill Goldberg, but I liked DDP and have followed his career from the start.*

I know how physically demanding wrestling is, and I always respected those guys as athletes and entertainers. I remember Diamond Dallas Page first as a manager and then as an announcer, and I was a big fan once he started wrestling. I really liked the Diamond Cutter.

I have never been one to celebrate in the end zone, but on that day, it felt real good, so I shot the Diamond Cutter sign and yelled, "Bang!"

It was pretty funny afterwards, since some people knew what it was, and others were asking me what I was doing out there. Plenty of us would get together on Saturdays before games and watch from our hotel rooms, but my friends know that on Mondays, I'm watching Nitro, *and on Thursdays, I'm watching Thunder.*

Wrestling was taking on a new role in our culture, and its acceptance was reaching segments of the population who never knew they could have so much fun watching TV with friends and family.

There were *Monday Night Nitro* parties taking place in homes and sports bars across America. Fathers were telling stories of Dick "The Bruiser," Black Jack Mulligan, and Mr. Wrestling I and II, instead of telling their sons about Willie Mays, Roberto Clemente, and the Robinsons . . . Frank and Brooks. Win or lose, there was always someone to cheer for, and someone else to boo with intensity.

Professional wrestling had something and someone for everyone to enjoy. The fan base was growing, and those who hid their enjoyment were now ready to admit that they had been watching all along. Walk into any mall or department store, and there are families wearing wrestling shirts and buying collectible merchandise and toys.

The merchandising of professional wrestling has been popular since the '80s, and the WWF did a good job of marketing during those years. I had a couple of Hulk and Jake

"The Snake" T-shirts during my years in the bar business, but typically, only the very top guys had collectible action figures or dolls made of their likeness.

Back in my earliest days in the AWA, my sister, Sally, was visiting her friend, Maureen, who has an amazing son who was three at the time. Liam was playing with his wrestling figures, and Sally was amazed that he knew all their names and the current feuds they were in.

SALLY FALKINBURG:

I was anxious to tell Liam that my brother was in wrestling, and when I did, he matter-of-factly asked who he was. "He's Diamond Dallas Page, the wrestling manager," I said proudly. Liam's response was: "Is he a rubber wrestling dude?" Maureen had overheard our conversation, and when she and I were alone, she said, "Tell Page he isn't sh*t until he's a rubber wrestling dude."

And Maureen was pretty much right, up to that point.

One of the friends I made in the early days of my career was Robbie Kanoff, a representative for several independent toymakers. Robby was responsible for my first action figure becoming a reality. One of the companies he represented, The Original San Francisco Toymakers, had a WCW licensing agreement, and Robbie suggested that Diamond Dallas Page be one of the characters for their new line of WCW superstars.

At the time the decision was made, nobody thought I would be a main-event guy, but Robby Kanoff had the balls to make dolls for a couple of mid-card wrestlers.

My first rubber wrestling dude and action figure was pretty good. It featured me doing a "Double Ax Handle" move with my arms chopping down when a button in the back was pressed. The thing that really cracked me up, though, was seeing my tattoos on a six-inch-tall, plastic doll.

It's amazing how many different types and styles of rubber wrestling dudes are available these days. The company, ToyBiz, has taken the action figure to many different levels. The figures are incredible now. They talk to each other with our voices, and can actually wrestle these days, but I'll always dig that first doll the most. After all, I had to get rid of that "monkey on my back" that my little buddy, Liam, hung on me.

Not only did The Original San Francisco Toymakers produce a DDP doll, but they also made one for my bro, Scott Levy, whose character, "Raven," was leading a new faction of wrestlers known as "Raven's Flock."

DDP and Raven were traveling partners and close friends. When Raven's character took a turn toward a more angry grunge character, the angle shifted. Raven claimed that his old friend and mentor, DDP, had turned his back on him, and his anger turned into a violent rage as he challenged DDP to a feud for his U. S. Heavyweight Championship belt.

"The Canadian Crippler," Chris Beniot, objected to Raven's challenge since DDP had promised Beniot the first shot at the title. The three wrestlers battled in different combinations, and had tremendously physical, hardcore-type matches. The feud lasted through the early winter months of 1998, before developing into a PPV *Triple Jeopardy* match.

During the feud, which eventually saw Raven take the U.S. title from Diamond Dallas Page, the nWo and Hollywood Hogan remained in Page's sights.

The Raven and Beniot matches were a different kind of brutal, and those feuds included a lot of interference from "The Flock." As far as I was concerned, I was working with the next superstars of World Championship Wrestling, including future titleholder Perry "Saturn" and cruiserweight champion Billy Kidman. One of the most innovative young guys in the business, Chris Kanyon, saw action in those matches, as did Reece, Horace Hogan, Scotty Riggs, and Van Hammer.

The most memorable and painfully entertaining match of the feud was the *Triple Jeopardy* Pay-Per-View match, which was a pretty crazy free-for-all. The match was all over the arena, and at one point, Raven and Beniot threw me through the lighting boxes which displayed the message: "Uncensored."

During the first half of 1998, I was either in a match with, assaulted by, or ambushed by every type and style of wrestler in the game—from the intense, hardcore style of Raven, where we used tables, ladders, and kitchen sinks on each other, to the tactical mat wrestling of Chris Beniot, who, pound for pound, is one of the toughest guys around. Saturn is a master of submission holds, and Kidman combined high-flying with technical mat skills. Wrestling Kanyon has always been challenging, and his style reminds me of a younger version of myself in the ring (only better). His creativity in the ring and his commitment make all of his matches entertaining and exciting for the boys in the back, as well as the fans.

My body was being hammered, and had been for awhile. During my feud with Macho, I was introduced to Doctor Ken West, an applied kinesiologist who I began seeing as a weekly ritual. Doc West is the very best on the planet, and has performed miracles on my body that allow me to continue the abuse. Kinesiology combines chiropractic medicine, nutrition, and Chinese methods of utilizing pressure points in the heeling process. Although I continued my regular deep massage therapy from Marcie Joiner, my visits to Doc West were no longer a ritual. They were survival. There wasn't enough time to heal, and even if there had been, I wasn't going to take time off while I was getting hotter.

Diamond Dallas Page was on a roll, and newspapers and radio stations were asking for more interviews. They wanted to know more about my Diamond Cutter and me. The controversy over the difference between Austin's "Stunner" and the "Cutter" had begun. The more people talked about it and the more they compared it, the better. My finish was "over."

HOLLYWOOD HOGAN:

The Diamond Cutter is an exciting and devastating finishing move that Page continually finds ways to execute. He's found ways to negotiate that move on all sizes of guys and from so many places. That one move alone makes him unforgettable and a constant threat anytime he is in the ring.

Times were good all around, and my Diamond Cutter

T-shirt was selling like crazy. It had my three-dimensional face framed by my hands forming the Diamond Cutter sign on it. As my shirts began to sell out of the arenas, dozens of new WCW licensees were considering me for their products, and WCW was selling more merchandise than ever.

Diamond Dallas Page was getting hot, and it seemed that his Diamond Cutter was popping up everywhere. Even pro bowler, Pete Weber, did an exaggerated celebration that included the diamond sign after striking out and winning a nationally-televised tournament. A band based in Atlanta named Stuck Mojo featured DDP and Raven in their video for their album's title song "Rising," and it was in MTV's rotation. DDP was being seen more and more outside the ring, and there were requests to see more of him and his diamond cutter.

In January of 1998, I was asked to be one of the celebrities at the Houston Tri-Star Sports Collectors Show. After a couple of great days of meeting and reacquainting myself with some of the sporting world's greatest legends, including Muhammad Ali, I looked forward to hanging with my bro's.

My greatest thrill was the opportunity to meet "The Man of the Century," Muhammad Ali. I always liked the talkers . . . especially

I knew that life was different now, but I had no idea that when I hooked up with my old bro, Bigg Rick Kolster, and my new bro, Ross Forman, for a night out in Houston, life would change again.

Neither of us are low-profile guys, and Rick is a strong 6'5" guy who trains regularly. He had shaved his head, and at a quick glimpse, looked like Bill Goldberg.

By this time, Bill Goldberg, the same guy I thought should be in professional wrestling years ago, was not only in wrestling, but was larger than life. "Goldie" was truly one of the biggest success stories to come out of wrestling. His football career was ended by a series of injuries, but once he made the decision to enter the "squared circle," the rest became history.

World Championship Wrestling and Bill Goldberg were giving fans a new alternative to the nWo. His undefeated streak had begun, and the chants of "GOLD-BERG . . . GOLD-BERG" were being heard around the country.

Bill busted his @$$ at The Power Plant and prepared himself to be the right guy, in the right place, at the right time. Although Goldberg went on to win over 170 straight matches, I still feel that his best days are ahead of him. His natural charisma and unbelievable intensity make him the type of performer who can captivate and entertain for years.

I loved being back in Texas, and when Jeff and Butch Rosenberg from Tri-Star invited us to the Rockets-Jazz game, it was that much better. I was jacked about seeing an NBA game with Ross and Bigg, and being able to see superstars Malone, Barkley, Drexler, and Stockton was awesome.

Ross Forman
WCW Magazine:

We had great seats, four rows behind the Jazz bench. Late in the game, Karl Malone stood up and took a position where he could look through the huddle at the crowd. He spotted us and flashed the Diamond Sign.

We popped, and when the game resumed, I told Page that he had to get him to do it again so that I could get a picture of it.

"Bro . . . what are you, an idiot?" Page asked. "How am I going to get him to do it again? He's Karl Malone!"

Karl "The Mailman" Malone
Two-Time NBA MVP:

Many times when there are athletes and celebrities in the stands, they go unnoticed and unacknowledged by us. That night, however, the game was such a blowout that when one of the guys said that DDP was in the stands, I looked for him in the crowd.

I have been a wrestling fan since I was very young, and I watched WCW regularly with my mother, brothers, and sisters. I wanted to be a pro wrestler way before I started playing basketball competitively, so seeing DDP was pretty cool.

When I found him in the stands, I flashed him the Diamond Sign.

Word came from arena officials that the Rockets and Jazz had invited us to the locker room after the game.

I was very impressed with Karl Malone, but how could I not be? I was a big mark for "The Mailman" as an NBA superstar, but that night, I could tell that he was one special human being. Watching him on the court and standing next to him made it easy to tell how committed he was to training, and his physicality and strength amazed me. I told him that he would be phenomenal in the ring, and offered to work out or train with him whenever he was in Atlanta.

I sensed that Karl wanted to know more about the world of professional wrestling, and could tell that we were on the same page in so many ways.

Karl Malone
NBA Superstar:

Page and I hit it off from the start. I told him that I was a fan of wrestling and that I respected what those guys did in and out of the ring. We talked about each other's training routines, and within a few minutes, he told me that I would be great in the ring.

I knew that Rodman had done it during the previous off-season, but I had never really thought about doing it myself. However, after hearing DDP, I started to consider it.

January was mid-season for Malone and mid-Raven feud-time for Diamond Dallas Page. Over the next few months, Page and Malone played phone tag, but finally saw each other when Karl invited him to the NBA All-Star Game.

DDP's trip to the 1998 NBA All-Star Game. (left to right) James Carmichael, Kevin Crimmins, Karl "The Mailman" Malone, Casey Collins, and Page. (Photo by Kaye Malone)

Because of my schedule, I literally had about an hour before my flight to New York to find three people to join me for the NBA All-Star Game. I was still in Atlanta, but I had spoken to Casey Collins, who works in the marketing department at WCW, and he was up for it and would meet me at Madison Square Garden.

Several calls to New Jersey found most of my bro's tied up for the day, but a buddy from high school, Kevin Crimmins, was able to make it, and was driving up the Jersey Turnpike toward the city.

I was on the fly when I got to the airport, and still had one ticket left when I got to my gate. I immediately went to a bank of pay phones, and after a few unsuccessful calls, in frustration, I said to myself, "I can't believe I've got a ticket to the All-Star Game, and I can't find anyone to go!"

I heard a guy behind me say, "You've got a ticket? Let me see it. I'll buy it from you right now!" I was laughing when I turned around and saw that it was a Delta Airlines representative known as a redcoat.

JAMES CARMICHAEL
DELTA AIRLINES CUSTOMER RELATIONS:

He immediately told me that he wouldn't sell it to me, but offered to give it to me. I had no idea who Diamond Dallas Page was. He told me that he was a wrestler and a friend of Karl Malone, but that he didn't have the ticket with him. He said if I really wanted it, after he picked the tickets up in New York, he would leave one waiting for me. I was getting off work soon, and I felt like the guy was for real, so I made plans to meet him in New York.

I knew that airline employees could fly standby, so I gave James all the phone numbers where he could reach me, and told him I'd see him in the seats after he picked up his ticket from will-call. Just as the game started, I received a page, and the message was that the redcoat was coming. Around halftime, I spotted James looking over the crowd.

JAMES CARMICHAEL:

I couldn't believe I was at the NBA All-Star Game in Madison Square Garden. On the floor were the greatest in the game—Malone, Jordan, Ewing, and many more. I looked up in the stands and heard "Hey, Redcoat! Yo, Redcoat! . . . Over here."

Within five minutes, I was sitting back enjoying the scene as I watched one person after another approaching my new friend, Page, for his autograph. I was surprised by the number of and the different kinds of people who knew who he was. There were kids, old ladies, plenty of guys, and lots of good-looking ladies.

It was pretty cool. James hooked up with Casey, Kevin, and me, and we were kicked back and loving it. The third quarter was about to start, and James casually asked me, "Dallas, are you somebody?"

I just cracked up, and told him, "Tonight was like winning the lottery for us, bro. After dinner, we're hooking up with Karl."

KARL MALONE
NBA SUPERSTAR:

Dallas introduced me to his buddies, and neither my wife, Kaye, nor I could figure out how they knew each other. When I heard that Page had just met the black guy that day at the airport, it blew me away. When James told me that he had never heard of Diamond Dallas Page, I couldn't believe it.

It showed me what kind of guy Dallas Page is. He's got one of the biggest hearts around, and was just being himself. Since something good had happened for him, he turned it around and made someone else happy too. It's simple. Page gives back and really treats people like he likes to be treated.

Karl popped when he heard how the four of us all wound up together that day. James told Karl that it wasn't until people had asked for my autograph that he began to think I might be someone famous, and he had no idea who DDP was. "The Mailman" immediately started cutting a promo. It was tongue in cheek, but Karl was real animated, dropping his jaw in disbelief.

"You don't know who Diamond Dallas Page is?" He repeated himself as he called to his wife, Kaye. "Kaye, he doesn't know who DDP is." Then Karl quickly turned back to James, extended his hand, and said, "Let me introduce myself. I'm Karl Malone."

It was a riot, and I nearly fell out of the chair. Karl was putting me over, and at the same time, he rolled right into a promo and sold it like a pro.

From that point until the end of the season, Karl and I stayed close. I asked him if he had given the idea of climbing into the ring any more thought. He said that he thought it would be fun, and was seriously considering it. I was jacked.

Before that, it was only light talk between us, more like we were just going to work out in the ring together. I never thought it would get so serious and become a reality so fu*king quick. I sensed that Karl wanted to make sure that he could do it right, and he wanted to know more.

I got Eric Bischoff on the phone and told him that Karl was interested. Eric had just watched the Jazz eliminate the Lakers, and saw how physical Karl was. He wanted to meet him as soon as possible, and within 48 hours, we had put together a deal for Karl Malone to live his dream with World Championship Wrestling after his season was over.

Herschel Walker, Karl Malone, and the rest of Diamond Dallas Page's fans knew that he had been distracted and ambushed by Hollywood Hogan during the previous year. Beginning with his turn to the nWo and throughout the Savage and Raven feuds, Hogan lashed out at DDP with an assortment of attacks. DDP finally reached his breaking point and directed his attention to Hogan.

During an interview with "Mean Gene" Okerland, Hogan and Dennis Rodman attacked me with metal chairs, knocking me down and out cold.

Basically, I identified Hollywood Hogan as the scum he had become since the formation of the New World Order. Diamond Dallas Page was willing to battle him one-on-one, anytime or anyplace.

NBA bad boy, Dennis "The Worm" Rodman, is to the general public and many fans of basketball and wrestling the epitome of the term "heel." Rodman had wrestled during the prior off-season wearing the colors of the New World Order.

The NBA season was entering the finals when Rodman missed a Chicago Bulls' practice to attend TNT's *Monday Night Nitro*. His absence created major media attention, and Rodman drew fines from both the NBA and the Chicago Bulls. "The Worm" was called a distraction by the press, and was publicly scolded by Bulls' coach, Phil Jackson, and Michael Jordan.

The Hogan and Rodman assault was intense, and the beating with the metal folding chairs was just a prelude to further altercations with Hogan.

With a showdown imminent between Hollywood Hogan and Diamond Dallas Page, another showdown began to heat up. Rodman's Bulls were meeting Malone's Jazz for the NBA championship. While the media's attention was directed at the possibility of the series being the end of Michael Jordan's career, the world saw Rodman and Malone banging it out under the boards.

KARL MALONE:

Just three months after meeting Page, he and Eric Bischoff were in my living room, and we had a deal that was going to help me live out one of my dreams. I respected what these guys did as athletes, and wanted to give it my all without seeming like I was invading their turf. Of course, I realized the "Dennis thing" would add to the drama of it all, but I just wanted to learn and be as good as I could be.

The deal was made while Malone and Rodman continued to battle on the court, and several times, they nearly came to blows during that final series of the season.

The media and general public were familiar with Rodman's off-court antics, and knew that he had wrestled before. The heat came heavy when word leaked that Malone was considering an off-season ring appearance with World Championship Wrestling.

Criticism of Karl Malone's decision came from all angles once the contract was confirmed. The local Utah press forgot about all the winning years of basketball he had brought to Salt Lake City, and everything he had done for the community. They were quick to judge what he planned to do during his off-season. Various media sources, including NBC sportscaster, Bob Costas, pompously ridiculed Malone and scoffed at the tens of millions of weekly viewers of professional wrestling. This was the same Bob Costas who had served as a ringside announcer at one of McMahon's early *Wrestlemania* Pay-Per-View matches.

Some members of the press use every opportunity to blast

anything and anybody who is associated with wrestling. I guess Bob Costas forgot about the exposure he had gotten and the paycheck he cashed when he needed it from wrestling. Bottom line is, I'd rather hear Marv Albert do a high school game than listen to Costas do play-by-play from a soapbox.

During the sixth and deciding game of the '98 NBA finals, Karl Malone answered his critics. After he made consecutive shots to draw the Jazz closer to the champion Bulls, Malone raised his hands in the Diamond Sign, and spoke to wrestling fans around the world. And in case they missed that camera angle, he did it again moments later.

When I saw Karl throw up the sign, I got jacked. I knew Karl well enough in that short time to know that he was committed to giving it all he had. We knew that the wrestling media would be critical if we were ugly in the ring, but Karl was determined not to let that happen.

The stage was set for a tag match between the nWo team of Hogan and Rodman and the working heroes of Diamond Dallas Page and Karl Malone. There was no doubt that the increased tension between Malone and Rodman would draw added interest. Within days of the match, the announcement and the angle were introduced on the greatest late-night showcase in television history—*The Tonight Show.*

The night after the NBA championship series had ended, Rodman appeared on *The Tonight Show* with Hollywood Hogan at his side. Dennis was as entertaining and outspoken as ever as he talked about the basketball series and his movies. Then Jay Leno asked him about wrestling. Rodman and Hogan took a few verbal jabs at Malone and me, and to everyone's surprise, we came out from behind the stage curtain carrying folding chairs. A scuffle began, and the four of us had to be separated.

For the first time ever, a professional wrestling angle was promoted on a network show; the top-rated late-night pro-

The nWo's Hollywood Hogan" and Eric Bischoff hi-jack NBC's Tonight Show

gram in the country. It was huge, and the excitement and hype kept getting better.

The next morning as America was waking up, the wire services, *USA Today*, and *ESPN's SportCenter* were reporting that two of the NBA's biggest stars were going to carry their on-court battles to the wrestling ring.

The official announcement was made in true Hollywood fashion, from the podium of Planet Hollywood in Los Angeles. World Championship Wrestling's Lee Marshall made the announcement that a match was set pitting the team of Hollywood Hogan and Dennis "Rodzilla" Rodman against Karl "The Mailman" Malone and Diamond Dallas Page. The match would take place on Pay-Per-View at the *Bash on the Beach* to be held in San Diego on July 19, 1998.

That press conference rivaled anything I had ever seen on TV. There was worldwide media coverage and over 40 television and video cameras. The flashbulbs were popping out of control as we posed for pictures and promo shots.

Prior to the match, Karl Malone was scheduled for Jay Leno's show. After the press conference, Karl and I went to the NBC studio and were waiting in one of the green rooms for Jay. Each room has its own bathroom, and while I was in the bathroom, Jay came into the green room.

I walked out and saw Jay on the couch talking to Karl as I was pulling up my zipper. Without missing a beat, Jay popped to his feet, looked back at Karl, and said, "Well . . . if you guys would rather be alone . . . "

We fell out laughing, and it doubled me over.

During the taping of the show, Jay ribbed Karl about the play-offs and his upcoming match with Rodman. "Who is this guy, Diamond Dallas Page?" he asked. As Karl explained Page and the Diamond Cutter, DDP made his second appearance on *The Tonight Show.*

I came out from behind the curtain and immediately got in Leno's face. I called Jay "Chin Boy" and told him to stick to doing what he did best . . . asking questions."

Jay Leno was dedicated to his training. (left to right) "Kanyon," Billy Kidman, Jay Leno, Rick, DDP, and Eric Watts all helped prepare Leno and NBA star, Karl Malone.

When "The King of Late Night," Jay Leno, told Karl Malone, "I'm a fan of wrestling, and I'll be watching," it was the biggest boost that the wrestling industry had ever received. Having Jay Leno's endorsement meant a lot to people who were unsure about how professional wrestling had evolved.

Newspapers, television stations, sports channels, and even straight newscasts were covering the story of the flamboyant Dennis Rodman and the normally reserved Karl Malone crossing over to the world of professional wrestling.

It had been one year since Page saw action in the main event with Randy Savage, and now he was in the middle of the biggest media frenzy ever directed toward professional wrestling. The mainstream press and viewing audience wanted to see good guy Malone beat the evil Rodzilla.

At the same time, the wrestling world wanted to see the "People's Champion," Diamond Dallas Page, settle the score with Hollywood Hulk Hogan, who was leading the wrestling world down the path of the New World Order.

KARL MALONE
NBA SUPERSTAR:

After I got over the jitters and awkwardness of being in the ring, I started feeling more comfortable. It was the most physically demanding workout I ever had, and emotionally tougher than anyone could imagine. The more I wrestled, the more impressed I was with the dedication of these athletes.

Karl Malone answered the bell every day that we trained. Billy Kidman, Chris Kanyon, and Eric Watts worked with us in the ring, and Karl hung with them at every turn. There is no doubt that he is an incredible athlete who has the determination and work ethic to do anything.

The professional wrestling industry was white-hot and burning up. Film crew after film crew wanted footage, and reporters came out of the woodwork to interview us. From ESPN to *USA Today*, and from *Entertainment Tonight* to the *NBC Nightly News*, the spotlight was on high.

Diamond Dallas goes toe-to-toe with Dennis "Rodzilla" Rodman.

ESPN's Charlie Steiner did a video piece on all the famous people who entered the world of professional wrestling for entertainment value. The list included Abe Lincoln, Babe Ruth, and even Muhammad Ali. Besides the active athletes like Rodman, Malone, and NFL future Hall of Famers Reggie White and Kevin Greene, many more professional athletes had showed interest in a ring career after their current playing days were over.

Rodman had generated publicity when he wrestled the first time, but this was way bigger.

We spent the last days prior to the *Bash at the Beach* away from the press, training at a private facility in Newport Beach, California. Karl Malone was ready, and had gotten in the best possible ring shape that someone could in such a short time.

The match itself was good by celebrity-match standards, although Rodman's tactics to slow the aggressive Malone down caused a delay in the initial action. Once the brawling started, Malone and Rodman showcased their athletic ability and dexterity. However, in true nWo fashion, Hogan's henchman, "The Disciple," interfered, resulting in a win for Hogan and Rodman.

KARL MALONE:

It was physically and mentally challenging, but, most of all, fun for me. I am very thankful that I had the opportunity to get in the ring, and I liked it. I will always be a fan of World Championship Wrestling, and will always have the utmost respect for what those guys do.

Page, Hulk, Eric Bischoff, and all the guys were great with the fans, and very professional in every way. Page and I became tight during that time, and have talked regularly ever since. People flash me the Diamond Cutter everywhere I go, and it's a pleasure to give it back.

Both wrestling federations were battling each other with record-breaking ratings. They were dominating cable's top ten programs, and often there were more Americans watching pro wrestling on cable in prime time than any other network programming.

Following the PPV victory, Hogan and Bischoff began to taunt Jay Leno for siding with Malone and Page. Bischoff used *Monday Night Nitro* to launch a parody of *The Tonight Show* where he was the host who mimicked Leno's monologues. The set was an exact replica of the NBC studio, down to the furniture. Hogan was a frequent visitor to the "*nWo Tonight Show*," and Bischoff even had a band supply the music leading into guest appearances.

NBC's *Tonight Show* retaliated when Leno brought a Hulk Hogan look-alike in for a series of interviews. He was a scrawny old man under five feet tall, dressed exactly like Hollywood.

The real Hollywood Hogan was incensed by the mockery, and Bischoff and Hogan crashed *The Tonight Show* during one of the satirical interviews.

Hogan and Bischoff came out of the audience and broke up Leno's bit before running him off the set. NBC cameras abruptly went to commercial.

When NBC's *Tonight Show* came back from commercial, there was no Jay Leno. Instead, it was Eric Bischoff behind the desk with Hollywood Hogan on the couch next to him. The nWo had hijacked network TV's legendary late-night show.

As Jay Leno approached Eric Bischoff at his desk from backstage, Diamond Dallas Page attacked Hogan from behind the couch, and a fight ensued. Leno then attacked Bischoff who was distracted by DDP's presence. The battle continued until NBC security took Bischoff and Hogan away in handcuffs.

As Hogan and Bischoff were being dragged away, I asked Jay Leno if he was ready to get in the ring to settle the score with the nWo. With the studio audience going crazy, Leno accepted, and another WCW angle was being featured on network TV. This time, it included one of the entertainment world's biggest stars.

This PPV battle would match the New World Order team of Hollywood Hogan, Eric Bischoff, and The Disciple (Ed Leslie) with *The Tonight Show* team of Jay Leno, Diamond Dallas Page, and bandleader, Kevin Eubanks, as support in the corner.

For the past few years, World Championship Wrestling has broadcast an outdoor Pay-Per-View event from Sturgis, South Dakota known as *Road Wild*. The match was held during the motorcycle rally, which is an annual retreat for bikers. The match draws countless fans, and some years, WCW has staged concerts with major national acts to accompany a full night of entertainment.

Neither the WCW nor Jay Leno were strangers to Sturgis. Leno is a recognized motorcycle rider, collector, and advocate. He has made several visits to the event, which draws over 300,000 bikers from around the world to the Black Hills of South Dakota.

This match would be another coup for World Championship Wrestling and Diamond Dallas Page.

Jay Leno's participation and the support of WCW would direct still more attention from millions of casual and potential fans to the entertaining world of wrestling. His appearance was considered a stunt, but at the same time, it was a ringing endorsement.

When Jay Leno went from watching wrestling to being a wrestler, it shocked Hollywood and the world. As much as WCW and wrestling in general had created matches with some of the greatest sports celebrities of our times, never had such a show business giant ever crossed that line and climbed into the ring.

Leno's request to have me as his partner was by far one of my greatest thrills and compliments. This angle was shot on the road with *Nitro* and *The Tonight Show* in Los Angeles, so the words "red-eye flight" were on the tip of my tongue daily.

Thankfully, the same trio of Kanyon, Watts, and Kidman, who had helped train and spar with Malone, worked with Leno. Jay was a consummate professional who took the training seriously, and never missed a session. Both he and Kevin Eubanks were committed to the task and gave it their total attention.

JAY LENO
HOST OF NBC'S *TONIGHT SHOW:*

The appearance was for charity, and the fact that it would be at Sturgis made it even more fun. I actually did some wrestling in high school and was a fan as a kid. That was back in the days of Bruno Samartino and Haystacks Calhoun. I found it to be entertaining, fun, and cartoon-like, and have always felt that it was part of America.

As I got to know the guys at WCW better, I found them to be regular guys who were incredible athletes, performers, and relentless workers. At the same time, they were good to their fans, and especially kids.

Hulk, Dallas, and all the guys I met were genuine in their efforts to meet their fans and sign autographs. I meet a lot of athletes, and often they don't have the same passion for their fans as the guys I met from WCW.

I looked forward to Sturgis, getting into the ring, having some fun, and raising money for charity.

I was more than happy to take the challenge of flying to the West Coast and chasing *Monday Night Nitro* and *Thursday Night Thunder* across the nation. I had done the same kind of thing during the match with Karl Malone, so when given the opportunity and challenge to do it again, I was ready. I saw this opportunity as a home-run shot.

Bischoff's version of *The Tonight Show* motivated me even more when he used the forum to verbally attack Kimberly. As the trip to Sturgis drew closer, I got revenge by destroying the entire set and banging! Bischoff with a Diamond Cutter on a *Nitro*.

I seldom worry in the ring, but I was worried for Jay. Even though he was in better ring shape than expected, I knew that the action could sometimes get very real in the ring. Even the most experienced guys get hurt every week in this business.

Kevin Eubanks was very impressive and was dedicated to training. Besides that, he plays killer jazz guitar. During the training, I got to know Kevin. He's one of the greatest guys and hippest cats on any coast. Maybe that's because he's from Philadelphia and spent his summers on the Jersey Shore.

KEVIN EUBANKS
MUSICAL DIRECTOR OF *THE TONIGHT SHOW BAND*:

I watched wrestling as a kid, and have watched regularly since Hogan and Page's first appearance on the show. But it wasn't until the announcement was made that I realized just how many people were watching wrestling. My friends were suddenly telling me who their favorites were, and asking me about different wrestlers and their feuds.

Heavyweight Champion at the time, Bill Goldberg helps DDP, Jay Leno, and Kevin Eubanks celebrate a victory over the nWo.

*I knew that Jay's involvement was big because wrestling
was becoming a topic in places it had never been.*

The match was staged before the largest outdoor audience
on Pay-Per-View that year, and was more impressive than originally thought possible. Hogan and Bischoff were formidable partners, but Leno relied on deceptive and clever moves to avoid dan-
ger. The hours of training seemed to pay off as Leno's timing and
teamwork with DDP were excellent.

Although it was Jay Leno who pinned WCW/nWo vice president, Eric Bischoff, it was a sneak attack by cornerman, Kevin
Eubanks, that set up the victory for DDP and Leno.

I think a lot of people were surprised by the muscles that Kevin
was packing, and when he delivered a textbook example of the
Diamond Cutter on Bischoff, the crowd went "road" wild. Leno made
the cover for the pin, and the match was yet another summer success story for Diamond Dallas Page and World Championship
Wrestling.

KEVIN EUBANKS:

*I was used to bodybuilding, but I was hurting for a few
days following the match. I soon realized that the cross-train-
ing that WCW wrestlers engaged in was far more than most
can imagine. Learning how to execute the Diamond Cutter
from various places in the ring kept me sore enough, so my
respect level rose from the very first day.*

*It was great fun, and I would jump at the chance to work
with Page and World Championship Wrestling again. The
experience went by quickly, and I am reminded of it often.
People flash me the Diamond Sign everywhere I go, from the
grocery store to Dodger Stadium.*

September saw the annual *Fall Brawl* PPV event take on a
new and bigger challenge for Diamond Dallas Page. The match
was called "War Games," and it took place in a "caged" format. A
chain-link cage was placed over the ring ensuring that all the com-
batants were confined to the ring area, and that no outside interference would determine the victor.

The main event saw three teams of three men battling to be

the one who would execute a pin fall. The winner earned a shot at the World Championship Heavyweight title that was held at the time by the undefeated Bill Goldberg.

Nine of the top superstars in wrestling vied for the chance to face Goldberg for the world title belt, including Brett Hart, Lex Lugar, Scott Steiner, The Giant, Scott Hall, Rowdy Roddy Piper, Stevie Ray, and Diamond Dallas Page. For added drama, this match marked the return of former WWF champion, "The Warrior," after several years of retirement. The Warrior was Hogan's long-time nemesis, and was included only to tamper with the nWo and Hogan's focus. Once the bell rang, it was every man for himself.

"War Games" was more an exercise in survival. With so many superstars in the ring at once, I looked for the right opening for a Diamond Cutter. I was able to catch Stevie Ray of the nWo with a blindside Diamond Cutter and . . . bang! . . . end of story.

I got my shot at the greatest achievement in the business, "Heavyweight Gold," and it came against my friend and the most devastating force in wrestling of 1998, Bill Goldberg.

Getting my shot at the title also meant that for the second straight year, I would be in the main event at *Halloween Havoc.* To me, that was a distinction all its own.

I entered the match as an underdog or longshot, and the answer to the question, "Who's next?" I knew that it was a shot at being the first to upset Goldberg and his streak, and I also wanted to be the answer to the question, "Who's first?"

BILL GOLDBERG:

When Page won the match at "War Games," I knew that with his work ethic, passion, and intensity, he would make the very best of his opportunity. Page is relentless at times.

Just one year after sharing the main event marquee with Randy "Macho Man" Savage, Diamond Dallas Page was again the challenger in one of professional wrestling's greatest showcases.

The match pitted two of World Championship Wrestling's most popular performers who had emerged in the top tier during 1998.

Since his debut in September of 1997, Bill Goldberg's rise was best described as meteoric. His undefeated career was designed on a long string of impressive and brutal matches that featured his signature "spear" and "jackhammer." With only a few exceptions, most of Goldberg's matches lasted fewer than five minutes, and he had seldom been challenged.

He, too, had aligned against the nWo. Like Sting, he helped scatter members of the New World Order when they were executing one of their patented ambushes. "Gold-Berg" had supported Page during the ongoing war against the nWo, and it seemed as if they were allies.

To that point, Goldberg's most impressive victories were over members of the New World Order. A victory over "The Giant" established him as a serious threat, and when he defeated Scott Hall, it set up a title match with Hollywood Hogan.

On July 6th, in the Georgia Superdome, in front of over 40,000 rabid fans and a nationally-televised *Monday Night Nitro* audience, the world saw Bill Goldberg defeat Hollywood Hulk Hogan for the world heavyweight title.

Goldberg was the talk of the sport, and along with Steve Austin of the WWF, was a poster boy for the wild popularity that professional wrestling was enjoying.

It always added to a feud when there was a natural clash of characters, but matching two driven people like Goldie and I made for a battle of pride and a match built on respect. The combination of Goldberg's size and strength was plenty to contend with, but eluding his spear was my main objective.

I watched as much tape as I could, but Goldberg's matches didn't show too many flaws. My training schedule was in full gear as I prepared my body for the type of punishment that I knew I would endure. I even made arrangements for Dr. Ken West to go with me to Vegas, not only to see what I did for a living, but to be available to adjust and treat me before and after my match.

I knew that I wasn't supposed to beat Bill Goldberg, but then again, I wasn't supposed to be a wrestler, a mid-carder, a main-event guy, or the . . . oh my GOOD GAWD . . . two-time, two-time Heavyweight Champion of the World, either. I prepared knowing that Bill Goldberg would try to end the match quickly, and I knew that the longer I battled him, the better chance I would have.

The majesty of the MGM Grand Ballroom and the sight and sound of announcer Michael Buffer in the center of the ring added to the magnitude and intensity of the championship match. Goldberg and Diamond Dallas Page were indeed "Ready to Rumble!"

The match lived up to the hype, and it was a great one, receiving much critical praise. It is also known as one of the greatest matches lasting less than 15 minutes. The main-event battle was filled with nonstop action and near pin falls. Each wrestler went full throttle and survived his opponent's finishing move. Page was one of the first opponents to ever stagger back to his feet following a Goldberg spear, and later, when DDP got Goldberg in position for a Diamond Cutter, Goldberg somehow managed to shake Page off of him.

Bill Goldberg retained the WCW World Heavyweight Championship title that night. Both men came out of the ring arm in arm, victorious in their quest to give everything they had, and to give wrestling fans a night to remember.

BILL GOLDBERG:

I don't think it was my longest match, but it was the first one that I knocked myself out in. We were both out on our feet at one point, and we maintained a high level of intensity the entire match. It was a great match and a great learning experience at that early point in my career.

It was that way with Page going back to even the early days of The Power Plant. When he worked in the ring with me, I learned more in an afternoon than I learned in weeks. He's been a positive influence on many guys, both in and out of the ring.

Our match at Havoc was a positive turning point in our careers, and like Page said, "The match brought us both to a different level." Our competitive spirits made it possible for both of us to express new dimensions.

I never felt like either of us could lose if we showed everyone why we deserved to be there that night. Eric Bishoff said it was special to have us emerge as major superstars in the same year, but the big picture was that both Goldie and I had answered our critics while staking our claims to a future in wrestling with our work in the ring.

Losing is never satisfying, but knowing that I gave 100 percent certainly is. I wasn't making any excuses for not winning the title from Goldberg, and there was nothing I would have done differently in preparation.

I didn't feel like I lost to Bill Goldberg that night, and when he lifted me up after I was counted out, the crowd's reaction made me realize that everybody won that night.

Ongoing feuds with Savage, Hall, Hogan, Hennig, and Hart established Page as a top guy. His *Triple Jeopardy* match, involving Raven and Chris Benoit, and his title challenge with Goldberg were rated in the top ten matches of the year.

In 1998, Diamond Dallas Page appeared in nine of the twelve Pay-Per-View matches telecast by Turner, and had become a top earner for World Championship Wrestling. His merchandise was selling, his ratings were high, and his image was positive. No one could deny his charisma and ability to entertain.

Diamond Dallas Page was a product of WCW. He was schooled in their training facilities and climbed their ladder to the top. Once given the chance, Diamond Dallas Page made sure that he held up his end of the deal, becoming a sales tool and profit generator for World Championship Wrestling.

With fame and celebrity exposure comes the notion by many that it is similar to winning the lottery. Many old friends asked me what it was like being around Page once he had the big bucks. After all, everyone had heard that World Championship Wrestling paid millions to secure the services of Malone, Rodman, and Leno; and everyone knows that Hulk and Savage make millions, right?

Yes, they do . . . but all the rest don't . . . and while Page was working in the same ring, he was far away from their tax bracket.

It was late 1998, and Page was being compensated based on his position in early 1997 when he emerged from his feud with

Eddie Guerrero. Page hadn't been offered contract renegotiations, and he never focused on what anyone else had earned, while his work-rate was one of the company's best. Page had to be reminded often that it wasn't his time yet. And although he was one of the highest-rated superstars, he was one of the lowest-paid wrestlers. And that's a fact.

There were no lawsuits, walkouts, or tantrums. He never complained on- or off-camera and never begrudged anyone for their salary. He knew his time was coming.

As 1998 came to an end, DDP prepared for a feud with the biggest man in professional wrestling, Paul "The Giant" Wight. Facing a man of Wight's size made for added concerns. To quote Paul Wight, "One thing about wrestling is for sure—there's nothing fake about gravity."

Page entered the feud knowing that an injury could affect his ability to fulfill any upcoming contract and that his career could be over before he reached superstar earnings. True, he could have dodged any real challenge and rested on his achievements prior to scheduling matches with the 7'2", 500-pound "Giant," but he is different. Page has always been different. And he will always be an anomaly.

Chapter Twenty

Giving Back And Getting Over

The journey has been life's greatest lesson, and whatever frustrations and disappointments I have endured have pretty much faded away. The string on the yo-yo has gotten shorter, but that's not to say that the ups and downs vanished when I got to the main event.

My real roots are in the bar business where I learned to create and develop an environment that energized people. From there, it was all promotion and hype. The immediate signs of success were how the crowd reacted or how hot the dance floor got. But, keeping a place hot and really being over in the bar business happens when crowds are created, new crowds are cultivated, and the place continues running hot.

The parallels between my life in wrestling and my life in the bar business were always there, although I realized it more as time went on. The bar business stoked my fire, but professional wrestling has been, and will always be, the vehicle that enabled me to attain most of my desires and reach my goals . . . for now.

There are plenty of people whose lives have been touched by the heart, soul, and sheer intensity of Page Falkinburg. But when his cause became a passion, he rallied the troops to help make it happen.

Probably the most prolific charitable program that Page has ever been associated with is his "Bang It Out For Books" program that started in the summer of 1998 to focus on the fight against illiteracy in America.

"Bang It Out For Books" began in Sturgis, South Dakota in 1998 during our annual trip to the *Road Wild* PPV. A year before that in Sturgis, I met a dynamic lady named Maryann O'Brien who worked for the computer firm, Gateway.

We speculated about the prospects of Diamond Dallas Page and Gateway showing kids the benefits of multimedia.

MARYANN O'BRIEN
GATEWAY MARKETING PROGRAM SPECIALIST:

I had such a jaded view of wrestling that I couldn't imagine any of these guys having an interest or being engaged in technology on any level.

When I heard Page was coming to Sioux City, Iowa, I organized an autograph signing for employees and their families.

On the morning of the signing, I was a bit worried about the turnout. It was snowing, and no one worked on weekends at the Gateway plant. By the afternoon, I wasn't embarrassed by the turnout at all. In fact, I was overwhelmed. It was incredible. Four hundred plus Gateway employees and their children showed up, including executives, members of management, and almost every other level of employee. Page was great with the crowd and signed autographs for over two hours.

Since that day, Page and I have been great friends. He will always be welcome in "Gateway Country."

Months later, Maryann was a guest at Page's birthday party held in Ft. Lauderdale. The event was more of a reunion for Page's friends from his days in the bar business. Meeting Maryann O'Brien was especially nice. She quickly became a bro, and her keen marketing sense gave us plenty to admire. It was at that first meeting that she helped give Page the direction that ultimately led to the formation of "Bang It Out For Books."

I respected Maryann's marketing ability, and when I asked her to meet with Kim and me to discuss a few ideas, I made sure to invite Smokey.

During that meeting, I discussed the growing opportunities in paid autograph appearances. If I were to become a part of that select circuit of wrestlers who were paid by the merchant, who then charged the fans, I wanted a portion of my fees to go to a charity. Maryann suggested that I target all of my donations to one area, rather than try to pick and choose from all the worthy causes. So, based on my past reading difficulties, it seemed logical that reading or literacy in general would become my focus.

It wasn't until August at the next *Road Wild* PPV event that Page, Kim, and Maryann saw each other again. It had been only one year since their first meeting, and it appeared that there might be an opportunity for Page to effectively get his message across. Page's ideas on how to give a donation were great, but, as usual, unconventional.

I knew that it would be hard to find an existing national charity with the same intentions as Page. Having literacy as his main focus made it easy to find schools and organizations that were short of funding and could use the help, but there were other factors that made it a bit more difficult. We knew that we would also have to sell the idea that a professional wrestler wanted to make a commitment to educate children at both a national and local level.

When I posed the various options to Page, he asked, "Isn't there some way we can cut through all the bullsh*t? How about if I just walked into an elementary school, put a thousand bucks on the principal's desk, and told him to buy some books for the kids with it?"

I thought about it for a few seconds, and started laughing.

The gimmick-man and "Prince of Promo" had mastered the notion that less is more. It was a simple solution . . . Page would just "Bang It Out For Books."

I spoke to Maryann, and while she was apologizing for not being able to help us more, she provided the inspiration and contact that gave the program validity.

She told me that Adam Hirschfelder of *Scholastic America* had an open ear to our proposal, but that she had experienced difficulty with many companies who were shying away from partnering with professional wrestling.

Smokey put our ideas on paper, came up with the name, and was committed to helping me create my own foundation to provide books to local schools. He told me about *Scholastic*, and I was jacked. *Scholastic* was the perfect match for "Bang It Out For Books."

Scholastic has been around for about 75 years, and although they are one of the nation's largest sources for educational books and multimedia materials, they also publish books for kids that are fun to read.

It was important to me to get across to kids that reading was an activity that could produce positive feelings. My focus was that reading was not just a school activity, and that if a kid had trouble reading like I did . . . there was help out there.

After talking to Adam Hirschfelder, I was encouraged that we could do something together. I put together a proposal based on my old bar training. It would be easier and faster if *Scholastic* could donate product rather than wait for us to develop something that might cost both time and money. It was similar in the nightclub business; if we could offset advertising or repair costs with free drinks or cover, we'd all benefit.

Adam loved the idea and gave us the green light to print a sign. He said that we could count on *Scholastic America* to match Page's cash donation with free books and educational material.

More bang! for the buck . . . and more books for the bang!

It was perfect. I would do an appearance, meet school officials and students right in their community, and then send them a check. *Scholastic* would then double my cash donation with books. Thankfully, Adam Hirschfelder had the guts and foresight to see that we had a good program, and that "Bang It Out For Books" could double the books and double the impression on the kids.

Over the next three months, Page did nearly 20 autograph appearances. Close to $40,000 in cash and materials were donated in the names of Diamond Dallas Page's program, "Bang It Out For Books," *Scholastic*, and *World Championship Wrestling.* It was also a credit to the various merchants and organizations that brought DDP in for autograph sessions to help their community.

Each appearance was a bit different, and in each town, DDP and his efforts were well-received. "Bang It Out For Books" was off and running like a wild horse until we reached Jackson, Mississippi.

DDP was scheduled to make a mall appearance, and the local elementary school system had been recommended by the merchant to receive the donation.

Two days prior to the signing, a representative of the school system informed us that they had elected to decline the donation,

In 1998, Page established "Bang It Out For Books"—a nationwide program to promote reading to elementary school kids.

since it was coming from a professional wrestler. The representative went on to say that since they had banned kids from wearing wrestling T-shirts in school, they felt there was a conflict.

I said, "Huh?"

As I wondered how free books and money to buy more could be a conflict for the kids, I scrambled to find a new school or organization to accept the money. By the next morning, a sports talk radio show had suggested we give the money to Vicksburg High School, since their library had recently been burned by arsonists.

Hours after confirming that our donation would go to the neighboring city of Vicksburg, the first school system called back. It seemed that there had been some terrible mistake . . . and they were accepting the donation after all.

It was one of the first times that Smokey saw how immediately negative people can be towards professional wrestling. I wasn't really surprised, although refusing to accept free books seemed bizarre, even to me. It was a hot topic in Jackson since, earlier that week, the state of Mississippi had been ranked way low in an education poll. The media was doing "man in the street" interviews, and there was plenty of heat. I agreed with Smokey that no matter what happened, Vicksburg High was getting the donation.

Smokey and I brainstormed an idea, and the North Park Mall Association helped by matching the $1,000 cash donation for their local school system. *Scholastic* was right there to pitch in, and they matched the cash with books. The result of a negative situation suddenly became doubly positive. To this day, Jackson is one of my favorite stops on that Deep South loop.

Christmas has become even more of a chance for Page to expand his charitable efforts into something much bigger than it was when he was in the bar business. After Page and Kimberly were settled in their home, they began to host an annual party during the holidays. Even the party had an angle—guests had to bring a toy for kids in the Atlanta area. The guestlist was a "Who's Who" of local WCW wrestlers and employees, and each year, the

Kimberly gives her wish list to Santa, who is Ron Reece. Reece suggested that DDP make the Diamond Sign before using his finish.

amount of gifts grew by leaps and bounds.

I think it was strange for the boys to see me in full Mr. Christmas form. My annual decorations were a cross between The Griswalds[1] and Macy's, and were probably nearly a spectacle by that time. Giving gifts to kids had become part of my holiday celebration since my earliest days in the bar business, so the "house party" was the solution.

KIMBERLY:

We had so many wonderful gifts for kids of all ages, and I found a very worthy new charity that was most grateful for the donations. The Children's Restoration Network is a group that not only feeds and clothes kids from troubled homes, but

---

[1] *The Griswalds-Chevy Chase's movie family in* Christmas Vacation.

provides education, job placement, and housing for single mothers who want to help themselves. Knowing that the gifts would help offset the demand was great, and the wrestling community and other friends helped while we celebrated Christmas in a big way.

Looking back, the first parties were the most fun, but they outgrew our home almost immediately. Over 225 people attended our third Christmas party, and our house was busting at the seams. We finally moved the party to a place that was better suited, and each year, more kids and families have benefited.

During Christmas of 1997, Page organized a wrestling event for charity at Polk High School in Atlanta that featured some future WCW superstars. The money benefited both the Polk High School athletic department and the newly-established Brian Pillman Memorial Fund. The main event saw DDP matched against Marcus "Buff" Bagwell of the nWo.

Many of the guys on that card are the current superstars of wrestling, and working with Buff is always fun for me. Marc and I go back to the lean days, and hanging with him

Jim Cox, of Atlanta's Children's Restoration Network, accepts gifts from DDP and Kimberly's annual Secret Santa Party.

can mean seeing sudden bolts of intensity that he isn't afraid to show up close sometimes. He's a tough, hard-nosed "sumabitch" Georgia boy who does not hesitate to confront any situation. Buff has a no-fear confidence and direct approach, and to top that, he has two brothers who make him look like the tame one from time to time.

Fans became familiar with Buff's mom, Mrs. Judy Bagwell, when she played herself in a series of cameo appearances during Buff's membership in the nWo. Judy Bagwell is just one of those moms who you know had her hands full with her boys. The Bagwell Brothers make Hollywood's bad boys, The Baldwin Brothers, look like the Osmond family. Her toughness and fortitude must be the source of Buff's "ever-ready" attitude. I had met Judy before at Polk High School, but throughout the night, I felt her looking at me as if she wanted to talk with me.

Finally, at one point, when I was away from everybody, she approached me and said, "Dallas, you don't have to answer this if you don't want to . . . but I just gotta know!" I couldn't imagine what she would ask. She then put her hand on her hip, changed her voice a bit, and, in a low southern drawl, said, "Are you as bad a 'molla-fu*ka' in real life as you are on TV?" She just cracked me up with her delivery, as well as her question. It was comical, and at the same time, it was huge being put over by the mom of three certifiably bad "molla-fu*kas."

Buff Bagwell suffered what could have been a serious and disabling spinal injury in front of the world in a *Nitro* match in April 1998. Not only has he worked his way back to a full recovery, but he continues to be "Buff the Stuff" and a huge fan favorite.

That night, while Buff was lying in the ring with the paramedics working on him, the air in the back got real heavy. We all have our own ways of dealing with the hard, cold fact that every time we climb into the ring, our careers and lives can be altered in any number of ways. I think most guys concentrate on being both physically and mentally prepared before they step out from behind the curtain, because once you start down that ramp, it's all about the reaction and getting over. That's really what anybody who ever got a taste of "the

Another Christmas ritual is the annual photo shoot for the Falkinburg Family greeting card. That's "Sophie" on the left and "Spooky" on the right.

show" in wrestling ever wanted—to stay healthy and to get over.

In the small central Florida town of Leesburg, an entire community was adopting Diamond Dallas Page as their newest resident and favorite son—so they thought.

The popularity of DDP went in a different direction when a scam artist and career criminal named Marvin Lee claimed he was WCW superstar, Diamond Dallas Page. He went on a four-day spending spree with a rubber checkbook.

This guy had a 54-page rap sheet, and must have been pretty convincing, because when I saw his picture, I was shocked. How anyone could have thought that this guy could get in a ring, let alone have the rap to make people open their wallets, homes, and businesses to him, was amazing.

Impersonating a professional wrestler in a con-game scheme was a first according to Alan Sharp of the publicity department at WCW. Marvin Lee was still at large when we first heard about his weekend in Leesburg. In a matter of days, he had managed to negotiate the purchase of Marty's Lounge, which he planned to rename "Diamond D's." He also ran up large bills at Marty's and the Budget Host Inn, and used bad checks for payment.

A local doctor actually had the phony DDP as a houseguest for a couple of days. But Marvin's shining moment and swan song came when he drove out of Phillips' Toyota dealership with a new, $32,000 Toyota 4Runner. The guy's pitch was so good, they never checked his credit.

The more I heard, the more I didn't like the fact that someone was signing autographs and impersonating me at the expense of other people. They finally caught the guy, and I guess he's watching *Nitro* from prison these days. However, I wanted to at least make good on the bogus autographs and give the people of Leesburg the chance to meet the real DDP.

Page visited Leesburg the next time WCW was in the area. He

signed free autographs for two hours at Phillips' Toyota, and met the people who had been scammed by Marvin Lee.

In lieu of an appearance fee, Page requested that a donation be made to the "Bang It Out For Books" program. With the help of *Scholastic* and Phillips Toyota, DDP donated $3,000 in cash and educational materials to the Arnold Palmer Children's Hospital Library in Orlando.

Negative publicity? Not a chance . . . just another hidden opportunity for "Positively Page."

Life is brutally honest sometimes, and there are many times in our lives when we are stopped in our daily tracks as a reminder of how fleeting the good times can be.

One of the toughest things to see is a child suffering while his family bravely maintains faith through it all. To watch the faces of sick children brighten when visited by a professional wrestler is remarkable. Through the years, so many of the boys have tried to call or send photos to give kids a reason to smile and look forward to seeing us on TV again.

I was once asked to call an eight-year-old boy who had been stricken with a rare form of leukemia. It is not easy to make those calls because of never knowing what condition the child or the family may be in on that day. But when I called eight-year-old Dustin Brown, I felt like I was talking to a well-adjusted adult. Although he had been through a lot, and was preparing for another bone marrow transplant, he was positive, optimistic, and spirited.

I realized that the young boy had no idea that his fight could not be won. But talking to Dustin that night energized me in such a way that two minutes into the conversation, I was a bigger fan of his than he was of mine.

Page gathered up nearly a dozen different autographed items for Dustin Brown. Some were pictures from Page and Kimberly, and others were samples of items that were to be released at Christmas. Whether it was a T-shirt or an issue of *WCW Magazine*, Page had inscribed a few positive words to his little bro,

Dustin. Page instructed me to send Dustin only a couple of things each week, so that we could brighten his days for as long as possible.

Over the months to follow, Page called Dustin's home or hospital bed to make sure he knew that DDP was in his corner.

Page has always been goal-oriented, and once he has attained success and validation, he develops a network. In both the nightclub business and wrestling, he learned the ropes, paid his dues, and worked himself to the point where he could contribute and make a difference in the lives of others.

He can go from the student to the teacher with great ease, but has always maintained his status as an "idea guy," who can help direct and advise others. Whether he was creating a bar promotion or repackaging a wrestler who he thought had potential, it became more than just a challenge . . . it became Page's entertainment.

As much as I am the shameless-but-proud self-promoter, I have always looked for ways to get the most out of every situation. All my life, I have been in businesses that were dependent on people with a vision and the quest to stay hot and get over. The bar business and wrestling provided plenty of outlets for my creative and, sometimes, wild imagination. And when I could develop an idea and help someone realize their potential, it worked for me.

I learned early on that the bar business and wrestling were often looked down upon by segments of society as temporary employment or less serious work. The broad talents of so many people I know have been underestimated. Hidden inside all of us are potential and passion, and finding and releasing these gifts is empowering and a whole lot of fun.

GLENN GILBERTTI
WCW SUPERSTAR "DISCO INFERNO":

Page's critics amaze me when they say that he is a self-serving promoter because I know that it's the most ridiculous statement I have ever heard. From the first day I met him, to

*this day, I have never seen anyone go out of their way to help
people like Page does. There have been many times when I
couldn't figure out why he was spending so much time helping
other guys instead of promoting himself. If he had spent as
much time self-promoting as he spent helping others, it would
be Page who is the wrestler who could become a governor or
president.*

*Page helped resurrect my character after I scrapped the
idea following a time on the indie circuit. It was Page who
helped me get an interview to show the tape of my character
and my work in the ring. Shortly after, I signed with WCW,
and I'm still "The Disco Inferno."*

STEVE "STING" BORDEN:

*Page always made an effort to help those around him,
especially the younger guys and those who were on their
way up. Anyone who has the capacity to help people is a
very secure person, and Dallas is one of those people. There
are guys who have been in the business a lot longer who lack
the guts and security to help others. Hats off to Page for
being someone who will lend a hand and make a difference
for the next wave of guys.*

*Page is also very supportive, and his positive attitude is
a constant. Often times, he is the first to approach a guy
following a match or an interview to express what he liked
about it. Even when something doesn't go as planned, he
will find a positive in the effort.*

*Sometimes, his positive twist makes me mad, but I'd much
rather be around people like Page. It's difficult to feel down
around him because his attitude helps me see the best in every situation.*

For some, Page's career and positive attitude have served as
examples that all things are possible. For others, he planted the
seed and never stopped providing whatever light he could to make
it grow.

BILL GOLDBERG:

I doubt I would ever have seriously considered a life in

professional wrestling after football if it weren't for Page. Page seldom lets anyone forget where he stands on something, and he told me often that I had a place in professional wrestling.

Page influences many, but to those who made the effort to strive for their personal goals and commitments, Page has been everything from inspiration to taskmaster.

SCOTT "RAVEN" LEVY:

Page and I have always had a love-hate relationship. We are very different, even though we are both bombastic, overbearing, obnoxious, and misunderstood at times. It is his sheer, unbridled optimism that blows my mind.

While Page and I disagree on many issues, we have mutual respect and concern for each another and our business.

He's like the demanding big brother I never had. We fight all the time, and most of the time, I think we are pains in each other's a$$es. But there is a deep-rooted, brotherly love that exists between us, and I wouldn't have it any other way.

Page's help and influence have been instrumental on several occasions in my career. They were major events for me, starting with Page arranging for my first tryout with World Championship Wrestling. After I worked in all three of the major federations, he helped me re-sign the largest contract I ever had with WCW.

If there is one thing that sets Page apart, it is that he wants people to succeed. Most of his critics have been silenced, and all that remains are people who are jealous that he is comfortable with himself and helping others. The ones who call him a shameless self-promoter are envious, since that is such a major part of what we are as performers. Because Page is so much better at it than everyone else around him, it has always created problems for him. Page is creative, and has a genuine passion to improve the product. He is successful at helping others, but he also has a knack for helping himself.

Everyone in his circle of friends will agree that Page Falkinburg left a positive impression on their lives. Often times, people see Page's passion, intensity, and the demands that he makes of himself, and it becomes their nature as well.

PERRY SATULLO
WCW SUPERSTAR "SATURN":

Page sets an example for so many guys. Only a few of us work as hard as Page, but it is a given that no one outworks Page.

We wrestle on a lot of days throughout the year, and the punishment to our bodies is unreal. But Page goes at TV speed and "balls to the wall" every match. Our job is to make people scream, and when we work with Page, we know there will be noise in the building.

Locking up with some of the new guys helped me learn different styles and challenged me physically. Sometimes, I noticed right away that someone had more to offer than could be seen on paper or at first glance.

CHRIS KLUCSARITS
WCW SUPERSTAR "KANYON":

I signed a temporary jobber contract with WCW, and was training at The Plant. During my first week, I met Page. There was never anyone of Page's caliber who trained as religiously.

I was a DDP fan even in his manager days in the AWA, and was thankful that Page took a liking to me. He is an example of the old-school integrity of the business, and he demands respect for the tradition of the guys who put us in the positions we are in today.

There is nothing Page will ever ask or demand of anyone, in or out of the ring, that he doesn't demand of himself.

I heard about this guy who was seven-foot-something and five hundred pounds. He was supposed to be a great athlete, and when I first met him at The Plant, we clicked immediately. He was polite and humble, and was the biggest son-of-a-b*tch I had ever met.

There was no doubt he had freakish size, but he was incredibly agile and more mobile than smaller guys.

When I challenged Paul "The Giant" Wight to show me how he would do an interview, he showed an incredible amount of charisma, cutting right into a promo like an old pro. No one has ever impressed me with a cold, off-the-cuff mock interview like Paul Wight.

Paul "The Big Show" Wight
Former WCW Superstar "The Giant":

I was brought in with the help of Hulk Hogan, but when I met Dallas on my first day of training at The Power Plant, I was very excited. I had been a huge fan of DDP's since I had worked as the world's largest furniture deliveryman.

During the first conversation we had, he said, "Alright, live camera . . . you and Mean Gene . . . give me the interview."

After that, Dallas Page took me under his wing and became more than just my mentor. He was a friend and partner who helped me to become a man. There were other guys who helped me in the ring, but Page became my motivator and the only guy who could build my confidence to the point where I could succeed in this business.

Page was responsible for putting me in the position to earn a contract with WCW. Not only did he help Eric Bischoff to see me in a different light, but Dallas Page prepared me mentally for my "make it or break it" debut.

Paul Wight's size alone created enough interest for World Championship Wrestling to showcase him as the next "Giant" in professional wrestling, and give him a limited contract to appear in a PPV event against Hulk Hogan. As much as it was a golden opportunity to shine in front of the wrestling world, it was also the match in which Paul Wight was measured and evaluated by fans, critics, and WCW.

There was plenty for Paul Wight to be nervous about going into that match. It was the largest crowd that "The Giant" had ever appeared before. I knew that the "next coming of Andre" hype had him concerned, but I also knew that stepping into the ring with the biggest name in the history of wrestling, Hollywood Hulk Hogan, had him scared. I didn't blame him. Who wouldn't be terrified to be put in that spot at his age?

I couldn't help but try to prepare him in whatever way I could for the mental challenge that he faced.

PAUL WIGHT:

I had the support of plenty of people, but Dallas had the sense, and was interested enough in me to know that I needed more than that. He walked right up to me and said, "Okay, Giant boy . . . I'm Hogan . . . now get on me." I grabbed at air, he countered my move, and I froze. Page's next words were, "Now what?"

Dallas Page is my mentor, and his opinions and guidance assisted me in getting to this point. He also helped make the battle with Hollywood Hogan become Pro Wrestling Illustrated's *Match of the Year, and me, their Rookie of the Year.*

DDP could be called a director of player development, a talent scout, and most often, a mentor to dozens of guys who are quickly becoming the superstars of World Championship Wrestling. However, his contributions often go unnoticed. From evaluating a new finish of a guy waiting for his shot to being available for an hour-long pep talk, Page is there for those he supports and calls his friends.

RAY LLOYD
WCW SUPERSTAR "BUZZ STERN"(FORMERLY "GLACIER"):

He is unlike anybody I have ever met, and I can truly say that without Page's friendship and attention, I would never have been given the opportunity for a contract.

Diamond Dallas Page's story is a ray of hope for every young or unknown wrestler. He is a living example of someone who has climbed past and through any limitations and roadblocks that have gotten in his way. He is an example for people everywhere not to let anyone ever say, "It can't be done."

Page has had an influence on me in so many ways, and I

am fortunate to be one of the guys who he has taken an interest in. Page is much more than a teacher to so many of the guys, and those he has helped in some way will be the superstars of wrestling for the next 20 years.

I grew up watching wrestling with my dad and twin brother. My dad was always supportive, and it was his dream to see me in the ring. My dad passed away before I got to the show, and he never got the chance to see me in the middle of a WCW ring, but I will always be thankful. Diamond Dallas Page Falkinburg helped me accomplish my dad's dream.

Just as I studied different wrestlers and their characters' performances in the ring and on the mic, I encouraged and expected the young guys coming up to do the same. That's where the whole thing started for me; I watched and studied the guys who dug the trenches and made a difference.

Kanyon showed relentless desire to learn and improve, and sometimes reminded me of myself. He's an "up north" guy who, before signing as a jobber with WCW, had worked in Memphis. We became friends while training often at The Plant, and he told me about a friend in Memphis who he wanted me to see.

I saw the guy on a tape, and was very impressed, so I mentioned him in passing to Eric Bischoff. Once I got the chance to see the guy in the ring, I knew that Billy Kidman would become something special.

Imagine the odds of a guy his size making the impact that he has—a tremendously talented high-flyer who didn't have the opportunity to compete like some of the smaller Mexican luchadores. Billy made the best of his shot, and has unlimited potential.

BILLY KIDMAN
WCW SUPERSTAR:

Without Kanyon getting to Page, I may never have gotten a chance. After Page saw me in the ring, his only comment was: "Wow!" He told me that he would do whatever he could to help me, and he has never stopped.

After he got the tape to Eric Bischoff, I was signed to my first contract over the phone. From that point on, he has been a constant supporter. Although his ideas are sometimes out there, nobody has a greater sense for this business than Page. In less than two years, Page helped me get to the show.

My greatest honor was when Page asked me to help with the training of Karl Malone, Jay Leno, and Kevin Eubanks. There are not many established guys who will stick their necks out for younger guys, but Page is different. He enjoys the pressure of taking guys to the next level.

Page has remembered each person along the way who contributed to the industry and to him personally. He maintains friendships and phone communication with many, and when he can show his appreciation, he does so in a variety of ways.

MIKE GRAHAM
PROFESSIONAL WRESTLING VETERAN:

I was out of wrestling completely for well over four years, and as it gained popularity, I knew I could still contribute. When Page called to ask if I missed the business, I told him that I was as ready to get back in as I could ever be.

There are many guys I helped along the way who brought my name up as a candidate for the booking committee or creative staff, but Page got me back into wrestling. Almost ten years after meeting this guy who hitched a ride in a pickup truck to be at one of my shows, he went to bat for me and revived my love for the business.

RANDY "MACHO MAN" SAVAGE:

Once a program is worked, it's usually over. Those involved usually move on to the next feud. That's fine with me, but when I returned home on Thanksgiving weekend from being on the road, there was a message that I never expected to receive.

It was from Page, and he was thanking me for the opportunity to work with me in a good, long program that helped him reach the next level.

It was one of the coolest things anyone had ever done. He

showed the world that he was a top guy, but was still thankful for every step along the way.

December 1998 was a monumental month for me, and one that will always be special. It began with Kimberly and I moving into our new home in Atlanta in a neighborhood and price range that I never expected to be in.

Kimberly found the perfect house while I was on the road, and we were able to spend Christmas and New Year's in our new home.

My road schedule was brutal, but when opportunities arose for me to conquer my fear of reading, wrestle on the Jersey Shore, or give more cash, gifts, and books to kids, I wanted to do it all.

With the formation of "Bang It Out for Books," the holiday season switched its focus to something other than just toys for kids. The logical alternative was for *Scholastic* to get involved and make the event bigger than ever. We had the full support of the Children's Restoration Network (CRN), which is a great organization in need of all the help it can get. The "Fourth Annual Diamond Dallas Page's Secret Santa Party" was a main event in more ways than one.

I felt it would be fitting for Mr. Christmas to read the holiday classic '*Twas the Night Before Christmas* so the children could learn that Christmas is a time for giving and bringing happiness to those less fortunate.

The "Secret Santa Party" took on a new life, and we turned the autograph session into an hour-long party for the kids and their parents. Kimberly was by my side for support, and she read too, as Smokey ran a slide show so the kids could follow along.

When Smokey suggested that I continue doing readings and speeches for kids, in addition to autograph signings, I knew that I would have a rematch with my fear of reading in front of people. Kids are very critical of each other, and I wanted them to know that I too had been teased about reading, but that I had beat it.

Getting Kimberly involved made it easier for me, and it also gave me so much pleasure to have my partner and love of my life by my side. I couldn't help being choked up that night knowing that it was Kimberly who had helped to expose my problem. She set me on the course to overcome my fears and enjoy reading as a part of my everyday life.

Diamond Dallas Page and Kimberly Falkinburg were captivating as they read to the audience of wide-eyed kids of all ages. Page began with a Christmas story entitled *Olive . . . The Other Reindeer* by Otto J. Seibold and Vivian Walsh, and had the kids leaning on every word. He was animated, relaxed, and flawless, never selling the fact that this was a place he hadn't visited in over 30 years.

Kimberly read the Dr. Seuss classic *How the Grinch Stole Christmas*, interacting with the kids as they recited lines from their

Christmas is a grand celebration for all the Falkinburgs. (back row) Brother, Colin; Mom, Elsie; Sister, Jamie; and Page. (front row) Colin's wife, Cathy; Sister, Sally; her husband, Paul Smith; and that's longtime family friend, Bruce, in a head lock.

1998 saw Page and Kimberly combine "Bang It Out For Books" *with their annual Secret Santa Party.*

annual favorite. By the time Page read the last words, " . . . and to all a good night!" the crowd knew they were seeing someone much different than the guy on TNT's *Monday Night Nitro*.

TONY PALLAGROSI
OLD BRO AND FRIEND:

Page's effort to help kids with reading fundamentals was being talked about more and more on the Jersey Shore. I spoke with Jon Bon Jovi, and had been contacted by Bruce Springsteen's assistant, Terry McGovern. They both expressed interest in Page's foundation.

I had also become more aware of money problems that many schools and educational programs were experiencing. When I looked closer, I found several programs that were in dire need of immediate funding.

Page suggested that a WCW charity wrestling match would be the best financial quick fix, and also a great way to bring attention to the needs of these worthy causes.

We selected three local programs that served as after-

school educational alternatives to the streets.

In a matter of weeks, Tony Pallagrosi, Page, and other WCW superstars had put together "Diamond Dallas Page's Reading, Rasslin', and Rock Extravaganza."

The ideas snowballed, and all the bases were quickly covered. A private reading hosted by Diamond Dallas Page would take place for underprivileged children at the nostalgic Royale Theater in Red Bank, New Jersey.

Tony told me that several celebrities who had homes in surrounding towns offered to join me in meeting and reading to the kids.

When I heard that Bon Jovi was going to be home during the holidays and had accepted Tony's invitation, I sat back and smiled, and thought about that night at Xanadu. No matter where his amazing talents lead him, Jon is just a terrific guy. Bon Jovi is now an accomplished actor, and continues to amaze me with his versatility and ability to keep it all real.

JON BON JOVI
JERSEY BOY:

I thought it was a great idea and a great way to give back to our hometown, and he was such a hero to the kids. What I didn't know was that Page had a reading problem that he did not overcome until late in his adult years. Seeing Page was the same as it had been every time we saw each other. It really didn't matter if I was on tour or he was champion of the world, we were just a couple of hometown friends who were happy to see each other again.

When Tony P. confirmed that Chaz Palminteri would join Jon and me at the reading, I popped. Chaz is truly an incredible story and an unbelievable talent, and his book and movie *A Bronx Tale* is one of my favorites. He wrote the screenplay and starred opposite Robert DeNiro in what I believe was an underrated, epic wise-guy film with a message.

Rolling Stone rock critic and biographer, Dave Marsh; screenwriter and director, John Sayles; and actor and writer, Daniel Wolfe were also present. They read stories and gave the kids their outlook on the meaning of the holiday season.

It was a tremendous thrill to be a part of it all, but the best thing was meeting each one of the kids and giving them gift bags full of toys, books, and school supplies.

TONY PALLAGROSI
CONCERTS EAST:

When Page told me that he was sure that we could get a quality card with WCW superstars for a Saturday night in Asbury Park, I was surprised. I knew that we had time and travel constraints, and there was also the WCW schedule to contend with. It was the Christmas season as well, and I doubted that anyone would want to be in New Jersey to wrestle for charity on a rare weekend off.

I put the word out, and my bro's were right there to make sure that this card was as big as it could be. The main event was a sneak preview of an upcoming PPV match that I was scheduled to have with The Giant, and that ensured a highly-publicized match. The rest of the card featured top superstars such as Raven, Kanyon, Saturn, Billy Kidman, Ray Lloyd, Alex Wright, Wrath, Konan, The Disco Inferno, and even Bam Bam Bigelow, who made his first WCW appearance in his hometown.

Scott Dickinson made the trip as the referee, and Danny Young was the WCW trainer on hand. Without "The Sarge" bringing the ring up from Atlanta and making sure we were technically sound, we would have been lost. Everyone gave up their free time to make the event a success.

Smokey did a great job as the ring announcer, and even my old friends, Donald "Beeda B" Ward and Smittee were on hand to help entertain the crowd.

I was sick with the flu, but I wasn't going to miss this for anything. I would have entered the ring on a stretcher if it had been necessary.

This visit to Asbury Park was another one of my dreams come true. As a kid, the Asbury Park Convention Center was the top venue in the area for concerts, speeches, and, oh, yes . . . wrestling.

This was the same old run-down building where my buddy, John Shipley, and I asked Greg "The Hammer" Valentine how to get into wrestling. Wrestling as the headlined main event with some of my very closest friends in the place where I first saw it live made it extra special.

I was completely run-down, had lost weight, and wasn't able to continue my workout regime due to the flu. Although I had so many positive things from 1998 to look back on, I was stressed, sick, and worn-out. I finally went to a doctor who told me my flu had developed into walking pneumonia, and I was even wearier.

We got the news that Dustin Brown had lost his battle with leukemia and passed away. I was down, saddened by the news, and disappointed about not getting the chance to

DDP's Reading, Rasslin', & Rock" charity event benefited after-school reading programs on the Jersey Shore. The celebrity line-up included (left to right) actor/writer Daniel Wolfe, actor/director/writer Chaz Palminteri, author Dave Marsh, director John Sayles, DDP, and musician/writer/actor Jon Bon Jovi.

The boys turned out to make Christmas better for the kids. (clockwise) DDP, John, Nitro Girl Spice, David, Jeremy, "Kanyon," "Disco" Andre, "Saturn," Scotty, and Billy Kidman (seated next to Page).

visit Dustin before he died. I was dragging my a$$ around the house, dreading the next road trip.

KIMBERLY:

I hated seeing Page so beat up from the road, the ring, and all the extra things that he heaped upon himself in such a short time. The benefits of the events were fantastic, and not only was Page able to give so much to so many during that holiday season, he was able to accomplish many of his goals. He overcame his fear of reading in front of people, and he returned to his hometown where he lit up the Asbury Park Convention Center as one of the biggest superstars in professional wrestling.

Page reminded me of his favorite movie character, George Bailey. I looked at my husband and saw a face that lacked the positive glow and eternal shine, and said, "You know, George . . . you've really have had a "Wonderful Life".

I'll never forget where I was standing when Kim said those words. The exact moment is locked in my memory and frozen in time.

It was the most positive thing that anyone could have said to me. It was so fitting that when I needed motivation and a lift, it would be my angel, Kimberly, who made me realize what life is really all about.

CHAPTER TWENTY-ONE

THE CRITICS, THE FANS, THE MEDIA,
AND OTHER FRIENDS

I have always had critics, and, most times, I draw a positive out of what they are saying to me. But when people said sh*t about me when they didn't even know sh*t about me . . . then I reacted. And sometimes, I overreacted.

MARK MADDEN
WRESTLING JOURNALIST:

Oh yeah, I was critical of Diamond Dallas Page, and I don't necessarily retract the things I said back then. And it's not like I was the only one who was on him, because he was awful at times. Really, the fact that he would have every heel gimmick going at once was enough of a reason not to take him seriously.

Madden was blasting me every chance he got, and the attacks came no matter what I did. It wasn't that I couldn't take what he was saying, but I just couldn't understand critical, bitter sh*t when I didn't think the fu*kin' guy was looking at a thing that I was doing. He was saying the same things over and over again, and buried "the ghost of DDP past." As far as I was concerned, it was old news. Mark Madden was relentless, and couldn't get over the old DDP.

I said things to him and about him that I wouldn't think of saying again. I was pi$$ed, and I "lost it" when I saw the same repetitive sh*t. The gloves came off, and I verbally attacked him and his weight. I was as vivid about his size as he was about my look. It was war, and it was fought over the Internet and on the WCW "900" hotline. And it was a shoot.

MARK MADDEN:

The perception was that Page was getting TV time because of his friendship with Eric Bischoff. Granted, Page wasn't the only one who may have had a job because of his friendship or association with Bischoff, but I was seeing Page an overbearing amount of time for no apparent reason.

The rabbit, the doll, the lottery, The Booty Man, he's broke, he's rich, it's his money, he's got a benefactor . . . his character seemed to change weekly.

Don't think it was the first time that someone had said that having Eric Bischoff for a friend made my path easier. And guess what? . . . I know that there will always be people who think they know the real story. Right now, there are people on the Internet, and maybe even in the locker room, who will say until the end of time that without Bischoff . . . I'd be nothing.

That statement used to bother me, but, early on, I knew that being Eric's neighbor made me work that much harder. It was motivation for me, and made the road more of an uphill path that made me even stronger.

Despite what Madden and those rag sheet writers had said to bury me with the fanatical but negative wrestling fans, I got myself to wherever I was at that point.

This "great debate" sparked some spirited conversation, and it seems that it is a topic that will always travel with the career of Diamond Dallas Page.

The rumor mill said that it was all because Page Falkinburg and Eric Bischoff were neighbors. The rag writers said it had to be because they knew and were sure of it. Eric was the lubricant to slide Page right up the ladder, and to lay it out there for the world to see DDP in a starring role. "A number one . . . king of the hill and top of the heap." Oops . . . that's the song about "making it" in New York, not Atlanta.

The reaction I got when I posed the question to the boys really didn't surprise me. They all know that the odds of becoming a top guy are slim in the world of professional wrestling. And, at the same time, they know it's easier to get "buried" at the bottom than it is to be "greased" to the top.

JAKE "THE SNAKE" ROBERTS:

Oh, that's the biggest bunch of bullsh*t. I knew that it would be ten times harder for Page to do anything with Bischoff in that spot. Page was under constant scrutiny, and he took even more heat for knowing Bischoff. Those who had issues with Bischoff may have used Page as a scapegoat at times.

"STAGGER LEE" MARSHALL:

It really isn't fair for that connection to be made because it wasn't something that Eric would have intervened in, even though I felt that Page was being held down at times. Eric was busy, and really had delegated the day-to-day wrestling duties in other directions.

There was an opinion that Page was "Eric's guy" because of the old-boy network that had been so prevalent in the sport, but the reality was that neither man played the game that way. If anything, their friendship made it more difficult for the opportunity that Page needed to open up. Both men knew that there was a faction who never believed that Page belonged.

There were plenty of people who doubted Eric Bischoff's experience and ability to run the company. Couple that with the legions of boys, both past and present, who never saw Page as anything but a walking gimmick, and the debate loses some steam.

CURT HENNIG:

I've known both guys since the AWA days, and I've heard all about the neighbor thing. Neither guy had anything to do with what each has accomplished. Bischoff had his own goals and vision, and that didn't have anything to do with Diamond Dallas Page.

It could go on and on, but why bother? Eric is my friend, and he and I haven't always agreed on things. But in hindsight, I wouldn't have wanted it any other way. Those who doubted me saw that my efforts and intentions were as real as I was.

I had learned enough about the business from day one to know that it was worse to have a door shut on you than to wait or to look for someone to open one.

ERIC BISCHOFF
FORMER WCW VICE PRESIDENT:

I really wasn't aware of or concerned with what anyone else thought about our friendship. I have never made any decisions based on what it did for me personally, or for anyone else. My concern was making decisions that were right for the company.

That being said, I feel that it was harder for Page because of the position our friendship put him in at times. There were many other things that caused Page to get three times the amount of crap than other guys got, and being neighbors just added to it. Many times, Page felt he was ready for his shot at moving up, but, at the time, I thought he wasn't.

Page was always driven to put himself in the position to be noticed, and when his opportunity finally came, he proved to all of us that he would be everything that he believed he could be.

The consensus of the dozens of wrestlers who were interviewed is that Diamond Dallas Page could not have been denied his opportunity due to his work ethic, desire, and constant improvement. Many of the answers were philosophical, and some were even political. Others seemed to be "eating crow" while they answered the question. But I think that Steve Austin summed it up best.

Steve "Stone Cold" Austin:

Ah sh*t, Page deserves all the credit in the world because he worked himself into the position he is in today. There was no reason for him not to be re-signed by Bischoff at the time, and I guess the proof is evident by where he is today. He's one of the best things going over there (WCW), and that is all due to him, not Bischoff or anybody else. He didn't need any help, and nobody could have stopped him. He worked for it.

While many were still reluctant to admit that DDP belonged, it was Mark Madden who ceremoniously "flipped" from ardent critic to admiring fan, marking the end of a bitter feud that waged for months.

Mark Madden:

I made one statement that seemed to get under DDP's skin more than anything else. I repeatedly wrote and said, "Whatever it was that DDP never had, he still hasn't got." And, up to that point, I was 100 percent correct.

His turnaround happened relatively quickly, and it all really started with the emergence of the Diamond Cutter. Page worked hard on every aspect of his character, and as awful as he was in the early days . . . he is that good now.

Page's work ethic has prevented him from falling into some of the traps that other wrestling performers seem to drift into. Most guys think that once they reach a certain point, they are good enough to last. Money tends to make them soft, and the contracts give a certain amount of security. Often, wrestlers seem to stall, and their motivation disappears.

But, for as long as I have watched and known Page, I have never known him to be satisfied. He constantly improved all facets of his game and ring work, and his interviews and overall psychology is good now . . . real good.

Page should be an example to many in the game today that hard work and a sincere love for this business can bring a wrestler to the top, no matter where they started.

Madden is a friend of mine now, and he is one of the few

bonafide journalists who is a wrestling critic who I pay any attention to. In the wrestling industry, there is too large a segment of the Internet and the "rags" who have too negative an agenda for me to be a part of. At the same time, some of my favorite people and the best ambassadors for our industry are writers, radio personalities, and even a few Internet columnists.

For many years, the monthly wrestling magazines were the only source of information for fans outside of the telecasts. Bill Apter, who is now with the hot new magazine *WOW (World of Wrestling)* has been a friend since the early days of DDP. Guys like Bill, Stuart Saks at *Pro Wrestling Illustrated*, and George Napolitano at *All-Star Wrestlers* have been positive forces in the industry.

For many in the wrestling reporting business, it's still a labor of love, and until recently, there was very little coverage unless the show was coming to town.

When that show comes to town for a televised event like *Monday Night Nitro* or *Thursday Thunder*, the WCW trucks roll in, and the production resembles a rock concert with a weekly schedule that is unmatched by any other televised sporting event. Both federations grind it out on the road with two televised events weekly, but, in addition, there are house-show loops in smaller cities and towns throughout the year. A monthly Pay-Per-View features the very biggest confrontations and the continuation of feuds between rivals. The spotlight focuses on the action in the ring, but there are countless others who make up the modern-day "Greatest Show on Earth."

So many people are a part of the overall production of each show, and the action begins way before the camera starts rolling. There are many people who dedicate themselves and make contributions to the product, and, so often, it's the camera angle, lighting, and announcing that help give the fans the very best entertainment. The announcer's table and the interviewers can have so much to do with the fans opinions of a wrestler. WCW has some legendary names holding the stick, like former champions Bobby Heenan and Larry "The Living Legend" Zybysko. It was Bobby "The Brain" who first put me over on the air, predicting that I would be a star one day, and "The Living Legend" actually took the time to work out in the ring with me at The Plant. Both Heenan and Zybysko have legions of young fans who, unfortunately, never got to see them wrestle. Both guys have made tremendous contributions in and out of the wrestling ring. All of the boys remember their first interview with "Mean Gene" Okerland, who is a fixture in the sport and one of my favorite dinner companions on the road. "Gino" is pure class.

It is especially huge to hear Michael Buffer calling you from the curtain as the crowd gets "rrrrready to rumble." And since I know you are thinking it . . . yes, Michael Buffer does have the very best job on the entire planet.

Announcers like Tony Schvionne, Mike "The Professor" Tenay, and Scott Hudson can offer spirited play-by-play, but they also act as pitchmen and shills who set up the angles and set the stage as the angles play out for the television audience. From ring announcer David Penzer to the referees and technicians who set up the pyro for the explosions, it is a traveling production that is made up of varied professionals all striving to be the highest-rated show in wrestling.

Through the years, Page surrounded himself with many solid friends, and, in turn, was a solid friend to many. He was accessible and grounded, and he managed to keep so many of us close, no matter where his journey took him.

His ability to find good in all types of people enabled him to cut through any preconceived notions that most people carry with them. It's no wonder that whenever people meet Page, they open up more than they normally would. Page makes people feel comfortable, and his genuine interest in their lives, lines of work, and goals makes it easy to want to know him better.

My circle of friends is a composite of all facets of my life. Often, when a person moves or changes jobs, friends, seem to get lost along the way. But there are so many people I have met along my journey who I want to know forever.

The nightclub business helped me develop friendships with some of the most hardworking, creative, and fun-loving

*My circle of friends includes my bro's from Auburn, Alabama—
(left) Myers Armstrong and his son, Todd (right). I get a bit of
R & R on Price Oil's boat "On The Prowl," Fishing and soaking
up the sun in Harbor Island in the Bahamas.*

people on the planet. I still talk to many of the people I worked
with over the years— bartenders, waitresses, and entertainers who have gone on to various successes. I met many celebrities while I was in the bar business and through my time
spent managing Smittee, but once wrestling exploded, I found
out that there were plenty of people in Hollywood who were
watching regularly.

I was a bottom guy when I was first introduced to Jason
Hervey backstage at a WCW event. I liked him from the
start, and he was more than just a mild fan of wrestling at
that point. His godfather was legendary wrestler, Terry Funk.

Jason played the classic heel older brother, Wayne
Arnold, on the long-running TV show *The Wonder Years*.

After knowing Jason for several years, I worked with
him and his partner, David Salzberg, on the production of
the WCW video *Feel the Bang*. The chemistry with us was
always natural, and the experience was a very positive one.
Later, when Jason and David told me about a script they
were working on called *First Daughter*, I knew he had found
a place for me beyond the wrestling world.

JASON HERVEY
MANDALAY ENTERTAINMENT:

Page captivated us, and we believed in him. When we shot the Feel the Bang *video, we knew that if Page were placed in a spot where people could see the real guy, they would embrace him like everyone else around him does. By filming him at The Power Plant, the place that symbolized the hard work and effort of getting to where he was, it enabled Page to draw people right in.*

It was the same when we cast him in the WTBS production First Daughter. *David and I knew it was just a matter of time before Page fit into something that we were doing, and we knew that Page would show his appreciation by being great in it.*

I have always had friends in the broadcasting business. Long before I was speaking into microphones regularly, radio people were partners in my quest to promote the nightclubs through the years. From the sales and promotion departments to the DJs who first gave me airtime when I was a middle-card guy, there are virtually dozens of personalities who I maintain contact with.

Cha-Chi LoPrete is a guy I came to know after being a wrestler for a few years, but I sure would have liked to hook up with him when I was in the bar business. "Chach" is a multitalented guy who I hit it off with the first time we met at WBCN in Boston.

How could I not like the guy? He has a quality daily wrestling segment on one of the hippest alternative rock stations in the country, and he digs Sinatra, Dean Martin, and Tony Bennett even more than I do.

In many ways, radio people share the same task as wrestlers or any other performer, and that is to get over, develop a fan base, and do whatever it takes to hold on to it once you get there.

Back when I was a bottom-guy wrestler and I was visiting Kimberly at school in Chicago, I began to listen to Mancow in the morning. He's a wise-a$$ who really has a wild sense of humor and an entertaining show that I listen to every chance I get.

Nationally syndicated morning radio DJ Mancow Mueller takes a studio Diamond Cutter.

Mancow's syndicated radio program is heard in over 20 markets, and is still based in Chicago. DDP has been a frequent guest on Mancow's show, but during the feud with the nWo, Mancow's allegiance wasn't quite what it appeared to be.

MANCOW MUELLER
WWW.MANCOW.COM:

I always liked DDP and his character in the ring, and when I first had him on the show, I was siding with him in his efforts against the nWo. But, I had also been a friend of Macho's (Randy Savage) for many years.

During the Page-Savage match at Chicago's United Center, I came to the ring with DDP, but swerved him when I hit him in the head with a pewter serving tray, which cost him the match. Savage got his hand raised, and left me in the ring, only to be cornered by DDP. With me begging for forgiveness from my knees, DDP persuaded me to get up, shook my hand, and went to hug me. The hug turned into a devastating Diamond Cutter that left me a little numb and a lot dazed for a couple of days.

I know that when I enter his arena, Mancow plays hard, so that night when he turned on me in Chicago . . . "The Cow" had to feel the bang!

Mancow is a world-class ballbreaker, and I quickly got hip to his radio games. I would be on the air, and he would have me on the line, but his volume was turned down so that I couldn't hear how badly he was cutting on me. Mancow is sharp, but I can break 'em back with the best of them. I had a friend who was holding his phone against his radio so I could hear all the sh*t Mancow was saying. (Nice try, Cow-boy.) He's a great guy who has become a friend, and I like Mancow's "push the envelope" kind of humor.

MANCOW MUELLER:

I've really gotten to know Page pretty well, and I can tell you that nobody who I have ever met or talked to loves his job more than Page. He is very secure with every aspect of his occupation, and handles himself better than most everyone around him in that business. He is, by far, the most fan-friendly celebrity that I have ever been around. He does it all for his fans, and has a keen sense of how not to forget where he came from and how he got where he is.

We can all learn and benefit from his positive attitude, his work with kids, and his enjoyment of life.

The number of radio programs that dedicate themselves, or at least a significant portion of their program, to wrestling is larger than ever. The show's callers and their questions are usually spirited, and although I hear crazy rumors and interpretations of what wrestling really is, for the most part, the fans are great and more knowledgeable than ever.

Many of these shows are in syndication and can be heard nationwide, like *Wrestletalk America,* which is hosted by my buddy, "Devious Doc," in Baltimore. There are many more that offer a forum for fans, as well as a stage for the boys to further promote upcoming matches. In the past few years, I've enjoyed getting to know James "Shadowe" Boone, who hosts *The Squared Circle* and my bro, Andrew, who hosts a show called The Pain Clinic. Of course, it's always a pleasure to talk wrestling with my main man at *Smitty's Sports Talk.*

Live interactive Internet shows are more popular than ever, and there are far too many columnists to mention, but I always dig the energy that "Diehard Derek Gordon" has when I do his show *And Justice for Brawl.* There are only a few Web sites that I pay attention to on a regular basis, and they are Al Issacs' and Remy Artega's site *scoopswrestling.com* and my old friend, Bob Ryder, at *1wrestling.com.*

The WCW site has come a long way over the past year, and the nightly live chat with Bob Ryder, Jamie Borash, and Chad "The Deliboy" Damiani gives WCW fans a chance to talk to a different superstar every night of the week.

One of the guys who I have become close to at WCW is Ross Foreman. Ross is the guy who was with me when I first met Karl Malone, and is someone who I have come to trust and depend on. Ross began as a freelance photographer and writer, and currently writes for *WCW Magazine* and contributes to *USA Today.* Ross has been with me for some of the most exciting times that I have had over the past few years, and has shot some of my favorite photos, including many that appear in *Positively Page.*

ROSS FOREMAN
WCW MAGAZINE:

Bro! Bro! Bro! That's a word that you hear quite frequently if you hang out with Page on any one of his jam-packed days. In all my years of feature writing and covering sports of all types, I have never seen an athlete more driven and intense. I've never been around someone who gets as much done in one day, and he really does have the kind of positive attitude that reflects on everyone he comes in contact with.

He has a tremendous ability to balance his life in the ring with his life as a man, and is an example for all of us. I am continually impressed with the way he accommodates his fans and his approach to his work, his friends, and his marriage.

But . . . I must tell you how absolutely whacked-out he is from the minute he wakes up until he goes to sleep at night.

In my travels, while dining with wrestlers, I have witnessed some of the largest food orders known to man. When WCW wrestlers order food, they might as well be ordering sides of beef, schools of fish, and acres of vegetables. But, for Page, it is not only what he orders . . . it's how he orders it. He is specific and precise when ordering, and someone can't help but wonder if the waitress and the kitchen can pull it off.

Breakfast is my favorite meal of the day, and, like we have been hearing for years, it is the most important one. My favorite breakfast stop on the road is the Cracker Barrel, but, in a pinch, a Waffle House will do the trick. Eggs are a great source of protein, so every morning, I have eggs . . . lots of eggs. And early in the day, I eat my "carbs," so I like to have pancakes too.

Ross Foreman:

Eggs and pancakes? Yeah right . . . It goes something like this . . . Eight eggs over lightly, but each egg must be cooked separately so that the whites are not touching each other. (Reason: He hates gooey egg whites.) No butter, only non-fat spray, and the eggs can all be served on the same plate as long as there is "no bonding of the eggs." Bacon cooked crisp and a stack of pancakes with blueberries and bananas in, not on, the pancakes . . . a bowl of fresh fruit, a large OJ, coffee . . . two refills, and lots of water. One more reminder that the blueberries and bananas must be cooked inside the pancakes.

So many of the people Page has met through the wrestling business have become close friends, and some of those friendships go way back to before his days of actually being in the ring. Like Jake Roberts, many of the boys remember Page's days in the nightclub and bar business with the wild nights of dancing and partying in Ft. Myers, but only Scott "Bam Bam" Bigelow knew Page when he roamed the streets of the Jersey Shore.

I first met "Bam" when we worked as bouncers in the clubs on the Shore. I knew about him before I met him, though. "Bam Bam" was always a big, tough kid who was "all everything" as a football player and wrestler at Neptune High, and he was tough on the streets too. How intense is he? Well, he started tattooing his head in high school, and entered wrestling several years before I became a wrestling manager. "Bam Bam" Bigelow has wrestled in the WWF, and while he was at ECW, he became known for his hardcore style. Since he has come to World Championship Wrestling, "Bammer" and I have had the chance to get as close as two Jersey Shore boys should be. Only now, we get to see a lot of each other.

SCOTT "BAM BAM" BIGELOW
WCW SUPERSTAR:

Page is my bro, and always has been. Page was very successful in the bar business, and while I began wrestling a lot younger than he did, his drive and blue-collar work ethic got him to the top. Page deserves everything he has achieved, but there was a time when I really didn't take his ring career seriously.

When Page was making his transition from manager and announcer to wrestler, the fans and media would ask me about him since he was a hometown guy. I cringed sometimes when I watched him. He was "the sh*ts" in the beginning, and I never thought he was going anywhere. Other than being a walking gimmick, I didn't see him ever challenging anyone for any titles.

Page has always had a solid character, and even when we were kids, he was a man. He's a straight shooter, no-bullsh*t type of guy in both his personal life and in the locker room.

There are too many sweet memories of those days when I was running Norma Jean's and traveling to the AWA and Florida Championship Wrestling tapings.

It was always good for us at the club when celebrities partied there, and it was exciting when wrestlers stopped by. The boys would visit the club in Ft. Myers whenever they were in Florida, and, of course, we would put them over huge. But after I entered the wrestling business, it became too much fun.

It really was obvious who the wrestlers were at that time, and, usually, the bar was so busy that I never had the chance to meet or get to know them as individuals. I remember "Sir Oliver Humperdink" being a great guy, and the first wrestling personality I met who was laid-back and subdued when he visited Norma Jean's.

The flip side of that coin was a couple of guys whose wrestling personas were more like titles than gimmicks. Back then, I never knew which guy was which . . . all I knew was that "The Nasty Boys" was an appropriate name.

BRIAN "NASTY" KNOBS
WCW SUPERSTAR:

Page was the "King of Clubs," and always had us "set up" when my Nasty Boy partner, Jerry Sags, and I visited Ft. Myers. That club was so hot, and it was all because of Page. From the DJ booth, he would get the crowd going crazy with his rap. I think the very first time we were there, Page made us judges for the "Hot Legs Contest," and it got crazier from that point on.

I remember being on the road with him years later and visiting a nightclub that wasn't "happening." The place was dead, even though there was a good crowd, and I started egging Page on to get the party going like he used to at Norma Jean's. Within a few minutes, Page was in the DJ booth like he had been doing it all along. The crowd lit up, and they saw DDP the wrestler as he was when we knew him in the beginning, promoting fun and making sure everybody was having a good time. Page has always been a friend, and, at times, he sure could be a fellow Nasty Boy.

In addition to Page's knack for finding fun-loving friends, he also finds ways to develop friendships that become business opportunities. He gets the most enjoyment when a friendship develops while helping each other pursue individual goals.

One of the best, and latest, examples of Page's knack for exploring business opportunities with friends is Kent Baklor. Radio personality "Devious Doc" introduced Page to Kent on a WCW visit to Baltimore in 1997. From that moment on, they looked for reasons to expand their friendship.

DDP with friend and partner, Kent Baklor, of Banker's First Mortgage Company.

Kent owns and operates Banker's First Mortgage Company, a company specializing in low-cost financing. He decided that if sports celebrities like Dan Marino and John Elway were having success as spokesmen for companies, why couldn't the most popular couple in wrestling.

KIMBERLY:

The opportunity for Page and me to represent a company that helps young couples get financing was exciting. We loved the fact that the commercial targeted people who might be reluctant to seek a mortgage or refinancing because of their occupations or the way they looked.

The 30-second commercial is running in regional markets across the country. It's pretty entertaining to see Kim and me as an average couple, along with my not-so-average job and my not-so-average look.

The book project known as *Positively Page* hit a serious speed bump just as the research was completed and the writing had begun. From the outset, Page wanted to maintain creative liberty to tell his real story, so we elected to write, produce, and market this book without the help of a major publisher. To do this, a financial partner was added. When unforeseen difficulties arose with the initial investor, Kent Baklor was there to pick up the slack and start the ball rolling again.

Kent provided the financial and emotional support necessary to make this book a reality.

Presently, I am working with Kent's wife, Diane, on an exciting new book project for children entitled *Positive Affirmations for Kids "A to Z with DDP."*

The thing I like most about working with the Baklors is that they want to have fun and make money while helping others accomplish their goals.

Volumes could be written and stories could be told for days about the relationships between celebrities and their faithful followers. Most people are quick to tell the stories of their brushes with greatness, and celebrities all have stories about "the time a fan came up to me in a restaurant and . . . "

But every celebrity approaches the idea of fame in a different way. While some stars are at ease and are good with fans, others seem rude or arrogant when they are actually just uncomfortable and shy.

Most times, when celebrities reach the point where they are easily recognized, their careers are pretty solid, as are their levels of fame. And what I have learned is that many movie and television stars, and even athletes and rock stars, can find a certain level of anonymity when they are in public.

People like Madonna, DeNiro, Seinfeld, and Brett Farve could sit next to someone at a restaurant in a pair of shades and a hat, and they may go totally unnoticed. But a top guy in professional wrestling has nowhere to hide . . . There is little chance that a Hogan, Savage, DDP, or Lex Lugar is going to be able to hide in a baggy shirt and horn-rimmed glasses.

For a professional wrestler, there is usually no escaping the gimmick.

All the boys deal with the fans in their own ways, and it really is difficult for me to judge anyone on how they do that. There is no doubt that the way the fans are viewed by the boys has a direct relationship to the level of the wrestler and the intensity of the individual fan.

Like I wrote earlier, in my eyes, Lex Lugar is truly the "King of the Road." Lex is someone who not only has a philosophical outlook about the fans, but is very dry, comical, and, at times, a bit "crusty" around the edges when he speaks of his years of being in the public eye.

Years ago, Lex told me about the "Four Stages of Stardom."

LEX "THE TOTAL PACKAGE" LUGAR
WCW SUPERSTAR:

First of all, I want everyone to figure it out, and then tell 10 friends that when I am out of the arena, I am not Lex Lugar. When I'm in an amusement park with my kids, I am not one of the rides, and when I am with my family, I will not take my shirt off to show you my "pecs." I don't want to hold your baby or listen to a play-by-play account of a match I had when you were growing up.

Of course, it is not that way for all the guys, and through the years, I haven't always felt the same way about the fans and their behavior. So, after many years of being on the road, I came up with what I believe is the definitive way to classify the levels of celebrity status: "Lex Lugar's Four Stages of Stardom."

THE ANTICIPATION STAGE - This is the first stage and one that stays with some guys throughout their careers. It usually lasts the first year or two, and it is most often seen as the period of time when you really hope that you get recognized . . . by anyone. In this stage, a guy will still look fans in the eye. He'll carry his own "Sharpie" to give autographs with, and he'll hang out in hotel bars on the road. A Stage One will introduce himself to every maitre d' and doorman on the planet with the hopes of getting a table or any other perks that come with being a TV wrestler.

THE AVOIDANCE STAGE - After awhile, those perks start to have "hassle" written all over them. The anticipation of be-

ing recognized develops into a major pain-in-the-a$$, and you find yourself entering malls at the service door, wearing sunglasses inside buildings, trying to insulate yourself in any way, and trying to protect the privacy of your family. It gets scary when you're in a mall. If even one person recognizes you, it's like all the others hear bongo drums calling to come in for the "kill." To go to ballgames, you need security, and you try to build a wall around your public life.

THE RECLUSE STAGE - After battling insurmountable odds, you finally relent to the fan intensity, reaching the point where you never want to leave the house. No matter what the reason is, you decide that you just aren't going out. This stage progresses to include many social and marital problems, ranging from cabin fever to acute paranoia. Stage three is a place where many guys exist, and often, they never leave their hotel rooms while on the road. If there was a way to have their food passed under the door to them, it would make a lot of stage three guys happy.

THE AGGRESSION STAGE - Stage four is a place where you really hope you never get to, but it is somewhat inevitable in many cases. In fact, for years, I have been stuck somewhere between stages three and four, and on a bad day, I have been known to cross over to a full stage four with fire in my eyes.

This stage can get ugly. The recluse snaps and decides that he will now go everywhere. No one or nothing will stop him or cause him to make any sacrifices. In stage four, you may actually look directly into a fans eyes, challenging him to say something stupid. Sometimes, in the aggression stage, you might have a glassy-eyed stare that accompanies a trance. You may ignore everyone around you and take the attitude that you are invisible. But then again, you may walk right over or through a crowd like they *are invisible.*

From my own experience, it is the fans who made it this way. It is hard to understand what it is really like to have that part of your life constantly tampered with, and I really don't care who criticizes me for my attitude about it. There is a time and a place for all that sh*t, and I determine when I feel like being accessible. I refuse to let anyone tell me when to turn the light on and off.

See . . . like I said, I'm somewhere between stages three and four, and there are lots of guys right there with me, although they may hide it better or are less than honest about their true feelings. Dallas is an exception to that rule. He's always "on," and he puts up with a lot of sh*t. But then again, he is in constant motion. I've seen Page ask a guy to walk with him and make that guy carry his bag to the gate, as he signs three things for the guy while the plane is waiting.

To hear Lex tell the "Four Stages" is a riot, and there is a whole lot of truth and conviction in his voice, although his tone is very comedic. Smokey loved it when he heard it, and we agreed that it had to be printed for all the world to see. But, in typical "Wordman" fashion, Smoke added Stage Five, and he calls his last stage, "Hey, remember me? . . . I used to be . . ."

Bottom line is, I enjoy who and where I am. I am truly living a dream and riding high. It is a wonderful life, and I am thankful for all the high and low places that the yo-yo has taken me.

CHAPTER TWENTY-TWO

THE LAST WORD . . . I DON'T THINK SO

There are so many factors involved with every success story, and everyone knows that it takes the help, guidance, and encouragement of people along the way.

But life has its swerves too. There are a certain amount of bumps along any road, and there will be dream-stealers along the way. Too many people will make more of an effort to tell you why it can't be done than to show you how to make it happen.

I remember Jake Roberts telling me that "jealousy has killed more people than war," and, unfortunately, The Snake's words are true.

Since I was a kid, I have always tried to find a way around those people. I have attempted to use everyday life as a tool to learn. Have I made mistakes? Damn right I have! Have I had some bad breaks? Yeah, probably.

But I have always tried to turn those negative darts into positive surges. When I incorporated that positive thought process into my everyday life, it helped me reach up for that "lightning bolt" and make my dreams become reality.

If there is one message that is conveyed from the writing of this book, and if there is one thing I hope is absorbed from my journey, it is that it can be done. Some called me a long shot, but deep down, many of them thought I had no shot. And that's okay . . . in fact, that makes it all sweeter now.

Some spoke out loud, and some said it behind my back, but I heard it all. They said that I either didn't have it . . . or I just didn't belong.

What I learned was that you can't let the people around you instill insecurity, no matter what they say or do to persuade you to quit believing in yourself. It's not a new concept, and there are many examples of people who persevered and chased their dreams despite critical comments.

I've spoken of my love for the spirit and the determination of Muhammad Ali and Satchel Paige. Their lives inspired greatness. Many of their hurdles came with the racial prejudices that were deep-rooted in America at the time. Ali shocked the world by rising from the streets of Louisville to become the greatest boxer who ever lived, and Satchel made it to "the show" at 42 years old and became "Rookie of the Year."

I really get jacked when I think of other people who were told that they couldn't . . . and did it anyway.

How about some of the biggest stars in entertainment, like Sylvester Stallone and Danny DeVito, or Howard Stern? Even someone like Ted Turner heard the words "no way" . . . but none of them were listening.

Stallone was a small-time actor, and *Rocky* was his dream. He wrote it, he believed in it, and he wanted to be in it. He knew that he was Rocky, even though all the insiders and "smart money" didn't see him in that spot. They liked his ideas, but they didn't want him. They didn't like the way he looked or the way he talked, and they didn't think he belonged.

They offered the struggling actor a million dollars over 20 years ago to back off and give up his dream, but he said, "No." Imagine having the balls to say "no" to a million bucks back then. Well, as I finish my first book, Stallone is working on *Rocky SIX*.

Do you think anyone believed that a 5'3" balding and

overweight hairdresser-turned-actor would become one of Hollywood's biggest stars and most influential producers and directors? Was Danny DeVito too small? Did he fit in amongst the pretty boys and glamour girls or any other pedigreed Hollywood stars?

I think he stands pretty friggin' tall as a guy who defied the odds and blazed the trail for all of us who know we can succeed.

Love him or hate him, you'll never forget (Hey, I like that!) Howard Stern. Radio's bad boy is another American success story. True to his conviction, he persevered through it all. He was fired and sued, he received hate mail and death threats, but he defied his critics and chased his dream to the top his way.

I know I'll get some heat from somebody for admiring Ted Turner, but even if I didn't appear on two of his networks every week, I would have to stand back and look up to him with great respect.

His story is a hard one to capsulize, but he overcame the suicide of his father, and basically took a billboard company and built an empire from it.

He took a down-and-out independent Atlanta television station and created the word "Superstation." When he told the world that he was going to broadcast news 24 hours a day, he was ridiculed and called a "wannabe." They all had him buried before he started. The networks laughed, and told him it couldn't be done . . . and they were wrong.

Another guy who I admire is my friend, Eric Bischoff. Eric's critics have been ever present, and although he is currently away from wrestling, his accomplishments helped shape the business and the wrestling world.

He was an out-of-work guy with a young family who was seeking a job in a business that he loved when he was hired as a fourth-string announcer. Eric was determined, and worked long hours with relentless passion to better himself and the wrestling business, and he succeeded in both. Not only did he make WCW competitive, he made the WWF work harder, making everybody money in the process. (You know, I think Vince should be sending Eric a check every week for bringing the best out in him.) Eric is still contracted by Turner, and is an asset to any entertainment company, so I doubt that we have seen the last of "Easy E." He loves the business too much, and can contribute to the overall product in many ways.

The people who achieve their dreams are the ones who are loyal to their commitment. For me, it was my refusal to be negative that kept me going. Staying positive and making the constant effort to work toward my goals has enabled me to be included with those who have faced what seemed like insurmountable odds.

In 1989, I heard a series of tapes called *Personal Power* by Anthony Robbins.

Basically, Tony Robbins suggested that if someone found something that they really want to do, but weren't sure how to get there . . . they should find someone who has done it, and then follow him.

I looked at the individuals who had made it in wrestling as talkers, like Classie Freddie Blassie, Captain Lou Albano, and even Handsome Jimmy Valiant. They were the ones I loved to watch on Gram's TV because they were the guys who could make a little black and white picture tube seem like it was in living color.

Later on, as wrestling was enjoying its run in the '80s, it was the flamboyancy of Dusty Rhodes, Superstar Billy Graham, and Jesse Ventura that set them apart from the other guys. They didn't need anyone else in the ring for them to get a reaction or entertain the fans.

In my opinion, the guy who is most responsible for what professional wrestling has become to the fans, the networks, and the merchandisers today is "Hollywood" Hulk Hogan. I'm not downplaying the impact of guys like Andre, Dusty, Flair, Funk, and Savage, to name a few, but Hulk pretty much paved the way for the rubber wrestling dude, cameo movie role, and wrestling T-shirt.

When I decided that I wanted to maximize my opportunity to remain in the business by expanding my focus to becoming a wrestler, I again went back to the conditioning that Tony Robbins provided.

Most longtime fans of wrestling and the reporters of the

ring will tell you that my style resembles Jake Roberts, and for the most part, I will agree. But there were others who I studied, including Hennig, Funk, and Savage. I can't forget Michael P.S. Hayes, either, because I dug what he did on the mic, as well as his look and style in the ring.

My point is that I had a plan and I followed it.

Do I think I belong in the spot that I'm in?

You can bet your a$$ I do! I know that I have contributed to this industry, and I proved that if you refuse to accept the negatives and keep yourself "in the game," it is possible to make good things happen. I finally "got paid" (as they say) in February 1999. I signed a contract that lasts for three years, and I have been fortunate enough to work my way into the mainstream of the entertainment world.

All that stuff makes a cocky kid a proud man, but my influence on the superstars of tomorrow is the contribution I am most proud of.

As far as the DDP character goes, it's like I've said in the ring and had printed on a T-shirt—"They'll love me . . . they'll hate me . . . but they'll never forget me." When I hang 'em up for good, I know I will look back with fond memories.

I am living my "American Dream."

I am asked all the time where I see myself when this contract is over. Interviewers ask me if I will continue to wrestle in WCW or if I'll attempt to make the transition to acting in movies and on TV. It's a pretty good bet that the ratings points that professional wrestling brings to the table will continue to provide opportunities for me, as well as for a lot of the boys.

As I complete this story, I am under contract with World Championship Wrestling until February 2002.

Will I wrestle after this deal is up? Not likely, but "never say never." Following this contract, I hope to return to the broadcasting booth and to be involved with World Championship Wrestling on a more limited basis. No, I don't mean booking, matchmaking, or whatever you want to call it. Instead, I plan to continue helping the superstars of tomorrow, and to be involved in character development and the promotion of professional wrestling.

Who knows where professional wrestling will go in the millennium, but I plan to be near it, whatever happens. Like Mickey Mantle, I hope to be able to remain with the team I played for throughout my career. But, I wouldn't hesitate to talk with any other federation or network that may be broadcasting professional wrestling in the future. Who knows? Maybe there will be a 24-hour wrestling channel in the next century, and I might be calling the matches of all the guys I helped along the way . . . who were never supposed to make it either.

I have no immediate plans to pursue Hollywood—California that is, but I do like visiting Tinseltown. Both Kimberly and I will continue to listen to offers to "act and react" to television or movie roles as they are offered, with the same attitude and intensity with which we approach all future business ventures.

There are so many things that I still want to experience, but one of the real pleasures in life has been my work with kids. "Bang It Out For Books" will always be one of my passions, and encouraging a good foundation for learning is a message that I always want to convey. But it won't stop there.

I want to help kids establish the kind of positive habits they need for their personal "blueprint for success."

Remember that no matter how much positive energy you have, or whatever motivational tools you develop, there will always be someone waiting to steal those dreams. They will tell you all the reasons why you can't succeed.

You may hear them say that you are too fat or too thin, too short or too tall, or that you are too green, too black, or maybe even too white. The opinion that I was too old to start up the ladder has followed me my entire career. It's a topic that has lingered for almost as long as the "Are you really married to Kimberly?" question.

So, critics, rag writers, and sh*t-slingers . . . how old is DDP? I've heard them say between 36 and 50.

I climbed into the ring in 1991 at the ripe young age of thirty-five years and five months. The year I was born, Eisenhower was president, and Elvis was "King." For the record, DDP's D.O.B. is 04-05-56 . . . so let's get it right.

My birthdays have all been great, but in 1999, I celebrated

my forty-third birthday on the White House lawn. I read to kids, out loud and in front of people, as a contributor to the Annual Easter Egg Roll with my wife, friends, and family by my side. Later that evening, I appeared on prime-time TV live from Las Vegas in a main-event match.

Hopefully, you have heard that you'll never make it or that you just don't have what it takes to reach your personal "main event" dreams.

As I said, it was Tony Robbins who made me see the power associated with the positive effects that a daily effort to excel has on people. There are hundreds of self-help authors and motivational gurus out there, but as far as I'm concerned, Tony Robbins is the "heavyweight champ."

He has not only helped improve the attitudes and lives of millions of people, he has helped *Release the Giant Within*[1] me. I have made an effort to take my positive approach to living life to its fullest with me throughout this journey.

You see, I have been studying and watching Tony Robbins, and, as far as I'm concerned, it's his "ring" that I will climb into next.

Hey, Tony! Get ready!

I know you can hear me knocking, and you know I'm coming in. So, lace up those big boots of yours because it's going to be me against you, two out of three falls for the "Motivational Championship of the World."

But seriously, I am ready to do whatever it takes to learn and prepare myself for the road ahead, and I can't think of a better mentor or person for me to follow than Tony Robbins.

In fact, I'm going to be a main-event headliner and a top guy in that arena. I have a vision that Diamond Dallas Page will be appearing at Madison Square Garden, and there won't be a wrestling ring to set up. I'll be there as a motivational speaker. Whether I am speaking to a room full of kids or in front of a major corporation, I plan to make a difference in as many lives as possible.

---

[1]Release the Giant Within *is the title of one of Anthony Robbins' best-selling motivational books.*

You know, through the years, I have had a bunch of nick-names. I've been called DDP, Dallas, Front Page, Double D, The Prince of Promo, Dutch, Dee Dee, Diamond, Dally, Page J, Diamond D, and even The Emperor. But if there is one thing that I want people to remember . . . it is that I am *Positively Page*, and that I *Refuse to be Negative* . . . which, by the way, is the title of my next book.